Getting Work

Pennsylvania Paperbacks

Getting Work

Philadelphia, 1840–1950

WALTER LICHT

UNIVERSITY OF PENNSYLVANIA PRESS
Philadelphia

Originally published 1992 by Harvard University Press
Copyright © 1992 by the President and Fellows of Harvard College
All rights reserved

First paperback edition 1999 published by
University of Pennsylvania Press
Philadelphia, Pennsylvania 19104-4011
Printed in the United States of America on acid-free paper

10 9 8 7 6 5 4 3 2 1

Library of Congress Cataloging-in-Publication Data

Licht, Walter, 1946–
    Getting work: Philadelphia, 1840–1950 / Walter Licht.
    p.   cm.
    Includes index.
    ISBN 0-8122-1719-5 (pbk. : alk. paper)
    1. Labor market—Pennsylvania—Philadelphia—History. 2. Working
class—Pennsylvania—Philadelphia—History. I. Title.
HD5726.P5L53   1992
331.12'09748'11—dc20   91-35021
                                                          CIP

To Gladys Palmer (1895–1967)

Contents

Tables

Preface

How did working people in a major industrial city secure employment in the past? How did that process change over time and vary at given moments for different groups of job seekers? Direct answers to these questions will be provided in the pages to come. En route, this book will stop and dwell separately on a series of interrelated topics bearing on working-class experience and the dynamics of the labor market.

"Getting work" is a marvelous umbrella-like issue; under its span can be found questions on a vast range of topics—the workings of the family; the role of culture in economic decision making; the relationship of schooling and job training to occupational attainment; the employment patterns and problems of young people; the legacy and meaning of discrimination; the function of intermediaries in the labor market such as employment bureaus and help-wanted advertising; and the impact of unions, technology, government regulations, and firm personnel policies on the structuring of work and work prospects.

The concept of getting work offers the opportunity not only to examine these and other subjects in a historical framework, but to look to explanations as well. The numerous issues that can be investigated under the cover of getting work are linked by a common problem: the need to account for variations in the experiences of workers in the labor market. There are two possible avenues of inquiry. The first is to concentrate on the level of individuals, or the so-called suppliers of labor. This path assumes that success and outcomes at work are invariably the result of personal initiative and competence. Standard economic thinking (and a good deal of the rhetoric of American politics) rests on this very assumption.[1] However, there are less voluntaristic ways of looking at individuals and experience in the job market. Personal good fortune and productivity can be envisioned as functions of education, training, and the personal capital that suppliers of labor accumulate and bring to the workplace.

They can also be viewed as functions of the expectations and values workers imbibe from their families, social groups, colleagues, and society writ large (enter Max Weber and the famous Protestant work ethic). Less free will is obviously imputed to the individual in these latter kinds of sociological explanations, but still the focus remains on the person and personal say and agency.

A second line of argument looks at forces and institutions far beyond the control of individuals. Workers can be pictured at the mercy of general economic circumstances, with the vicissitudes and structure of the economy shaping and limiting work histories and possibilities. A larger societal view can also fix on the role of government in establishing the contours of the labor market and on customary social practices—institutionalized sexism and racism, most notably—in limiting personal options. A stress on such controlling forces need not remain on a macro level. Intermediaries in the labor market, unions or employment bureaus, for example, play their roles. Most important are the firm itself and the buyers or so-called demanders of labor; how employers judge and set standards for both hire and the internal allocation of labor within companies greatly affects personal choice and chance.

An extended analysis of the merits and flaws of the above perspectives would be superfluous for the purposes of this book. The various explanations are rather resources for constant consideration. This study in fact begins with a synthetic and eclectic notion: that getting work is a process shaped by general economic conditions, personal means and decisions, agencies within the labor market, firm strategies, and state policy. I will assess the changing character and relative significance of structural, personal, and institutional factors in employment experience.

The conceptual framework also provides the organizational principle for the book. In the first chapter I establish the context; the time is the last half of the nineteenth and first half of the twentieth centuries and the place is the industrial city of Philadelphia. I draw a brief socioeconomic portrait of Philadelphia to highlight certain aspects of the city's history that greatly affected the lives of men and women seeking and obtaining employment there. I then move to the personal and look at the demographics of entrance to the job market—when young people began working, how first and subsequent jobs were secured, and the relative accessibility of employment opportunities.

In the third and fourth chapters I examine various agencies in the labor market influencing the hiring process. The third chapter is devoted to the controversial and complex question of schools and work, the fourth to the history and role of apprenticeship programs, unions, employment bureaus, and help-wanted advertising. The role of firms in structuring work opportunities is the subject of the fifth chapter. In the sixth I look at the labor market as a political entity and study the state as both employer and shaper of employment conditions. In the seventh chapter I return to the personal and focus on the problem of losing work. Unemployment and irregular employment were constant features of working-class existence in Philadelphia during the period under study and they forced various kinds of coping strategies. The job search became a seemingly perpetual activity.

This book began as an extension of an earlier study of mine on the organization of work on mid–nineteenth-century American railroads.[2] I originally intended to investigate whether employment patterns and personnel practices discernible on the early railroads applied to other industries and in other time periods. To that end I began to pursue research on labor relations in firms in the city of Philadelphia. That effort was then promoted but also vitally transformed when I was asked to join a large-scale research project funded by the National Institute of Education, "The Organization of Schools, Work and Family Life in Philadelphia, 1840–1920" (Grant 9-0173). Professor Michael Katz of the University of Pennsylvania was the principal investigator of the project and I would like to thank him for his initial invitation and continued support and collegiality. Our research progressed thanks to funds from the National Institute of Education. During the project's tenure I worked closely with Professor David Hogan of the Graduate School of Education at the University of Pennsylvania; he has been a constant source of ideas and advice.

This book owes its greatest debt, though, to an extraordinary corpus of studies on labor force participation and industrial relations in the Philadelphia metropolitan region. These studies were conducted by Gladys Palmer and her associates at the Industrial Relations Department of the Wharton School of the University of Pennsylvania from the 1920s through the 1950s. The discovery of Dr. Palmer's printed reports and her manuscript records forced me to rethink my original objectives and helped me to reconceive this book. *Getting*

Work is dedicated to Gladys Palmer, a pioneer in labor economics research who was never properly heralded in her own time. I should add, too, that Dr. Palmer's papers were left in the custody of Professor Ann Miller of the University of Pennsylvania, and I thank her for allowing me such easy access to them and for encouraging me continuously. Dr. Eugene Erickson of Temple University was responsible for the computerization of data collected by Gladys Palmer and her associates in 1936, material that forms a key part of this work, and my appreciation extends to him as well.

In addition to the National Institute of Education, I received research support from the National Endowment for the Humanities and the University of Pennsylvania. I was also fortunate to have been invited to spend a year as a fellow at the Hagley Library in Wilmington, Delaware; for making that year a most enjoyable and productive experience I want to thank Glen Porter, Elizabeth Kogen, Michael Nash, and the entire Hagley Library staff. A joint grant from the Andrew Mellon Foundation and the National Endowment for the Humanities paved and paid my way at the Library.

During the course of my research I was also granted access to the records of many firms still in operation in Philadelphia. I would like to thank the following individuals for their time and support: Leo Kuehl of Brown Instrument Company of Honeywell, Incorporated; H. K. Taylor and Robert Taylor of Ellisco Incorporated; Lynne Walker of Herder Cutlery; Claudette Johns of the Insurance Company of North America (now CIGNA); Edward Hueber of Kelley & Hueber; Christian Spahr of Lea & Febiger; S. E. Firestone of McCloskey Varnish; Percy Lanning of Perseverance Iron; Walter Smith and Carol Wojtowicz of the Philadelphia Contributionship; Judy Delcolliano of the Philadelphia Gas Works; John Remmey of the Richard Remmey Son Company; William Hipp of Schmidt's Brewery; George Kallish of Swoboda and Sons of Transcontinental Leather, Inc.; and Harvard Wood and Harvard Wood, Jr., of H. C. Wood Incorporated. Records in the Historical Society of Pennsylvania and the Urban Archives of Temple University also proved invaluable and thanks are due to archivists there, particularly Frederic Miller at Temple.

I would like to thank Columbia University Press for granting me permission to reprint revised portions of my article, "Studying Work: Personnel Policies in Philadelphia Firms, 1850–1950," in Sanford M. Jacoby, editor, *Masters to Managers: Historical and Comparative Perspectives on American Employers* (1991). At Harvard University Press, I would like to thank Aida Donald for her continued support and Lauren M. Osborne for a perfect editorial touch.

Any number of individuals, including many students of mine, also deserve mention, but I will single out two for special words of appreciation. During the course of the research and writing of this book I participated with Philip Scranton on several Philadelphia history projects and I have profited greatly from his knowledge and understanding of the city's development. Whole classes of students served as research assistants, but one student, Alan Brophy, labored intensely, and I remain appreciative of his help. Finally, it is customary to thank spouses and children for providing needed and welcome distractions while completing book-length manuscripts; this book was in fact a distraction from my more important family life, and my love and thanks are due to Lois and Emily for sustaining me once again.

Getting Work

1 · Particularities

Consider the histories of these four Philadelphians: William Rees, Timothy Ragan, Jean Bally, and William Deacon. In 1936, during the Great Depression, they and 2,500 other workers from Philadelphia provided biographical and occupational information to researchers investigating the getting and losing of work.[1]

William Rees was born in England in 1878. At the age of six he migrated to Philadelphia with his family. Seven years later he left school and obtained a job as a bobbin boy at the worsted mill where his father and a brother worked. Over the course of the next forty years Rees remained a weaver, but was in and out of work fourteen times; eight of his severances were due to layoffs. His longest stint of work, ten years, had been at a Brooks Brothers plant; participation in a strike led to the end of his tenure there.

Between jobs, Rees normally walked the streets of the city looking for openings. Sometimes he would get lucky and, as he noted, "stumble in just when they need[ed] a weaver." On one occasion, he was walking past a mill when "[I] saw a man through a window whom [I] knew. [He] asked what [I] was doing and [I] said that [I] wanted a job. [My] friend told [me] to come in . . . [He] found the boss weaver and [I] was given a job." Friends often helped Rees locate employment in this way, but in most instances, work was secured through direct application to mills. The process was never easy. Rees mentioned that once he had walked almost four miles from his home on Olney Street to a factory on York nine mornings in a row "because the foreman said that he was going to put [me] on any morning." On the ninth morning he discovered that another man had been favored instead. After that he did not look for work for several months. "Things like that takes the heart out of you," Rees reported.

Timothy Ragan, unlike William Rees, was a native Philadelphian. Born in 1887, he left school at the age of twelve, and as he related,

1

"did not have a hard time" finding a job in the cardroom of the Dobson woolen mill. Ragan quit within a month, however, "to try something else." He hoped to learn a trade, and his cousin helped him secure a position as a blacksmith's assistant. Slack times left him unemployed again.

Ragan next applied for a job at the Midvale Steel Company but stayed with the firm less than two months, finding the work "too heavy and too hot." After several months without employment, he was able to locate a position as a machinist's helper at the Philadelphia Navy Yard. He was eventually upgraded to machinist's status without having to proceed through the normal channels of apprenticeship and he worked steadily at the Navy Yard until 1927. In that month he suffered an unspecified injury and was forced off the job for five months.

When Ragan returned to the Yard he was unable to resume his normal duties and had to take a lower rating as a machinist's helper once again. Ragan noted that he was greatly embarrassed by his demotion and that he did not let his friends or relatives know of his plight. With the Navy's massive furloughing of civilian workers during the depression, Ragan found himself unemployed again between 1931 and 1935 and had only just been taken back at the Yard at the time of his interview. Ragan felt strongly that machinists should be judged and classified not according to their formal education, whether through school or apprenticeship, but solely on the basis of their experience and ability.

Jean Bally's story and testimony are less involved. She was born in Scotland in 1905. She left school at the age of fourteen and a year later obtained a job through family connections as an office clerk in a shoe factory in Glasgow. The following year she migrated to America and settled in Philadelphia, where a brother, a sister, and several cousins worked as weavers. One cousin working at Cochran's carpet mill inquired on her behalf for employment and six weeks later Bally commenced working in the city. For the next fifteen years she labored on and off as a weaver with periods of intense work broken by periodic layoffs. Bally in most instances obtained new positions through information and contacts provided to her by her cousins. As she related to her interviewers, one cousin was a weaver at the Axminster Company, another knew the boss at Folwell's, and another was a foreman at the Nelson Carpet Company. Within these boundaries she lived her working life in Philadelphia.

William Deacon was one of the youngest workers canvassed. He was born in Philadelphia in 1914. He was a high school graduate whose schooling had included industrial education courses in the machine trades and woodworking. Deacon obtained his first job at the Radio Corporation of America as a coil winder during a strike; he had been referred to RCA's personnel department by the Junior Employment Bureau of the Philadelphia Board of Education. After six months of employment, however, he was laid off. He then looked for a new job and secured a position two months later as a cabinet inspector at General Electric after responding to a newspaper advertisement. He had been employed for only three months when he was laid off again. After several months of unemployment he was rehired by RCA as a coil winder, a position he still held at the time of the WPA survey. In 1936, William Deacon was thus at an early stage in his working life.

Encapsulated in the testimony of these four Philadelphians is the subject matter of this book. Most of the issues are there: the role of family connections in hiring, the question of schooling and occupational history, the importance of personal decision making and exigencies in employment experience, the place of government in the labor market, the function of placement agencies, and the ever-present and pressing problems of unemployment and uncertain employment.

The experiences of William Rees, Timothy Ragan, Jean Bally, and William Deacon varied, but they shared one thing in common, and that was the city of Philadelphia. These four individuals sought employment, plied their trades, and lost work in a city with a particular history. Economic and social developments in the city greatly affected the chances of those seeking and securing opportunity there. There was nothing peculiar to Philadelphia's evolution; the city shared and still shares features with many other major commercial and industrial centers. The particularities are crucial, however. The personal fortunes of the working men and women who came to thrive and persevere in Philadelphia's labor market cannot be understood without first attending to the context.

A rich hinterland, an enterprising merchant community, and ready markets for the goods processed and crafted in the city transformed Philadelphia into a major commercial entrepôt within one hundred years of its founding by William Penn as a haven for persecuted

Quakers.[2] By the time delegates convened in the city to write the Declaration of Independence and a decade later the Constitution for the new republic, Philadelphia had become second only to London in both the volume and value of the products shipped in and out of its port. Philadelphia's commercial fortunes plummeted, however, in the early nineteenth century, as the city lost trade to its chief rival, New York.[3] Rather than enter a long-term period of economic stagnation—a fate suffered by other prosperous colonial seaport towns—the city embarked on a new direction that would mark its history for the next 150 years. It became a major manufacturing center.

The task of chronicling Philadelphia's rise to industrial supremacy is not simple. There is no single invention, entrepreneur, event, or circumstance that can be designated as the prime mover or essential part of the story. There are no particular moments or stages of development to be noted, either. Tales of British industrialization can start, if incorrectly, with James Watt and the creation of the steam engine; those of New England's industrial development with Samuel Slater and his Pawtucket, Rhode Island, mill, or with the Boston Associates, who built the great mill towns of Waltham and Lowell, Massachusetts; and those of American manufacturing growth in general with Eli Whitney's inventions or the construction of the railroads. There are key happenings in this way of presentation and then endless repercussions and derivatives. Philadelphia's case must be visualized differently; industrialization occurred in that city as a steady mushrooming of enterprise.

Although the stories of thousands of initiatives must be told to render Philadelphia's industrial history, these individual efforts do add up to a whole. By the mid-nineteenth century, the city's industrial structure had a definite character with great implications for the men and women who sought employment there. At least four features are apparent and noteworthy. The first is product diversity. While upwards of 40 percent of Philadelphia's work force came to be engaged in garment and textile production, the city was not identified with any single manufactured good (unlike Lynn, Massachusetts, and shoes, Pittsburgh and steel, or Detroit and cars). An amazing array of items poured from its workplaces. Philadelphia became known for its boots and shoes, hats and caps, iron and steel, machine tools and hardware, locomotives, saws, lumber and wood, furniture, shipbuilding, chemicals, drugs, glass, fuel, jewelry, papermaking, paints and varnishes, printing and publishing, metal items, bricks and tiles, and fine instruments.[4] A longer list could be produced; these goods represent products in which the city led the nation both in volume and quality of production. Even in textiles—a major segment of the city's economy—there was an extraordinary variety. Philadelphia was a center for cotton, wool, and silk spinning; cotton, wool, and silk weaving of cloth and ribbon; lacemaking, carpetmaking, hosiery, dyeing, and textile finishing. Within these categories, particularly carpet manufacture, further distinctions could easily be drawn.[5] Similarly, the garment trades were involved in the production of everything from basic men's and women's wear to fancy ties, gloves, and braided epaulets.

A diversity of work settings is another mark of Philadelphia's industrial base. The goods produced in the city issued from a variety of sites. A visitor to the city in 1850 who cared to look would find one segment of Philadelphia's work force toiling in factory buildings and operating water-powered, or in some instances steam-powered, machinery. More typical was the small manufactory, a place where workers created wares with hand and foot-driven machines. Artisan shops still dotted the landscape and in certain trades production continued according to ancient craft practices and standards far into the twentieth century. Hidden from view was another kind of small workplace, the sweatshop, where semi-skilled and unskilled workers produced standardized goods on an assembly-line basis. Also obscured from the visitor's eye would be the extraordinary amount of work performed in homes, usually on the basis of outwork, but also for direct use or peddling in the streets.[6]

The mere labeling of five different work settings renders little justice to the complexity of Philadelphia's production system. A visit to a mill building one year might find one firm operating there with a force of machine operatives; the next year the same structure might be subdivided with various businesses producing on either a manufactory, craft, or sweatshop basis. With any given good, moreover, production could be conducted in a variety of settings. In 1850, about 3 percent of all hats and caps manufactured in Philadelphia were produced in factories, 41 percent in manufactories, 40 percent in sweatshops, and 16 percent in artisan shops; thirty years later, according to census takers, headwear was still being manufactured in diverse settings in the Quaker City, although factory production had increased dramatically. Finally, a given good during its production might pass through several settings; the line between mill, shop, and home was hazy. In textiles, a fiber might be combed in a home on an outwork basis, spun in a mill, woven in a manufactory or home (handloom weaving, particularly of carpets, remained an institution in Philadelphia into the twentieth century), and then dyed and finished in a shop. Diversity of products and work settings made Philadelphia's industrial history complex and particular.[7]

Specialization is a third component of the structure and story, specialization in both operations and products. Fully integrated firms existed in Philadelphia, but they were more the exception than the rule; those that were established also often engaged in the production of custom goods. Philadelphia's textile industry provides the clearest examples of specialization. In Lowell, Massachusetts, major investors financed the building of multi-purpose factories; in each new factory, raw fibers were cleaned, carded, spun, and woven into cloth and the fabric was finished and packed, all under a single roof. Separate establishments emerged as the pattern in Philadelphia, with independent manufacturers engaged in either the spinning, weaving, dyeing, or printing of cloth. Moreover, rather than produce standardized coarse fabrics, as in New England, Philadelphia's segmented textile producers chose to enter high-quality product lines. From the city's textile work sites came high-grade cotton, wool, and silk yarns, fancy dress cloth, upholstery and drapery, custom carpets, and finely dyed and calico printed fabrics.[8]

Speciality items, in fact, marked all industrial production in Philadelphia. Iron and steel producers in the city concentrated on the production of high-quality iron and grey steel and on custom forgings and castings. Machine building firms prospered by catering to the individualized needs of their customers. Garment and shoemakers made fancy wear. Philadelphia became known as a place to purchase the finest dental instruments, measuring gauges, cutlery, varnish, and tools. Even large-scale, fully integrated firms, such as Baldwin Locomotive, Stetson Hat, and Midvale Steel, thrived by manufacturing small-batch custom goods to the specifications of their many clients.[9]

The small-to-medium-sized family owned and managed enterprise was the fourth critical feature of Philadelphia's industrial development. Job seekers in Philadelphia through the first decades of the twentieth century typically found work in small proprietorships. In 1880, for example, there were 9,163 firms in operation in the city. Sixty-two percent of these employed between one and five workers, another 24 percent between six and twenty-five. Large enterprises with employment greater than fifty accounted for but 8 percent of all businesses, and the number of truly large firms, with personnel exceeding five hundred or a thousand, could be counted on the fingers of one hand. In 1880, the average industrial worker in the city labored in a unit of approximately twenty employees.[10]

Smallness went hand in hand with family owned and managed businesses, and it was the family firm or partnership that came to predominate and proliferate in Philadelphia. Figures for the textile industry in the city during the nineteenth century are revealing. In 1850, 322 companies operated in the trade; 272 were owned by single individuals, 37 by partners and 13 by corporate entities. In most instances, these corporations were owned privately, with the corporate form adopted for legal reasons rather than for capitalization.[11] Two decades later the number of corporate textile businesses had grown to 17 percent of the total, but still more than two-thirds of the firms producing yarns and fabrics in the city were owned by single persons.[12] Philadelphia remained a noncorporate town through the mid–twentieth century and the persistence of small-scale proprietorships lent a particular paternalistic quality to work relations on the Philadelphia shop floor.[13]

Diversified manufacture in products and work settings, segmented establishments, a high proportion of employment devoted to the production of specialized (mostly non–durable) goods, and the prevalence of small-to-medium-sized family owned and operated firms, characterized Philadelphia's industrial system as it materialized in the nineteenth century. Two questions emerge concerning economic developments in the city. How did the city switch so successfully from commerce to industry and build a strong manufacturing base? And why did Philadelphia's industrial structure take its particular form? The answer to the first question is fairly straightforward. All the necessary conditions for industrialization were present: trading traditions and experience, availability of resources, easy access to markets, and ample supplies of technological information, entrepreneurial spirit, and skilled labor.[14]

The particular character of the city's industrial system requires less certain explanations. The absence of a major waterfall first precluded the building of large, totally mechanized factories. Philadelphia did have the Schuylkill River, and where the river moved rapidly, as in the borough of Manayunk, large mills were built, but the power entailed compared poorly with Lowell's Merrimack. Most of Philadelphia's early mills were built on the banks of small streams and creeks, and that fact limited operations. Philadelphia firms, in fact, at a relative disadvantage, looked to solve their energy needs with steam power earlier and to a greater extent than their counterparts in other areas; as a result, the city became a center for steam engine construction, with forty-four companies in the trade by the 1840s, and also a major consumer of the anthracite coal now mined in its northern hinterland.[15]

Philadelphia's long history of artisanal work also played a role. Craft production during the colonial period laid a base for industrialization and set a direction. What is notable in the city's manufacturing history, for example, is not the activity of merchants in the gathering of outworkers into merchant-created centralized shops and factories, but the building and expansion of firms by artisan entrepreneurs. The artisans turned manufacturers also had on hand a plentiful supply of skilled workers, and that proved an incentive to rely on hand labor in the production of custom goods. In New England, a scarcity of such labor power served as an inducement for the building of mechanized facilities and engagement in coarse wares production. Philadelphia, known as a craft center from an early date, also attracted further generations of skilled immigrant workers and potential small-scale operators, thus perpetuating the process.

The advantages of specialized production are a third consideration. Competing with large-scale manufacturers—whether New England textile mills or, eventually, Pittsburgh steel combines—would have proven disastrous for Philadelphia proprietors. Rather than produce standardized goods, they profited by entering specialized, high-quality markets. Their small size afforded a flexibility that allowed them to shift into new lines with order and market changes; abundant skilled labor further facilitated the process. The Philadelphia production system rested on the advantages achieved through specialization rather than the benefits that can accrue to scale.[16]

Specialization also bred greater diversity of production. Fully integrated businesses deliberately avoided reliance on other enterprises; from raw materials to finished products, goods were shaped under a single roof. In Philadelphia, every separate spinning mill bred a weaving concern and vice versa; fabric makers further gave opportunities to machine builders, dyers, and finishing companies. A small shipyard similarly dealt with blacksmith shops, foundries, rope works, and tanneries. Philadelphia's small, flexible enterprises were both producers and consumers, and they relied on the demand for their products not only outside the city but among themselves. Christian Schrack, for example, established a varnish manufactory in 1815; to survive he chose to perfect a product that he could sell to coach makers. He eventually became a major supplier to the Baldwin Locomotive Works, thus cutting his specific niche in the marketplace. Such an example illustrates again the perpetuating potential of the Philadelphia industrial order.[17]

A final partial explanation of Philadelphia's particular industrial history lies in the behavior of the city's merchant elite. The promoters of large-scale manufacturing in New England were the grand accumulators of commercial wealth during and after the Revolution. Philadelphia's great mercantile families sponsored a few industrial experiments, but generally they placed their surplus capital elsewhere: in further trade, banking, canal and railroad construction, and mining development.[18] Their specific investment proclivities remain something of a mystery and cannot be fully explained by their Quaker heritage and reserve.[19] Whatever the reasons, the opting of Philadelphia merchants out of the industrial arena had definite implications. It created a capital scarcity, a further limit on the building of large enterprises, but also a vacuum. Aspiring native-born artisans and enterprising immigrant skilled workers and proprietors would fill the void and build Philadelphia's production system.[20]

The Philadelphia system of industry was intact as early as the mid-nineteenth century. The structure of the city's economy remained remarkably unchanged for the next hundred years. A visitor to the city in 1950 could easily cite the same characteristics to describe Philadelphia as a traveler of a century earlier. When studying major developments in American economic history during the last half of the nineteenth and first half of the twentieth centuries—the emergence of the corporation, the horizontal and vertical integration of enterprise, the advent of bureaucratic management, the rise of capital goods industries, and the growth of a nationally based and standardized marketplace—it is not to Philadelphia, but to Cleveland, Chicago, and Detroit that the scholar goes for examples. Philadelphia in developmental terms reached a plateau by the time of the Civil War and a major shift in character would not occur until after World War II.

History was not completely frozen, however, and although the continuities may be more striking than the transformations, the changes must be mentioned. First, there were the normal ups and downs of the business cycle. The Philadelphia economy was ever fluctuating and susceptible to market and political disturbances and influence. The War of 1812, for example, made for boom times in the city, but depressed conditions followed thereafter as the British dumped cheap goods on American shores. In 1819, during the first significant depression of the many that would occur during the nineteenth century, there were reports that 20,000 Philadelphians were seeking employment, out of a work force of 64,000.[21] Severe downturns in the late 1830s and in 1857 similarly spelled financial and personal disaster in the city. Full-fledged prosperity, however, returned with the Civil War and the passage of high-tariff legislation; Philadelphia mills, shipyards, and arsenals produced to capacity. The massive depressions of the 1870s and 1890s brought large-scale unemployment again; 60,000 Philadelphians were out of work in 1893, for instance, and the dispossessed took to demonstrating in the streets.[22] Industry perked up in the first decades of the twentieth century, and World War I was a special boon to Philadelphia manufacturers. The changing fortunes of the textile industry in the 1920s, however, served as a harbinger of the general bad times to come in the 1930s. War would then bail the city out once more. Structural continuities can thus be pointed to, but business activity and conditions were rarely static in the Quaker City.[23]

The post-1870 period also witnessed significant long-term shifts. New industries emerged, adding to the diversity of production. Discoveries of oil in western Pennsylvania after the Civil War turned Philadelphia into a leading fuel refining and shipping center.[24] Fifty years later the city would house the three largest manufacturers of radios in the country and production of electrical appliances in general became a new source of employment.[25] Electrification in industry,

Particularities • 11

itself, represented a change, although steam remained a major source of power into the twentieth century and many firms, operating in a typically flexible way, relied on combinations of steam and electricity.[26]

The declining status of the textile industry in Philadelphia represents perhaps the most critical change in the production system established in the city during the early 1800s. Alterations in fashion began to affect rug manufacturers as early as the first decades of the new century and the tumble continued at full pace in the 1920s. A taste for hardwood floors and linoleum damaged the entire rug industry, but Philadelphia was placed at a further disadvantage when interest in custom rugs gave way to demand for cheap, standardized products.[27] Woolen and silk manufacturers faced similar competitive pressures, but would be dealt an even more fatal blow with the coming of synthetics. In one instance, a change in fashion actually stirred business activity. The wearing of shorter skirts by women in the Roaring Twenties insured prosperity for workers and mill owners alike in the full-fashioned silk hosiery trade. The boom, however, would not last; the depression of the 1930s curtailed production of stockings and the development of nylon late in the decade would spell an ultimate end.[28] In general, the Philadelphia textile industry (including garments), the single largest source of employment in the city, succumbed to large-scale producers of standardized threads and fabrics (and clothes) operating in increasingly modernized facilities in low-wage areas of the country, namely the South. Had a market for specialized goods maintained its strength, the city's mill owners might have survived as they had a century earlier when faced by competition from New England.[29]

The decline of the textile industry in the 1920s in Philadelphia was a sign of a general deindustrialization to take place decades later.[30] Yet, the story should not be hastened unnecessarily, for as late as the 1950s the city remained a major manufacturing center. Textiles had suffered losses, but during World War II, 40,000 workers were still gainfully employed in the trade.[31] Philadelphia's contribution to the nation's manufacturing had declined to 3 percent of the total (half of what it once had been), but this was still substantial given the geographic expansion of industry, and by 1950 employment in the city's ten major industries far exceeded percentage figures for the country as a whole.[32] Perhaps the best sense of both the persistence and stability of Philadelphia's manufacturing base can be rendered by the following statistics. In 1800, 42 percent of the city's adult population was occupied in industrial pursuits; 150 years later, at mid-twentieth century, the industrial work force comprised 46 percent of the city's laboring populace.[33]

The particular features of Philadelphia's industrial order also remained apparent. The scale of operations in the city certainly increased during the late nineteenth century and first half of the twentieth—while the average worker in Philadelphia in the 1880s labored in a concern of twenty employees, his or her counterpart in 1930 could count an average of 53 co-workers on the shop floor. Still, small-to-medium-sized firms proliferated. In 1930, out of a total of 5,760 manufacturing companies, only 28 employed more than 1,000 workers, and 100 employed more than 500. Ten years later, census enumerators discovered that 30 percent of Philadelphia's industrial labor force worked in facilities of less than 100 employees, 50 percent in plants employing 100 to 1000, and 20 percent in large-scale works employing more than 1000. These figures can be compared with those in cities such as Chicago and Detroit, where 67 percent and 50 percent of all industrial employees, respectively, labored in huge firms of 1000 or more.[34] Similarly, proprietorships and partnerships prevailed. Competition did force a number of consolidations, but still by 1945 few branch plants of national corporations could be found operating in the city, and a survey completed in 1941 revealed that only 38 percent of all manufacturing enterprises in Philadelphia were owned corporately (and most of these were privately held and involved local investors).[35] That the city never developed capital goods industries explains to a certain extent the relative absence of corporations.

A plethora of goods still issued from Philadelphia's work sites as well, and specialization and flexibility continued to mark operations. Radios, televisions, light electrical appliances, and fine electrical measuring instruments joined the complex product mix; they were manufactured in firms that were able to meet custom small-batch orders. Such firms remained reliant on the city's skilled labor base.[36]

The period 1800 to 1950 then forms a whole: it is Philadelphia's age of industrial enterprise. While substantial changes occurred during this 150-year period, the structure of Philadelphia's economy remained relatively fixed. Wholesale transformations would transpire during the post–World War II era: industrial employment would decline precipitously—100,000 manufacturing jobs were lost in the city in the decade of the 1970s alone; venerable family owned Philadelphia firms would be purchased by national corporations and operations subsequently liquidated; once-proud industrial neighborhoods would decline and newcomers to these areas would find no jobs available; and white-collar and service-sector work in larger, bureaucratically managed enterprises would increase and predominate, thus providing new employment, but never involving the production of the quality goods that once flowed from Philadelphia's custom manufactories.

There is no longer anything unique about the nature of economic activities in Philadelphia. A distinct production system prevailed in the city from the early 1800s to the mid-twentieth century, from the age of Jefferson to the age of Truman. Individuals contributed to the building of Philadelphia's industrial order—the efforts of proprietors and skilled workmen alike were as important as natural resources and market forces. But the structure in turn also shaped individual experience in profound ways. Philadelphia was a particular place and working in the city had particular advantages and disadvantages. The system not only affected the conditions under which people labored but also determined to a great extent who exactly came to be employed there.

Economic opportunity and expansion first generated population growth. In 1800, close to 68,000 people resided in the original rectangle of a city established by William Penn and the surrounding villages that were to be incorporated in 1854 to form the modern urban complex known as Philadelphia. By the time of that consolidation, the population of the area had increased six-fold and on the eve of the Civil War the city housed more than 500,000 people.[37] The late nineteenth century would witness a doubling of residents, with census takers counting close to 1.3 million Philadelphians by 1900. The population would then grow to and plateau near 2 million in 1930; characteristically, rates of increase began to decline as Philadelphia's place in the national economy slipped. Soon the city would give way and become the country's second, third, fourth, and finally fifth largest metropolis.[38]

In-migration by and large accounted for the vast increases of population after 1800. Yet Philadelphia did not receive a random sample of migrants. The city's particular opportunity and economic structure shaped the process. Philadelphia, for example, never attracted massive numbers of foreign-born immigrants, and among the major manufacturing cities it remained the one most identified as a city of native-born workers. In 1880, Irish, German, and English-born migrants represented 42 percent of the entire work force of the United States and were majorities in most industrial areas. These groups comprised only 30 percent of Philadelphia's laboring population in that year.[39] Conversely, native-born laborers with native-born parents accounted for more than 55 percent of the city's working population. Only five other cities, all significantly smaller—such as New Haven, Connecticut, and Wilmington, Delaware—had higher percentages of native-born wage earners than Philadelphia.[40]

Philadelphia did not become a prime magnet for migrants from overseas for a number of reasons. The decline of commerce and the port and the failure of the city's business community and political leadership to develop adequate passenger line service and publicity made the city a less accessible point of entry for immigrants.[41] Passenger steamers from southern Europe first entered the harbor only in 1909, and during the country's peak period of immigration (1900 to 1915) Philadelphia never directly received more than 12 percent (and sometimes as little as 3 percent) of the numbers disembarking in New York City in any one year.[42]

A more significant explanation lies in the kinds of jobs available in the city. Philadelphia quickly garnered a reputation as a center for craft work. The production of specialized goods required skilled labor, and commentators in the nineteenth century quickly developed the sobriquet "Philadelphia Mechanic."[43] British- and German-born weavers, loom fixers, pattern makers, molders, and machinists easily secured employment along side their native-born counterparts, but immigrants without craft experience had a more difficult time. The railroads, the anthracite coal fields north of the city, and the steel mills of western Pennsylvania (or the automobile plants of Detroit and stockyards of Chicago) attracted unskilled labor, particularly from southern and eastern Europe, to a greater extent. Philadelphia's production system made for a particular ethnic mix.[44]

The industrial order of the city also had implications for the employment of women. Light industrial jobs prevailed in Philadelphia and this opened opportunities for greater female labor force participation. In 1880, single and married women constituted less than a quarter of the nation's work force, but close to one-third of Philadelphia's industrial workers. In some industries, such as textiles, garments, and hat and paper making, females accounted for clear majorities of employees.[45] Immigrant women, moreover, held an advantage over their male kinsmen. A young Irish woman living in Philadelphia in 1851 wrote back to friends in her homeland that "No female that can handle a needle need be idle [here]."[46] Irish young ladies found work in light industries and as domestics, while Irish men found but common day labor. As a result, the proportions of Irish women to men in Philadelphia increased steadily during the nineteenth century. By 1880, for every 10 females there were 7 males, and, among twenty to twenty-nine-year-old Irish immigrants, for every 1,000 women there were but 582 men.[47]

Finally, the very strength of the city's economy proved a severe weakness as well, and this weakness had an equally profound impact on the experiences of working men and women in Philadelphia's labor market. Philadelphia entrepreneurs profited by entering specialized markets. Remarkable opportunities existed in this sphere even for immigrants. In 1880 more than 75 percent of all the textile firms conducting business in the city were owned and operated by manufacturers of immigrant background (at a time when the foreign born comprised 30 percent of the total population).[48] Yet, custom markets were and still are also characteristically unstable—seasonality and the very tenuousness of demand made for uncertain fortunes, and as easy as entrance was for proprietorship in Philadelphia, so was bankruptcy and failure.

The mortality rates of firms in Philadelphia were extreme during the nineteenth and early twentieth centuries. The city once proudly boasted of the number of venerable firms in operation for more than one hundred years—in 1950 there were 171 such firms to celebrate—but below the noted survivors were thousands of businesses that had opened and failed without much fanfare and as a matter of daily course.[49] Of 126 textile firms in operation in the industrial neighborhood of Kensington in 1850, for example, many started by enterprising immigrants, only 23 were still in business ten years later (new ones, of course, cropped up to fill the void).[50] Similarly, a major study of 6,198 businesses conducted in 1930 discovered that less than one-fourth survived the period under investigation, 1915 to 1930.[51] A clear relationship existed between the size of an operation and the ability to keep one's doors open. Small custom workshops—Philadelphia's claim to distinction—were particularly at the mercy of the marketplace.

Uncertain business made for uncertain employment. Philadelphia offered a variety of work opportunities: from sweatshop to artisan shop, mill, plant, and even entrepreneurship. A large proportion of production, however, in all these settings, was geared to specialized markets, and that made for a common experience and problem. Few Philadelphians during the nineteenth and early twentieth centuries could count on constant work.[52] Firms frequently went out of business, but even in normal times, irregular commerce led to frequent job furloughs. Underemployment and unemployment were also key, if less glorious, features of the Philadelphia industrial system.

Citizens of the Quaker City had to cope. Women and children worked in large numbers in the city, not only because jobs were available to them in light industry, but because their incomes were needed for family survival, especially when layoffs were a pervasive reality. Philadelphia in fact had the largest percentage of families with more than one breadwinner of all industrial cities.[53] Philadelphia similarly was known as a city of homeowners. Homeownership indeed was widespread among the city's working population, but not only because it was possible. Owning a home could serve as a hedge against irregular employment. Boarders taken into the home and outwork performed in the home could provide much needed income.[54] Finally, high labor turnover and people constantly out of work had a negative effect on productivity and raised the potential for social unrest; business and community leaders in Philadelphia were also forced to cope with the particularities of Philadelphia's industrial order.[55] The getting and losing of work was a personal and political issue.

Who came to the city, who joined the labor force, the conditions under which people worked, the ability of families to make ends meet, the problems faced by managers and politicians alike—all were matters shaped by Philadelphia's production system. William Rees, Timothy Ragan, Jean Bally, and William Deacon sought and re-sought employment in this special context.

2 · Entering the World of Work

Timothy Ragan began working at the age of twelve. William Rees took his first job at thirteen, Jean Bally at fourteen and William Deacon at sixteen. Family and friends came to the aid of William Rees and Timothy Ragan in their first searches for work; later they had to rely on their own resources and determination. Family connections were a constant in Jean Bally's occupational history, while William Deacon counted on schooling and school placement services in his passage into the labor market. These stories conjure up images, particularly of bygone times. In the past, people went to work in their early teens if not before, and there was but a short juncture between childhood and the adult world of employment. An extended free-wheeling (and, some would add, free-loading) adolescence is a modern phenomenon. Similarly, in traditional society, people relied heavily on kin and close personal acquaintances in their economic activities; today, impersonal institutions and rules and regulations also affect and buffer experience. William Deacon's story, in this regard, is different from the others. He is seemingly a twentieth-century figure, educated and trained in a trade at school, who began work at sixteen after high school graduation and used a formal employment agency to secure work.

How accurate are our images? How representative are these stories? When did people in the past enter the world of work and how did the age of entrance vary for different groups within the society? Similarly, how did workers generations ago secure jobs and how did that process vary within the work force? These are the key questions of interest in this chapter as the focus shifts to the actual experiences of working men and women in the larger Philadelphia industrial system. I will also consider the question of access to jobs. Did all workers live in convenient reach of employment opportunities? Was simple geography a factor in occupational attainment? Finally, I will

17

treat a distinct situation—the employment histories of black Philadel-phians, which make, in every respect, a separate story.

During the spring and summer of 1903, a dramatic confrontation attracting national attention and involving the question of child labor in industry unfolded on the streets of Philadelphia. In April of that year, the city's Central Textile Workers Union announced a cam-paign to improve working conditions in the local textile industry, especially for those below the age of fifteen, who comprised more than 25 percent of the work force. High on the agenda of the union was a reduction in hours of work from sixty to fifty-five a week without concomitant losses in pay. The essential health and well-being of youngsters in the mills, the union argued, required short-ened hours of toil. After weeks of fruitless petition and negotiation, the union called a strike for May 29. More than 90,000 workers subsequently walked off their jobs, forcing the closing of 636 textile firms in the city. It was one of the largest strikes in American history to date.[1]

Mary Harris, better known as "Mother Jones," then added to the drama. The fiery labor advocate and organizer arrived in Philadelphia in early June and convinced strike leaders to make child labor the central issue. On June 17, she organized a parade and demonstration to Independence Hall, with 50,000 adult striking workers led by 7,000 working children. Two weeks later she called for a children's protest march from Philadelphia to Oyster Bay, Long Island, the summer retreat of President Theodore Roosevelt. On July 7, with a full press contingent in tow, Mother Jones's army of young Philadel-phians left the city, only to receive a mixed reception on the road. They arrived at their destination on August 1 with their numbers greatly depleted and found the President unavailable. The march gar-nered great publicity, but little else. The textile strike of 1903 dragged on ineffectually for three months after the children's march, when union executives declared an official end. The issue of child labor, however, did not disappear from the public's eye.

Middle-class reformers soon assumed the cause. One prominent group of civic leaders formed the Pennsylvania Child Labor Commit-tee for the express purpose of lobbying for stricter enforcement of existing legislation on child labor and for new standards. To promote further reform, they released a series of reports containing striking photographs and statistics detailing the exploitation of young people at work. A study of Philadelphia night messengers created the greatest stir, with tales of twelve-year-old boys working nine-hour night shifts, fifty-four hours a week, for an average weekly compensation of $4.12.[2] The time the young boys spent at saloons and other places of ill repute during the evening also received due note. The moral health of child laborers, however, was not the sole health concern; other reports issued by reform groups gave evidence of serious physical disorders—anemia and respiratory infections—suffered by children in the labor force.[3]

The high point of publicity on the issue would come during the week of December 9, 1906, when more than twenty-five thousand Philadelphians crowded into the city's Horticultural Hall on Broad and Locust Streets to view "An Industrial Exhibit," which dramatized with shocking photographs the use and state of child labor in Philadelphia industry.[4] The Consumers' League of Philadelphia sponsored the display. This organization was led by Florence Sanville, a Progressive era reformer and author of several studies on labor conditions and affairs, and Scott Nearing, a young economist and emerging muckraker, who would gain notoriety a decade later for being fired from the University of Pennsylvania for his radical views on capitalism and peace and again a half-century later for his example and advocacy of living a simple, self-sufficient life on the land. Progressive reformers in the Pennsylvania Child Labor Committee and the Consumers' League succeeded in having Philadelphia dubbed "The Greatest Child Employing City," and pressure soon mounted on local and state politicians to curb child labor through compulsory school attendance laws, to regulate it through work certification procedures, and generally to improve conditions in industry through stricter hours and safety inspection legislation.[5]

The warnings and fears of Philadelphia's Progressive era reformers were justified. The employment of young people in Philadelphia was a growing phenomenon. Despite an increase in the building of school facilities and public campaigns on behalf of common school education, the percentages of children at work increased dramatically over the last half of the nineteenth century (see Table 2.1). At least for youngsters above the age of twelve, all age levels were affected.[6] While 3 to 4 percent of all thirteen-year-olds worked in 1860, for example, more than 20 percent of their numbers joined the work-a-

Table 2.1 Labor force participation, percent of young white men and women in Philadelphia, 1860–1900

	1860			1870		
Age	At Home	In School	At Work	At Home	In School	At Work
Males						
12	18	80	2	19	74	7
13	25	72	3	27	62	11
14	43	49	8	30	50	20
15	44	43	23	24	35	41
16	37	21	42	25	18	57
17	26	10	64	20	10	70
Females						
12	22	75	3	22	72	6
13	31	65	4	28	64	8
14	40	52	8	36	48	16
15	43	34	23	38	33	29
16	55	15	30	45	19	36
17	48	8	44	50	7	43

Source: United States Manuscript Schedules, 1860–1880, 1900. For 1860–1880, I relied on the data bank of the Philadelphia Social History Project, which includes information for the entire black, Irish-born, and German-born populations living in Philadelphia in 1860, 1870, and 1880, and a sample of one-sixth of the white, native-born population in 1860 and 1870 and one-ninth of this group for 1880. Information for 1900 comes from a

day world forty years later. Among fourteen year olds, the jump was as great, from 8 percent at work in 1860 to more than 40 percent by century's end. While older youngsters, fifteen to seventeen years of age, had always worked in greater numbers, their respective proportions in the labor force rose as well. The growth of child labor in Philadelphia, however, apparently did not occur at the expense of losses in school attendance. The percentages of young people remaining in school at each age interval remained fairly constant. The numbers of youngsters neither at work or in school and presumably at home (or in the streets causing the notorious trouble detailed in nineteenth-century newspapers and novels) declined in direct relation to increases in work force participation. Most children by the turn of the century were either on the job or in the classroom, their options now narrowed and defined.

Table 2.1   (continued)

	1880			1900	
At Home	In School	At Work	At Home	In School	At Work
Males					
13	77	10	12	79	9
14	66	20	10	67	23
16	48	36	12	43	45
18	37	45	10	29	61
16	17	67	11	16	73
14	10	76	10	11	79
Females					
12	77	11	16	81	4
19	70	11	20	60	20
38	51	21	24	45	31
39	31	30	23	28	49
36	18	46	27	15	58
44	10	46	29	9	62

separate systematic random sample of 1 percent of all households in the city and a 10 percent random oversample of new immigrant groups (Italians, Poles, Russians, and Austro-Hungarians) and African-Americans. Young people living alone were excluded from this analysis.

The above cited figures apply to young white males, but the increase in child labor over the course of the nineteenth century commonly held for all groups of young Philadelphians. The numbers of young women at work grew in the same increments. Eight percent of all fourteen-year-old girls in Philadelphia could be found laboring in 1860; 20 percent by the turn of the century. Among the city's various ethnic groups the same increase held true (see Table 2.2). Approximately one-third of Irish and German-born fifteen-year-old males in the city were at work in 1860; twenty years later, two out of three were recorded by census enumerators as gainfully employed.

A general increase in the labor force participation of young people in Philadelphia is thus manifest in the late nineteenth century. By the time that both labor leaders and middle-class reformers raised on high the scandal of child labor, young people between twelve and

Table 2.2 Labor force participation and school attendance, percent of thirteen- and fifteen-year-old male and female Philadelphians, 1860, 1880, 1900, by ethnicity

	1860		1880		1900	
	In School	At Work	In School	At Work	In School	At Work
Thirteen-Year-Old Males						
NWA	77	0	70	21	71	20
Blacks	62	9	66	23	80	10
Irish	71	6	55	18	60	20
German	51	10	29	57	★	★
Irish2			64	34	59	33
German2			62	30	72	25
Italian					★	★
Italian2					58	33
Russian					55	30
Russian2					86	14
Thirteen-Year-Old Females						
NWA	64	4	80	11	70	15
Blacks	59	13	64	24	70	6
Irish	66	7	50	30	★	★
German	59	1	39	54	★	★
Irish2			67	23	54	21
German2			52	21	63	29
Italian					21	29
Italian2					60	20
Russian					44	19
Russian2					64	7

Source: See Table 2.1. In 1880, census enumerators began gathering information on parents' place of origin, allowing for a determination of ethnic background of second generation immigrants.

Key: NWA = Native-born White American; Irish2, German2, etc. = 2nd Generation; ★ = Extremely small numbers in sample.

seventeen comprised more than 15 percent of the city's entire working population, a critical mass not easily hidden from view (and in certain trades, like textiles, a prominent mass indeed).[7] While the across-the-board growth in young people at work is of essential note, important distinctions existed among different groups of young Philadelphians in both rates of school attendance and employment. Who then went to work and who went to school?

Table 2.2 (*continued*)

	1860		1880		1900	
	In School	At Work	In School	At Work	In School	At Work
Fifteen-Year-Old Males						
NWA	50	19	49	43	30	57
Blacks	38	39	28	62	44	50
Irish	34	37	20	70	20	40
German	23	32	0	93	★	★
Irish2			29	61	23	71
German2			23	69	27	61
Italian					8	85
Italian2					0	100
Russian					25	75
Russian2					50	40
Fifteen-Year-Old Females						
NWA	42	19	46	29	39	35
Blacks	29	33	42	41	28	56
Irish	21	32	13	59	★	★
German	27	24	15	31	★	★
Irish2			27	43	24	58
German2			8	51	27	57
Italian					★	★
Italian2					★	★
Russian					19	64
Russian2					★	★

Age was one critical factor. In 1880, 75 percent of all seventeen year olds in Philadelphia could be found on the job and only 10 percent in school; the numbers were reversed for twelve year olds. At every point in time and for all groups, there prevailed a clear relationship between age and work force participation. Birth order also played a role. Fourteen-year-olds who were first-born children generally worked; their contemporaries who had older working brothers and sisters remained in school.[8]

Important similarities and differences emerged between young men and women. From ages twelve to fifteen, boys and girls in Philadelphia entered the labor market in equal proportions. For ages sixteen and beyond, however, the percentages of young men at work became distinctly greater. In 1880, more than 75 percent of all seventeen-year-old males earned a living, while less than 50 percent of their female counterparts could be found at work. The relatively lower entry rate of teenage girls into the labor force, however, was not matched with concurrent increases in school attendance. Men and women of that age attended school in similar numbers; larger proportions of young women stayed at home, presumably to take care of younger children.

The socioeconomic standing of the family had as great an impact on prospects for schooling and work among young people as age. Throughout the late nineteenth and early twentieth centuries, for example, upwards of 70 percent of the thirteen- and fourteen-year-old sons and daughters of Philadelphia proprietors and professionals attended school; 50 percent of the children of that age group of skilled workers in the city had the good fortune of attending school; and only 40 percent of the young people whose fathers occupied unskilled positions could be found in the classroom (see Table 2.3). Class differences held across time and age level and, with few exceptions, also across ethnic divides. For example, in the year 1880, among thirteen- and fourteen-year-old American-born children of American-born parents, 75 percent of those whose fathers were professionals or proprietors attended school; 60 percent of those whose fathers were skilled workers were in school; and 38 percent of the children of unskilled laborers were in the classroom. Similarly, among Irish-born thirteen- and fourteen-year-old children of Irish-born parents, practically every child from upper-status households attended school; 67 percent of those whose fathers were skilled men were in school; and only 40 percent of the children of Irish common day laborers were in the classroom. Whether measured by father's occupation, property holding, or personal wealth, the socioeconomic standing of the family proved in multivariate analysis to be the most salient factor in deciding a young person's fate as worker or student.[9] Ethnic differences in particular tended to fade when controlled for by class.

There are a few exceptions and qualifications to the above general statements. Within all socioeconomic groupings, black young men and women had the highest rates of school attendance and the lowest in labor force participation. German-born children and American-born children of German parents, conversely, across all class divides, had high numbers at work and relatively low percentages in school. Parents of German heritage, whatever their social standing, either valued work over education for their children or else controlled occupations and lines of work that they chose to have or easily could have their children inherit at early ages; the dominance of German immigrants in certain trades and businesses in Philadelphia makes the latter possibility most plausible, although the two explanations are not mutually exclusive. The use of apprenticeship as a substitute for schooling by Philadelphians of German ancestry is a related issue of importance to be discussed in a subsequent chapter.[10] The cases of black Philadelphians and Philadelphians of German background are the only two, it should be noted, where the factor of ethnicity or culture remains distinct across socioeconomic categories. Even the notable and oft-cited rates of high attendance at school by immigrants of Russian Jewish descent appear less remarkable when they are controlled for class standing of parents.[11]

Three other details modify the general portrait. Among immigrants in Philadelphia's population, families either naturalized or in residence in the United States for more than five years tended to send their children to school to a greater extent than did newer arrivals.[12] In the same vein, children born in America to immigrant parents were much less likely to join the work force than their first-generation counterparts. Finally, young immigrant women were more likely to go to work and not attend school than women of American-born parents, and that fact apparently held across class divides. Women of German heritage in particular had low rates of school attendance.

Which young people then stayed in school in the past? Which young people entered the world of work? In Philadelphia, white males from families on the lowest rungs of the socioeconomic scale, American-born or immigrant, generally entered the labor force in the greatest numbers; blacks and young men and women from more comfortable backgrounds stayed in school or at home. There were broad exceptions to this pattern, and individual, contingent situations should not be forgotten, either. A father's death or unemployment could force a young man of any background into work; the death of a mother similarly could take young women out of the labor force and back to the home to tend to child care and the running of the household. If sufficient diaries and letters of Philadelphia's working

Table 2.3 School attendance rates of thirteen- and fourteen-year-old male and female Philadelphians, 1860, 1880, 1900, by father's occupational status and ethnicity

Father's occupational status/ethnicity	Males, 13–14 Years of Age		
	(percent in school)		
	1860	1880 .	1900
Professional/			
proprietors (total)	71	65	74
NWA	82	75	86
Blacks	60	80	★
Irish	100	100	★
German	25	★	★
Irish2		67	75
German2		57	67
Italian			★
Italian2			★
Russian			71
Russian2			100
Skilled (total)	52	51	54
NWA	51	59	46
Blacks	72	62	★
Irish	69	67	★
German	42	13	★
Irish2		64	46
German2		38	70
Italian			13
Italian2			33
Russian			40
Russian2			63
Unskilled (total)	42	37	50
NWA	60	38	43
Blacks	59	51	★
Irish	30	40	★
German	50	33	★
Irish2		41	52
German2		13	50
Italian			★
Italian2			★
Russian			47
Russian2			★

Source: See Table 2.1.
Key: NWA = Native-born White American; Irish2, German2, etc. = 2nd Generation; ★ = Extremely small numbers in sample.

Table 2.3 (*continued*)

Father's occupational status/ethnicity	Females, 13–14 Years of Age (percent in school)		
	1860	1880	1900
Professional/			
proprietors (total)	69	70	64
NWA	70	88	68
Blacks	57	100	★
Irish	60	★	★
German	63	33	★
Irish2		93	50
German2		50	43
Italian			★
Italian2			★
Russian			17
Russian2			75
Skilled (total)	56	48	47
NWA	64	65	51
Blacks	72	67	★
Irish	25	33	★
German	26	22	0
Irish2		48	39
German2		40	63
Italian			11
Italian2			25
Russian			36
Russian2			46
Unskilled (total)	40	59	41
NWA	43	29	33
Blacks	48	59	★
Irish	43	29	★
German	10	★	★
Irish2		50	56
German2		33	33
Italian			43
Italian2			★
Russian			25
Russian2			★

people existed, such personal events and considerations might temper our faith in the general conclusions reached by statistical analyses of vital records. Certainly the testimony of Timothy Ragan, William Rees, Jean Bally, William Deacon, and the 2,500 other workers interviewed during the Great Depression provides ample evidence of the role played by circumstance in people's lives.

The general pattern of youth employment that can be constructed does provide an important clue to the expansion of child labor in the nineteenth century. Why did the institution grow? Why did not school attendance become a more universal phenomenon? Expansion in industrial production and jobs provides one answer. In fact, Philadelphia's light industries offered prime opportunities for the young to be employed. Labor force participation rates, moreover, proved fairly sensitive to business cycles and general levels of employment. Figures for the relative numbers of young men and women at work dipped, for example, in 1860; the city was still feeling the impact of the depression of 1857. An extremely large drop in youth employment similarly can be charted during the 1930s.[13] In other words, the young came into the work force as employment opportunities expanded (and left accordingly with the onset of bad times); that accounts to a great extent for the notable increase in child labor in the late nineteenth century.

Only one part of the story is thus told, however. An additional explanation lies in the high rates of work force participation of boys and girls from poor families. Opportunity and availability of jobs may have pulled, but necessity also pushed the young into work. Low wages made it impossible for unskilled adult male workers to support their families on their own incomes and irregular employment both contributed to and exacerbated the problem. Budget analyses for Philadelphia in the late nineteenth century reveal that working-class families suffered a more than $100 shortfall in income over expenses. In 1880, the yearly expenses of the average household came to an estimated $564, at a time when the mean yearly income of male adult workers was $441.[14] Money from second and third breadwinners was an imperative for family survival; with wives and older daughters needed for child care and home production, the burden fell to boys and younger girls. Estimates for 1880, in fact, reveal that children employed in Philadelphia contributed as little as one-third and in some instances as much as one-half of total family monetary resources. (With these figures in mind, the demand by trade unionists during the period for the so-called family wage for adult male laborers, compensation that would cover all family expenses and eliminate child labor, is clearly understandable.)[15] Poor families faced an additional bind necessitating child employment. As either renters or owners of small row homes, they were unable to house relatives and boarders, an important source of income for families in the middle and upper rungs of the socioeconomic order.[16] The reasons for an increase in the labor force participation rates of young people in the late nineteenth century are then fairly evident.

Less straightforward are explanations for the decline in child labor during the first four decades of the twentieth century. Many answers are available. Technological change at the end of the nineteenth century, including increased mechanization and automation, reduced the demand for unskilled labor, particularly the labor of the young.[17] Rising standards of living, most notably during the Progressive era and the 1920s, made families less reliant on children's income and allowed parents to send their young to school for longer periods of time. Certainly the passage of compulsory school attendance laws and other legislation banning the employment of youngsters spelled a death knell to a scandalous practice successfully attacked by reformers. Increased respect for the value of education in general placed more children in school than at the workplace.[18]

The problem in finding a single or simple answer for the reduction in youth employment in the twentieth century is that the decline was gradual and progressive. Had a sudden overall shift occurred, one or more of the above explanations might be most critical. In 1910, 63 percent of all Philadelphia young people between the ages of fourteen and nineteen were gainfully employed; a decade later the figure stood at 55 percent, by 1930, 43 percent, and 1940, 31 percent.[19] Technology did not play a role; in Philadelphia, significant changes in either techniques of production or occupations did not occur in this period and jobs traditionally occupied by young workers continued to exist; certainly the steplike quality of the reduction in the labor force participation rates of teenagers precludes a structuralist kind of explanation.

Youth employment may have declined in different decades for different reasons. The drop from 1910 to 1920 can probably be attributed to the passage of compulsory school attendance legislation in

Pennsylvania in 1915, which forbade the employment of children under the age of fourteen and required strict work certification procedures for fourteen- to sixteen-year-olds. The reduction in the 1920s may have been the result of gains in real income and more widespread acceptance of schooling as a critical resource. The large decline during the 1930s rested on high rates of unemployment and a complete absence of openings for young workers as well as implementation of federal codes first under the National Industrial Recovery Act of 1933 and later the Fair Labor Standards Act of 1938 that prohibited employment of young people below the age of sixteen. Law and economics converged in this way to gradually eliminate an institution that had actually expanded during the nineteenth century.

A final issue on youth employment concerns the nature of the jobs held. For the most part, young people in Philadelphia occupied menial or unskilled positions (see Table 2.4). Significant differences, however, prevailed for different groups of young workers. Girls held low-level jobs to a far greater extent than boys. White American-born young men of American-born parents occupied skilled jobs in greater proportions than black and immigrant young men. (White American-born young women held a similar advantage with regard to other younger women, but still faced gender discrimination.) No visible changes in the nature of jobs held by young people occurred over time—with one notable exception. In 1850, nearly 30 percent of all young black males in the labor force worked in skilled positions; by the end of the century upwards of 90 percent of young black men at work were engaged as unskilled laborers. The declining fortunes of African-American youngsters in the Philadelphia industrial system will be a part of their separate story.

First experiences in the labor market varied for different groups of young Philadelphians. The children of the poor entered the world of work in great numbers at early ages; American-born white youngsters generally had access to better jobs. How young people secured their first positions also varied, and here the career histories of Timothy Ragan and the other 2,500 Philadelphia workers canvassed by researchers from the University of Pennsylvania in 1936 provide unique information.[20]

These researchers, under commission from the Works Progress Administration, gathered data on employment histories from workers in four representative industries: textiles, hosiery, metal trades, and radio manufacturing. Although not randomly selected, the group canvassed reflected well the gender and ethnic composition of the work force with the exception of black Philadelphians; African-Americans found few jobs in the industries covered and only seven appear in the survey. The respondents ranged in age from 17 to 77; the oldest had started work in the 1870s. As a group they began their working lives at an average age of 15.2 years, although characteristic generational differences prevailed. Those who first entered the work force in the last quarter of the nineteenth century began working at an average age of 14.3 years; respondents who were first employed between 1900 and 1920 assumed their first jobs at an average age of 15; and the youngest in the sample began working on average at 16. Across all age cohorts, those who had stayed in school longer entered into work later in their teens. Figures obtained from the interviews on age of entrance into work and level of education manifest clearly both the progressive decline of child labor in the city and the impact schooling generally had in changing the basic demography of work force entry.[21]

How did respondents to the survey actually secure employment? In their accounts of their experiences in the labor market, at least seventeen distinct methods of obtaining jobs are noted. They can be grouped into four categories: family connection, personal connection, personal initiative, and formal agencies or institutions. Since complete career information was included, important distinctions between first and subsequent positions can also be drawn (see Table 2.5).

On their first entrance to the job market, 27 percent of the participants in the WPA survey obtained work through the direct intervention of family members—parents, siblings, and other kin. Another 25 percent utilized non-familial personal connections, relying on the assistance of friends, neighbors, and even politicians. The largest number, 40 percent, secured their first jobs through their own initiative, presenting themselves directly to their prospective employers. The remaining 9 percent took advantage of various institutional mechanisms—newspaper and radio advertisements, employment agencies, and school referral services. These figures place into perspective the role of family intervention in securing work. A sizable minority of workers in the WPA survey owed their initial employ-

Table 2.4 Skill levels of Philadelphia males and females, twelve to seventeen years of age, 1860, 1870, 1880, 1900, by ethnicity

	1860			1870		
	% White Collar	% Skilled	% Unskilled	% White Collar	% Skilled	% Unskilled
Males, 12–17 Years						
NWA	27	53	20	25	38	37
Black	3	18	79	3	10	87
Irish	15	52	33	11	34	55
German	20	57	23	17	53	30
Irish2						
German2						
Italian						
Italian2						
Russian						
Russian2						
Females, 12–17 Years						
NWA	5	26	69	6	32	62
Black	1	19	80	1	6	93
Irish	4	56	41	6	32	62
German	3	48	49	6	41	53
Irish2						
German2						
Italian						
Italian2						
Russian						
Russian2						

Source: See Table 2.1.

Key: NWA = Native-born White American; Irish2, German2, etc. = 2nd generation; * = Extremely small numbers in sample.

ment to the helping hand of kin, but family connection did not represent the dominant means of job procurement.

The role of family is further tempered by looking at labor market experience beyond initial employment. Few workers in the survey remained with their original employers for long periods of time. Mobility, in fact, marked their entire working lives, and getting work was a constant activity. How the respondents obtained work also changed significantly over the course of their careers.

Family connection, in particular, declined in importance in later

Table 2.4 (continued)

	1880			1900		
	% White Collar	% Skilled	% Unskilled	% White Collar	% Skilled	% Unskilled
Males, 12–17 Years						
NWA	26	34	40	21	28	51
Black	3	10	87	3	9	88
Irish	14	32	54	11	22	67
German	11	59	29	5	62	33
Irish2	12	34	54	14	33	53
German2	21	42	37	16	40	44
Italian				5	55	40
Italian2				17	68	17
Russian				16	53	31
Russian2				21	21	58
Females, 12–17 Years						
NWA	8	30	62	16	33	51
Black	1	9	90	0	11	89
Irish	3	33	64	★	★	★
German	7	30	63	0	42	58
Irish2	8	31	61	13	37	50
German2	8	38	54	13	40	47
Italian				0	78	22
Italian2				8	75	17
Russian				8	71	21
Russian2				10	67	23

efforts at securing work. While more than 25 percent of those interviewed in the WPA canvass mentioned the assistance of kin in obtaining their first jobs, no more than 12 percent reported family help in subsequent job searches. In addition, for those workers who relied on the intervention of family members, the role of parents diminished over time. Siblings and other kin played a more critical role. Retirement and death obviously rendered parents less significant in their children's later employment efforts. Methods of obtaining work in general, and the role of family connections specifically, cannot be properly assessed then without proper regard to the stages of the occupational life cycle.[22]

Table 2.5 Methods of getting work, Philadelphia workers, 1870–1936

	First Job		Intermediate Jobs		Job Held in 1936	
	N	%	N	%	N	%
Family connection	367	27	117	10	146	12
Parents	173	47	26	22	27	18
Siblings	90	24	32	27	46	31
Other kin	104	28	59	50	73	50
Personal connection	340	25	333	30	403	32
Friends	314	92	291	87	347	86
Neighbors	22	7	5	1	6	1
Former supervisors	2	1	34	10	45	11
Political pull	2	1	3	1	5	1
Personal initiative	555	40	566	50	576	46
Standing at factory gate	33	5	23	4	32	5
Written application	169	30	147	26	200	34
Walking from factory to factory	353	64	396	70	344	60
Institutions	123	9	113	10	124	10
Newspaper ads	47	38	60	53	47	38
Radio ads	5	4	1	1	0	0
Union hiring hall	2	1	9	8	11	8
Employment agency	22	17	34	30	58	47
Junior employment service	26	21	4	3	1	1
School reference	21	17	5	4	7	5

Source: Interview Schedules, 1936 Gladys Palmer Survey for Works Progress Administration.

Personal connections actually increased in relative importance over working life, with one-third of the participants in the survey noting the assistance of acquaintances in later job searches. Here the growing influence of supervisors and foremen is particularly noteworthy. Workers frequently moved to new positions with their supervisors when the latter transferred to new firms. Others secured work through the fortunate circumstance of meeting former overseers when applying for new jobs. Taking advantage of such networks obviously was only made possible after gaining both entrance to trades and the good favor of one's foreman.

Philadelphians also relied more heavily on their own pluck and perseverance in subsequent employment efforts, with little change in the specific methods of personal initiative used. Finally, the percentage of workers relying on formal institutions remained constant over the course of careers, with a steady 10 percent of those surveyed owing their first and later jobs to various agencies. Among those relying on such assistance, there was a growing use of employment bureaus over time and, not surprisingly, a decline in the importance of school referral services. Schools played a greater role in initial employment than in later career experiences. Again, the importance of specifying the point in the working life cycle is made clear by the testimony of the WPA survey respondents.

The survey data also allow for the drawing of finer distinctions. Methods of getting work not only varied by career stage, but also by gender, birthplace, generation, education, skill level, and trade. Men and women, for example, secured their jobs in basically similar ways (see Table 2.6). Family connection proved equally important for both in initial hiring and less important in subsequent employment efforts. Men and women also used institutions in similar, steady ratios. The key difference emerged in the categories of personal connection and initiative. At all stages of their careers, female workers relied to a greater extent on the assistance of friends and neighbors and less on personal initiative. The percentages here hint at what can be found in the interviews: that women were less likely to present themselves alone and directly to employers than men, less likely to stand at factory gates or wander the city looking for work, and conversely, were more reliant on non-familial, gender-specific networks based on the block, neighborhood, and work. "My girlfriend got me the job" was a common refrain.

When place of birth is considered, the similarities among the various national groups are more notable than the differences. With few exceptions, workers of all different national origins canvassed in 1936 relied principally upon personal initiative to secure their first jobs. British-American workers reported the greatest resort to family connections, and, surprisingly, Italian and Irish respondents reported the fewest uses of kinship networks. These findings challenge various commonly held assumptions about the behaviors of individuals from these backgrounds. Also, mythic institutions such as the padrone system are brought into question. Mention of the system is conspicuously absent from the interviews with workers of Italian heritage,

Table 2.6 Methods of getting work, Philadelphia workers, 1870–1936, by sex, nativity, age, education, and occupation

	First Job					Intermediate Job					Job Held in 1936				
	N	Family cnctn. %	Personal cnctn. %	Personal init. %	Insts. %	N	Family cnctn. %	Personal cnctn. %	Personal init. %	Insts. %	N	Family cnctn. %	Personal cnctn. %	Personal init. %	Insts. %
Total	1385	27	25	40	9	1129	10	30	50	10	1249	12	32	46	10
Sex															
Male	984	28	22	41	9	822	10	28	52	10	925	11	30	50	10
Female	401	23	31	38	8	307	11	35	45	9	324	25	40	36	10
			C = .10 (.00)					C = .07 (.10)					C = .12 (.00)		
Place of birth															
Philadelphia	909	26	26	41	7	697	10	33	49	9	826	13	36	42	9
Rest of USA	143	29	25	38	8	135	14	22	52	13	128	7	21	56	14
Germany	49	22	18	41	18	48	8	25	54	13	58	9	38	41	12
*Germ.-Am.	23	30	30	35	4	19	26	26	37	11	15	7	27	67	0
Italy	39	23	26	51	0	21	14	33	33	19	35	3	14	69	14
*Ital.-Am.	16	13	13	69	0	16	0	31	62	6	16	25	19	44	13
E. Europe	41	32	27	39	2	47	13	26	55	6	51	8	28	53	10
*E. Eur.-Am.	27	19	30	41	11	24	4	29	58	9	26	8	31	54	8
Britain	46	35	11	48	7	56	5	25	59	11	42	7	12	71	10
*Brit.-Am.	20	40	20	35	5	23	13	4	74	9	13	8	46	31	15
Ireland	13	15	31	46	8	12	8	25	50	17	11	0	27	64	9
*Irish-Am.	4	25	25	25	25	3	0	33	67	0	3	0	67	0	33
Other	17	35	35	24	6	15	20	13	40	27	15	7	40	40	13
*Other-Am.	5	20	60	20	0	7	0	43	57	0	8	13	50	37	0
			C = .16 (.00)					C = .20 (.00)					C = .22 (.00)		

Age in 1936															
17–29	609	24	29	35	12	380	13	37	27	10	607	15	35	40	9
30–44	467	25	22	47	8	441	9	28	33	11	434	10	30	51	10
45–77	309	34	19	42	5	308	8	23	59	9	308	8	31	49	11
		C = .17 (.00)					C = .16 (.00)					C = .12 (.00)			
Years of schooling															
0–5	125	34	20	42	4	129	8	31	56	6	122	5	28	53	14
6	139	32	24	38	7	134	10	31	52	8	133	10	28	53	14
7	185	29	23	43	6	168	12	35	45	8	150	15	33	43	9
8	529	26	23	43	8	440	11	30	50	10	475	11	35	44	9
9–16	401	23	29	35	14	258	11	26	50	14	363	13	32	44	11
		C = .15 (.00)					C = .11 (.32)					C = .11 (.18)			
Industry															
Textile	216	34	16	47	3						155	12	34	49	5
Hosiery	192	29	39	30	3						283	18	46	27	9
Metal trades	233	26	28	38	8						577	9	29	54	9
Other Manuf.	151	17	23	46	14						53	15	36	34	15
Building and construction	27	41	22	30	7						17	12	0	41	47
Trade and commerce	127	41	18	47	17						13	15	15	61	8
Government, util. offices	32	9	22	56	22						51	2	24	55	20
Service	5	80	0	20	0						5	20	20	40	20
Agriculture	36	36	31	25	8						8	36	11	50	0
Other trade	33	52	24	18	6						87	12	23	54	12
		C = .31 (.00)										C = .30 (.00)			

Table 2.6 *(continued)*

	First Job					Intermediate Job					Job Held in 1936				
	N	Family cnctn. %	Personal cnctn. %	Personal init. %	Insts. %	N	Family cnctn. %	Personal cnctn. %	Personal init. %	Insts. %	N	Family cnctn. %	Personal cnctn. %	Personal init. %	Insts. %
Skill level															
Skilled	85	39	26	37	6						560	10	32	48	10
Semiskilled	513	28	27	40	5						511	14	34	44	8
Unskilled	110	36	30	25	8						47	6	36	36	21
Apprentices	147	28	22	40	10						8	25	0	50	25
White collar	179	18	16	47	19						10	10	40	20	30
Other	256	24	16	40	12						86	12	22	55	12
			C = .21 (.00)										C = .15 (.00)		
Full-timer or part-timer															
Full-time	1003	25	25	41	9						917	11	32	47	11
Part-time	536	30	25	37	8						332	13	34	45	8
			C = .05 (.37)										C = .04 (.55)		

Source: See Table 2.5. Absolute figures along rows change because of missing information. Contingency coefficient C is given as measure of association, with level of statistical significance given in parentheses.

Key: Hyphenated Americans in this instance refer to European-born workers whose first jobs were secured in America. Family cnctn. = family connection. Personal cnctn. = personal connection. Personal init. = personal initiative. Insts. = institutions.

who reported securing their first jobs through personal initiative to a far greater extent than other groups of workers.[23] These turn-of-the-century immigrants may have been more isolated and reliant on their individual wits than is commonly assumed, especially in a city in which a high premium was placed on skill and where the skilled trades remained fairly closed to newcomers.

Over career time, the similarities between workers of different national origins also overshadowed the differences. Family connections declined in importance for all groups, with the sole exception of Italian-Americans, and reliance on personal initiative increased. Dependence on institutions increased marginally for American-born workers in the survey, but increased substantially for respondents of Italian and Eastern European heritage. The growing use of formal agencies by immigrants late in their working lifetimes can be attributed to generational and educational factors.

The time at which workers entered the labor market, in fact, played a significant role in methods employed to secure work. Participants in the WPA survey who first gained entrance to the job market in the late nineteenth century relied to a greater extent on family connections than their twentieth-century counterparts, and, conversely, reported minimal use of formal employment agencies.(Since these agencies, by and large, did not exist at the time, these findings are not surprising.) Over the course of their careers, all age cohorts registered less reliance on familial intervention. This points to the greater importance of career time over historical time. No matter to which generation the survey member belonged, help from kin decreased over the working life.

There is one notable exception in the age data. While the utilization of institutions remained constant for the two twentieth century cohorts in the survey, there was a distinct increase in the use of formal services by the oldest generation of workers. This runs counter to the expectation that workers born into a mature industrial society would be more likely to rely on formal mechanisms. William Deacon served as an example of a so-called modern figure at the outset of this chapter. In fact, it was the oldest workers in the survey who over the course of their careers depended increasingly on institutional help.

Education adds an additional twist to the story. On initial entrance into the job market, those with the most years of schooling tended to use formal services more and family connections less than those workers who had left school earlier or had no formal education (here a sense of modernization is confirmed). This relationship held, though not in as strong a fashion, for subsequent positions, but then an odd reversal occurred late in the workers' careers. On last jobs secured, the survey members with the least amount of schooling reported the greatest use of formal agencies. Late in their careers, in other words, workers with little education sought institutional assistance in securing new employment. Since a similar finding was discovered for older (versus younger) workers, a question arises as to which was the more important factor, years of schooling or generation. Actually, these factors prove of equal significance. The greatest resort to formal employment agencies was recorded not just by the oldest workers, but more specifically by the oldest workers with the fewest years of schooling. This exactly fits the histories of the Italian and Eastern European immigrants mentioned earlier who, among the different ethnic groups, reported the most frequent use of institutions in obtaining jobs. Thus, older immigrants who did not have the advantages of education encountered difficult times late in life in securing new positions and required the help of agencies.[24]

There was actually a two-tiered world of employment services in operation in Philadelphia during the late nineteenth and early twentieth centuries, a point that will be fully illustrated in Chapter Four. The youngest workers with the most years of schooling were the first; they had access to job referral offices in school and presumably ample knowledge of other such services that were part and parcel of the modern order. Second, the oldest workers with the fewest years of education—and a disproportionate number of immigrants fits into this category—found themselves late in life on line at public and private hiring agencies, an option of last resort for them.

Finally, information in the 1936 WPA canvass provides an opportunity to determine the relationship between methods of obtaining work and the character of the work sought. Survey members who entered the work force in their later teen years tended to occupy skilled and white-collar positions to a greater extent than those who began working at earlier ages; this is hardly surprising, for children of twelve or thirteen years with little or no education would only be eligible for the most menial jobs. While a relationship existed, then, between age and occupation, no distinct pattern emerged between methods of securing employment and the trade, skill level, and full-

or part-time nature of the positions acquired. However, one or two exceptions deserve note. On first entrance to the labor market, for example, skilled workers and particularly those seeking jobs in the building and construction industries relied heavily on family connections—family networks of hiring were obviously important in these fields. Conversely, those gaining jobs in trade, commerce, government, and white-collar work in general used formal agencies to the greatest degree. Over the course of workers' careers, there was a definite drop in the importance of family intervention for all trades and skill levels, but continued high use of formal agencies for those in search of office work. Changing occupational structure in this way apparently contributed to a slight but noticeable shift in the mechanisms of job procurement.

Several conclusions on the dynamics of securing employment can be drawn from the WPA survey. At least one-fourth of the respondents depended on kin in obtaining their first jobs, but family connection declined in importance over the working life. Most Philadelphians relied on their own personal initiative or increasingly over careers on the help of personal acquaintances. In only approximately one in ten attempts at finding work was a formal employment agency employed. Survey members born in the twentieth century and those with the most years of schooling tended to use institutions to the greatest degree, although older immigrants who had little or no education found themselves dependent on such services later in their lives. Those in pursuit of white collar work also used employment services to a relatively large extent. Other distinctions emerged— female workers relied more on friends than the males—but in general the similarities in how various groups of Philadelphians operated in the labor market in finding work outweigh the differences that can be cited.

The patterns of getting work discernible in the testimony also match the little that can be determined through generalization about the hiring practices of firms in Philadelphia. In 1931, the Philadelphia office of the Pennsylvania State Employment Service conducted the first apparent study of recruitment procedures of businesses operating in the city. The agency gathered information from 1,591 companies. Ninety percent of these firms reported that hiring occurred entirely through company facilities; only 10 percent noted the use of outside services, and of these close to 60 percent employed agencies in less than 25 percent of all hirings. In recruiting workers, the great majority of companies relied on lists of former employees, applications "at the gate," and recommendations of workers presently on payroll. The use of public and private employment exchanges and that of help-wanted advertising in local newspapers were reported as last resort measures and usually involved highly selective posts. The general informal nature of the hiring process was also particularly manifest in another piece of information obtained by the State Employment Service. Of the 1,591 firms in the canvass, only 9 reported the existence of an established personnel department in charge of recruitment; another 42 noted the establishment of separate employment offices, while in 1,540 companies (97 percent), the function of hiring rested totally in the hands of individual managers or supervisors.[25]

General employment conditions could affect and alter company methods of recruitment. Another Philadelphia survey of hiring practices, conducted ten years later during a period of war-induced labor shortages, found a majority of firms resorting increasingly to advertisements and private and public employment agencies.[26] Normal ad hoc processes did not suffice when workers were in short supply. Recruitment practices could also vary by the nature of the jobs to be filled. Participants in the 1936 WPA survey who sought white-collar posts reported greater use of formal hiring services. Not coincidentally, a study conducted in the late 1930s on the recruitment of clerical help in small offices in Philadelphia reported primary resort to employment agencies for staffing positions. Only 8 of the 150 small firms canvassed noted reliance on worker recommendations and, specifically, the use of kin networks.[27]

The recruitment of office workers differed for a number of reasons. Offices were generally located in center city Philadelphia; this precluded neighborhood-based hiring and made the process impersonal from the start. Traveling downtown to find office work was in fact a daunting experience, particularly for young women from industrial areas.[28] Employers of white-collar labor, moreover, had no reason to invest time in training recruits in such standardized skills as typing, stenography, and filing. Clerical workers acquired their expertise in outside institutions, public and private schools and business colleges, and referral services either part of or separate from these institutions could measure and attest to their competence. White-collar firms thus contracted out the function of evaluation of applicants to other agencies. This was particularly useful when conditions required hiring temporary help. Manufacturing concerns, on the other hand, located in industrial and residential districts such as Kensington, Manayunk, and Germantown, trained workers on the job, particularly for small-batch or custom work; the process was inherently social from the beginning and plant superintendents and foremen accordingly relied on neighborhood and family contacts in recruitment. As white-collar work has increased, as offices have become larger and the pools of office labor have grown, personal and familial connections may have become more important in the hiring process. The absence of detailed surveys on current employment practices in Philadelphia permits only speculations on the subject.

The ways in which Philadelphians found work, then, generally match the methods employed by firms in the city in securing their labor. Do the findings from the WPA canvass of 1936 correspond to other studies on job search conducted in other places and times? From the 1930s through the 1970s, researchers completed thirty-four surveys in various towns and cities in the United States on the question of methods of obtaining employment.[29] Unfortunately, these studies asked only about present positions held and were not attentive to change over career or historical time. A certain consistency, however, is apparent. In most surveys, 35 to 45 percent of all respondents have reported securing work through direct application to companies and another 35 to 45 percent through the intervention of friends or relatives (these latter figures are slightly lower than for the WPA survey). The remaining 10 to 20 percent of those canvassed obtained jobs through institutional means (a higher use of agencies than that recorded for Philadelphia in 1936). These general figures hide important distinctions. Context proved important; one study conducted in Detroit in the 1960s found, for example, that 40 percent of those sampled secured employment through union hall hiring lists. A gradual increase in the use of formal employment services over the last forty years, though, is manifest when figures from the thirty-four studies are compared. Still, for the vast majority of workers either one hundred years ago or today, jobs have basically been found in roughly equal proportions either through personal connections or personal initiative.

W. E. B. DuBois may have been the first scholar to notice and note that, in northern industrial cities, black youngsters entering the world of work experienced a distinctly different process than did their white counterparts. In 1896, DuBois accepted an invitation to join the faculty of the sociology department of the University of Pennsylvania as an assistant instructor. He had recently earned a doctoral degree at Harvard—the school's first black Ph.D.—and completed additional course work on social science concepts and methods in Europe. As part of his appointment at the University of Pennsylvania, DuBois was asked to conduct a study of the conditions of Negro life in Philadelphia.[30] The University had operated a settlement house in the city's seventh ward, which had increasingly become a black ghetto, and reformers in Philadelphia, many connected with the school, had drawn links between political corruption in the district and the neighborhood's growing social and economic problems, including rising rates of poverty, unemployment, and crime. DuBois received encouragement to investigate. From his efforts emerged one of the first great classics of American social science research, DuBois's *The Philadelphia Negro*.

DuBois did not have access to the kinds of manuscript census materials that would have allowed for precise comparisons between the school attendance and labor force participation rates of young blacks and whites in Philadelphia. His own in-depth survey of the seventh ward convinced him that African-American children were in school or at home and not at work to a far greater extent than both their American-born and immigrant white counterparts. This finding was puzzling. Black family incomes were on average the lowest in the district. Why then did not black children earn money to contribute to the family economy? DuBois offered an explanation. He resorted not to demographics—black families were no smaller than white—nor to culture. He did not argue that black parents placed greater value on schooling than on their children's potential for income earning. Rather, the answer was to be found in discrimination. Black youngsters simply could not secure jobs because they were black. As he wrote:

> [The] absence of child labor . . . is not voluntary on the part of the Negro but due to restricted opportunity; there is really very little that Negro children may do. Their chief employment, therefore, is found in helping about the house while mother is at work.[31]

DuBois's explanation requires some correction. African-American children did not merely idle away at home. High levels of labor force participation of married black women made it necessary for black girls to stay at home for the purposes of child care, but black children in general also attended and remained in school in disproportionately large numbers. At least for the late nineteenth and early twentieth centuries, black classroom attendance figures indicate great faith and belief on the part of black parents in the power of education for their children, undoubtedly part of the reason black youngsters were to be found more in school than at work.[32] DuBois, however, did point to the more critical reason: the denial of employment on the grounds of color. Racism kept teenage blacks from serving as second and third breadwinners, but this was not a phenomenon peculiar to the young. Systematic exclusion of African-Americans from industrial jobs in Philadelphia marks the city's history through the Second World War. Black Philadelphians, young and old, in effect never became part of Philadelphia's particular economic order. Their experiences within the labor market form a separate narrative and on this point the historical evidence is staggering.

Discrimination in hiring affected many groups in Philadelphia. American-born Philadelphians occupied skilled and white-collar positions to a far greater extent during the nineteenth century than various newcomers to these shores, though by century's end the children of immigrants began to match older-stock Americans in their occupational achievements. Women, too, continually held jobs on the lowest rungs of the job ladder. The case of blacks in the work force presents a different kind of story, for African-Americans were almost completely absent from Philadelphia industry.[33]

Major firms in the city, for example, made a practice of not employing black workers and certainly not black youngsters through the 1930s. The Budd Company, Bendix, Cramps Shipyard, and Baldwin Locomotive, with combined work forces of over 35,000 employees, hired not a single black (not even in the most menial positions) until the late 1930s.[34] The Crown Can Company, the machine building firm of William Sellers, and the Quaker Lace Company, fixtures in the city's economic landscape, also hired no blacks. Smith, Kline, and French, the 3,000-employee pharmaceutical works; J. G. Brill, the manufacturer of streetcars and other mass transport vehicles, also with 3,000 employees; and General Electric, with 6,500 workers on payroll in the city, employed less than forty-five African-Americans among them.[35] In the textile industry during the 1930s, with total employment ranging upwards of 45,000, census enumerators could locate only 280 black employees, all holding janitorial positions.[36] Where blacks did find employment in industry, moreover, as at the Frankford Arsenal, they often worked in segregated areas and used segregated facilities.[37] At the Sun Shipyards, just south of the city, black workers built ships separately in the so-called colored yards.[38]

Only a handful of industrial firms in Philadelphia experimented with the use of black labor. In 1916, the Pennsylvania Railroad hired for the first time more than 1,100 black maintenance-of-the-way men and based them in camps along the line near the city; before that time, only a score of black laborers in Philadelphia had found work in the railroad trade.[39]

Only five other major companies were known to employ blacks: Atlantic Refinery, Franklin Sugar, Westinghouse, Disston Saw, and Midvale Steel.[40] The last case provides the most intriguing story. Of all the manufacturing firms in the city, Midvale Steel was the only one to build a reputation as an employer of black labor. By 1917, the company's payroll included more than 4,000 African-Americans.[41] Employment of black workers at Midvale had begun in the late 1890s and was the result of a deliberate initiative on the part of an individual mentioned by DuBois in *The Philadelphia Negro* as a "crank"—none other than Frederick Winslow Taylor. The Midvale Steel Company occupies a place in American business and economic history for any number of reasons, but not least of all for serving as the site of Taylor's most publicized experiments in scientific management and time-and-motion studies. In an effort to prevent "soldiering," concerted actions by workers to break piece-rate drive systems, and talking and "clannishness" among employees, Taylor fixed on a solution: integrate the work force with blacks. Workers would spend less time socializing and more in production. The irony here is great. Significant opportunities for blacks opened at Midvale Steel, the most important employer of black labor in Philadelphia, because of the efficiency schemes of Frederick Taylor. The story, though, has an odd, or perhaps not so odd, coda. Midvale remained a critical employer of African-Americans, but within a decade of their initial hiring, managers of the company began to place them in segregated sections of the plant. So much for Taylor's experiment.

There was little irony involved in the two other ways in which industrial opportunities emerged for blacks in the Quaker City. Black job seekers could benefit as much from strikes and wars as from the machinations of the likes of Frederick Winslow Taylor. The first black women to be employed on an ongoing basis in the city's large garment trades secured their jobs in 1910 as a result of their strike-breaking activity. Expansion in clothing production during World War I led to further openings for black needleworkers and a citywide walkout of garment makers in 1921 gave employment to an estimated additional three hundred; few of these latest recruits, however, retained their positions at strike's end.[42] World War II proved another and more important boon to blacks seeking work, and, as will be shown later, the war period witnessed the first large-scale reversal in discriminatory employment practices in Philadelphia and the much belated entrance of blacks into the city's industrial fold.

The place of strikebreaking in the black employment experience should not be exaggerated. Garment strikes in 1910 and 1921 can be cited; there are other examples, such as the quilt manufacturer who in 1916 replaced his male white work force with black women because the men were "Bolsheviks . . . who wanted more money and shorter hours," and the scheme hatched by the National Hosiery and Underwear Manufacturers Association of Philadelphia to transport black girls who were in training in knitting mills in Enfield, North Carolina, to Philadelphia to work at low wages in city mills (it is unclear whether this plan was ever implemented).[43] Large-scale importation of black strikebreakers never occurred in Philadelphia, however, and it is probably one reason why the city, with the largest African-American population in the north by the late 1910s, did not experience the racial tensions and riots that scarred other northern industrial areas during the first decades of the twentieth century. Blacks remained outside the Philadelphia industrial system in more ways than one.

The plight of black workers in Philadelphia cannot be attributed simply to lack of training or schooling. Black youngsters recorded the highest rates of school attendance throughout the early twentieth century. Blacks generally were denied admission to formal apprenticeship programs in the city; in fact, a survey taken of skilled African-American workers revealed that most black craftsmen in Philadelphia had been trained in the South.[44] Still, even highly skilled black workers experienced severe discrimination in hiring. A census of the black community in the 1850s taken by Quaker officials, for example, indicated that 40 percent of those blacks trained in specific crafts could not find work in their chosen trades.[45] Black shop owners and businessmen, as a result, served as the sole employers of black skilled labor. In 1910, all seventeen trained African-American printers in the city worked in black-owned printshops and for black newspapers.[46]

The inability of trained black workers to secure employment in Philadelphia eventually attracted the concern of public school authorities. In an effort to improve the job prospects of black students, officials in the Philadelphia Board of Education began in the 1920s to encourage the enrollment of black youngsters in commercial courses. A lackluster record of placement induced a survey of employers in 1940.[47] The Board asked sixty firms to provide information concerning current practices and prospects for the employment of black graduates of commercial course programs. Eighteen of the sixty firms refused outright to consider the idea. Eight of these noted "personal disapproval" of blacks, five expressed fears of adverse employee reactions, and five others fear of negative customer response. Another twelve firms admitted they had never considered the hiring of blacks, and twenty-one were noncommittal. Five companies offered to interview selected black candidates, one firm refused to participate in the survey, and three companies reported that they already employed black clerical help—five black workers in all.

African-Americans, even educated and trained members of the community, found no place in Philadelphia industry throughout the nineteenth and early twentieth centuries; they apparently had limited access to job openings in the burgeoning white-collar sector in the modern era. Where then did blacks find employment? The main answer lies in domestic service. In his survey of the seventh ward in Philadelphia in the 1890s, DuBois discovered that 60 percent of all black working men and 90 percent of all black working women earned their livings as domestics. Those figures generally hold for the city at large and remain constant over the next forty years.[48] In comparison, less than 30 percent of all white immigrants and 10 percent of all American-born workers in Philadelphia during the period could be found in service.[49] Blacks also tended to occupy domestic positions throughout their working lifetimes, while for whites, domestic work represented a passing stage into what was considered more desirable and less demeaning factory, office, and sales work.[50]

For African-American youngsters, too, domestic service loomed as the sole opportunity; seven out of ten of the relatively few black youngsters in the labor market during the nineteenth century held domestic jobs.[51]

Blacks thus functioned in a separate labor market in Philadelphia. They occupied mainly domestic positions. Black males not in service found day labor jobs, largely in hauling and carting. The small population of skilled workers found employment in black-owned businesses and the even smaller group of black professionals—doctors, lawyers, and ministers—served their community. There were exceptions; the hiring of 4,000 black workers by Midvale Steel is the most notable.

Prejudice and discrimination, and not lack of schooling, provide the most important explanation for the unique black employment experience in Philadelphia. Blacks today in northern urban areas are identified as prime holders of hospital maintenance, food preparation, and orderly jobs. Yet it was not until World War II that the first African-Americans began to work in Philadelphia hospitals that catered to white patients. Fears that blacks carried disease excluded them from employment in positions now commonly held by them.[52] Employer "disapproval" of blacks kept them separated.

Resistance by white workers, both informal and organized, also contributed to the problem. In the 1850s, a charitable organization, the Philadelphia Society for the Employment and Instruction of the Poor, attempted to persuade firms in the city to hire black workers. The effort met with little success, largely because of opposition from white employees. As Joshua Bailey, member of the board of managers of the society, noted in a diary entry of January 10, 1853:

> Employers expressed themselves willing to receive such a one (a colored man) into their shops, but they cannot dare to do it knowing the opposition such an act would meet with from their workmen who will not consent to work with colored people.[53]

The arrival of immigrant groups from Europe exacerbated the situation. Instead of pushing African-Americans up the occupational ladder, immigration forced their exclusion from trades they had previously occupied. An article in the *Daily Sun* in November 1849 discussed the results of competition for jobs between Irish and black workers on Philadelphia's docks:

[There] may be, and undoubtedly is, a direct competition [between
the Irish and blacks] as to labor . . . The wharves and new buildings
attest to this fact in the person of our stevedores and hod carriers . . .
When a few years ago, we saw none but blacks, we now see nothing but Irish.[54]

Figures from available censuses confirm the reality of the above
observations. Between 1847 and 1850, the percentage of hod carriers
and stevedores in the black population fell from 5 percent to 1 percent; in absolute terms, the number of black hod carriers fell sharply
from ninety-eight to twenty-eight and stevedores from fifty-eight to
twenty-seven.[55]

The arrival of immigrants from northern Europe in the 1840s and
1850s coincided with a decline in the employment prospects of black
workers. The percentage of African-American youngsters holding
skilled jobs, for example, dropped precipitously after 1850. The number of black skilled workers in general able to ply their trades also
fell. In the special Quaker census of the black community in 1838,
23 percent of the black craftsmen polled reported not being able to
practice their craft because of "prejudice against them." By 1856, 38
percent of the black artisans were "compelled to abandon their trades
on account of the unrelenting prejudice against their color."[56] The
opposition of white workers to the hire of African-Americans in
Philadelphia continued to have an impact into the first half of the
twentieth century. In 1932, a study of 172 firms in the metal trades
in the city with a combined employment of 39,000 people discovered
but 286 black workers in the entire industry (all hired as helpers).
When employers were asked about these low numbers, the most
frequent explanation was "to avoid antagonizing white employees."[57]

Pressure for exclusion of blacks by white workers could also take
an organized form, and here the trade union movement in Philadelphia played its role. Either through custom or through precise exclu-
sionary clauses in their charters, unions in the city generally excluded
blacks from membership. A study in 1910 estimated that out of a
population of 63,000 as few as 200 blacks held union cards, and these
men were primarily members of all-black labor associations, such as
the brotherhoods of hod carriers and hotel workers (both ephemeral
organizations).[58] Among white unions, only the Cigarmaker's Union
included blacks on its membership rolls.[59] Twenty-five years later,
the number of black unionists in Philadelphia still stood at less than

1,000.[60] Exclusion from union membership, of course, also meant exclusion from union-regulated apprentice programs and from trades where the closed shop prevailed. Such practices could go to extremes. In 1918, a plant superintendent in a photoengraving concern approached the photoengravers union for approval to hire a "colored boy" to wash plates for proofers. Recruiting white youngsters for the job had proven difficult. Union officials flatly and summarily denied the request.[61]

The non-participation of blacks in the Philadelphia industrial order eliminated them from consideration in such surveys as the WPA canvass of 1936. A comparison of patterns of getting work between black and white workers is not allowed in this canvass and information on the subject is wanting. In 1919, however, the Consumers' League in Philadelphia interviewed close to 200 black female industrial workers, and one question involved methods of securing employment.[62] Of the 141 respondents who answered this question, 63 percent reported the help of fellow employees in obtaining their present positions (no distinctions were drawn between friends and relatives); a surprisingly large number, 29 percent, noted finding their jobs through want ads; 1 percent through employment bureaus; and the rest through a variety of means. The high use of newspaper advertisements is striking and, as will be shown, the help-wanted ad was actually a basic component of the separate labor market in which black Philadelphians once operated.

The market in general did not function on behalf of blacks in the city. African-Americans, young and old, should have been employed in greater numbers in Philadelphia industry; their labor, after all, could have been purchased cheaply, so favoring whites unnecessarily boosted the wage bill of employers. Employer prejudice and white worker resistance—that is, racism—combined to undo the not always benevolent but nonetheless normal workings of the marketplace. For blacks, relief would have to come through extra-market forces, first through concerted pressure by black church leaders and organizations like the National Association for the Advancement of Colored People and the Urban League to increase the hiring of blacks in Philadelphia, and second and most important, through the ultimate intervention of the federal government.[63]

Any discussion of job search must finally consider the question of accessibility and geography. Did workers in Philadelphia, young or

old, live in convenient reach of jobs fifty and one hundred years ago?
In our own day and age, distance from employment opportunities
and poor transportation access have been cited as prime reasons for
the high unemployment rates of minority groups living in ghetto
areas, and particularly minority teenagers. Is this a problem unique
to our own times?

Before 1950, all Philadelphians had easy access to jobs. As evidence, first consider the rather depressing testimony of one job seeker
in 1915. He had been interviewed by researchers preparing a report
on employment conditions in the city. The man, who goes nameless,
described one day's travel in search of work after being laid off from
an unskilled position in a hat factory:

> I got up at 5:30 and went to Baldwin's and was told no help was
> required. From there, I went to Hale & Kilburn at 18th and Lehigh
> Avenue and met with the same answer. I then walked to 2nd and
> Erie Avenue to Potter's Oil Cloth Works, and they needed no help.
> Then to the Hess Bright Company, at Front and Erie Avenue, and
> again met with the same result. Next I came back home at 2nd and
> Lehigh Avenue for a meal. In the afternoon, I went to Edward
> Bromley's; no help needed; from there to a firm at American and
> Girard Streets, with the same result. Then I recalled at the Barnett
> File Works, again with the same result. I tried two other places in
> the neighborhood, whose names I have forgotten, and none had
> any work. Often I would go out and after meeting with bad luck
> day after day, would say to myself at night, "the job has got to
> find me," but the next morning I would feel differently about it.[64]

In his hunt for work, this Philadelphian walked approximately
eight miles. He covered a six-square-mile area through the Spring
Garden, Northern Liberties, Logan, and Kensington sections of the
city. He did not find a job, but that is not the point here. Within
one hour's walk, this job seeker traveled through a dense area of
employment, where jobs proliferated, if not openings. For the average worker in Philadelphia during the nineteenth century, in fact,
there existed within a one-mile radius of his or her home approximately sixteen thousand industrial jobs.[65]

Physical accessibility, of course, did not guarantee employment,
as the above tale shows. Black Philadelphians, most notably,
throughout the nineteenth century actually lived in the greatest proximity to manufacturing jobs. Within one mile of residence of the

average black worker could be found more than twenty-three thousand industrial positions. The equivalent figure for German immigrants is approximately nineteen thousand jobs, and for Irish immigrants and American-born workers approximately fifteen thousand.[66] The full impact of institutionalized racism is manifest in these numbers. The group with the greatest access to industrial opportunities experienced the least success and most obstacles in achieving employment.

The close proximity of Philadelphians to work in the past can also be illustrated with estimates on the average distances traveled on the journey to work. In the mid-nineteenth century, most residents in the Quaker City walked each day between six-tenths of a mile and one mile to their jobs. The only group to live at greater distances to the workplace were a small vanguard of white-collar personnel who could afford private or public transportation, the latter being horse-drawn streetcars charging fares amounting to 10 percent of the average daily wage in Philadelphia. In abandoning the increasingly congested, immigrant-inhabited city for newly opening residential areas both within and outside the city's boundaries, these workers also represent a pioneer cohort of suburbanites.[67]

Distance traveled to work increased by the early decades of the twentieth century, but most industrial workers still lived near sites of employment. A study of one hosiery mill in the 1930s revealed that 70 percent of the employees resided within a two-mile radius of the factory and practically the entire labor force walked to work.[68] Another canvass of women workers in the mill district of Kensington found that one-half lived within fifteen minutes of their places of employment and that only one in three used private or public transportation.[69] A series of other surveys conducted on employment conditions during the crisis decade of the thirties similarly produced estimates that the average worker lived within 2.8 miles of his or her work, or within a forty minute walk. Job tenure, moreover, was found to be inversely related to distance of residence from workplace, an indication that once workers secured and were able to maintain employment, they would move even closer to their jobs.[70]

Particular groups of laborers in Philadelphia also lived in extreme proximity to work and formed distinct occupational communities. In trades where businesses tended to cluster, workers resided within short distances of places of employment. Brewery men, for example, congregated in Northern Liberties and in another neighborhood near the Schuylkill River, appropriately dubbed Brewerytown, within blocks of most of the breweries. Other industries in which both firms and employees clustered included sugar refining, shipbuilding, leather making, carpets, locomotives, apparels, boots and shoes, printing and binding, and jewelry. In decentralized trades, on the other hand, such as building and construction, tool and machine manufacture, and food preparation, workers lived at greater distances from work and in less segregated neighborhoods.[71]

Since World War II the distances between residence and work have increased greatly and commuting has become the norm. Widespread ownership of automobiles, suburban real estate development, the federal government's promotion of metropolitan highway construction, and urban decay and unrest have combined to lengthen the journey to work (in a not dissimilar manner to the first stages of suburbanization in the mid-nineteenth century). Accessibility to jobs, however, has not been affected; suburbanites find jobs, minority residents in the inner city encounter difficulties. Again, the question proves to be more one of social rather than physical distance.

The plight of today's ghetto residents, inhabiting neighborhoods in Philadelphia once brimming and now empty of work opportunities, particularly manufacturing jobs, can be attributed to problems of social distance—who is favored for hire, who gets work—but the changing industrial geography of the city has also played a role. In the first hundred years of Philadelphia's history, workplaces centered around the port. The next hundred years witnessed the filling in of the downtown with retail stores, offices, and small workshops, but also the building of mill districts around the core. Access to water power and open space necessitated the construction of mills away from the densely occupied center city.

The third century of Philadelphia's history would see a further dispersal of industry with the building of sprawling plant sites north, south, and west of the mill districts in the remaining undeveloped areas. The movement of the Baldwin Locomotive Works in 1928 from its 4-square block complex at Broad and Spring Garden Streets, practically smack in the center of town, to a 616-acre site 12 miles south of the city, represents a key example. Several generations of locomotive workers had lived in a distinct community in the neighborhood surrounding the original works. Now commuters would comprise the work force of the the newly located suburban plant facility.[72]

The creation of industrial parks at the edges of the city occurred at the same time that production in the mill districts ground to a halt; here the gradual erosion of the textile, hosiery, and garment trades is crucial. As a result, not only have many manufacturing jobs disappeared, but those that remain have become decentralized. In the 1920s, two-thirds of all industrial positions in the Philadelphia metropolitan regions were located in the city proper, and 60 percent of these could be found within a three-mile radius of the central business district. In the 1980s, less than 40 percent of the remaining jobs in industry in the area are within the city's boundaries.[73] The latest immigrants to Philadelphia, mainly blacks and Hispanics, came to reside in low-rent mill districts just when these neighborhoods were experiencing severe employment loss; their access to new suburban plant jobs is limited as well. Here physical distances compound the social disadvantages racial minority groups experience in getting work. The multiple dilemmas of Philadelphia's newest arrivals are unique.

Philadelphians in the past entered a labor market structured by the city's particular industrial system. Workers in the city remained equally in the grasp of this system in one critical way. That young people in general rushed into the work force in great numbers when opportunities expanded and left in a similar rush with the onset of bad times is an indication that the fate of workers in the city remained fundamentally tied to the vicissitudes of the market economy. Yet experiences did vary. The children of the poor left school and entered the world of work earlier than children from more comfortable backgrounds; men operated in the labor market in different ways than women; American-born youngsters had access to the best jobs; older immigrant workers without the advantages of education faced great difficulties in securing jobs and along with workers entering the system in the twentieth century, utilized institutionalized services to the greatest degree; young workers of German heritage apparently had their distinct employment histories. These particulars qualify a generalizable portrait of economic activity in the city; experience in Philadelphia's industrial order again varied, values and social background mattered. Yet, none of these specific cases compares to the extremely specific story of African-Americans in the Quaker City. Black workers inhabited a separate world and operated in a separate labor market (possibly judged and rewarded among themselves according to merit and productivity, but not on an individual or neutral basis when compared with whites). Fixed practices and customs determined personal fortunes and outcomes.

Finally, few Philadelphians entered or functioned in the labor market anonymously. Blacks wore the badge of color; most youngsters entering the world of work in the late nineteenth and early twentieth centuries relied on familial and personal connections in hire. But institutions also existed to aid individuals. The role of various intermediary agencies in the labor market—schools, unions and employment services among others—will now be examined in greater detail.

3 · Schools and Work

American schools are in perpetual crisis. Hardly a decade passes without a new onslaught of reports with the same dire conclusions: the public schools in the United States are failing to educate American school children, American school children are failing to learn. Critics from across the political spectrum join the fray. Conservatives forever warn of moral decay and the dangers of permissiveness and lax standards; progressives, in turn, speak against formalism and elitist practices and in favor of instruction both relevant and individualized. Consistency rarely marks this discussion. In defense of all that is worthy in Western intellectual traditions, one conservative may espouse classical education; another, with an eye more to the imperatives of the modern economic order, may champion practical learning and vocationalism. Liberals similarly divide. In the name of egalitarianism and democracy, common and standardized teaching can be supported by some, education tailored to the individual by others. For entirely different reasons, ideological opponents can be found favoring the same programs and reforms. Faced with recurring diagnoses, suggested cures, and confused debate, historians can only greet the latest best-selling jeremiad with both skepticism and bemusement.

Popular dialogue on the state of American education is echoed to a great extent in ongoing scholarly arguments on the place and function of public schools in American society. Academic discussion hinges on interrelated questions of intentionality and consequences. How and why, for example, have the schools become structured as they are? Who bears the greatest responsibility for educational policy and practice? Moreover, what exactly have the schools accomplished? Which groups have benefited from public schooling? Which groups have not?[1]

A benign and celebratory view of the American public school interprets common school education in this country as a triumph of liberal reform. Public school advocates created and maintain public schools to insure the existence of an informed citizenry, to inculcate common values and knowledge in our heterogeneous population, and to provide equal access to opportunity. Against awesome odds the schools have succeeded, by and large, in achieving their original promise. A less sanguine interpretation sees the schools as the creation of specific interest groups, particularly those concerned with molding an effective work force for an expanding capitalist economy. The schools for some scholars have served the function of training new generations of workers in requisite technical skills. Others view the school as playing a more significant social role, one that includes engendering habits of discipline and obedience and encouraging natural acceptance of a world of authority, hierarchy, competition, and differential rewards. Even according to this less idealistic point of view, the schools have succeeded and fulfilled their initial intent.

The development of the American school can also be treated without reference to original conception. What transpires in public schools can thus be envisioned as a function of organizational demands, of bureaucratic decision making, and, in a more dialectical vein, as part of the continuing tensions between local politicians and school administrators, administrators and parents, administrators and teachers, teachers and parents, and, not least of all, teachers and students. The realities of human behavior in complex settings provide a better explanatory handle on the course of events than recourse to ideals and official objectives. Results are also inevitably mixed in this view of the world.

An even more ambivalent perspective would almost entirely discount the impact of schooling. In this way of thinking, natural ability, personality traits, social background, family dynamics, the vicissitudes of the economy, adult experience, circumstance, and pure luck are considered more significant in personal history and fortune than whatever individuals take from or are given by schools. The impact of the school, in other words, should never be overestimated.

Finally, one scholarly debate about American education has completely avoided the question of how and why the schools operate as they do. Interest here is focused entirely on results and measurements of outcomes. The exact extent to which more years of schooling translate into occupational achievement and greater income is at issue.

In this chapter I will address the various questions and arguments raised in public and scholarly debates on American education by looking specifically at schools in the city of Philadelphia and their connection to the world of work. The school can be treated as an institution in the labor market, an intermediary that funnels young people into and through the work force. As already noted, the mere extension of schooling in Philadelphia in the late nineteenth and early twentieth centuries changed the basic demography of entrance to working status. School placement services facilitated this process for a minority of Philadelphia youngsters. Yet how significant have the schools actually been in the lives of the citizens of the Quaker City? How important have the schools been as an agency in the labor market?

Answers to these questions require a look at both intentions and results. The following need to be established: the degree to which deliberate efforts were made in Philadelphia to link schools to the demands and workings of the city's economy; when initiatives in that direction occurred and who sponsored them; and of course, the ultimate and exact influence and effectiveness of such initiatives. A complex world of vocational education did emerge in fact in Philadelphia involving public, parochial, and private schools and training in both industrial and commercial pursuits. However, these programs developed in an unsystematic fashion, amid conflict and without consensus. As will be shown, the impact of schooling in general and vocationalism in particular proved to be limited. Uncertain efforts and commitments guaranteed uneven results.

The notion of linking schooling to work can be traced in Philadelphia as far back as early colonial times. William Penn called for the creation of public schools in his new settlement in order that young people "be taught some useful trade or skill."[2] Benjamin Franklin, Philadelphia's great institution builder in the eighteenth century, similarly championed "useful" learning and criticized traditional Latin grammar school education.[3] With the exception of the building of a number of private academies and municipal pauper schools, there was little accomplished, however, in the way of education—practical, classical or otherwise—in the Quaker City until the 1830s, when Pennsylvania legislators established a state-wide system of public common schools.[4]

Advocates of school reform in the 1830s did not have direct material ends in mind, but their new schools were to serve a definite purpose. They did not connect the establishment of common schools to the emerging industrial order, for example; they had different and greater social objectives. Free universal schooling, school reformers argued, was necessary to protect republican government and values, provide equal access to opportunity, and promote social mobility based on individual initiative and achievement. "In a republican government, no voter should be without the rudiments of learning," Samuel Breck, chief sponsor of common school legislation persuaded his fellow assemblymen. "Let all [children] fare alike in the primary schools, receive the same elementary instruction, imbibe the republican spirit and be animated by a feeling of perfect equality."[5] Thaddeus Stevens, future abolitionist, radical advocate of economic and political rights for the eventually freed slaves of the American South, and Breck's legislative ally, seconded the argument. "If an elective republic is to endure for any great length of time," Stevens warned, "every elector must have sufficient information, not only to accumulate wealth and take care of his pecuniary concern, but to direct wisely the Legislature, the Ambassadors, and the Executive of the nation." Stevens further argued that the common schools would allow for the social mobility of all citizens, but particularly "the meritorious poor." Once in place, "we shall no longer see the struggling genius of the humble obstructed . . . but . . . see them reach the farthest goal of their noble ambition. Then the laurel wreath would no longer be the purchase of gold, but the reward of honest merit."[6] For Stevens and others, the establishment of universal public schooling in Pennsylvania represented an anti-aristocratic, petty bourgeois project writ large and not a specific industrial capitalist endeavor. The schools would serve to prepare young people for life both as citizens in a republic and as individual actors in a competitive marketplace.

The original mandate of the public schools did not necessarily translate into a specific curriculum, but the democratic republican thrust of the charge presented a challenge to classical learning. School officials in Philadelphia initially moved in a practical direction, but not without difficulty. In 1838, for example, city school controllers opened Central High School for Boys as a cornerstone of the their new school system. A competitive examination was established to determine entrance to Central, a procedure that allowed Central's administrators to shape curricular goals and programs in the city's lower schools.[7] Alexander Bache, the first principal apppointed at Central, set the way for the school in its first half-century of operations. Central, Bache declared, should prepare boys for "the pursuits of commerce, manufacture, and the useful arts."[8]

Bache and his successors instituted courses in modern languages, natural sciences, elocution, trigonometry, surveying, navigation, bookkeeping, and phonography (the Pitman method of shorthand).[9] These offerings served Central's students well, for throughout the nineteenth century the great majority of Central's alumni occupied positions upon graduation in commerce and industry, with only a small minority bound for college. Nevertheless, developments unfolded at Central with discord. The competitive entrance examination system instituted by Bache became an instant source of contention; charges of elitism and unfair grading standards brought protests from neighborhood lower schools and the eventual creation of a mixed geographical quota and open competitive system. Bache and successors also faced continued opposition from classicists on the school's faculty who spoke against tipping the balance of the school's curriculum too precipitously toward vocationalism. This particular battle would continue at Central for a good hundred years after its founding without clear resolution.[10]

A less controversial early initiative on practical education in Philadelphia occurred in the city's public night schools. In 1849, a group of prominent Philadelphians petitioned the controllers of the city's schools to open night classes for "apprentices and young men."[11] The intent here was only in part pedagogical. Night life on the streets of Philadelphia by the mid-nineteenth century had become most raucous; the schools could be used to contribute to greater social order by engaging restless male teenagers in wholesome activity. School board officials subsequently established an Artisan's Night School with a full panoply of technical courses. Enrollment was restricted to apprentices and journeymen, and they received instruction in geometry, calculus, penmanship, mechanical drawing, physics, chemistry, and steam engineering. This effort represented the first full-fledged vocational experiment in public education in Philadelphia and occurred three decades before vocational classes became fixed features of day-time programs. Other night school endeavors followed, and by the 1880s they had unceremoniously served more than 20,000 students.[12]

The cause of vocational education received significant attention and credibility from the Great Centennial Exhibition of 1876 held in Philadelphia. A demonstration in the Russian pavilion of the Moscow Technical School shop classes developed by Victor Della Vos attracted particular acclaim and forced intense discussion among educators in the city and throughout the country. The Russian manual training institute was hailed by some as an appropriate model for schools in an industrializing society and castigated by others as antithetical to the values of a democratic republic. The exhibit produced specific calls in Philadelphia for practical instruction in daytime classrooms and even for the creation of special separate industrial schools.[13] In 1879, Edward T. Steel, a textile manufacturer and outspoken advocate of manual training in the public schools, assumed the presidency of the city's board of education, and his appointment placed the issue clearly in view.[14]

The time was ripe for initiatives on vocational education. In 1880 Charles Leland, an English educator, approached school officials in Philadelphia with a proposal to establish a manual arts school for children of elementary school age. Leland, follower of the British philosopher and social critic William Morris, had participated in the revived English handicraft movement and helped establish several manual arts training centers in his native country.[15] School board officials were sufficiently impressed with Leland's suggestions to authorize the opening in 1880 of an Industrial Arts School. Students and teachers from neighboring elementary schools could visit the new school for instruction in design, modeling in clay, wood carving, carpentry, metal work, and embroidery. Leland, however, did not intend for the school to serve strict vocational purposes. Exercising the hand and eye were as important as training the mind for him. "The aim of the school," he insisted, "is the development of the perceptive and creative faculties of the whole individual, and the training of the muscles into facile dexterity."[16]

The success of Leland's enterprise brought pressure on Philadelphia school board members to open additional manual arts schools. In 1885, school officials voted funds to establish for older boys the Philadelphia Manual Training School, where instruction was offered in mechanical drawing, pattern and tool making, wood turning, rorging, and soldering.[17] The principal of the school, William Sayre, however, went out of his way to explain that a trade school was not the intention. The Philadelphia Manual Training School's "purpose," he noted, "is not to make mechanics, but to train boys for manhood. It is a fitting school for life and for living." Sayre envisioned a "symmetrical education" of "thinking and doing."[18]

For Leland and Sayre, manual learning served no necessary practical ends. Classical education involved a false dichotomy between the physical and the mental; in their way of thinking, hand and mind were interrelated and demanded equal and simultaneous stimulation. Other advocates of manual training held to different positions, but all participants to the quickening debate on practical education in the public schools in Philadelphia immediately went on record against narrowly structured trade schools; a class-based educational system in which the children of poor and working families were to be tracked into separate vocational schools was ideologically and politically unacceptable.

Edward Steel, President of the Philadelphia Board of Education in the 1880s, and a prime mover in the revising of the classical curriculum, also argued that manual arts instruction did not aim at trade training.[19] But unlike Leland and Sayre, he saw the new manual arts centers as serving another social purpose. Industrial and urban transformation, he wrote, had spawned social divisions and tensions. During the economic depression of the 1870s, in particular, Philadelphians had witnessed anarchy wrought by "the reckless and desperate of the unskilled against property."[20] Young people needed to learn respect for labor, and classical learning failed in this regard to meet the demands of the modern order. The manual arts schools would play an important role in encouraging socially acceptable behavior.

Steel's reasoning was influential. When the Philadelphia Board of Education approved the creation of two new manual arts training schools in the early 1890s, they were placed in neighborhoods with growing immigrant populations. Those schools, a board report argued, would help to transform a "class [of children] most difficult to reach" by inculcating habits of diligence and punctuality.[21] Charles Leland, not to mention William Morris, had different objectives and visions in mind for manual arts education.

By the 1890s practical education had emerged as an overt political issue in Philadelphia, a matter discussed in public forums and related to greater community good and order. The cause of manual arts and trade training also became entwined in a larger movement for social reform in the city and this increased its visibility. A number of groups spearheaded the reform effort, with the the Public Education Association leading the way.[22] Highest on the agenda of the reformers was the creation of a nonpartisan, totally centralized city board of education. Localism had marked public educational affairs in Philadelphia since the enactment of state laws creating common schools in the 1830s. Under the original legislation, voters in each ward of the city—and the number of wards had grown to fifty-two by the turn of the twentieth century—elected neighborhood school boards. Until 1867, each sectional ward sent one member to serve on the central board of controllers; in that year, a new state law provided for the appointment of central school board members by the Court of Common Pleas, an effort aimed at divorcing politics from the overseeing function.[23] Central authorities had always assumed responsibility over the city's single high school, Central High, and in this way they exerted indirect control over the primary school curriculum (officials on the city-wide board had also taken charge of evening school programs by the early 1870s). Still, power remained dispersed, with neighborhood boards maintaining significant determination over the hiring, supervision, and firing of teachers as well the day-to-day operations of the lower schools.

More than twenty-five years of agitation by reform groups and charges of corruption and mismanagement would lead to the passage in 1906 of state legislation stripping the ward school boards of all effective authority. A twenty-one–member central board of education was created, composed entirely of officials appointed by the Common Pleas Court. This new governing body received powers to centralize and control all decision making about curriculum and personnel.[24]

Reformers also sought to have a strong central manager placed in charge of the school system. They achieved this objective before the revamping of the board's structure and authority. In 1885, Philadelphia Board of Education President Edward Steel succeeded in overcoming local opposition to the appointment of a school superintendent. When he subsequently announced the selection of James MacAlister, former head of the Milwaukee public schools, reform groups registered enthusiastic approval. MacAlister was not only a proven central administrator, but also an outspoken advocate of manual arts training.[25]

Compulsory school attendance laws emerged as a third cause of educational reformers. Exploitative conditions in industry, the pressing imperative to introduce immigrant children to American ways and institutions, and the need to guarantee a sufficient body of students demanded the passage of legislation requiring minimum years of enrollment in classes. In 1895, reformers lobbied successfully for the enactment of Pennsylvania's first compulsory school attendance law, which mandated that young people between the ages of eight and thirteen spend at least sixteen weeks during the academic year in school. A decade later, a revised bill would require full school-year attendance for all children below the age of fourteen. Compulsory attendance was also immediately linked by reformers to the question of practical education. With a broader constituency, they argued, the schools had to present relevant and tangible subject matters and materials. Centralized and professionalized management of the schools, compulsory school attendance laws, and practical education became a related three-part clarion call for Philadelphia reform groups.[26]

Opposition soon surfaced to reform legislation, and managerial and curricular change came neither smoothly or uniformly. Politicians representing immigrant working-class communities, for example, successfully blocked and qualified the passage of compulsory school laws in Pennsylvania over a fifteen-year period at the turn of the century. Such laws, they argued, were insensitive to the economic needs of working families and the cultural traditions of newer-stock Americans. One such opponent called attendance laws "class legislation of the dirtiest, filthiest kind" and Democratic Party governors in the state vetoed such bills accordingly.[27] The centralization of decision making within the school system drew equal fire from neighborhood groups and their legislative representatives; despite the efforts of civic leaders and numerous Philadelphia reform organizations, the city remained until 1905 the last bastion of local school control among the nation's major municipalities.[28]

The question of centralization also affected discussions and decisions on curricular change. Local school boards, for example, refused to adopt manual training courses advocated by central board members and top administrators on the grounds that their authority was being usurped.[29] Teachers, too, petitioned against new practical course offerings; in opposition, they defended both their right to set the curriculum and the value of liberal arts education.[30] Reformers similarly found little support for vocationalism from local politicians. City council representatives, for example, repeatedly refused to appropriate funds for the creation of new manual arts schools. In part their stalling signified a general aversion to the spending of public monies on education. They also blocked efforts that hinted at any strengthening of the authority of central school managers.[31] Local politics so frustrated reformers that both Philadelphia Board of Education President Edward Steel and Superintendent James MacAlister, forces behind centralization and practical education and men closely associated with such groups as the Public Education Association, resigned from their posts in protest in the 1890s. Their immediate successors owed their appointments to their taking clear positions against reform.[32]

Trade unionists added their voices of opposition and apprehension to trade training and curricular change in the schools. Organizations representing employers, such as the Philadelphia Association of Manufacturers, the Chamber of Commerce of Philadelphia, and the Philadelphia Board of Trade, had taken official and repeated stands on behalf of practical education, and labor groups were wary of their intentions. In their public pronouncements, business leaders warned that the training of young workers should not be left to the discretion of willful skilled mechanics or, worse, radicals on the shop floor; the schools could teach both proper values and skills and, by increasing the number of competent workers, break what was perceived as the monopoly power of the unions.[33] Trade union officials in Philadelphia reacted in kind in the face of such official positions taken by the business community, testifying locally as well as in the halls of the national Congress against trade education in the schools.[34] At times, this debate spilled beyond a mere war of words. As early as 1886, the question of hiring trainees from manual arts schools emerged as a key issue in a series of strikes in the garment industry in the city.[35]

Conflict then marked developments in practical education in Philadelphia in the last decades of the nineteenth century, but there was a good deal of conceptual confusion as well. Advocates of manual training disagreed among themselves as to the purposes of such instruction; some grounded their arguments in pedagogical theory, others in social necessity. Whether manual arts instruction was to be offered in separate schools with distinct clienteles or in all schools in a universal fashion also remained an issue of debate. Advocates of practical study similarly drew a sharp distinction between manual training and trade training, generally favoring the former as part of a general education—the hand and mind had to be exercised simultaneously—and opposing the latter as too narrow and potentially at odds with the goals of the common school system.[36] The lines drawn, however, were often hazy.

Political tensions and intellectual ambivalence guaranteed that matters would be resolved in a hybrid way. In the first two decades of the twentieth century, vocational education and not mere manual training would become a fixed feature of the Philadelphia public school system, but an uneven and somewhat contradictory effort prevailed. Advocates of straightforward trade instruction asserted themselves in the first years of the new century, arguing forcefully that the realities of the modern economic order demanded an absolutely practical education. Murrell Dobbins, president of the city's Master Builders' Exchange, a trade association of construction firms, assumed a leading role here. Immediately after receiving an appointment to the Philadelphia Board of Education, he moved to have a "mechanical trade school" established in the city, a separate institution to train high-school youngsters in carpentry, plumbing, plastering, electrical construction, bricklaying, iron work, and painting. The school opened in 1906 with the name of the Philadelphia Trade School and it represented a clear departure from the manual arts instruction introduced during the prior decades.[37]

At the same time, however, that Dobbins succeeded in establishing strict trade education, other school officials were forcing efforts in a different direction. In 1908, school board President Henry Edmunds ordered a reevaluation of the manual arts schools created during the 1880s and 1890s. Their cost alone raised problems for him, but, more crucially, Edmunds worried that as "separate institutions" the schools fomented strong feelings of "class prejudice" in the minds of students and parents. Children from all walks of life should attend the same schools, he insisted, to further mutual understandings and democratic practices and ideals.[38]

Edmunds delegated the task of restructuring Philadelphia's schools to a newly appointed superintendent, Martin Grove Brumbaugh.

Brumbaugh was professor of pedagogy at the University of Pennsylvania, a leading figure in the Public Education Association, and, after his tenure as superintendent, a Progressive-era reform governor of the commonwealth.[39] He moved to resolve tensions. He advocated manual arts instruction in comprehensive elementary schools, general shop work in comprehensive junior high schools, and continued mechanical arts and vocational instruction in the senior schools. Most important, he followed Edmund's policy lead in abandoning the separate manual training schools and creating new universal, but internally differentiated, district high schools. Students of varied backgrounds would walk through the same doors and inhabit the same buildings—ostensibly part of the same interacting and mutually supportive democratic mass—but once inside would follow curricula suited to their respective interests and abilities. Each comprehensive school would offer separate academic and practical course programs.[40] This seemed an appropriate solution for schooling children in a diverse, industrializing democratic society. As Henry Edmunds explained in a 1915 report celebrating his and Brumbaugh's accomplishments:

> Educational opportunity has broadened in scope—true American democracy lies not in equality of condition but in equality of opportunity. This idea of democracy permeates our school policy. Classification closely adopted to the individual pupil has been secured through an enlargement of school organizations. Academic, manual training, commercial and home economics courses in high school—all on a four-year basis and conducted in a composite school organization, give equality of opportunity for various types of pupils who enter these institutions.[41]

While Edmunds and Brumbaugh oversaw the phasing out of the manual art schools and the building of new comprehensive differentiated high schools, surprisingly they did not dismantle the Philadelphia Trade School established by Murrell Dobbins. In fact, a separate Trade School for Girls would be opened in 1916, specializing in instruction in garment making and millinery work. The Philadelphia Trade School would eventually be consolidated with Central High School in 1919 as part of the comprehensive secondary school movement, but other separate trade schools would be conceived and constructed in the next decades.[42]

Vocationalism as an educational reform actually ran its course during the 1920s in Philadelphia. Practical education became a fixed element of public schooling during the period 1880 to 1920, although pure classical education had never been a singularly accepted or practiced ideal in the city. In spite of this increase in vocational education, the connection between schooling and work remained loose. As of 1920, youngsters in Philadelphia's public schools received some instruction in handicrafts in elementary school and some woodworking and other shop classes in junior high. The comprehensive senior high schools offered mechanical arts courses and limited trade training; more deliberate trade education was available in the city's separate trade schools.[43] But Philadelphia never reached a full commitment to technical and occupational education on the order of European countries. Political conflict and financial constraints limited developments to a certain extent; the difficult question of what constitutes a proper education in a democracy and the politics of that question limited action as well.

Vocational education is taken synonymously with the preparation of young people for employment in industry. The efforts by reformers and school officials in Philadelphia to tie public schooling to the world of work, however, involved more than the attempted training of students in the mechanical trades. Commercial course degree programs, career guidance and job placement services, and night classes for young working adults represented less controversial but important aspects of vocationalism that are easily overlooked.

The training of young people in commercial skills emerged in Philadelphia as a general issue for a singular reason: it concerned the question of what role the public schools in the city would play in the education of young women. Benjamin Rush, the nation's first great philosopher and an intellectual leader in Philadelphia during the late eighteenth and early nineteenth centuries, may have been the first to connect learning for women with business expertise. In prescribing a school system for the city, Rush wrote on the necessity for educating women: "[A] woman should have some knowledge of figures and bookkeeping in order to assist her husband while he is alive and be executers [*sic*] of his will."[44] In fact, whenever school officials or reformers in the city raised the subject of schooling for girls, they stressed practical education.

After school authorities established Central High School for young men in the late 1830s, debate commenced in Philadelphia on the creation of a similar institution for girls. Opposition emerged immediately and far outweighed support; opponents argued that there was no inherent reason or demand for advanced education for girls and that the expense was unwarranted.[45] School board controllers soon dropped the idea, but supporters of schooling for young women kept the issue alive in the only way available to them. Teacher training represented the sole appropriate form of learning for females at the time and women's advocates used this as grounds to argue for the establishment of a normal school in the city. As a result of their efforts, school officials bowed to pressure and opened the Philadelphia Girls' Normal School in 1848. Young women could enjoy the advantages of continued schooling, in other words, but specifically for training in a trade.[46]

The Philadelphia Girls' Normal School proved to be more popular than expected, and with increasing demand for teachers, enrollments in the school swelled. Overcrowding by the 1880s forced new debates on the school's future, and when the school board voted to build a new boys' high school and move the normal school to Central High School's large facilities, the issue of expansion brought the question of women's education into the limelight. Officials of the normal school, most notably its principal, forcefully argued that the school should simply continue to fulfill its original mission, that of training teachers.[47] Representatives from the Public Education Association offered a different vision. They had been influential in founding the Manual Training High School for boys in 1885, and advocated the creation of a similar institution for girls. The imperatives of the economy and the need for greater social order, PEA reformers argued, demanded the establishment of a school to prepare and socialize young women either to occupy positions in industry or to be better and more efficient homemakers. PEA President Charlotte Pendleton even proposed that young women educated in the manual arts would have an uplifting influence on factory life in helping to still shop floor radicalism; they could also be trained to be good supervisors and shop forewomen.[48] A report issued by the organization in 1893 placed the potential role of a transformed normal school bluntly: "If you educate one hundred girls in such a school . . . we are ready to let the economic question of labor settle itself."[49] Other groups and individuals joined in petitioning for a women's manual arts high school. Widespread support actually existed on the school board for such a venture, but the effort was stopped in its tracks when ward representatives on the city council, never too willing to direct more public monies toward education, vetoed the plan as too costly.[50]

Graduates of Philadelphia's Girls' Normal High School, many of them practicing teachers, presented a third plan for a new expanded girls' high school for the city. In four major petitions submitted to the school board and in a flood of letters to local newspapers, they lobbied for the creation of a straightforward academic high school or, at the very minimum, the inclusion of a college preparatory track in the overall curriculum of a new school. In these representations, alumni spoke openly of their frustrations with the educations they had received. One letter signed by 223 graduates concluded, "deeply feeling our needs, we covet for them [future enrollees] much more comprehensive training."[51] Support for academic education also came from various women's civic organizations; notably included in all petitions, however, was also support for commercial education. As one petition to the board beseeched, graduates of the new girls high school should be able "to pursue any avenue of higher culture or business opportunity open to them."

Superintendent James McAlister moved to reconcile the different approaches to a new girls' high school for Philadelphia by recommending a differentiated curriculum for the new institution. When Girls' High opened in 1893 on the grounds of the old Central High School, students were offered a three-track program consisting of a so-called General Course, which served as the teacher training component, a Classical (college preparatory) Course, and a Commercial Course. The largest number of students, approximately 40 percent, opted for commercial studies and this program remained as popular for the next fifty years. The business curriculum as initially conceived included commercial geography, penmanship, and business forms in the first year; commercial arithmetic, shorthand, and business correspondence in the second; and commercial law, bookkeeping, shorthand, and typing in the third and fourth.[52]

Demand for commercial courses at Girls' High School served as a precedent for school officials in Philadelphia to institute similar programs in boy's schools as well. In 1898 a department of commercial education was created at Central High School; Central now had a differentiated curriculum despite faculty pressure to maintain the venerable institution as an academic school. Four new high schools opened in the first decade of the twentieth century included business courses as well as industrial and academic programs. When a second girls' high school, the William Penn School for Girls, was founded in 1909, the curriculum included only commercial and manual arts classes and the purposes of the school were clearly vocational. As principal Cheesman Herrick boasted in remarks at the schools opening ceremonies:

> [T]he school and college of the Eighteenth Century took as their motto "I believe;" the school and college of the Nineteenth Century, "I believe and I think;" but the school and college of the Twentieth Century have taken as their motto, "I believe and Think in Order that I May Work;" in other words, our education tends, and rightly, to become vocational.[53]

Commercial courses grew to be a major component of the public education system in Philadelphia. School officials instituted business courses in the new junior high schools established in the 1920s. By 1940, fourteen of the city's sixteen comprehensive senior high schools offered commercial training programs; three vocational schools also provided instruction in office practice. Approximately 40 percent of students enrolled in Philadelphia public high schools in that year were pursuing commercial course degrees.[54] Although business education had first emerged as part of the discussion on the proper education of young women, young men were only slightly less inclined to choose the commercial track. Business courses became part of the public school curriculum in a relatively quiet way. They apparently posed a lesser challenge to both democratic and egalitarian values and classical academic traditions than did mechanical trade instruction. They provided the opportunity for white-collar employment, for assumed upward mobility, and never provided fuel for political debate.

As the public school's role in preparing young people for work became more explicit, the schools emerged as a definable agency in the labor market. During the first decade of the twentieth century, school officials in Philadelphia also established vocational guidance programs and job placement services that rendered the schools an even more important direct intermediary in the city's employment marketplace. Developments here, however, unfolded without great deliberation and the ultimate impact of these efforts was limited.

Compulsory school attendance legislation forced school leaders into action. Under a set of laws passed between 1897 and 1915, the school board in Philadelphia was not only charged with pursuing truants, but also with issuing employment certificates for students leaving the system between fourteen and sixteen years of age and providing assistance in their searches for work.[55] Responsibility for the latter task fell to a new agency established in 1915, the Junior Employment Service.[56] Budgetary constraints, however, soon left the JES without funds or a staff; into the breach stepped an organization that would play a key role in the creation of school vocational guidance services in Philadelphia.

The White-Williams Foundation traced its origins to the year 1800, when its predecessor the Magdalen Society was founded in Philadelphia to provide counseling and shelter to wayward girls. For more than one hundred years, the Society operated a house of refuge in the city (with mixed success), but in 1915 a decision was made to revive and reorient the organization's work. Young women had to be reached at early ages and in schools, officials of the organization began to argue; they had to be encouraged to remain in school and be offered information on employment and career prospects and possibilities if early entrance to the labor market was unavoidable. The Society could play an important role in guiding young women and preventing waywardness by providing such counsel. With the change in purpose came a change in name.[57]

In 1917, the newly christened White-Williams Foundation offered to fund the salaries of two staff members of the Junior Employment Service, who would advise students on job opportunities. In that same year, the principal of the McCall School asked school authorities to appoint a vocational counselor to the school and the Foundation agreed to support that position as well. In 1919, when a deficit in the school budget threatened a complete closing of the JES, the Foundation stepped forward again to provide personnel and equipment and to adminster the program.[58] The JES would be returned to the formal jurisdiction of the Philadelphia Board of Education in 1925, but only after the staff of the White-Williams Foundation had left its mark on the operation.

The new expanded role of the Foundation in these years necessitated hiring new personnel, and the trustees of the organization recruited a corps of young men and women, trained in the new social sciences and social work, who envisioned their service to the public schools as a great mission and experiment. They invited faculty from the psychology department of the University of Pennsylvania, for example, to develop and administer intelligence and vocational aptitude tests. Generating and organizing data on school leaving patterns and employment trajectories emerged as another key pursuit.[59]

Representatives from the Foundation also worked with the small staff of the Department of Vocational Education and Guidance, an agency established by Philadelphia school officials in 1914 to coordinate manual instruction in the elementary and junior high schools in the city. Foundation staff members convinced school leaders to create vocational guidance courses as necessary adjuncts to the sewing and shop classes offered in the lower grades. By the 1920s a curriculum for young children had been developed on work in the city and the nature of available jobs, as well as a series of programs for highschool students on employment opportunities. The White-Williams Foundation similarly funded the writing of a score of pamphlets on Philadelphia industry, which included complete descriptions of jobs and general requirements for hire.[60] School officials, however, realized that these initiatives in vocational guidance introduced a dilemma. As a published curriculum guide in vocational education warned Philadelphia teachers: "Especial care must be taken that the material is not presented in such a way as to make children want to leave school and go to work."[61]

The White-Williams Foundation eventually withdrew from its position of direct influence on school policy and affairs. By the early 1930s, the Philadelphia Board of Education operated five Junior Employment Service offices; employers sent notices of openings and requests for recruits to the agency, students underwent interviews and received referrals to jobs.[62] The Department of Vocational Education and Guidance continued to apppoint counselors to schools and supervise their work and to develop and oversee the vocational guidance curriculum. Individual school principals and teachers, however, had great discretion over the implementation and quality of programs, and in some respects this was a result of the original unclear division between the staff of the White-Williams Foundation and school officials. As a survey in 1937 which found vocational guidance efforts in the Philadelphia public schools to be haphazard at best concluded, "Guidance work in Philadelphia did not develop as a result of any definite program initiated and sponsored by a central authority. It was largely the result of individual initiative by a high school principal or a classroom teacher who saw a particular need for it."[63]

School job placement services and vocational guidance programs thus became part of the public education system in Philadelphia as a consequence of changing compulsory school attendance laws and the work of Progressive-era social reformers, rather than through the deliberate planning of school officials. Compulsory attendance laws also played a role in one other aspect of practical education in the city—the school board's night school program. Public school night classes for young working people in Philadelphia had been a fixed institution in the city since their inception in the 1850s, and they always had a vocational cast. The 1915 Pennsylvania Child Labor Act greatly increased the importance of continuing education in the city. This legislation required that working children fourteen to sixteen years of age with employment certificates issued by the schools attend continuation classes after work for at least eight hours a week during the school term. The new law forced school officials to expand their evening programs and keep open nineteen school buildings. By the mid-1920s, more than 10,000 working youngsters were enrolled in classes each year. While math, English, and civics were required, the emphasis of the course work was practical. Boys could take mechanical drawing, business practices, typing, electrical wiring, and wood and metal work. Girls were offered classes in dressmaking, millinery, cooking, typing, and business in addition to home management. The implementation of vocational education in continuation night courses occurred without incident and on a comprehensive basis, unlike that in day school programs.[64]

The educational order created in Philadelphia during the nineteenth century stretched far beyond the public schools. Leaders within the city's growing Catholic community built a separate parochial school system, and secular private institutions of learning proliferated as well. In these settings, attempts were also made to link schooling to the world of work.

The first Catholic schools in Philadelphia were founded in the late eighteenth century. Local parishes established schools for young children and private donations allowed for the creation of several Catholic academies.[65] An expansion in the number of Catholic school facilities in the city occurred in the 1830s, mirroring developments in the public sector and occasioned by the arrival of tens of thousands of Catholic immigrants from Ireland. Catholic children enrolled in newly created parish schools received instruction in reading, writing, arithmetic, and, of course, religion.[66]

The expansion of Catholic education in Philadelphia occurred in an unsystematic fashion. The decision to open a parish school rested with the parish priest, and Catholic private academies for older children were completely autonomous institutions. In the 1850s, the Right Reverend John Neumann launched the first efforts to unify and coordinate Catholic schooling in the city. He first created a city-wide board of education, which representatives from each parish with a school were invited to join. The Bishop of Philadelphia served as the board's first presiding officer. However, until the 1890s this central agency developed little in the way of uniform policies.[67]

Concern for dwindling enrollments in the parish schools forced a restructuring of Catholic education in the last decades of the nineteenth century. The reordering of the public schools in that period served as both a model and a threat. Surveys revealed to Catholic leaders that although 20 to 25 percent of all youngsters of elementary school age in Philadelphia attended parish schools, these numbers declined precipitously for older children. Of greater concern was the reality that only between 10 and 20 percent of all Catholic families opted to send their children to Catholic schools. Newly arriving Polish and Italian immigrants stayed away in troubling numbers. Catholic schools had reputations for overcrowding and poor sanitation, and with innovations in the public sector parochial schools could only survive with major new initiatives.[68]

Change required leadership from the top. In 1890, the central board representing the parishes voted to create an administrative staff to develop a uniform curriculum and standardized policies regarding personnel, attendance, grading, and examinations. Within a year, newly hired administrators issued directives regularizing the work of the parish schools. In 1895, the board established a group of inspectors to oversee the schools, and in 1901 the power to appoint principals and teachers was lifted from local priests and placed in the central board's hands.[69] Most important, in 1894 the board selected Father Philip McDevitt as the first superintendent of Catholic schools in the city and, in a similar manner to his counterparts in the public realm, he moved to renovate and manage Catholic education in a determined way.

Superintendent McDevitt placed the building of a diocesan high-school system at the top of his agenda. Parish school officials had added grades to local schools to accommodate older children, but by the turn of the twentieth century, private Catholic academies remained the only avenue to pursue for a Catholic secondary education. McDevitt pushed for the creation of new high schools to lure Catholic families into the fold; operated on a citywide basis, these schools would act to upgrade and standardize the curriculum and practices of the decentralized feeder parish schools—in other words, they would play the same role initially envisioned for Central High School in the public school system. In launching a secondary school structure, McDevitt could also cite the authority of the American Council of Bishops and their call for establishing Catholic high schools throughout the country.[70]

An attempt to found a Catholic high school in Philadelphia actually predated Superintendent McDevitt. In 1890, diocesan school officials opened Roman Catholic High School for Boys, the first secondary Catholic school under central or non-parish control in the United States. When McDevitt was appointed superintendent in 1894 he resolved to make Roman Catholic the flagship of the new system and the key to the future of Catholic education in the city. McDevitt insisted that Roman Catholic had to attract older Catholic students away from the public high schools and that its greater appeal would rest on forging a curriculum "eminently practical" in character.[71] Almost two decades before Martin Brumbaugh created the comprehensive but differentiated public high school in Philadelphia, McDevitt instituted a three-track program at Roman Catholic. Students could pursue academic, commercial, or mechanical course work, though all students had to be exposed to manual and business training instruction. (Religious teaching, of course, remained a staple of the curriculum.) McDevitt's system, however, did not unfold without opposition; as with schools in the public sector, attacks on centralization came from local parishes where parents and parish school officials voiced concern for their diminishing hold on educational decision making.[72]

Diocesan high schools represented a top priority for McDevitt in sustaining Catholic education in Philadelphia; emphasizing vocational learning, and particularly commercial training, loomed as a second important means toward competing successfully with the public schools. Before 1900, religious instruction had been the defining characteristic of the Catholic schools in the city. Manual arts work had been offered in special Catholic schools for orphans and delinquents, and in the 1880s sisters in various Catholic academies and extended parish schools had taught typing, shorthand, and bookkeeping; these efforts were the extent of vocational teaching in the parochial schools.[73] After 1900, Catholic schools deliberately tied learning to the job market, particularly to the world of white-collar work. In 1901, the Philadelphia diocese's central board of education opened the Bishop Neumann Business School, the first of sixty such institutions in the city, which offered a three-year program in commercial skills. Many of these schools would ultimately be merged to form four-year comprehensive schools with the business track representing the core of the curriculum.[74]

Commercial education further emerged as a key element and concern when Catholic school officials moved to create a separate set of high schools for Catholic girls. They opened the first, the John W. Hallahan Catholic Girls' High School, in 1912, and the purposes of this institution were unambiguously vocational. According to the school's original handbook, the school "aim[ed] to develop a Catholic who is vocationally prepared with the acquisition of efficiency in at least one type of gainful employment sufficient to permit a graduate to secure an initial position or to profit by further instruction and learning to lead to further gainful employment."[75] Business courses and religious instruction dominated the curriculum at Hallahan. Catholic parents could send their daughters to the new high school with the knowledge that the school provided a proper moral environment and certificates of graduation that represented a ticket to hire in the growing office sector of the city's economy.

In the 1920s, Catholic school officials in Philadelphia opened additional comprehensive girls' Catholic schools and new regulations added to the status and prestige of the commercial track. Students now had to pass academic courses with high grades as a prerequisite to pursuing the business program.[76] Local school leaders also encouraged the brightest and most ambitious of the girls to enroll and, as a result, young women in commercial programs in Catholic girls schools in Philadelphia had the highest rates of graduation of all students in the city in parochial and public schools alike.[77] The Catholic girls' schools in Philadelphia became in this way the feeding grounds to white-collar employers and direct agents in the labor market; they represent probably the clearest attempt to link schooling and work in the city in terms of intention and in practice and impact as well.

Catholic school leaders grafted vocational education onto the Catholic curriculum without the debates or dilemmas manifest in the public realm. Vocationalism apparently was compatible with religious instruction and the Catholic schools were not challenged by the issue of fashioning a proper course of learning for citizens of a democratic republic. Catholic authorities also saw a perfect match between practical schooling and their clientele, boys and girls of immigrant families; there were always the private Catholic academies for the children of better established families in the Catholic community.

Vocationalism also flourished without great commotion in a third segment of Philadelphia's educational order, private secular institutions. Private trade schools abounded in the city, though they had been established for quite varied reasons. The furthering of science and technology and republican principles inspired the formation of one set of schools. In 1824, for example, a group of budding manufacturers, inventors and professors of engineering science, helped found the Franklin Institute for the Promotion of the Mechanic Arts. The namesake of this new association provided its originators with a vision of a nation populated by enlightened, engaged, scientifically minded, mechanically inclined, independent producers and citizens. The institute offered lectures and issued publications; the founders also opened a high school that originally was to serve only the sons of Philadelphia artisans. The mechanics school of the Franklin Institute remained in operation for close to one hundred years and functioned as a critical source of technical training in Philadelphia.[78]

Leaders of the Franklin Institute also helped spawn a number of other notable Philadelphia centers for vocational education during the nineteenth century. In 1850, Institute directors assisted in the establishment of the Philadelphia School of Design for Females and in 1877 joined in the founding of the Philadelphia Museum of Art, with the clear intention of establishing a museum school dedicated to industrial arts instruction. In 1884, a branch of the museum school was reorganized into the Philadelphia Textile School, with the encouragement of the city's textile manufacturers' association; a donation from a wealthy industrialist would eventually see this initiative develop into the Philadelphia College of Textiles. The creators of the Philadelphia Textile School, however, had different intentions than their predecessors connected with the Franklin Institute. This new school was not conceived for the sons of artisans, but rather as a place where sons of mill owners and other prospective managers and proprietors could receive hands-on experience with textile equipment and further education in the economics of wool, cotton, and silk production.[79]

Other technical schools came into being in the city with the same purposes of promoting a technically capable managerial class. In 1853, the Polytechnic College of the State of Pennsylvania was established in Philadelphia. Classes in civil, mechanical and mining engineering were offered, but for the expressed purpose of creating "professional directors" of industry.[80] Still, the notion of creating and maintaining an educated and competent producer class persisted. In 1891, Philadelphia's leading financier, Anthony Drexel, left a sizable legacy to create an "Industrial School." The education of young women from the city's working classes in the sciences and mechanical arts was one of Drexel's prime concerns. When the school opened in 1892, more than 150 girls were enrolled. The school soon became coeducational and underwent a vast expansion, with new offerings in electrical engineering, machine construction, and architecture. Drexel Institute was transformed into a college in the first two decades of the twentieth century. The new college pioneered cooperative education programs—with students dividing their time between course work and actual working situations—and for one hundred years, Drexel, through its direct links with Philadelphia firms, has been a prime agent of mobility for Philadelphia youngsters from middle-class and working-class backgrounds into engineering and highly skilled technical jobs.[81]

Concern for children in unfortunate circumstances and for wayward youngsters in the city spawned a second group of private vocational institutions. Here, manual arts training and trade instruction were seen as a means toward personal redemption and lessening dependency. As early as 1826, overseers of the House of Refuge in Philadelphia introduced courses for young residents in bookbinding, basketmaking, and chair caning, with the aim of encouraging moral reform. Children enrolled in the Pennsylvania Institute for the Instruction of the Deaf and Dumb and the Pennsylvania Institute for the Instruction of the Blind similarly received instruction in shoemaking, cooking, spinning, and other crafts, to promote industrious habits and prepare them for useful, autonomous lives in society.[82] Practical training was even envisioned as an imperative for young men preparing for service in the ministry. In 1829, the Presbyterian minister John Monteith established the Philadelphia Manual Labor Academy in Germantown; Monteith insisted that the spiritual development of clergymen required exercise of the hand and eye as well as the soul.[83]

The notion that trade education could help troubled children went beyond such scattered efforts to the establishment of several venerable institutions. In the 1820s, Stephen Girard, the leading financier of his day, left his legacy to create a school for poor, white male orphans. The original plans for Girard College called for a "mechanical education" and the erecting of workshops for the "cultivation of mechanical skill." Girard's school opened in 1840, but for the first twenty years school officials did not implement manual training programs. In the 1860s, instruction began in typesetting, printing, carpentry, electroplating, and telegraphy, and under the forceful leadership of a new departmental head of "Industrial Science," Girard College became a manual arts and polytechnic institute. The school for orphans also succeeded in securing ties with local manufacturers and by the turn of the twentieth century school officials spoke metaphorically of an education at Girard as a classical apprenticeship.[84]

Anxiety over the spread of teenage gangs in the city in the 1840s and the number of rowdy, idle adolescent males on the streets similarly led to the the founding of the Spring Garden Institute in 1852. Free reading rooms, a circulating library, lectures, and classes in drawing and design were to be offered for the "improvement of young men in their leisure time . . . whose circumstances have deprived them of moral training and mental culture."[85] Financial difficulties forced the institute to languish during the first decades of its operations, but an important reorganization occurred in 1877.

Impressed by the vocational education displays at the Centennial Exhibition, a number of leading manufacturing companies, including the Baldwin Locomotive Works, donated monies to transform the Spring Garden Institute into a center for instruction in the mechanical trades and draughtmanship. A full complement of courses and shop classes began to be offered in the early 1880s, and in the next forty years more than thirty-five thousand students would take advantage of the programs and certificates offered at the institute. Major employers in Philadelphia began sending foremen and workers to the school for further training. The textbooks developed by the faculty became the standard for learning and were assigned in technical schools throughout the country.[86]

The desire for "proper training and education of youth in industry and economy" brought into existence a third important and enduring private vocational school, the Williamson Trade School.[87] Isiah Williamson, a successful merchant and investor, bequeathed his fortune in the 1890s to the creation of a residential academy where boys from poor backgrounds would be fed, clothed, lodged, and taught basic reading and writing as well as woodwork, bricklaying, masonry, and plastering. Apprenticeship had been a prime experience in Williamson's upbringing and the deterioration of the practice served as the motive for his founding of a new institution. The trustees of Williamson's school argued for decades about the extent to which trade education would dominate the curriculum, but the school's reputation flourished on the basis of its vocational training programs.

Fear of social disorder brought notable private vocational schools such as Girard College, the Spring Garden Institute, and the Williamson Trade School into being. Concerned Philadelphians launched scores of other, more ephemeral efforts similarly aimed at redeeming children in trouble. A directory of such initiatives would include the Southwark Mechanics Institute and the Industrial Home for Girls, created in the 1850s; the Lincoln Institute, founded in 1866 for sons of Episcopalian soldiers killed during the Civil War; the St. Francis Industrial School, established in 1886, where orphan boys learned carpentry, plumbing, and stonecutting as well as Christian ethics to help "reconcile capital and labor"; the Philadelphia Protectory for Boys (1898); and the Wanamaker Institute of Bethany College (1891), financed by John Wanamaker and intended for "worthy" poor boys and girls. In addition, both the Philadelphia Young Men's Christian

Association and Young Women's Christian Association established courses respectively in mechanical drawing and practical electricity and dressmaking, typing, bookkeeping, and stenography.[88]

Two other private vocational school initiatives need to be added to the list as well. They are the Institute for Colored Youth and the Berean Training and Industrial School, both founded to assist black youth in Philadelphia. Just as African-Americans generally were excluded from the industrial order in the Quaker City, they fared poorly in terms of educational opportunities, despite the importance the black community placed on schooling. Vocational education programs, both in the public and private realm, had been conceived in part to assist disadvantaged youngsters—the orphaned, the wayward, the immigrant; in Philadelphia access to even these possibilities was severely limited for blacks. Efforts at industrial education for black young people had to emerge entirely from within the black community.

Laws passed by the Pennsylvania General Assembly at the turn of the nineteenth century provided for the establishment of schools for the poor; in practice this meant schools for white pauper children. Intense lobbying by the Pennsylvania Abolitionist Society—a group responsible for founding several private schools for black children—led to the opening of the first public school for blacks in 1822.[89] School board officials authorized the creation of seven additional "colored" schools by mid-century, all operated on a segregated basis and housed in older facilties formerly populated by white pupils. Segregation became the letter of the law in 1854 with the passage of a state statute and remained official policy until 1881, when a local court ruled that legalizing separate school facilities violated the equal protection clause of the Fourteenth Amendment.[90] Segregation in the Philadelphia schools continued in practice, however, and actually was furthered and rationalized under the reform administration of Superintendent Martin Brumbaugh during the first and second decades of the twentieth century. Relying on the results of newly developed and administered intelligence tests, Brumbaugh argued that the poor test results of African-American students justified separate educational efforts; segregated schools, he noted, also kept open employment opportunities for black teachers, who by custom were not assigned to schools with white students. Brumbaugh's initiatives came at the exact time of a four-fold increase in the population of black students in the Philadelphia school system. There was massive in-migration of black families to the city during World War I and the 1920s, and the children of these latest arrivals found themselves crowded into the few black schools in the system, leading to average class sizes of between forty and fifty students. The general policy of segregated learning would not be reversed until 1937, when public school officials, facing pressure from a politically mobilizing black community, made integration of the system as a prime goal.[91]

While vocational training had been held out by school administrators and reformers as a panacea for disadvantaged white children, such aid, ironically, was not offered to black youngsters. Blacks could not enroll, for example, in the first public manual arts schools established in the city in the 1880s and 1890s, nor would they be granted admission to the trade and commercial schools opened in the next three decades. In 1891, black students attending the James Forten Public School at Sixth and Lombard Streets, where blacks had been enrolled for sixty-three years, were actually transferred from this school to one several streets away; the Forten School was then closed and re-opened as the James Forten Elementary Manual Training School, a school intended to assist in the Americanization of the growing immigrant community in the neighborhood. African-American parents waited until 1910 for the school board to found the first black school with an industrial arts curriculum; reports soon followed, however, of various deficiencies in this school's program when compared to similar initiatives in white communities.[92] These developments, oddly, transpired in Philadelphia at a time when the notion of trade training for blacks as advocated by the likes of Booker T. Washington was receiving official sanction on the national level among white civic and political leaders. W. E. B. DuBois, it should be noted, remained consistent, and as part of his general attack on Washington's seemingly accomodationist positions and strategies, he criticized even the few efforts at introducing industrial arts programs in black public schools in Philadelphia.[93]

Blacks in the city also had little recourse to private vocational institutions. Girard College, the Spring Garden Institute, and the Franklin Institute, through either explicit policy or custom, accepted only whites, and by the 1920s only a handful of black students could be found at Drexel, the Wanamaker Institute, and similar centers of trade training. A move to fill the void thus needed to come from within the city's black community.

The Institute for Colored Youth had been established by a group of Quakers in 1842 to train African-American teachers. The school attracted a good number of students, but directors of the institute were always cognizant of a glaring contradiction: few schools at the time, public or private, would hire black teachers. Pressure slowly mounted for a revision of the curriculum and the Centennial Exhibition in Philadelphia convinced new school administrators that industrial education would be a wise course to pursue. In the 1880s, popular classes in dressmaking, cooking, carpentry, bricklaying, shoemaking, millinery, printing, plastering, tailoring, typing, and shorthand were introduced, and the Institute emerged as a singular resource for young black adults in Philadelphia.[94]

The Quaker directors of the Institute for Colored Youth throughout its transformative years, however, had misgivings about the new directions of the school. They hoped to maintain teacher training as the Institute's prime function and focus. A series of political imbroglios followed and in 1903 a decision was made to sell the school's property in the city and open a new school with less of a trade emphasis in Cheyney, Pennsylvania, a rural location in Delaware County. (This would be the beginnings of Cheyney University.) Students enrolled in industrial courses at the Institute were then encouraged to transfer to the newly founded Berean Training and Industrial School, which would soon fill the vacuum in trade education for young black Philadelphians created by the closing of the Institute for Colored Youth.[95]

The Berean School had been established by Reverend Matthew Anderson in 1899 in the basement of the Berean Presbyterian Church. Philadelphia department store owners John Wanamaker and Isaac Clothier helped finance the venture, initially opened for the purpose of educating and training "minors and adults in cooking, carpentry, upholstery, sewing, millinery, or any other kinds of manual or industrial employment."[96] School officials later added classes in shorthand, bookkeeping, tailoring, and printing. The practical aims of the Berean School were further revealed in 1912 when officials introduced courses in shirtwaist making, after several garment manufacturers in Philadelphia expressed their willingness to begin employing blacks as garment workers. The Berean Training School became the most important private industrial school for blacks in the city and continues to serve the Philadelphia black community to the present day.

The furthering of science and republican ideals as well as concern for social order and the plight of unfortunate and disadvantaged young white and black men and women generated during the nineteenth century a world of private vocational schools in Philadelphia. Another kind of private vocational school enterprise joined the fold in the late nineteenth century and came to predominate in the twentieth: the private trade or business school operated for profit. A survey conducted in 1936 revealed 55 such schools operating in the city, offering training in 28 different trades—from bartending and beauty culture to electrolysis, embalming, horology (watch making), interior decorating, massage therapy, and welding.[97] Such schools were tenuous enterprises. The 55 private training firms surveyed in 1936 had survived the depression of the 1930s; 130 such schools had been plying their trade in 1929. Of the 55 survivors, the greatest number, 18, were business schools.

Thomas Peirce established the first business school in Philadelphia in 1865, the Peirce College of Business. By the late 1890s, close to a thousand men and women were enrolled in Peirce College courses.[98] Peirce had few competitors at the time, but in the first decades of the twentieth century a score of similar ventures would appear. The business schools in the city generally welcomed all customers. Only three schools in operation in 1936, for example, required high school diplomas; eleven actually maintained simple open admission policies. The schools varied in their offerings as well. Most taught typing, filing, stenography, and basic secretarial skills; four provided special instruction in accounting procedures, and five in bookkeeping practices. Students in these schools typically enrolled for eight- to ten-month periods and tuition fees ranged from $150 to $250 a course, substantial figures for the time. Students completing courses received certificates of competency and thirteen of the eighteen schools operated free placement services to assist graduates in obtaining employment.[99]

This history of vocationalism has dealt to this juncture only with intentions, with conceived efforts to tie schooling to the world of work. The impact and results of these initiatives have not yet been considered or measured. Several points are clear now purely on the level of intentionality. First, practical education has had a long history in Philadelphia. While key developments unfolded between 1880 and 1920, linking schools to work always had a claim in the city. In fact, classical learning never occupied in Philadelphia a dominant place in educational theory or practice. Second, to concentrate only on the public realm or mechanical instruction loses sight of the breadth of the undertakings. Classroom instruction connected to work activity came to be offered in public and parochial schools in the city and private institutions of all sorts and involved instruction for employment in both industry and commerce. Third, the relationship between economic and curricular change is not straightforward in Philadelphia. To be more precise, it is difficult to account for the growth of vocationalism in Philadelphia's public and parochial schools in the late nineteenth and early twentieth centuries by simple reference to transformations in the city's industrial base or labor markets. The city did not undergo significant economic change during the period. A new kind of work force was not needed. Fears of social disorder in fact provided greater cause for initiating programs of practical instruction than any technological imperative. This leads to a fourth issue regarding the chief actors in promoting vocationalism. The business community in Philadelphia certainly spoke in favor of manual arts and trade training, but the role of school reformers and administrators appears more critical. The tie between vocational education and school-system building both in the public and parochial school realm must be fully appreciated. Bureaucratization, professionalization and vocationalism went hand in hand; for Martin Brumbaugh and Father Philip McDevitt, the success of the structures they were building depended on a clientele, and that clientele had to be offered a tangible education; social reformers and social scientists provided school managers with ample arguments and justifications, some seemingly philanthropic in nature, others clearly based on fears of social unrest. Finally, events transpired unevenly, and an educational order fully geared to the workplace did not materialize in Philadelphia. Localism (local control of educational policy making and local financing of schools); democratic values, traditions, and politics; class antagonisms; intellectual confusion; and concern for liberal arts learning made a hybrid system of vocationalism inevitable.

The historian does not have at his or her command easy means to assess accurately the actual value of schooling in occupational achievement—to go beyond the question of intentions. Assembling sufficiently large, representative samples of Philadelphians from different eras, gathering social and demographic background information for those selected, and tracing their ensuing educational and job histories presents formidable obstacles to the researcher. Relating levels of education to vocational attainment in a general or certain way is simply not possible. From a historical standpoint, the question can only be approached in a composite fashion. One issue to consider is that of school attendance.

Universal attendance in school came only gradually in Philadelphia. The percentages of youngsters enrolled in schools during the nineteenth century remained fairly static, while the numbers of young people at work grew. By 1900, one-third of all thirteen year olds could be found on the job, as could a majority of fourteen to seventeen year olds. Compulsory school attendance laws, changing attitudes toward education, and gains in real income raised the proportion of fourteen- and fifteen-year-old youngsters in school to 90 percent by 1930, but still less than 50 percent of their sixteen- and seventeen-year-old counterparts could be found in classrooms. When the law in Philadelphia allowed young people to work, they chose work over school in great numbers. Any evaluation of the role of schools in occupational attainment must first take the following into account: that at least for the first one hundred years of common school education in a city such as Philadelphia, not all young people accepted the assumed advantages of classroom enrollment.

The social determinants of school attendance also have to be taken into consideration. The socioeconomic standing of families of school-age children had an enormous impact on prospects for schooling. With few exceptions, the children of professional parents and proprietors enrolled in school programs to a far greater extent than did the children of skilled and unskilled workmen. This can be seen in general figures and also in individual school statistics. Central High School had an especially elite student body, but even in schools of lesser reputation and status enrollments did not reflect the social composition of the city writ large.[100] At the William Penn High School for Girls in 1910, more than 30 percent of the students came from families whose fathers were businessmen and professionals; at the time, no more than 10 percent of Philadelphia's population could be classified as such.[101] Even at Southern High and Manual School, another product of the vocational school movement, more than 30 percent of the boys in attendance in 1910 came from upper-class backgrounds.[102] Again, qualifications are in order in assessing the role of schools: attendance was not universal and children from working-class backgrounds have historically had the most loose allegiances and connections to the school order.

Another consideration is high drop-out rates, which accompanied uneven levels of school enrollment. In 1941, school officials in Philadelphia estimated that upwards of twenty-five thousand young people were leaving the city's school system in any given year; of these, close to 60 percent left prior to graduation with no intention of returning.[103] That figure, high as it may seem, roughly approximates precise calculations available from school-level studies. Research conducted at Kensington High School, for example, during the 1930s revealed that 50 percent of all entering classes to the school failed to complete four years of course work.[104] A similar study at Germantown High School indicated a drop-out rate of 47 percent.[105] For an earlier time period, the first decade of the century, and a different kind of school, Central Manual Training High School, recent research indicates a similar leaving rate of 49 percent.[106]

Quite characteristically, school leaving occurred as soon as youngsters reached the legal age for securing employment. A report prepared by the White-Williams Foundation in 1919 noted that the vast majority of applicants for work certificates requested papers within a few weeks of their fourteenth birthdays.[107] When the school leaving age was raised to sixteen in the 1930s, students just turning sixteen left school in the greatest numbers.[108] When they could leave, many young people in Philadelphia opted out of the school order.

Vocational education programs in the public schools in Philadelphia operated with the highest rates of turnover of students. At Northeast High School in the 1920s, the drop-out rate of the nearly 70 percent of students taking the industrial arts curriculum was twice that of students enrolled in academic and commercial course tracks.[109] A study conducted, also in the 1920s, in an unnamed school in Philadelphia similarly revealed an 80 percent leave rate for students pursuing mechanical arts degrees; a 55 percent drop-out rate was recorded for the school at large.[110] At the Edward Bok Vocational School in the 1940s, only 30 percent of the students in each entering class stayed to graduate; most of those who left did so within the first and second years of the school's program, again within a short time of their turning sixteen.[111]

The low rates of school completion by students enrolled in industrial education programs raises a general question about the sizable drop-out rates recorded in Philadelphia's public schools. A high proportion of students enrolled in mechanical trade courses came from working-class backgrounds; that they left school in great numbers to work and contribute to family income is not surprising. A number of studies conducted in Philadelphia during the 1930s and 1940s also indicated that students tracked into vocational education programs tended to be classified as below average in intelligence and that their teachers had low expectations for their academic progress—a second explanation for high rates of school leaving.[112] Financial necessity, poor academic performance, and lack of interest emerge then as reasons for the drop-out problem, but which factor figured most heavily in Philadelphia? School officials and social investigators, in fact, devoted a good deal of attention to the matter, but a clear answer is not manifest in their studies.

In 1920, the White-Williams Foundation conducted the first known survey of school drop-outs in the city. Five hundred thirteen youngsters applying for work certificates and intending to leave school were interviewed. When asked why they were leaving, 49 percent of the youngsters merely responded that "They Did Not Like School"; 37 percent indicated "Financial Necessity," and 14 percent offered a variety of other reasons.[113] Two years later, school officials launched their own study. Three hundred ten students who had left South Philadelphia School for Girls in 1920 were canvassed. Fifty-seven percent listed academic difficulties and lack of interest in school as their reasons for not completing their education, 24 percent said they had to work or help out in the home, and 20 percent provided a series of other explanations. Nineteen (6 percent) of the young women, though, mentioned that they planned to return to school and complete their course work for graduation.[114]

Changing economic circumstances could change the kinds of responses recorded by investigators looking into the problem of school leaving. In the midst of the depression of the 1930s, 250 girls who had left Kensington High School were asked for their reasons. More than 60 percent answered that they needed either to secure work to supplement family incomes or to help out directly in the home; only 16 percent noted a lack of interest in schooling.[115] Clearly, academic difficulties or disinterest and financial necessity loomed as the most important ingredients in high school drop-out rates, and their relative significance varied across time and the particular circumstances of different groups of students. Successful experiences in school, however, did matter; as several studies of Philadelphia public school students indicated, students with superior records stayed in school and graduated in far greater numbers than those with below-average grades.[116] Success bred success. Still, for a sizable proportion of school-age children in the Quaker City—perhaps half—schooling for either economic or academic reasons did not represent, at least before the 1950s, an essential or appealing opportunity and experience.

For those supplying labor in Philadelphia in the past, schooling apparently did not convey necessary advantages. From the demand side—that is, from the standpoint of employers—formal education had mixed value as well. Firms engaged in manufacturing, for example, and in need of industrial manpower rarely relied on the schools for workers or put great stock in what potential employees could learn in school. Companies hiring clerical help, on the other hand, found the schools a vital agency in labor recruitment and training.

In public pronouncements and associational activity Philadelphia manufacturers may have appeared to be strong advocates of vocational education, but in private they showed little faith in the schools. A study conducted in 1916 in 262 millinery firms in the city, for example, revealed that not a single company established educational qualifications for employment. Less than 2 percent of the largely female work force in the industry had graduated from high school; 61 percent even had less than six years of schooling. Millinery employers generally held to the opinion that the trade could be learned only on the shop floor.[117]

A survey two decades later in an even more skilled field, the machine industry, measured similar results. Managers of 172 companies employing approximately 39,000 workers provided information on the education and training of their personnel.[118] Fifty percent of the firms reported having no educational requirements for hire; another 40 percent preferred recruits with some high school education but not necessarily certificates of graduation. For 15 percent of the firms, a junior high school degree was sufficient, and only 5 percent of the companies actually required vocational school training. Furthermore, of these 172 machine trade firms only four administered mechanical tests in judging applicants for jobs. The great majority of companies expected new workers to acquire their skills under the tutelage of foremen and experienced hands. Only seventeen company managers reported ever contacting schools or school agencies in search of labor, and only a few revealed any knowledge of the vocational education curriculum in the Philadelphia public schools. A number expressed respect for private schools in the city, particularly the Williamson Trade School. The machine industry represented a venerable and vital sector of Philadelphia's industrial order, yet as of the late 1930s the industry had few ties to the city's educational system.

A final study conducted in the 1940s attests to the disjuncture between the public posture of the manufacturing community and daily practice. Wartime shortages of skilled labor had brought the issue of the training of young people in mechanical pursuits to the fore in Philadelphia. One survey generated out of this concern canvassed twenty major companies in the city, including Westinghouse, General Electric, Brill, and the Radio Corporation of America, and found that all these firms relied heavily on shop-floor instruction of recruits; only six companies reported favoring graduates of public and private vocational education programs for hire. The particular production needs of the businesses required direct on-the-job training by plant managers.[119]

In a number of instances, Philadelphia manufacturing firms did try to strike up a relationship with public schools in the city to facilitate trade education of young workers, but the limited success of these ventures illustrates the realities that made for uncertain links between business enterprises and the schools. In 1913, for example, the Philadelphia Typothetae, a trade association of printing concerns, attempted to establish a cooperative work program between the Philadelphia Trade School and printing firms in the city; the experiment was aimed at students enrolled in continuation or evening classes. The initiative collapsed when officials in the organization could not decide whether trade instruction should be offered primarily on the shop floor or in the classroom and whether it should be taught by company officials or school instructors.[120] In 1920, a similar effort was made to create a supervisors' training program at Northeast Evening High School. The firms involved in this plan soon reneged on their commitment; foremanship, they later insisted, could only be learned on the job.[121]

A grander cooperative scheme was launched by the Philadelphia Metal Manufacturers' Association in 1926. This organization had been formed two decades earlier for the express purpose of breaking the hold various metal workers' unions had on the trade. Increasing the number of skilled workers in the field was an important objective of the association, and to this end a pact was negotiated with the Philadelphia public school board to establish a Cooperative Apprentice Plan. Youngsters under this program received release time from school to work in certain designated firms and receive trade instruction; school officials created special after-work and Saturday classes for students in the program in order that they could finish all course requirements toward graduation. The program, however, operated for only a few years and never involved more than two hundred young men.[122] A fatal flaw doomed the initiative. Enrolled students rarely finished their course work; they learned that good wages could be earned through full-time employment in the firms to which they had been assigned. The companies, for their part, collaborated in the undermining of the cooperative plan, gradually engaging the student apprentices as regular employees.[123] Given the opportunity, students again chose work over schooling; given the opportunity, firms chose to train their new workers completely in their own way.

Philadelphia's particular production system contributed to the general lack of reliance of Philadelphia manufacturing firms on the city's educational order. Small-batch, custom production required specialized skills and constant retooling; few firms had great faith in the ability of the schools to train workers for their specific needs. In fact, school officials received cautions against great investments in vocational education. The United States Navy, for example, maintained sizable production facilities in Philadelphia and employed thousands of skilled workers. In the late nineteenth century, the Navy decided to train its civilian work force in Philadelphia in special apprenticeship programs. Navy officials advised local school administrators that existing public school vocational education programs could not possibly give potential Navy employees the skills to perform the specialized tasks involved in shipbuilding and repair. They would prefer that recruits instead be better instructed in reading, writing, and math in the city's schools.[124] A report prepared for the school district in 1940 on the manpower needs of local manufacturers reiterated the same point. Few Philadelphia firms expected the schools to equip young people adequately for the kinds of industrial employment available in the city; the schools would do better to impart general knowledge and habits of discipline.[125]

Industrial education in Philadelphia then did not serve the purposes of either the suppliers or purchasers of manual labor. Today, few believe that the skills taught in vocational education classes bear any relationship to the expertise required for existing or future jobs. Recent studies conducted by the United States Department of Labor and other researchers confirm the irrelevancy of most present-day manual arts classroom instruction; jobs have become either so unskilled that they require minimal shop-floor training or so technical that intensive, long-term learning has to take place in the plant.[126] Evidence from Philadelphia on the actual function of industrial education programs in the past raises doubts about whether such initiatives have ever had great impact. Two realities limited their role: young people in the city needed full-time work and left school when offered it; employers, given the nature of manufacturing production in the city, preferred to train their personnel directly.

An entirely different situation prevailed for commercial course instruction in the city's schools. In business classes in Philadelphia's public, parochial, and private schools, young people developed standardized skills easily and directly transferable to the office: typing, stenography, bookkeeping, and the use of office addressograph and billing machinery. School programs proved advantageous to employers of clerical help; companies did not have to spend substantial time or money training new workers (no need, in other words, to teach typing on the job). A growing body of graduates of commercial course programs—largely female—also provided an ample, relatively inexpensive, and replaceable labor pool.

By looking at the different credentials established for hire, it is easy to see that white-collar employers forged closer connections with the educational order than did manufacturing firms. Two surveys conducted by the Women's Bureau of the Department of Labor in 1930 and 1940 reveal that between 52 and 56 percent of all firms engaging clerical help in Philadelphia required high school degrees of their recruits; less than 5 percent of the companies canvassed had no policy with regard to educational achievement.[127] Small firms especially insisted on prior instruction and training; clerical staff in these offices needed to perform varied tasks. One study of 150 small offices in Philadelphia thus reported that 80 percent of these firms required high school degrees and 40 percent preferred college graduates.[128] The commercial course degree then represented a ticket to white-collar employment, and this fact is reflected in the levels of education attained by clerical workers in the city. Interviews with 4,368 office employees in 1932 indicated that 14 percent had attended college, 37 percent graduated from high school, and another 44 percent completed at least two years of high school course work; only 14 percent had not gone beyond grammar school, and this group was employed largely as messengers and for other low-skilled office tasks.[129]

Any evaluation of the actual impact of vocational education programs thus must make a distinction between industrial and commercial course programs. A critical link emerged between white-collar employment and school instruction and certification. The most deliberate tie may have been forged, though, by the city's Catholic schools, for no where was there a clearer or more successful intention to connect the curriculum to the world of work. Catholic schools deliberately prepared their best high school students—particularly the girls—for office employment and built relationships with firms to assist in job searches. As a result, parochial school students received favorable consideration in hiring. The Bayuk Cigar Company, for example, sought with little success to recruit clerical help from the public schools. The company's personnel manager then contacted the St. Boniface Business School and graduates of that program came to dominate the office.[130] Interviews conducted in the 1950s by Gladys Palmer (Industrial Research Department, Wharton School, University of Pennsylvania) with personnel officials of such major Philadelphia firms as Smith, Kline, and French Laboratories; American Stores; and the Insurance Company of North America revealed similar relationships with Catholic schools in the city. The parochial schools, recruitment officers testified, trained their business students well, provided information on applicants in a comprehensive and deliberate way, and prepared students for interviews.[131] As H. W. Flecktner of Bayuk Cigars noted, "Girls from Catholic schools appear well groomed for employment interviews in contrast to the sloppy appearance of girls from other sources."

Philadelphia's public schools did not provide as well for their students. The Junior Employment Service had been established, primarily through the foresight and largesse of the White-Williams Foundation, to render job information and referrals to public school students in search of work. From its inception, the agency was underfinanced and understaffed and communications and cooperation between JES and the city's high schools remained "uneven and sporadic," as one investigator found.[132] Employers in Philadelphia generally were unaware of the existence of the service and only a small group of firms arranged to forward notices of job openings.[133] Moreover, school officials discovered that, despite publicity efforts, students themselves had little inkling that assistance in securing employment was available to them. Less than one-half of those students leaving school before graduation registered with the JES; surveys indicated that the others simply did not know that the school system operated a placement bureau.[134] Black students here faced additional obstacles; those that knew of the JES and signed on with the service found the all-white staff either unwilling or unable to help them find work.[135]

Thus, young people leaving the public schools in Philadelphia before 1950 were left basically to their own devices, with the schools providing little in the way of direct or indirect assistance in procuring employment. A partial explanation lies at the level of intentions. A consensus never existed in Philadelphia to have public school policy and practice systematically tied to practical ends—that is, to work. An absence of clear direction and financial stringency in general in the funding of education led to ineffective programs and initiatives. Commercial education courses represented an important exception; business classes in Catholic schools in particular offered a definite commitment to practical education and a practical curriculum with definite results. Uneven levels of school attendance, high drop-out rates, and the propensity of Philadelphia manufacturers to train workers on the job and not rely on the schools, are other important aspects of the story. The issue here is not whether schooling should or should not be linked to work, but rather, that this connection was never soldered in Philadelphia. The schools may have inculcated habits of discipline and acculturated students to a world of hierarchy and differential rewards, but that theory is actually impossible for historians to prove. Given that a sizable proportion of young people in the Quaker City had weak allegiances to the schools, great doubt has to be cast on this contention as well. If the schools did have a clear role, it was in raising the age of entrance into the job market, in affecting basic changes in the demography of work.

In the early 1940s, public school administrators in Philadelphia all but admitted that school attendance did not convey necessary benefits or advantages. Researchers for the system had just followed several large samples of students for two-year periods after they had either graduated or dropped from the rolls. The results of the investigation had definitely been colored by the extended economic depression, but the findings were still dismaying. Investigators reported that, although 41 percent of those who had graduated from academic programs continued their educations in college or other institutions of higher learning, 25 percent of their peers were unemployed and seeking work one year after receiving their degrees. Among graduates of industrial education programs, 51 percent had found jobs; 49 percent remained unemployed. Graduates with commercial course degrees fared slightly better; only 33 percent had not been able to secure employment. The fortunes of the school drop-outs were decidedly worse; of their number, 60 percent had failed to obtain work. With these figures in hand, school officials concluded that, while the schools' ability to affect favorably the prospects of its students might be limited and influenced by events far beyond the control of educators, a clarification of goals and a commitment to new efforts and initiatives were in order.[136]

The unclear relationship between schooling and work can finally be seen in the lives of William Rees, Timothy Ragan, Jean Bally, William Deacon, and the 2,500 other Philadelphia working men and women interviewed in 1936. These Philadelphians had varied educational histories. As a group, they averaged 7.8 years of schooling; slightly less than 75 percent had attended grammar schools for eight years or less, and while more than 25 percent pursued secondary school education, only 7 percent of the entire sample secured high school diplomas. Extended years of schooling, moreover, did not translate into occupational stability or achievement. Philadelphia workers with the fewest years of schooling were as likely to be employed regularly and obtain job promotions as those who stayed in school into their late teens. Another kind of learning opportunity, though, did prove important in work experience—apprenticeship. Philadelphia workers receiving formal apprenticeship training had clear advantages in employment. Apprenticeship, like schooling, can be considered an intermediary in the labor market, a practice that affects the chances and possibilities for getting and keeping work. If the school's place in the occupational histories of Philadelphia's working people remained uncertain, did other institutions, such as apprenticeship, play a greater role?

4 · Agencies

In theory, the labor market consists simply of suppliers and purchasers of labor; they negotiate terms of employment directly and on an individual basis. In reality, different groups of workers enter the exchange process with different prospects and advantages, and there are various customary practices and established agencies that act to benefit certain job seekers and not others. This chapter will consider such formal intermediaries in the labor market as apprenticeship programs, unions, public and private employment bureaus, and newspaper help-wanted ads.

The history of apprenticeship can be traced back to ancient Egyptian, Greek, and Roman times with scattered evidence of fathers binding their sons to artisans to have them educated in skilled trades.[1] Apprenticeship became institutionalized in western Europe in the thirteenth century with the creation of the guild system; in receiving the official right to limit entrance to trades, organized craft groups established formal training programs.[2] When the guild system began to disintegrate two centuries later with the expansion of commercialized activity, national sovereigns moved to bolster the threatened apprenticeship system with state regulations. In England, laws passed in the late sixteenth century established a compulsory seven-year apprenticeship for young men who wished to enter trades and granted to local officials the authority to bind orphans and children of the poor to master craftsmen who were to provide for their lodging, board, and trade instruction.[3]

British settlers transported British laws, customs, and practices to the new world. In Philadelphia, the city council enacted legislation in 1716 regulating apprenticeship arrangements, with provisions for registering indenture contracts with city officials. The council also established a board of guardians to oversee the dispensation of relief to the growing population of poor people in the city and the city guardians received authority to apprentice children under their aegis to local artisans. With the growth of craft production in colonial Philadelphia, the apprenticeship system flourished, and by the middle of the eighteenth century, approximately five hundred new apprenticeship indentures were being filed each year with municipal authorities.[4]

The apprenticeship system went into eventual eclipse in Philadelphia and elsewhere; any number of explanations have been offered for the demise of the institution. The American shores, for one, proved an unsuitable environment for apprenticeship. A relative abundance of land and scarcity of labor guaranteed that any attempts to regulate labor (at least, white labor) would fail. With opportunities abounding, apprentices characteristically reneged on their contracts and went in search of less restrictive employment. The American Revolution further contributed to the erosion. Young men left their benches in artisan shops in droves to join the patriots' cause; the democratic fervor unleashed by the upheaval provided additional problems for masters in their efforts to control their charges.[5] Finally, and certainly most important, the expansion of the market economy and increasing demand for cheap, standardized goods during the first half of the nineteenth century destroyed artisanal production and practices. New entrepreneurially minded manufacturers began to produce on an assembly-line–like basis, with unskilled wage labor that they hired and fired at will. In the emerging industrial capitalist order, there was no place for apprenticeship. The frontier, the democratic ethos, and industrialization thus combined to undermine the institution.

Explanations are readily available to account for the decline of apprenticeship. Documenting the demise of the institution, however, remains a difficult task. Ongoing tallies on apprentices were never compiled. Certainly literary evidence exists to substantiate the erosion of the practice in Philadelphia. The *Mechanics' Free Press,* for example, the city's leading labor newspaper in the antebellum period, is filled with letters from apprentices complaining of poor treatment at the hands of their employers and of their being reduced to the status of common day laborers.[6] Similarly, directors of Girard College, the school for orphans endowed by the financier Stephen Girard, faced a telling dilemma. Girard had stipulated in his will that students enrolled in the school be bound out in their teen years to local artisans. Administrators of the college found the task of locating master craftsmen who would take on apprentices increasingly difficult and they abandoned the idea in the late nineteenth century.[7]

Scattered evidence that attests to the decline of the apprenticeship, however, should be balanced by records indicating the actual and surprising persistence of the institution. The drawing of several distinctions is initially helpful here. Apprenticeship took various forms. The education of professionals—lawyers and doctors, most notably—occurred entirely within the context of apprenticeship before and after the American Revolution. Professional schools had not yet been founded and young men, usually from upper-class backgrounds, seeking entrance to the professions learned their trades while in service to experienced practitioners. Professional training of this sort persisted in Philadelphia and elsewhere late into the nineteenth century.[8]

On the opposite end of the socioeconomic scale, another kind of apprenticeship arrangement also remained in practice. Municipal court authorities continued into the twentieth century to oversee the binding out of children in trouble and those in unfortunate circumstances to local artisans. Whether youngsters in these categories were ever afforded the trade instruction prescribed by law remains an open question. The public apprenticing of children only came to an end with Progressive-era attacks on child labor and the enactment of legislation making school attendance compulsory.[9]

The craft apprenticeship represents the third manifestation of the system. A young man bound to a master craftsman for a four-to-seven-year period of service, residing in the master's household, receiving instruction in highly skilled labor, preparing for eventual masterhood—this is the portrait normally associated with apprenticeship. In contrast to professional and public indenturing, this type of apprenticeship usually involved young men from middling or respectable working-class backgrounds. In Philadelphia, craft apprenticeship did not pass into extinction either; nor did the notion that a young person's general and vocational education could best be fulfilled while in service and at the workplace. The practice persisted, but the nature of the institution and the experience did change.

The gradual eclipse of artisanal production in Philadelphia doomed the traditional shop apprenticeship. As administrators of Girard College discovered, the opportunities for placing young men under the

long-term tutelege and care of master craftsmen in the city evaporated over the course of the nineteeenth century. Two new kinds of
apprenticeship programs, however, emerged to fill the vacuum: the
first, created and administered by businessmen as part of their companies' operations; the second, initiated and overseen by organized
working people through the agency of their trade unions. These two
systems originated and evolved in distinct ways but sustained the
system.

A number of business leaders in Philadelphia attempted to rescue
the practice of apprenticeship from oblivion and fashion formal training programs for their new large-scale enterprises. The most notable
case in point is that of the Baldwin Locomotive Works. Matthias
Baldwin began manufacturing his famed locomotives in the city in
the early 1830s, and within two decades his work force had grown
to 1,400 men. The production of custom engines required highly
skilled labor, and guaranteeing an ample supply of trained hands
emerged as a constant problem for the firm. Matthias Baldwin personally instituted an apprenticeship program to alleviate the situation.
Baldwin was a religious man, whose experiment with modern apprenticing was motivated as by much by ethical concerns as by economics.

Surviving records of the firm indicate that between 1856 and 1868,
Baldwin signed indenture contracts with 344 young men and their
parents. During that period, his apprentices comprised between 10
and 20 percent of the entire Baldwin task force. The average apprentice began his training at sixteen and agreed to serve for five years
with the company. The standard wage schedule started apprentices
at a weekly pay of $2.25 and provided for a 25 cent increase each
year. Baldwin actually withheld a small portion of the weekly compensation and these saved earnings were awarded to each apprentice
upon completion of their indentures. Deductions and fines for ab-
sences, tardiness, and disorderly conduct, however, reduced these
final payments for a majority of Baldwin's trainees.[10]

Baldwin provided no lodging for his apprentices—an obvious
break with the craft system—and most of Baldwin's charges lived at
home, with local families, or in boardinghouses surrounding the
plant. Baldwin officially promised to train his recruits in the skilled
trades. The largest number of young men were specifically prepared
as machinists; others received instruction in blacksmithing, molding,

boilermaking, and carpentry. Appproximately 80 percent of the firm's apprentices completed their five-year terms.[11] The minority who reneged on their contracts did so toward the end of their service. As Baldwin sadly noted in a letter, "There is one period in our Boys time we always consider critical. It is when they have made considerable advances in their business and have an idea they can go into the world as journeymen and earn wages. This happens about the age of 19 and 20. At this time they are apt to feel they are [finished with their training]."[12] Baldwin, it should be noted, made every effort to locate runaways and even secure indemnities from their parents. For the most part, his charges remained loyal; during a major strike at the plant in March of 1860 only one apprentice joined the work stoppage.[13]

Throughout its history in the Philadelphia area, the Baldwin Locomotive Company offered premium jobs and employment and apprenticeship at the firm were considered quite desirable. Consequently, Matthias Baldwin could favor the applications of boys with respectable credentials and recommendations, including the sons and relatives of regular employees in good standing with the concern. As part of a service to his customers, Baldwin also agreed to train young workers from companies purchasing his engines. (Baldwin produced heavy machinery for use in Cuban sugar mills and, as a result, a group of Cuban youngsters joined the ranks of the Baldwin apprentices in the 1860s.) In general, Baldwin's trainees came from relatively secure backgrounds. Sixty-four percent of them came from families whose fathers were skilled workmen; the fathers of another 20 percent were professionals or small proprietors, and only 16 percent had fathers who occupied positions as day laborers.[14]

The Civil War severely jeopardized Matthias Baldwin's experiment with industrial apprenticeship. His young recruits either enlisted or were drafted into military service and Baldwin tried in vain to win exemptions for them and his general work force. A number of recruits did finish their training during the war years and several others returned from the military to resume their service. Still, the program appears to have gone into decline during and after the war, and when Matthias Baldwin died in 1868 his succeeding partners, for reasons not noted in surviving firm records, decided to abandon the system. The education of young workers in the firm would be handled informally over the next thirty years.

In 1901, Samuel Vauclain, who had risen to the general superintendency of the Baldwin works and would later become an influential and outspoken president of the company, decided to initiate a new apprenticeship program. Vauclain established a three-tiered system of formal training. Seventeen-year-old boys who had completed at least eight years of schooling could apply for indentured service. They would agree to bind themselves to the company for four years, attend work regularly and receive shop floor instruction and supervision, and complete three years of night school courses in algebra, geometry, and mechanical drawing. The firm opted not to establish a school on the premises; recruits were expected to go to local public schools or private trade schools, the latter at Baldwin's expense. A second program existed for high school graduates, who could become apprenticed for three-year periods and who agreed to two years of extra school training in mechanical drawing and specification writing. A third level of indenture was established for graduates of colleges and technical schools who wanted instruction in practical shop work.[15]

Under the three systems, recruits applied to a superintendent of apprentices who supervised their indentures and made all assignments. All apprentices were placed on rotating schedules; they served in all shops and areas of production and only in their last year did they concentrate on a chosen specialty. Upon completion of their terms, recruits were given bonuses of $100. The Baldwin Company experienced great success with Samuel Vauclain's program of industrial apprenticeship. In 1909, the firm reported that between 85 and 90 percent of all accepted applicants to the program had satisfactorily completed their obligations and been hired as full-time workers. The concern's perennial problem of insuring an adequate supply of skilled hands had been solved. As company officials noted, "It is no longer necessary to go outside of the works for any talents desired."[16]

The subsequent history of Vauclain's experiment is difficult to determine. In 1916, Baldwin executives, in testimony to a special presidential commission on industrial relations, announced that they had abandoned formal apprenticeship programs in the company. They would no longer make distinctions among young men hired by the firm.[17] Other evidence indicates that parts of Vauclain's plan remained in place through the late 1940s. High school graduates could still become apprenticed to the firm and were still required to take supplemental course work; their service, however, now tended to be limited to particular production areas. In some instances, persisting apprentice arrangements at Baldwin became modified by agreements reached between the firm and various craft unions.[18] After 1916, however, the effort never approached the comprehensive scale of the program envisioned and established by Vauclain. The Baldwin story, then, is one of repeated efforts to institute programs of industrial apprenticeship—neither the idea nor the practice of apprenticeship disappeared—but the sustenance of these efforts remained problematic.

Other venerable firms in Philadelphia followed Baldwin's lead in creating industrial apprenticeship programs. To guarantee continued supplies of skilled workers, founders of both the Disston Saw and the John B. Stetson Hat companies developed apprenticeship systems at early stages in their enterprises' histories. In both instances, apprenticeship programs emerged as features of larger paternalistic efforts. Managers at Disston and Stetson actually maintained apprenticeship practices on a more regular basis than at Baldwin's, but, as at Baldwin, such formal training initiatives eventually came to be controlled and administered by trade unions.[19]

Surveys conducted in Philadelphia during the second and third decades of the twentieth century reveal a proliferation of lesser-known management-created apprenticeship programs in the city on the order of those at Baldwin, Stetson, and Disston. The Atlantic Refining Company, E. G. Budd Company, Midvale Steel, General Electric, Westinghouse Electric, Curtis Publishing, the Pennsylvania Railroad, Cramp's Ship and Engine Building Company, Fels [Soap] and Company, and David Lupton's Sons Company, among others, all had apprenticeship systems in place by the 1920s.[20] These firms typically set up programs of three or four years' duration. To be eligible, young recruits had to have finished eight years of schooling; none of the above firms required a high school diploma for admission. In addition to training on the shop floor, apprentices had to attend classes for an average of five hours a week. While their course work tended to be technical in nature, apprentices in a number of businesses also received instruction in English, math, economics, and even history. While some companies built classrooms within the walls of their plants, most arranged to have their indentured workers take classes in public school evening programs or local technical institutes and YMCAs. Apprenticeship thus survived in Philadelphia in this fashion.

The notion of educating young workers on company premises gained favor among another set of Philadelphia businessmen who nevertheless saw no particular need to establish actual apprenticeship programs. John Wanamaker, the city's great retail sales merchant, assumed the lead in what would become known as the "company school" movement. Wanamaker began in business in 1861 as the operator of a small clothing store. In the late 1860s, he decided to expand his enterprise, largely through product diversification, and in 1876, amid great fanfare, he opened a grand emporium in an abandoned depot of the Pennsylvania Railroad.[21] Wanamaker emerged in the city and the nation as a pioneer in retailing, consumer services, and advertising, and also in personnel management. He developed innovative administrative structures for his complex business, new recruitment and employment practices and training programs, and a host of employee benefit packages that would establish him as a champion of business paternalism; not coincidentally, he also became a vehement opponent of trade unions.[22] The education of young people concerned him greatly and here he saw his store playing an important role.

In 1878, Wanamaker started classes for young employees in his store; the classes covered methods of salesmanship, mathematics, ethics, and public speaking. In 1890, he founded an in-store school, complete with a full-time principal and teachers.[23] Boys and girls went to classes from eight to ten in the morning before attending to their jobs. Wanamaker's new school had a definite military air. Students wore uniforms, supplied free of charge by Wanamaker, and were called cadets. He also provided musical instruments and drilling equipment to form a marching band. In fact, a battalion of young store workers would later serve bravely in the Spanish–American War.

On March 12, 1896, Wanamaker's store school officially became known as the John Wanamaker Commercial Institute; the Commonwealth of Pennsylvania would eventually charter the institute with a new title, the American University of Trade and Applied Commerce. John Wanamaker had clear ends in mind for his school that went beyond the immediate needs of his business. As he noted, the school was planned so that "the United States shall reap a harvest of healthy, educated, contented men and women, fit for conditions peaceful and prosperous, instead of leaving them to socialist anarchies, ignorance and poverty that breed discontent and crimes."[24]

At its peak the school enrolled three hundred young men and women (in separate classes) and had twenty-four teachers on staff. Courses were given in reading, writing, math, English, spelling, stenography, commercial geography, commercial law, music, French and German, and business methods; a summer camp was also established for participants. Students received grades for their course work and these grades determined their prospects for promotion within the store. Wanamaker proudly publicized the results of his endeavors, but his successors were less enamored of the institute. They gradually phased the school out in the 1920s; they could not provide the full education for fifteen- and sixteen-year-olds required by the state after the passage of compulsory school attendance laws. In-store vocational training programs for sales and office clerks, buyers, and department heads remained important features of the firm and models for the industry.[25]

A number of other Philadelphia companies opened similar schools. Wanamaker's chief competitor in merchandising, Strawbridge & Clothier, operated a rival school and also established a student work-cooperative program with several public high schools in the city.[26] The Bell Telephone Company and the plumbing supply firm of Haines, Jones, and Cadbury created much discussed plant schools as well.[27] These Philadelphia companies joined a national movement. In 1913, leading businessmen in the country formed the National Association of Corporation Schools, an organization intended as a clearinghouse for information about schools established by and for companies.[28] In the bulletins of the association, Philadelphia firms figured prominently. The company school movement, however, began to wane by the 1930s. Economic hard times demanded stringent measures, and firms soon jettisoned these costly programs; compulsory school attendance laws also forced company school students into regular classrooms on a full-time basis. Straightforward industrial apprenticeship programs weathered these developments and prevailed over the company schools.

Businessmen generally established apprenticeship programs in Philadelphia for two reasons. The need to guarantee an ample supply of skilled workers trained in the specific demands of companies provided one important incentive. In addition, the desire of some executives to engender greater loyalties among workers encouraged them to experiment with a variety of paternalistic efforts, including the formal schooling of recruits. Not all business leaders, however, were prompted by these two reasons. During the late nineteenth century, manufacturers in various trades in Philadelphia banded together into associations to lobby for protective legislation, curb ruinous competition within industries, and collectively counter the power of workers organized into unions. To break the control of craft unions in the city, trade association officials specifically established new and different apprenticeship arrangements and made subsequent employment in trades incumbent on passage through association programs and non-union membership. The Philadelphia Metal Manufacturers Association and the Philadelphia Master Plumbers Association, for example, created trade-wide, association-administered apprenticeship programs and thereby kept the the recruitment and training of machinists and plumbers tightly monitored.[29] Subsequent trade union victories, in certain instances, placed these efforts under joint association and union management. The institution of apprenticeship, then, survived in Philadelphia not just through the initiatives of individual businessmen, but also through collective action.

The United States Navy provides one final example of the role of employers in maintaining apprenticeship. In the 1790s, the Navy Department chose Philadelphia as a major site for ship construction. Initially, the Navy contracted with local craftsmen who in turn hired their own apprentices and journeymen to build vessels. In the nineteenth century, Navy officials gradually assumed direct management of Naval operations in the city. The recruitment and training of the thousands of hands needed emerged as a distinct problem. A loose apprenticeship system was instituted and apprentices first appear on the employment rolls of the city's Navy Yard in 1895. In 1912, local administrators received permission to establish a Navy Apprentice School. Four-year training programs were created for toolmakers, shipfitters, machinists, electricians, patternmakers, steamfitters, riggers, plumbers, molders, blacksmiths, sheet metal workers, painters, cabinetmakers, joiners, sailmakers, and shipsmiths. Navy officials also reached agreements with the Philadelphia Board of Education to furnish instructors for classes in English, mathematics, science, and mechanical drawing. Young civilian workers had to pass civil service examinations before acceptance into the program and their tenure and placement depended on successfully completing tests at six month intervals. The Navy Department's apprenticeship program in the city served as a model for private employers throughout the country; the program was greatly expanded during both world wars, effectively meeting the Navy's severe wartime needs for skilled labor, and remains in place to this day.[30]

The maintenance of apprenticeship practices in Philadelphia through managerial initiative—whether on an individual or a collective basis, in private or public enterprises—tells only one piece, albeit a large one, of the story. Of equal if not greater importance is the role played by the city's working people. To protect both the status of their jobs and the jobs themselves, organized workers in the Quaker City made the establishment and control of apprenticeship programs a key demand. In fact, apprenticeship emerged as an issue for them immediately with the changes in productive relations wrought by industrial development.

With the expansion of market activity and the breakdown of craft traditions and practices, employers in Philadelphia began to hire young unskilled workers to perform menial tasks on the basis of the wage and with no other obligations than to compensate them for the work performed. In the skilled trades, journeymen reacted by demanding stricter controls on the hiring and training of new recruits to prevent the inundation of their work with cheapened labor. If their collective strength was sufficient, they could refuse to produce until shop owners agreed to their conditions of employment.

Philadelphia journeymen led the way in not only forming the country's first trade unions to back their demands, but also in their attempts to control the labor market. The first constitution of the Philadelphia Typographical Society, drafted in 1802, thus provides the earliest known inclusion in a union's regulations of a provision for limiting entrance to the trade by establishing periods of apprenticeship. "No person shall be eligible to become a member of this society," the constitution reads, "who shall not have served an apprenticeship satisfactory to the board of directors, to whom he shall make application in person and they shall thereupon proceed to the election by ballot, and if the candidate shall obtain a majority of two thirds of the board present, he shall then be declared a member of this society, and receive a certificate thereof."[31] Although the printers of Philadelphia did not succeed in this early period in establishing closed shops in their trade they did lay the basis for a new form of apprenticeship arrangement and experience.

In the late 1820s and early 1830s, the city of Philadelphia witnessed an upsurge in trade union organizing and activity, including notable strikes and labor political agitation. The hiring of unskilled workers to replace experienced journeymen remained a vital issue and the establishment of apprenticeship agreements and strict ratios of new recruits to veteran workers figured in a number of work disputes and walkouts.[32] Skilled workers, however, once again did not possess the power to dictate terms to their employers. The proliferation of workshops generated by an expanding market economy presented an enormous obstacle to controlling various trades; a decade-long severe economic downturn, beginning in 1836, further effectively destroyed the city's union movement and allowed employers the upper hand in structuring work relations.

New unions of skilled workers emerged in the 1850s and 1860s. Establishing fixed periods of apprenticeship, limits on the number of young men permitted to enter into service, and prohibitions on the employment of non-apprenticed workers emerged as common and constant demands of organized journeymen in this period. When able to dictate terms to their employers, craft unionists in Philadelphia during the late nineteenth century did achieve contracts that invariably included strict provisions on apprenticeship. High demand for skilled labor, the relatively small number of workers and specialized firms involved in many cases, and the persistence of artisanal values and traditions contributed to the organizing successes of various craft unions in the city at the time.[33] For example, highly skilled lace workers formed the Lace Curtain Operatives Union in 1892. Within a year's time, the entire body of 560 skilled lacemakers in Philadelphia had joined the organization and the union proceeded to exert tight controls in the industry. Manufacturers who needed to enlargen their work forces because of increased orders had first to seek permission from the union, and union officials oversaw the subsequent training and apppointments of these new employees.[34]

In the twentieth century, craft unions generally began to assume direct roles in the administration of apprenticeship programs and certification of workers. In the early years of the century, for example, photoengravers in Philadelphia succeeded in organizing their trade and achieving a closed shop. The union zealously guarded apprenticeship arrangements: a five-year apprenticeship was established through contract and young men seeking to apprentice in the industry first had to seek approval from the union (the union also gained veto power over the discharges and releases from indentures). The photoengravers further decided to institute and conduct their own technical classes during the evenings to supplement the normal shop floor instruction.[35] Apprenticeship programs inspired and managed by unions thus came to take their place alongside the initiatives launched by employers.

By 1921, a young man seeking to apprentice himself in Philadelphia could consult a partial listing of opportunities compiled and published by the Public Education and Child Labor Association of Pennsylvania. He would learn that he could apply directly to such firms as E. G. Budd and General Electric and join company-established programs; or to the Metal Manufacturers Association, the Employing Bricklayers' Association, the Master Stone Cutters' Association or the Master Plumbers' Association to participate in trade-wide programs instituted by associated employers; or to the Bricklayers Union of Philadelphia, the Brotherhood of Carpenters and Joiners, the Brotherhood of Painters, the Amalgamated [Sheet] Metal Workers, the Bookbinders' Union, the Amalgamated Lithographers, or the Philadelphia Photo-Engravers' Union to enter training programs totally controlled by unions, with classes offered in union halls by and for union men.[36] Skilled workers in the craft trades in Philadelphia tended to be the most successful in regulating apprenticeship in their trades, but similar kinds of arrangements were achieved in the 1930s and thereafter by industrial workers with unionization in such mass production industries as hosiery and electrical goods manufacture.[37]

The unions in Philadelphia assumed control of apprenticeship not only to protect jobs and wages, but also to maintain their strength. Just as some managers sought to initiate training programs to break the power of organized workers and instill loyalty to companies among young recruits, trade unionists too looked upon apprenticeship arrangements as opportunities to mold a corps of staunch union men. In establishing union-administered apprentice programs for young brewery workers, the United Brewery Workmen's Union in 1906 thus resolved that "the apprentices should become members of our organization from the day of their employment in the brewery, thereby preventing them from becoming traitors during lockouts or strikes."[38]

In industries where organized workers had achieved a closed shop, young men seeking entrance to trades first had to seek admission to the unions. "All boys, before being allowed to go to work," the constitution of the Hat Finishers' Union read, "must appear in person at a meeting of the board of officers consisting of the president, vice-president, secretary, treasurer, and finance committee and have their names registered on the books of the Association."[39] The union then placed recruits into apprenticeship positions as openings emerged. Through custom or explicit policy, sons of union members received preferred treatment. The constitutions of the Stonecutters' Union and the Plumbers' Union in fact included specific provisions that sons of members would be the first enrolled in apprentice programs.[40] With an article in their union by-laws, window glassworkers made it impossible for anyone other than the kin of members to be offered training in the trade. "No member of the Association," their constitution stipulated, "shall teach his trade, whether flattener, cutter, blower or gatherer, to any other persons excepting his own son."[41] Agreements reached by building contractors and the Philadelphia Plasterers' Union put a slightly different twist on the matter; by contract, apprenticeship rolls were first to be filled by the sons of employers and then the sons of union members.[42] Apprenticeship, then, particularly in the case of union-administered programs, was not an opportunity available on an equal basis to all young Philadelphians.

The extent to which apprenticeship survived in theory and practice in the Quaker City can be vividly revealed in the lives of William Rees, Timothy Ragan, Jean Bally, William Deacon, and the 2,500 other Philadelphia workers surveyed in 1936. Thirty percent of the men and women canvassed in the study reported having had formal apprenticeship training.[43] Unfortunately, researchers did not inquire whether these Philadelphians served under programs administered by management, trade associations, or unions. Whatever the form, the canvass clearly indicated that apprenticeship as an institution had not disappeared in the city. Workers born in the twentieth century were in fact as likely to have been apprenticed as their older colleagues.

Apprenticeship is normally associated with craft work and male workers, and on the question of trade and gender, the 1936 survey contained a number of other surprises. While apprenticeship remained a male preserve—35 percent of the male workers reported having served as apprentices—a small group of women, 13 percent of the total, had actually been trained through formal apprenticeships. Similarly, while more than 50 percent of those workers entering the metal trades had been apprenticed, a not unexpected finding, 44 percent of the workers hired by hosiery firms had also had apprenticeship training—an indication that the practice was as much a part of industrial as of craft work.

The 1936 canvass revealed too that apprenticeship generally was not a substitute for schooling. Young men and women who had completed high school were as likely to have served as apprentices as their counterparts with only grade school educations. But here there was one notable exception. Youngsters of German ancestry had among the lowest rates of school attendance in Philadelphia (see the census figures presented in Chapter 2). The 1936 study showed that German-Americans had served in apprenticeship programs in greater proportions than had other ethnic groups. More than half of the surveyed workers born in Germany or in America of parents of German origin reported receiving apprenticeship training. The German-American case is explained not so much by an aversion of the parents toward formal schooling, but rather by the particular work patterns of this ethnic group. Workers born in Germany came of age in a nation where craft practices in general, and apprenticeship training specifically, persisted; once in Philadelphia they soon dominated skilled trades, such as the metal works industry, where apprenticeship as an institution also endured. Family values and networks and good prospects for employment acted as incentives for their children to follow in their footsteps. Young Philadelphians of German background thus left school at relatively early ages and served apprenticeships in significant numbers.

The connection of apprenticeship and ethnicity to type of work is seen in several other instances. In the 1936 study, relatively large numbers of Philadelphians of Italian and Eastern European ancestry surprisingly reported training through apprenticeship. Their dominance in employment in the hosiery trade can account for these results. The near total exclusion of black Philadelphians from hire in the city's industries as well as their denial of membership in unions similarly explains what the Armstrong Association referred to in 1919 as the "meager opportunities for apprenticeship" that existed for young black men and women in the city.[44] African-Americans entering the world of work were thus denied a vital advantage, formal job training, that might have opened more doors of employment to them.

Apprenticeship indeed proved a great aid for the 2,500 Philadelphia workers surveyed in 1936. Forty-three percent of the group reported moving to skilled and better-paid and better-respected positions over the course of their working lives. A clear relationship existed, though, between apprenticeship training and occupational mobility. Sixty-two percent of those who had served an apprenticeship rose during their careers, while only thirty-five percent of those who had not been apprenticed had been similarly promoted. This relationship held across all age cohorts—that is, that among young workers, those with the advantages of apprenticeship were more likely to have risen even in early stages of their working lives than had their counterparts without such training. More notably, while apprenticeship emerged as the strongest predictor of occupational attainment with the exception of gender—few women in the study experienced upward job changes—years of schooling on the other hand had *no* bearing on the vocational histories of the workers canvassed. Philadelphians with less than sixth-grade educations were as likely to have achieved better positions as those with high school diplomas.[45] In this survey, education mattered in occupational achievement, but not regular schooling. *Apprenticeship* education proved to be the key ingredient in employment success. The results of the 1936 survey here complement the findings presented in the previous chapter: that only loose ties were forged between the educational order in Philadelphia and the world of work and that schooling had mixed and unclear benefits for the working people of the city. The study also suggests that learning on the shop floor deserves an equal place in discussions and considerations on education as learning in the classroom.

One exception to the above claims, however, needs to be highlighted. Apprenticeship training did not enhance the employment possibilities of all Philadelphians, and an important case in point is women. Thirty-five women, 13 percent of the total number of women surveyed in 1936, reported serving formal apprenticeships.

Of these, only one moved to a better position during her tenure at work. Seventy percent of the male workers who had completed apprenticeships, on the other hand, attained promotions during the course of their careers. Apprenticeship apparently did not serve as significant an aid for women as it did for men. The institution of apprenticeship thus survived in Philadelphia—in changed form, no doubt—but it remained an institution of importance by and large for Philadelphia workers who were white and male.[46]

The attempt by organized working people in Philadelphia to protect their jobs though the institution of apprenticeship raises a larger issue, that of the role played by trade unions in general in affecting transactions and outcomes in the labor market. Philadelphia occupies a central place in the chronicle of trade-union activity in the United States; at least before the 1880s, key events in the organization of labor in the country occurred in the Quaker City. Philadelphia witnessed the formation of the nation's first trade unions and served as the site for the first strikes and union contracts and for the first great legal case involving the rights of workers to organize, the Cordwainers' Conspiracy Trial of 1806. From the city emerged the first Workingmen's Party in the country, the first central trade union council, the leading trade union newspapers of their day, and such important movements as the National Labor Union in the 1860s and the Knights of Labor in the 1870s.[47] After the 1880s, the union presence in Philadelphia remained strong, but critical events in trade-union development would unfold in other locations. The next age's great labor confrontations would occur in the new industrial heartland stretching from Pittsburgh to Cleveland, Detroit, and Chicago, and would involve mass-production workers in the large-scale, bureaucratically managed corporations that remained largely foreign to the Philadelphia scene.

The city may occupy a key place in the lore of American trade unionism, but the question of the role that Philadelphia unions played in the local job marketplace remains an open issue. Here, famous events have to be set in perspective with actual numbers. Before the 1930s, best estimates are that for any given period no more than 10 percent of those employed in the city were affiliated with labor organizations.[48] A great surge in unionization did occur during the 1930s and 1940s in Philadelphia, as elsewhere. The newly created

Congress of Industrial Organizations brought millions of mass-production workers onto union rolls after 1936. Union membership continued to swell, and surveys after World War II revealed that more than two-thirds of all Philadelphia workers labored under union contracts; one canvass even placed the number of production line workers in the city covered by union agreements at the 90 percent level.[49] While the union presence in the city dated back to the early nineteenth century, any assessment of the role played by trade unions in the labor market in Philadelphia must begin with the understanding that only late in the city's industrial history did a majority of workers in the area come under the union banner.

A 10 percent overall figure of union membership before the 1930s does hide notable pockets of enduring labor strength in Philadelphia. In certain trades, unions achieved and maintained at relatively early dates substantial control over terms of employment. Highly skilled Philadelphia workers in industries with a few small-to-medium-sized firms were the most successful. The 2,000 weavers in the city's custom upholstery and drapery trade and the 600 photo-engravers in the printing industry, for example, formed closely knit unions that exerted great authority at the workplace.[50] Other examples can be cited, but here too perspective is in order; even the most skilled of craft workers could watch their labor organizations dissolve. Concerted employer counteroffensives had their effect. A deliberate initiative by the Metal Manufacturers' Association in the first decades of the twentieth century to rid the industry of labor organizations, for example, wiped out nearly all traces of unionism among well-organized patternmakers, molders, and finishers.[51] Economic downturns could prove equally disastrous to successful labor organization—the depressions of the 1830s and 1870s decimated burgeoning trade-union movements. A striking single example is provided by the Power Loom Body Brussels Carpet Weavers' Mutual Defense and Benefit Association, a group founded in 1891 by highly skilled weavers, mostly of English descent, who wove custom Brussels and Wilton rugs. The union enjoyed great organizing success in the industry and control over jobs, particularly while Philadelphia rug manufacturers were themselves enjoying prosperity during the first decades of the twentieth century. In the 1920s, however, demand for custom rugs declined precipitously—parquet floors, linoleum, and broad carpet were in vogue—and Philadelphia's custom rug industry virtually disappeared; so, too, did the protective association of the industry's weavers.[52] Deindustrialization in recent times, the massive loss of manufacturing jobs suffered in Philadelphia since the 1950s, has contributed in a similar way to the vast decline in the union movement's presence and power in the city since its apex in the late 1940s.

Certain realities, then, must balance any evaluation of the role played by unions in the labor market. In seeking improved terms and conditions of work for their members, however, established unions in Philadelphia did initiate measures affecting employment in the city, and these efforts deserve mention. To strengthen the leverage of organized workers, for example, unions attempted to limit entrance to trades through union-created and administered apprenticeship programs. The total number of jobs involved is impossible to determine and could not have been sizable until the greater unionization of the work force. Yet in Philadelphia, unions, specifically those in the building trades, of bookbinders, photo-engravers, bakers and confectionery workers, cigar makers, machinists, marble workers, and brewerymen operated effective apprenticeship systems in the late nineteenth and early twentieth centuries.[53]

Apprenticeship represented only one of the measures enacted by trade unionists that had an impact on the job marketplace. A more important initiative affecting far greater numbers of workers involved the assuming and controlling of the actual hiring process. Unions in Philadelphia attempted to become agents of employment. This effort was aimed not just at restricting openings, but more significantly at dealing with a basic problem for workers in the city: the irregular and uncertain nature of work opportunities. Custom production and seasonality—basic features of Philadelphia industry—guaranteed that perennial furloughing and underemployment were inescapable realities of working people's lives. Trade unions demanded power over job placement to prevent oversupplies of labor and also to see that work was spread equally and fairly among workers during the frequent slack times.

The union hiring hall represented the great goal in this area, but its establishment in Philadelphia by trade unionists did not come easily, and even where it was instituted the results were mixed. A prime example is provided by the building trades. Various craft unions achieved strong footholds during the early decades of the twentieth century. Seasonality in construction made control over hiring and the allocation of work a vital issue. By the 1930s, when the first extensive surveys on the subject were conducted, unions of sheet-metal workers and marble and tile setters had achieved complete control over employment. Employers could only hire men supplied by the unions, and union business managers assigned workers completely on the basis of seniority. A slightly different situation existed for asbestos workers, steam fitters, welders, plumbers, gasfitters, and electricians. Either by contract or through custom, employers were expected but not necessarily bound to call the unions of these tradesmen when openings occurred. They could advertise for non-union help if the respective unions could not supply workers, and only in certain instances would these recruits automatically become union members. The allocation of jobs through union lists was also handled less systematically. On the other hand, the unions representing structural iron workers, bricklayers, plasterers, stone masons, cement finishers, carpenters, painters, decorators, and paperhangers performed absolutely no employment services. Even in this highly unionized trade, the uneven development of union practices toward controlling the labor market corroborates the mixed portrait of union influence in all trades.[54]

In one industry in Philadelphia, printing, the union role in employment remained unambiguous. Philadelphia printers organized their trade at an early stage and instituted tight union work rules. In fact, one of the first instances of the establishment of a union hiring hall in the United States can be found in the records of the Journeymen Bookbinders' Trade Society of Philadelphia. That organization's constitution, written in 1833, includes the following article: "There shall be a house of call appointed for the trade, at which a book shall be kept for mutual confirmation. Employers stating vacancies in the establishments required to be filled; journeymen out of employ, stating their name and branch in the trade."[55]

By the twentieth century, practically all employment in printing establishments in Philadelphia had come to be handled by unions. Five printers' unions—the Photo-Engravers, German Typographia, Paper Rulers, Lithographers, and Blankbook Workers—had completely organized their branches of the trade and the allocation of work was entirely controlled by officials of these organizations. For a second group of unions—the Women Bindery Workers, Plate Printers, Press Assistants, Web Pressmen, and News Pressmen—

regulation of employment only covered union shops in the city. Two other unions, the Typographical Union and Independent Pressmen's Union, also provided an employment service, but members of these two groups had the right to seek jobs on their own. In three instances, the unions of the electrotypers, stereotypers, and power-diestampers, the respective organizations had not formally assumed hiring roles because the small number of specialized workers involved never faced problems of slack times or limited work. Despite these variations, the printing industry in Philadelphia presents a textbook example of trade-union control of the labor market.[56]

The attempt by organized working people in the Quaker City to regulate employment extended beyond craft work and skilled workers. In the garment trades in Philadelphia, unions made concerted and successful efforts to control the allocation of jobs. Here, initiatives were aimed not at restricting entrance to work but at protecting the jobs of people in an industry where layoffs due to seasonal factors or poor business conditions were endemic. By the 1930s, contracts reached between garment manufacturers and the International Ladies' Garment Workers Union, for example, specified that all hiring be conducted through the union's office. Officials of the ILGWU developed a complicated bookkeeeping system that monitored job allocations. Separate unions for cloakmakers, skirtmakers, pantsmakers, and clothing cutters established similar procedures.[57]

The Amalgamated Clothing Workers' Union in Philadelphia created the most impressive union employment bureau in the trade. The ACWU founded a labor exchange in November of 1929 which soon managed the distribution of jobs for more than 22,000 workers. Employers signing contracts with the union accepted the duty to report all openings to the union office. Members registered with the union and were referred to jobs on the basis of both seniority and length of time out of work. The ACWU prided itself on its efficient record-keeping system, and many employers found it convenient to have the union handle recruitment for them. As in other instances of union control of hiring, garment manufacturers did retain the right to reject workers referred to them by the union, but rarely did so.[58]

The Amalgamated Clothing Workers' Union also devoted substantial time and money to assist groups of garment workers who traditionally had little contact with unions and little control over the terms of their employment, namely, men and women of the needle trades who toiled at home under contract or in tenement and row-house sweatshops. The union successfully persuaded major manufacturers in Philadelphia to suspend outside contract work and bring all aspects of production into the factories (where full complements of workers would labor under standards agreed to by employers and the union). The ACWU also reached an agreement in 1932 with a group of outside contractors who accepted union scales of payments and other conditions. The Amalgamated Clothing Workers' Union in Philadelphia in this way helped to eliminate the sweatshop system in the garment trades in the city, several years before effective government regulations would be written on the federal level to end the practice.[59] The ACWU also provides a prime example of the ability of an industrial union to achieve control over the market for labor involving mass-production workers.

Not all organized working men and women in Philadelphia, however, succeeded in regulating employment opportunities in their trades. In the 1880s, brickmakers, textile workers, and hatter finishers in the city demanded union control over hiring, but their pleas fell on deaf ears.[60] The Tapestry Carpet Workers' Union secured union hiring hall procedures in the first decade of the twentieth century, yet the union itself did not survive the collapse of the industry in the 1920s and subsequent factionalism within the organization.[61] The American Federation of Hosiery Workers similarly reached an agreement with hosiery manufacturers in the early 1930s that included a provision that "There shall be established a joint employment bureau." The union succeeded in attaining a firm foothold in Philadelphia, but a labor exchange for hosiery workers was never created.[62] Unlike the garment trades, the sixteen unions involved with textile workers in Philadelphia assumed no role in employment. They founded no hiring halls, kept only loose records of the employment histories of their members, gathered no information from employers on job openings, and relied on custom and local mill owners' personal relationships with workers to govern the distribution of work during both busy and slack times. Though differences in industrial structure, geography, and the ethnic compositions and trade-union traditions and experiences of the respective workers involved offer possible explanations, the actual reasons for the dissimilar policies and practices of Philadelphia's garment and textile trade unions remain unclear.

The motives for seeking control of the hiring process thus varied. In craft trades where work was steady, such as printing, union power over employment, like apprenticeship regulation, represented an effort to limit access to jobs. In skilled trades marked by irregular work patterns, such as construction, authority over hire constituted a means to both restrict entrance and spread work equitably, especially during slack times. For mass-production workers and common day laborers in industries where employment fluctuated widely, union control over job placement brought a modicum of fairness in hiring to the workplace. The classic union hiring halls for longshoremen and merchant marines that emerged on the waterfront in Philadelphia and other cities during the 1930s, as well as the labor exchanges established by clothing and garment worker unions in the same period, helped curb various corruptions in the hiring process, such as nepotism and payoffs for jobs. These innovations also guaranteed protective conditions for veteran workers, and institutionalized spreading and sharing of work.

In Philadelphia, where custom production and seasonality made underemployment a chronic problem, work sharing became a vital ideal and practice for organized working people. Dye workers in the city as early as the 1880s included in their union's work rules the stipulation that "The working time shall be apportioned among all the hands as far as practicable."[63] Photo-engravers at the turn of the century similarly achieved contracts with provisions for reductions of hours and work sharing during slack periods.[64] In one of the first agreements reached in the garment trades, garment manufacturers in 1914 agreed to divide work equally among all employees during the off-season.[65] Unionized electrical workers likewise won a key demand in early bargaining in the radio industry in the 1930s that called for reductions of work to twenty hours a week if need be to see that as many workers were retained during slow times.[66] This had an enormous impact on the work experience. As one employee of the Philco Radio Company testified to investigators from the Industrial Research Department of the Wharton School at the University of Pennsylvania: "There is a difference since the plant was unionized. Instead of overtime during the rush season and then lay-offs, there are now alternate periods of full-time and part-time work."[67]

Union control over hiring could then have the varying and seemingly contradictory impact of both limiting and spreading employment. In fact, any final assessment of the role played by unions in the labor market in Philadelphia must be balanced and mixed in character. Before the 1930s, unions affected the occupational experiences of perhaps 10 percent of the work force in the city; among the 2,500 Philadelphians interviewed in 1936 by WPA canvassers, less than 1 percent reported having secured jobs through union hiring halls at any point in their careers.[68] Yet, in the skilled trades, union control of the labor market and the limiting of access to jobs were undeniable. Trade-union involvement with the great majority of workers in Philadelphia came late in the city's industrial history and, with the erosion of the city's industrial base after 1950, lasted for but a relatively brief period. Here, the story is less one of the monopolization of jobs and more one of the amelioration of employment conditions in general and specifically the guaranteeing of equitable divisions of work opportunities.

In one instance, trade union policies and practices in Philadelphia contributed to an already deteriorating and unfortunate situation. Formal exclusion of blacks from union membership in certain instances and customary discrimination in others limited possibilities for employment for even skilled African-Americans and kept blacks in general from the kinds of protected work circumstances white workers achieved through successful union campaigns.[69] The trade union record for women workers in Philadelphia is slightly better, industrial unions in the garment trades and electrical goods manufacture enhancing their jobs in the same manner as for their male counterparts.[70] Trade unions occupy a definite place in Philadelphia's official history; Philadelphia alternatively occupies an important place in the general history of American trade unionism. But were unions in the final analysis a critical agency in the city's labor market? Did they have an notable impact on the experience and process of getting work? Ultimately, their very uneven and limited role has to be emphasized in any answer.

In theory, little should stand between the individual job seeker and a potential employer. The employment bureau is a classic example of an intervening institution in the labor market, but its appearance can easily be squared with theory. There are natural obstacles— barriers of geography and distance or poor information flow, for example—and employment agencies emerge to facilitate connections between job seekers and employers. The actual history of employment bureaus in Philadelphia, however, defies such straightforward understanding. Agencies did emerge in the city, but for remarkably diverse reasons.

Reformers from the White-Williams Foundation, for example, helped to institutionalize the Junior Employment Service of the city's school system out of concern for wayward adolescent girls. The Metal Manufacturers' Association of Philadelphia established an employment office during the first decade of the twentieth century for the machine and metal trades not to increase the information flow or to facilitate better contacts between job seekers and firms, but specifically to weed out union activists and sympathizers from employment.[71] Unions in Philadelphia launched job placement services as well, and again the fluid workings of the labor market in the city were not in mind. Unions expanded their roles into employment work in the name of fairness and greater job security and protection. Employment bureaus came to occupy a definite place in Philadelphia's labor market; in tracing their history, the broad range of initiatives and motives must be stressed.

Private gain represented one incentive; there were profits to be made in the business of providing employment assistance. In 1756, William Meyer opened in Philadelphia perhaps the first employment office in the Western hemisphere. Meyer advertised that for an established fee he could supply employers with journeymen, apprentices, common day laborers, and slaves.[72] The business of labor contracting continued to flourish in the nineteenth century. Employers in Philadelphia encountering difficulties in recruiting workers could seek the services of John Welsh, Robert Taylor, Andrew Craig, or George McHenry during the antebellum period.[73] These men, who were either merchants, packet ship line owners, or direct labor agents, established contacts in Ireland. There they arranged and paid for the transport of Irish immigrants to the city. Their profits consisted of the fees charged both recruits and employers minus costs of shipping. The practice of labor contracting was open to various abuses—false advertising, exorbitant charges, and, in certain instances, writing into the contract long-term labor services at a time when indentured servitude had been legally abolished in most states, including Pennsylvania. The system sparked a good deal of political debate. As a result, Congress, during a period of severe wartime labor shortages in 1864, passed legislation legalizing but also regulating the importation of foreign workers under contract. The matter did not rest there, for congressional action spurred two decades of agitation by the nation's trade-union movement for the abolition of the contracting system. In 1882, Congress, facing such pressure, officially banned the system.[74]

The official outlawing of labor contracting did not spell an end to the practice. Illegal recruitment and transport of foreign workers and their "sale" to employers in the United States continued beyond the pale of the law. The so-called padrone system provides a notorious example. Padrones, men of influence in the Italian immigrant community, arranged for the passage of Italian workers across the Atlantic and their placement in low-paying jobs in factories or in common day labor. Kickbacks and other favors due to these job bosses left the subjects of the system exploited and in a constant cycle of debt.

The existence and workings of the padrone system, however, have always been matters of dispute. Progressive-era muckraking reporters and government investigators painted lurid portraits of the padrones, confirming impressions held by older-stock Americans of the unpleasant and corrupt ways of the immigrant community and adding grist to arguments for immigration restriction. Evidence for padrone activity, however, is wanting, and for Philadelphia and other American cities many researchers have concluded that the system was more myth than reality. Few immigrant ships carrying Italians in fact docked in Philadelphia; the city never served as a base for the extensive recruitment of Italian labor. More important, immigrants of Italian ancestry soon succeeded in building political careers and machines in Philadelphia, and it proved to be politicians and not labor contractors who effectively distributed jobs to new arrivals from the homeland—particularly, public-sector work in street paving and cleaning, utility-line construction, and work at the municipal gas houses.[75] The absence of any mention of the padrone system in the WPA interviews reinforces a skeptical view of the subject.

Labor contractors—from colonial merchants to early twentieth-century padrones—operated no ordinary job placement services. The men and women they recruited in foreign lands were bound to long-term service and fealty. Legislation banning the practice, the growing abundance of labor in American cities, and the eventual curtailing of immigration ended more than two centuries of massive legal and illicit contracting of foreign workers (at least on the East Coast).

With the demise of the practice, another kind of private employment bureau came to the fore. By the first decades of the twentieth century, more than 100 private companies in the employment business could be found listed in commercial directories for Philadelphia. These firms acted as agents both for local job seekers and for companies in need of workers and turned a profit by charging fees to both sets of clients. By the mid-1930s, 185 private employment agencies plied their trade in the Quaker City.[76]

Two kinds of commercial employment agencies operated in Philadelphia in the nineteenth century, one involved with the placement of service workers and day laborers and the other with office, technical, and professional personnel. An example of the former is provided by the C. G. Odell and Co. Employment Bureau, a firm established in 1852. Odell's advertised in a widely distributed circular that "We can promptly furnish Male and Female *Help,* both Protestant & Catholic of Every *Nationality*." The company further informed the public that it operated a "Male Department" able to supply "coachmen, waiters, grooms, footmen, valets, courriers, clerks, farmers, gardeners, porters, bell boys, hall boys, errand boys and useful men" and a "Female Department" placing "cooks, houseworkers, laundresses, chamber maids, waitresses, seamstresses, nurses, teachers and small girls." Odell's also promised "References Thoroughly Investigated" and added a somewhat mysterious message: "Our means for obtaining Help are varied and extensive, and if parties will leave their orders entirely with us, we can generally (if given reasonable time) give satisfaction."[77]

A seemingly more respectable kind of employment firm soon joined Odell's in the field. These companies mailed letters to commercial and professional offices in Philadelphia offering to furnish them with trained and responsible personnel. The Stenographers' and Bookkeepers' Association, for example, could provide "a thoroughly competent Stenographer, Typewriter, Bookkeeper, Entry Clerk, Bill Clerk or Office Assistant"; the Office Service Company specialized in the placement of bookkeepers, accountants, and auditors; the Quick Service Company dealt with "experienced bookkeepers," although their letterhead advertised "Furnishers Of All Kinds of Help"; and the Business Service Company, whose motto proclaimed, "Right Men For Right Places," operated a "Department of Salaried Positions for Executives, Sales, Clerical, Technical and Professional Men."[78]

These firms vouched for their clients' educations, expertise, and trustworthiness, and in certain cases offered to administer intelligence and personality tests and provide results. The integrity of traveling salesmen seemed to be a particular issue of concern; employment companies supplying referrals for sales agents informed interested parties of their abilities to construct and render supposedly accurate psychological profiles.

In Philadelphia as elsewhere, employment bureaus furnishing day laborers and service sector workers outnumbered job placement firms involved with white-collar positions. Among them, there emerged a set of agencies that deserve note. By the early 1930s, no fewer than forty private employment agencies in the the city specialized in the provision of "Negro Help," primarily female domestic workers.[79] Black Philadelphians occupied a separate labor market in the city and nowhere is this more evident than in the role of employment bureaus in the experience of African-Americans in getting work. Sixty percent of black men and upwards of 90 percent of black women in Philadelphia before World War II held domestic service jobs. White employers rarely hired African-Americans directly. Race prejudice required an intermediary, a referral agency to vouch for the reputation of the black job seeker. Conversely, blacks in search of work, knowing full well the mores and sentiments within the white community, rarely felt free to approach white employers in a straightforward fashion. As a result, employment bureaus generally came to play a significantly different and more critical role in the hiring process for blacks than for whites.

Reliance on private employment companies unfortunately placed black Philadelphians in additional jeopardy. "Negro Job Offices" were notoriously corrupt and exploitative. Fly-by-night enterprises taking fees from recruits one day and closing their doors the next dotted the black community. Other agencies demanded substantial percentages of the wages earned by clients once employed. Many Philadelphia employment companies dealing with black labor also recruited for domestic workers in the South, particularly in Virginia and the Carolinas, and paid for their transportation to the city (recalling early labor contracting). Several months of wages were then due to the agencies and not a few resorted to holding the baggage of the young women involved as collateral. Employment firms in the city also offered black recruits lodging, charging them exorbitant rents.

There were even reported instances of agencies placing young black girls as maids in local brothels and luring them into prostitution.[80]

The sordid practices of black employment bureaus provided fuel for Progressive-era reformers, black and white, and calls for the regulation of the industry soon emerged. The damning exposés of reform-minded social investigators may have been shaped by their repugnance and misreading of the ways and lifestyles of various working-class newcomers to the city, but a problem did exist, and here members of Philadelphia's black community began to take matters into their own hands. Bleak employment prospects for African-Americans in general and the exploitative role of private employment agencies pushed leading black organizations to focus greater attention on vocational issues and to establish nonprofit job placement services. The Armstrong Association of Philadelphia (the Philadelphia chapter of the National Urban League) assumed a commanding role in this area. In 1912, officials of the association approached manufacturers in the garment industry with pleas to open their doors to black workers. As a result of this initiative, five hundred black men and women were placed in shirtwaist factories throughout the city. The Association then entered into negotiations with the Pennsylvania Railroad, which led to the hiring of one hundred black track repairmen, the first blacks to be employed by the line since the company's inception sixty years earlier. In 1915, the Association expanded its role. In addition to striking agreements with particular firms, the organization opened a full-fledged employment service that handled referrals for domestic as well as industrial jobs. For the next thirty years the Association remained the key source of employment assistance for the Philadelphia black community.[81] Other groups joined in this effort. The Philadelphia branch of the National Association for the Advancement of Colored People, although it did not operate an employment bureau, also pressed local businessmen to hire black workers. An initial victory occurred during World War I when executives of SKF Industries agreed to NAACP demands to integrate the company's work force.[82] Three decades before presidential orders and federal legislation would break racial barriers to employment, black groups in northern cities such as Philadelphia were organizing to end hiring customs and policies that benefited only white job seekers.

Private employment bureaus proved inadequate and corrupt not only for blacks in search of work but for white job seekers as well.

A variety of nonprofit placement services appeared to offer more reputable assistance and to fill a void. Tales of young women preyed upon by employment agencies and their general plight in the labor marketplace moved religiously inspired staff members of the Young Women's Christian Association in Philadelphia to open job referral agencies in branch Ys. By the late 1920s, nearly five thousand young women were registered with YWCA placement offices in the city and close to half of their numbers would be hired for domestic service work by households or firms that regularly filed requisitions with the Ys.[83] Philadelphia's Armstrong Association and Young Women's Christian Association operated the most extensive nonprofit social service placement bureaus in the city. The Young Men's Christian Association of Philadelphia also maintained an employment office, smaller in scale, as did such organizations in the the the city as the Big Brother Association, the Family Society, the Knights of Columbus, and various local churches and social settlement houses.[84]

Reform-minded groups created nonprofit employment services as much to facilitate contacts between job seekers and employers as to deal with such pressing social problems as racial discrimination and the moral evils and corrupt practices facing young people, particularly young women, in finding work in the modern industrial city. Philanthropic job placement agencies, however, were joined by another set of noncommercial employment bureaus—adding to the complexity of initiatives and motives. The Philadelphia Manufacturers' Association and the Philadelphia Textile Manufacturers' Association, two leading trade associations of employers in the city, for example, operated employment offices in much the same manner and for the same purposes as the Philadelphia Metal Manufacturers' Association. Professional societies, such as the Philadelphia Technical Services Committee, a joint organization of engineering associations in Philadelphia, also maintained a free job placement bureau for engineers and draughtsmen. Charity schools such as Girard College established employment offices to match the efforts of private business schools as well as the Junior Employment Service of the city's public school system. A range of nonprofit and nonfee placement services, alternatives to private, commercial ventures, became available then for Philadelphians in search of work.[85]

The illicit practices and inadequacies of private, for-profit employment agencies spurred reform-minded groups in Philadelphia not only to create philanthropic services but also to demand government regulation of commercial enterprises. State legislators in Harrisburg, Pennsylvania, responded by passing a series of laws at the turn of the twentieth century that required the licensing and inspection of private employment agencies. Legislation further established the maximum fees agencies were allowed to charge clients and required that fee schedules be posted. Private employment bureaus could now be fined for false advertisements and promises and for other faults discovered by state inspectors. Progressive-era reformers could celebrate another victory over unbridled and unholy private market activity, but enthusiasm was short-lived. New investigative reports issued during the second decade of the century proved that abuses still abounded.[86] The next call would be for a direct rather than a regulatory role for government and the creation of a Pennsylvania-wide system of state-administered labor exchanges.

By the time reformers and legislators in Pennsylvania had begun to discuss the need for a statewide system of public employment offices, nationally based government job placement services had already been in operation, in some cases for decades, in Western European countries such as Germany and Great Britain. In the United States, New York City had founded an experimental, short-lived public labor exchange in the 1830s; the federal government and various states had created agencies in the last half of the nineteenth century to advertise and recruit for workers in Europe, particularly during periods of labor shortage; and Ohio became the first state in the country to establish a system of public employment bureaus in 1891, although on a limited basis.[87] This represents the sum total of deliberate government initiatives on labor mobilization and distribution in the nation through the first decades of the twentieth century.

Two developments led to the enactment of legislation in 1915 that allowed for the creation in Pennsylvania of a state system of public employment services. A severe economic recession in late 1913 and 1914 accompanied by high levels of unemployment provoked a good deal of debate and study in the commonwealth. An influential report commissioned by the Mayor of Philadelphia that pointed to critical informational barriers between employers and job seekers provided one impetus for legislative action.[88] Continuing investigations into the corrupt practices of commercial employment agencies added additional weight to arguments on behalf of public labor exchange.[89] Proponents fixed on two major justifications. A modern economy, they reasoned, required an organized and rationalized labor market; the particular plight of women in getting work also necessitated government intervention. "The labor market for women is much farther from standardization than that for men," noted a report by the Pennsylvania Department of Labor and Industry, the agency placed in charge of the state's new labor bureau. "Women have suffered more than men from unfair charges and moral dangers under the system of unregulated private agencies." The commonwealth's program of job placement services owed its genesis as much to the belief that unemployment would be alleviated if the state facilitated contacts between suppliers and purchasers of labor as to then current notions of womanhood and concern for the experiences of women when working outside the home.[90]

The first state employment office in Pennsylvania opened on October 1, 1915. As American industry began to prosper by providing armaments and other goods to war-torn European countries, the demand for labor in industrial states such as Pennsylvania soon surged. The case loads of the newly established public job placement service expanded accordingly as firms utilized all available means to recruit workers. After the entry of the United States into the confrontation in Europe, Pennsylvania's employment offices were incorporated into the United States Employment Service operated by the United States Department of Labor. The country had in place for the first time a national system of labor exchanges established for the express purpose of coordinating the country's manpower resources with wartime production needs. At war's end, however, Congress withdrew support for the USES and Pennsylvania remained one of a few states to maintain public employment services into the 1920s.

A new national emergency would witness a second and permanent incorporation of Pennsylvania's job placement offices into a national system of labor exchanges. As one of many measures enacted to combat the great economic depression of the 1930s, Congress passed in June of 1933 the Wagner-Peyser Act, a law providing for a joint federally and state-funded and state-administered system of labor bureaus. Massive unemployment would be countered, proponents argued, with the government intervening as matchmaker between job seekers and employers. The Wagner-Peyser Act remains the basis for the public employment services that exist in our own time.[91]

Utilization of Pennsylvania's system of public job placement offices (both state and federal) fluctuated widely during the first quarter century of their operation. Throughout the First World War, between 1,000 and 1,200 Philadelphians made application each month at local branches. In 1920, however, following a period of postwar economic dislocation, the number of men and women registered with the public employment service multiplied eight-fold, and in December 1920 more than 24,000 people in the city sought the state agency's assistance. By the late 1920s, monthly totals had dropped to around 300, partly because cutbacks in funding had greatly reduced the operations of the bureau. The Great Depression and an expanding initiative following an increased federal government role pushed the registration of job seekers to new highs. Throughout the decade of the 1930s, between 5,000 and 10,000 Philadelphians applied for work at local employment offices each month. In June of 1933, at the height of the economic crisis, no less than 35,000 men and women established files with the state service. The numbers dropped late in the decade and then rose again during World War II as employers facing shortages of labor posted a new round of job openings.[92]

The number of posted positions at state employment offices thus fluctuated as dramatically as did the registrations of men and women in search of work. In April of 1916, for example, 438 job openings were listed in Philadelphia branches of the public employment service; six months later, officials of the bureau could post 1,725 positions. During the depression of the 1930s, job openings numbered about 500 per month, with the exception of January 1934, when 1,400 jobs were available. In general, a ratio of three applicants for every position registered prevailed during the 1920s; that balance shifted during the depression years to as much as thirty-five job seekers for every listed job opening and an overall average ratio of ten to one. These figures, however, have to be placed in an additional perspective. As officials of both private and public employment agencies discovered, a job posting did not automatically translate into a job placement. For a variety of reasons, the number of positions posted was always significantly greater than the number of applicants eventually hired. Figures provided by the Pennsylvania State Employment Service indicate that less than half of the jobs listed by the agency ever became filled. The place of public employment services in the labor market in Philadelphia was thus limited.[93]

Data collected by state officials and by social investigators provide further information on the clientele of public employment agencies. Which groups of Philadelphians utilized or were forced to resort to state job placement offices to the greatest extent in their searches for work? During the 1920s and 1930s, 75 percent of the registrants in the city were men and 25 percent women, a close approximation of their relative proportions in the labor force. Among men, 80 percent were white, 20 percent, black; among women, 60 percent were white and 40 percent, black.[94] The proportion of black Philadelphians among those on line in public employment offices was more than twice their proportion in the general working population. The percentages of black applicants also grew notably over the period.

Registrants for jobs at state placement services in Philadelphia represented a relatively older group of workers as well. The men averaged close to thirty-six years of age, the women, thirty-three. The applicants also tended to have low levels of schooling and skills. They had remained in school an average of eight years and 60 percent had not completed grammar school.[95] They also reported being out of work at least a year on average and previously occupying unskilled or semiskilled positions. Among the men, laborer, delivery man, truck driver, domestic servant, and office clerk were the most frequently listed titles for last employment; among the women, domestic, clerk, and factory operative were the positions most commonly reported.[96] Philadelphians who registered with state job placement agencies were thus among the least employable of job seekers.

An odd disjuncture between the kinds of jobs listed at public employment offices and the composition of the applicant pool also prevailed, a situation which further compounded the problems faced by those groups of workers who utilized the service in the greatest numbers. From the early 1920s through the 1940s, for example, the great majority of job openings listed in state employment agencies in Philadelphia had definite specifications for the race and sex of the person to be hired. While black women comprised 40 percent of the female registrants, only 19 percent of all jobs listed for women indicated a preference for an African-American employee; similarly, black men represented 20 percent of the male applicant pool, but only 10 percent of the jobs posted for men specified that blacks would be hired.[97] White women actually faced favorable chances at the public employment office. White women constituted approximately 15 percent of all the applicants. During the 1930s, between 30 and 50 percent of all jobs listed in Philadelphia's public employment offices sought the services of white female employees.[98]

A further divergence existed between the skill levels of most registrants and the types of positions posted. While unskilled workers comprised the great majority of applicants to the public employment service in Philadelphia, the six occupations most frequently listed in notices of job openings included, in order: laborer, domestic servant, machinist, tool and die maker, waiter or waitress, and carpenter.[99] The needs of employers who registered jobs with the public employment service matched in some respects the skills of the applicant pool; but it is also clear that the demand for skilled workers remained high in the city—employers in search of machinists, tool and die makers, and carpenters had to resort to public job placement agencies—and a complete match between the supply of and demand for labor did not materialize. Workers most requiring public assistance in getting work thus entered an agency not fully geared to their particular circumstances.

The experiences of Philadelphians in public employment bureaus rendered in official state reports is echoed in the testimony of the 2,500 workers interviewed in 1936 by WPA investigators. Only a small number reported using job placement services, public or private. Less than 1 percent of those surveyed noted resorting to employment agencies in their first encounters in the labor market; only 5 percent mentioned use of such services in later job searches. The oldest workers in the canvass and workers with the fewest years of schooling reported registering with placement services to the greatest extent.[100] Still, only a small minority of these Philadelphians had contact with employment bureaus. Employment agencies of various kinds and with different purposes—and not just economic—came to occupy a position in the labor market of the Quaker City, but, at least before 1950, their impact was limited. There is again one important exception. The role played by such organizations as the Armstrong Association in securing jobs for African-American workers proved critical and essential for the members of that community.

If all else failed—if family and personal connections, school referral services, private or public employment bureaus, and just knocking on doors proved wanting—with a penny in the nineteenth century and a nickel in the first half of the twentieth, a Philadelphian in search of work could purchase a local newspaper with page-long listings of job openings. The newspaper help-wanted ad is a favorite conceit of politicians. When challenged by reporters to explain a lack of response on their part to evidence of rising unemployment, a frequent practice is to wave the classified section of a newspaper and point to an abundance of jobs begging to be filled. The fault, it is inferred, lies with the less-than-vigilant job seeker. The newspaper want ad is a familiar part of everyday social life and an agency in the labor market whose history and function deserve scrutiny.

The familiar help-wanted ad became an institution in Philadelphia local papers only late in the nineteenth century. In 1850, the two most prominent newspapers in the city, the *Bulletin* and the *North American,* contained no want ads. The Philadelphia *Inquirer,* which commenced publication in 1860, included nothing resembling a want ad until the 1890s. The *Public Ledger,* the city's most popular journal in working-class neighborhoods, did carry employment notices, help-wanted as well as situation-wanted ads. Readers of the May 1, 1850, issue, for example, could find a non-alphabetized listing of eighty-five ads announcing job openings.

The *Ledger* remained for the next four decades the only newspaper in Philadelphia to print help-wanted notices, although the *Bulletin* occasionally listed openings in its "Personal" column. Advertisements in the *Ledger* increased in number gradually. Eighty-seven ads could be found in the May 1, 1860, edition of the paper; ten years later, the number had reached 200. Advertising of that magnitude required a classification system and by 1870 ads in the *Ledger* were divided into female and male categories. During the depression of the 1870s, the number of listings declined; as economists would soon learn, counting the lines of help-wanted advertisements in local newspapers offered a fairly reliable means of gauging changes in overall employment. Returning prosperity brought increased notices in the 1880s, and the *Ledger* reacted by alphabetizing listings of jobs for the first time, still with separate lists for men's and women's jobs. By the early 1890s, the *Ledger*'s employment pages contained more than 500 notices each day.[101]

The Philadelphia *Inquirer,* however, soon replaced the *Ledger* as the city's most important source of help-wanted advertising. The *Inquirer* first accepted ads for job openings in 1888, but maintained only a small listing; readers of the May 1, 1890, edition of the paper could find just ten employment ads. The paper then expanded the initiative, announcing the establishment of an "Employment Bureau." For 50 cents, an employer could place an ad in the *Inquirer* and use the paper's Bureau to interview prospective workers. The paper soon dropped this service, but in its place offered free advertising to both job seekers and employers. An editorial in the journal on May 1, 1892, explained that the paper intended to play an active role in combatting unemployment in the city as part of its greater social commitments. This proved to be a temporary promotional effort—soon fees would once again be demanded of purchasers of advertising space—but by the late 1890s the *Inquirer* easily surpasssed the *Ledger* in help-wanted listings. The paper with increased notices also introduced an innovation, classifying jobs by type ("Agricultural," "Professional," "Personal," "Trade," "Transportation," "Manufacturing," and "Clerical") and then alphabetizing them under each heading, again separately for men and women.

Apparently help-wanted advertising sold newspapers, because the *Public Ledger* did not take the *Inquirer's* challenge lightly. The newspaper countered with a new and supposedly more useful job classification system and began running articles comparing its coverage with that of the city's other daily papers.[102] In November 1905, the *Ledger* further began to offer free help-wanted advertising space. This had the immediate effect of increasing the number of notices, but by 1910 listings in the paper had dropped to an average of forty-two ads a day.

Advertising in the *Inquirer* continued to surge. The May 1, 1910, issue contained just under one thousand help-wanted ads. A new challenger appeared when the *Bulletin,* too, began to run the ads, and by 1920 the two journals between them printed more than two thousand notices a day. The increase in the number of help-wanted ads in Philadelphia's two most popular papers in the first decades of the twentieth century did not reflect an actual expansion of employment, but rather an increase in the use of advertising as a means of recruiting labor. Before and after that time, fluctuations in the number of ads closely reflected changes in overall employment levels. In specific years, for example, notices tended to be highest in the months of April, May, and September and low during the winter and midsummer months. During the 1920s and 1930s, labor economists spent a good deal of time studying want ads as indicators of the demand for labor; they discovered strong correlations between changes in employment and advertising space. Ads tended to increase and decrease as hiring rose and fell. Not surprisingly, relatively few notices of job openings could be found in Philadelphia newspapers during the depression years of the 1930s; the papers filled with ads once again as the nation and the city geared up for the production of wartime goods in the early 1940s.[103]

Newspaper job listings reflected not only employment levels but also the occupational structure of the city, with one major exception. On May 1, 1920, the *Inquirer* and the *Bulletin* printed between them 2,400 job notices. The proportions of agricultural, professional, trade, and manufacturing positions listed directly matched the proportions of such jobs in the city as a whole. For example, 55 percent and 59 percent of the openings listed for males in the *Bulletin* and the *Inquirer,* respectively, were manufacturing jobs; at the time, 52 percent of all men in the labor market in Philadelphia occupied industrial positions. Similarly, 25 percent of the jobs for women in the *Bulletin* and 33 percent of those in the *Inquirer* were factory positions at a time when 34 percent of the female labor force in the city was engaged in manufacture.[104]

Not all categories of work followed this general trend. For example, there were relatively low numbers of positions listed under transport. The major exception was the category of domestic servants. For both men and women, the proportions of listings for personal service jobs were double their proportions for the labor force as a whole. In 1920, 5 percent of all men in Philadelphia occupied such positions, but 10 percent of the want ads seeking male workers were for household help. Likewise, 25 percent of the female work force was engaged in domestic labor but more than 45 percent of the want ads were for domestics. In addition, 2 percent of all listings were actually ads for employment agencies, many of which specialized in domestic work.[105] The help-wanted ad thus shared an important history and characteristic with the employment agency: both institutions operated significantly in that tier of the labor market involved with domestic service work.

The connection between domestic employment and the want ad also had implications for the gender composition of the jobs listed in the classifieds. Drawing distinctions between men's and women's jobs was a fixture of the help-wanted ad from its inception and re-

mained so into the 1960s, when legislation and judicial rulings officially banned the sex typing of occupations. Throughout the late
nineteenth century and the first two decades of the twentieth, jobs
listed for women either equaled or outnumbered openings advertised
for men. At times, the number of female positions could even be
twice those advertised for male job seekers. In the May 1, 1900,
edition of the *Public Ledger,* for example, 120 ads appeared in the
column for women, 69 for men. A reversal in this pattern occurred
after the First World War, when positions for domestic servants began to decline; notices for all women's jobs declined proportionately.
Throughout the decade of the 1920s, in fact, between two-thirds and
three-quarters of the help-wanted ads appearing in both the *Bulletin*
and the *Inquirer* were for men's positions.

In general, throughout the late nineteenth and early twentieth centuries, ads for clerical and domestic service positions occupied greater
space under the columns for women's jobs in the classifieds than for
the men's; notices for professional, transport, and manufacturing
posts dominated the latter. Although the number of openings listed
for women ·declined overall in the 1920s, the various periods of
expansion in employment and increased help-wanted advertising
during the decade saw notices for women's jobs increasing at faster
rates than those for men's jobs. Boom times brought increases in the
hiring of clerical and domestic service workers and a rising demand
for female labor. Clerical jobs were particularly sensitive to economic
conditions, and as women found new opportunities there, demand
for household help rose accordingly.[106]

While categorizing positions by gender remained a constant in
help-wanted advertising in Philadelphia from the 1860s to the 1960s,
the use of racial and ethnic descriptives increased only in the late
nineteenth century and did not become a fixture until the first decades
of the twentieth. In 1860 or 1870, ads frequently included the following specifications: "sober, industrious man," "stout hearted boy,"
"reliable girl," or "decent young woman." By 1890 or 1900, a majority of notices contained racial or ethnic requirements as well: "colored
girl to do light housework," "Protestant childnurse sought," or "a
German or colored woman to cook."

Jobs for women particularly became associated with racial and ethnic specifications. In 1870, 19 percent of the positions advertised for
men and 18 percent of the openings listed for women in the *Public*

Ledger included mention of racial or ethnic qualifications. By 1910, 40 percent of the male jobs and 62 percent of the female had such specifications, and ten years later, 36 percent of the men's positions and 75 percent of the women's made such references.

Ads for domestic servants included race and ethnic requirements to the greatest extent. An increase in the proportion of help-wanted ads devoted to household labor thus partially explains the growing proportion of jobs associated with cultural requirements, especially in women's positions. The growing racial and ethnic categorization also reflects the increased racial thinking and stereotyping that occurred worldwide at the turn of the twentieth century, coinciding with massive inter- and intra-hemispheric labor migration flows and the misappropriation of Darwinian principles to explain and justify social distinctions and orderings.

Non-domestic service positions also included racial and ethnic criteria, although to a lesser degree. Ads for construction jobs requested Italian and Polish workers or read "Laborers—colored come, ready for work." Manufacturing positions had the fewest mentions of such descriptives; only 3 percent of the notices for factory operatives in the *Inquirer* and the *Bulletin* specified race or ethnic qualifications. Ads for clerical positions, on the other hand, frequently noted a cultural preference, usually "Protestant preferred."

The connection between Protestants and clerical employment is illustrated in a somewhat amusing set of letters that survives in the records of the E. C. Beetem & Son Company, a prominent carpet manufacturing firm. In mid-March of 1913, the company placed an ad in the Philadelphia *Inquirer* announcing an opening for a "sober, Protestant bookkeeper" (in keeping with the stereotyping of the day, that is probably a multiple redundancy). Beetem & Son received sixty-eight responses to the advertisement, the great majority of which made a point of emphasizing the high moral character and religion of the applicant.

> I am a mason. I am married and do not use tobacco or alcoholic drinks. I am willing to work for a moderate salary to show worth.[107]
> I am a high school graduate and have had eleven years practical experience in accounting departments of several large corporations . . . I am a Protestant and have excellent references to offer. I am a married man.[108]

I am speedy, accurate and systematic as regards work; ambitious, energetic, forceful and hustling as to nature.[109]

I am married, 40 years of age, Protestant, strictly temperate and am positive I can fill this position to your entire satisfaction.[110]

I am 19 years of age and have complete [sic] a course in Book-keeping in a business college, and I have had 3 years experiences as a bill clerk with a mfg. concern. I am a member of the Episcopal Church.[111]

I am a Protestant, Presbyterian.[112]

Finally, in addition to skill level, sex, race, and ethnicity, help-wanted ads in Philadelphia at certain times specified one other qualification: willingness to work as a strike-breaker. During a strike of rapid transit workers in 1910, which mushroomed into a city-wide general walkout, the classified pages of the *Inquirer* and *Bulletin* were filled with ads placed by firms in search of men to operate idle machinery. One notice read: "Boilermakers and boilermakers' helpers to take the place of men on strike . . . standard pay; free transportation and board."[113] The hiring of strikebreakers was a politically contentious issue and some firms attempted to set the record straight in their notices. "This is not a strike-breaking advertisement," the Central Railroad of New Jersey noted in an ad placed in the *Inquirer* seeking yard brakemen during a labor confrontation in 1920. "Men are not wanted to take strikers' places. The vacant places to be filled are those where men have quit the service. No strike has ever been ordered or declared. Organization men are on the job. The vacancies to be filled are permanent positions."[114] The great industrial battles of the age were thus also fought on the help-wanted pages of the daily newspapers.

Who actually used newspaper help-wanted ads and to what effect are difficult matters to resolve. If the 2,500 workers interviewed by WPA investigators are any measure, only a small percentage of Philadelphians in the past secured employment through the classifieds. Less than 4 percent of the respondents reported obtaining either their first or subsequent jobs through a want ad. There were only slight distinctions between this small minority and their fellow Philadelphians who found work in other ways. The oldest members of the sample—those born before 1892—tended to use help-wanted notices to a slightly greater extent than the younger; Philadelphians occupying clerical positions relied somewhat more heavily on the newspapers than workers in other trades; and, probably of most interest, with the exception of Irish and British-born workers, not a single immigrant Philadelphian reported securing a job through the want ads.[115] Obviously, facility with the English language played an important role here.

The 1936 survey does not provide the means to determine the place of help-wanted ads in the experience of black Philadelphians in the labor market. There are indications that blacks in the city in fact found jobs through the newspapers. A survey of 141 black women conducted in 1919 by the Consumers' League of Pennsylvania, for example, revealed that 29 percent had secured employment through a job listing in a local paper.[116] Another investigation completed two decades earlier also concluded that the classifieds represented an important service to black job seekers.[117] The existence of "for colored" worker listings—particularly for domestic help—in newspapers is sufficient indication in this respect that help-wanted ads represented a signficant agency in the process of getting work for blacks. African-Americans required such intermediary institutions to find work because racial prejudice effectively prevented personal and direct contacts with prospective employers.

With the possible exception of blacks, the help-wanted advertisement apparently did not play a notable role in the securing of employment for most Philadelphians in the last half of the nineteenth and first half of the twentieth centuries. This finding is confirmed in a number of contemporary studies conducted in firms on methods of recruiting labor. One canvass completed in 1931 and involving close to 1600 companies indicated that 25 percent of the firms had at one time or another placed notices of job openings in local newspapers. Yet over 90 percent of these companies also reported that hirings mostly took place at the gate with plant managers and superintendents in charge.[118] Responding to a want ad obviously did not guarantee a job.

Twenty-five percent of Philadelphia firms resorted to newspaper want ads at some point to recruit labor. Survey research in the second and third decades of the twentieth century also revealed that only 10 percent of all companies in the city posted listings of job openings in public employment offices; 1 percent made use of private employment agencies; only 2 percent made contact with school referral services—in fact, few businessmen were even aware of the existence of the Junior Employment Service or familiar with the curriculum of the public school system, vocational or otherwise; and 7 percent dealt in some manner with trade unions in the city in facilitating hiring.[119] These figures testify that before World War II the labor market in Philadelphia had not become institutionalized; that is, individual prospects for getting work did not depend on connections to these various agencies.

Some qualifications to this general conclusion, of course, are in order. Schools, unions, and employment agencies certainly assisted individuals as well as particular groups of workers, but the impact of these institutions was uneven and never definitive. In a few instances, however, the role of agencies in the labor market needs underlining. Employment bureaus, newspaper want ads, and, most important, political action groups, proved essential resources in the searches for work of black Philadelphians; conversely, apprenticeship programs and unions hampered their progress. Apprenticeship for white male workers, on the other hand, remained a key practice and institution in Philadelphia and, perhaps of all the agencies in the labor market, apprenticeship had the greatest impact.

5 · Firms

Firms in Philadelphia played a less ambiguous role in the labor market than did schools, unions, employment bureaus, and other mediating agencies. The employment policies and practices of businesses in the city directly affected the prospects and fortunes of Philadelphia job seekers. Decisions made by employers on recruitment worked to the advantage of certain individuals and groups of workers and to the detriment of others. There are any number of obvious cases in point. First and foremost, manufacturing companies in Philadelphia, with few exceptions, did not hire blacks. Whether this was the result of overt racial hostility on the part of managers, simple misperceptions and misunderstandings, or bowing to pressure—organized or otherwise—from white employees, the outcome was always the same. Blacks in the Quaker City were systematically denied access to essential employment opportunities.

Employers also favored particular job seekers for reasons other than race. "Protestant Bookkeeper Preferred," as the ad read, represented a practice that placed Protestants (that is, Protestant males) in high-level white-collar positions in firms in the city; in the same manner, young female graduates of Catholic girls' high schools were sought for lower-echelon clerical posts. A German-American manufacturer of fancy silk products similarly might hire only his compatriots; a plant superintendent of a cotton textile mill by custom might employ workers solely from the surrounding neighborhood. Sex typing of jobs likewise opened up certain opportunities for men and usually less skilled and poorly compensated jobs for women. Some employers in Philadelphia adopted policies of strictly barring married women from employment; older workers, both men and women, faced definite obstacles in their searches for work.[1] In all of the above instances—and others could be mentioned—firms made choices that enhanced and eliminated chances for employment for different sets of workers without consideration for individual abilities, or, as economists would have it, particular marginal productivities.

The conclusion that the firm's role in getting work was and is critical is self-evident. The mere statement, however, overlooks a complex reality. Employment practices of businesses vary, and in a city with as diversified an economy as Philadelphia a wide range of practices would be expected. Practices also change. In this chapter, I will assume that firms are important and look beyond that supposition to examine how and why companies differed in their personnel policies. Moreover, I will offer a general look at employment procedures, not just an investigation of hiring practices. The actual concern will be with the formalization of practices, and by formalization I mean consideration and implementation of deliberate policies on the recruitment, training, disciplining, rewarding, promoting, firing, and retiring of labor. When and why did firms in Philadelphia begin to forge regularized employment procedures, and in what kinds of companies and which trades did such procedures come to emerge and prevail? Two score case studies of labor relations in companies in the Quaker City will provide material for this examination and the means to further an understanding of the processes of getting work.

There is no dearth of theories to account for variations and changes in the employment practices of firms. Standard microeconomics, for example, would first draw attention to the issue of costs. The high costs of labor turnover, labor shortage, and unionization, microeconomists would surmise, force companies to develop deliberate initiatives to recruit and reward labor and thus engender greater loyalty and diligence among workers. Human capital theorists would point to technological and occupational shifts, which can produce a need for new technically trained and socially motivated work forces; in these instances, programs are required to improve the human capital resources of the firm. Standard macroeconomic thinking, whether of the Keynesian or monetarist kind, actually provides little help in understanding the course of structural changes within enterprises; inputs affect outputs, because internal arrangements and social relations have no necessary form.

Sociological explanations are also available. A culturalist perspective might point to the role of custom and tradition or ideas and values in spurring enterprise directors to certain actions. In Philadelphia, with a large population of Quakers and a sizable number of leading Quaker businessmen, family owned and operated firms proliferated and persisted, so this kind of argument is not easily dismissed. As will be shown in this and the following chapter, a concern for harmonious relations and ethical standards did help shape decision making on personnel matters in a number of instances.

Organizational theorists would provide other kinds of sociological answers. Followers of Max Weber might stress the imperatives toward greater degrees of hierarchy, specificity, and rationality within organizations and the role that increased size and complexity might play in fostering departmentalization in general and the creation of specialized offices for handling employment concerns in particular. Another kind of organizational perspective would place less emphasis on the inevitability of bureaucratic development and point to the creative work of middle-level managers, their efforts to control market conditions as much as respond to them, and their personal interest in seeing to the maintenance and expansion of their prerogatives and realms of control. The personnel function can be envisioned here as the protected and growing offspring of professionally trained personnel executives.[2]

The above kind of organizational perspective might be countered by a Marxist answer, although on the question of the formalization of employment practices there is no single Marxist understanding. Marxists of different stripes would share the assumption of inherent tensions between managers and managed over the extraction of surplus labor and in turn profits, thus making the management of labor a continual issue. Management systems do evolve, and in terms of modern personnel practices a Marxist explanation would point to the significance of the rise of the corporation and the subsequent need to restructure incentives and make for careers within firms, with the elimination of possibilities for independent producership. This top-down form of argument rests on an assumption of management's imperative and ability to control.[3]

Within the Marxist framework there are also more dialectical ways of envisioning the process. A first would be to stress fully the role of conflict in spurring executives to develop new strategies aimed at engendering greater labor discipline and fealty; a second would be to see the push for greater procedures and programs actually and singularly coming from below, that is, from the laborers; and in a third, formalization would be pictured as part of converging and negotiated attempts by both directors of work and the directed to secure more regularized employment conditions.[4]

The recent work of so-called labor market segmentation theorists in fact displays this kind of mixed Marxist view on the subject. Their argument goes as follows: labor conflict, pressure, or intractibility forces those firms operating in regularized markets where costs for administrative mechanisms can be passed on to consumers to develop technological and ultimately bureaucratic methods of control—sometimes this occurs not through actual threat but through the foresight of corporate figures recognizing the need for stabilized relations. Less well-heeled firms conducting business in competitive situations and unable to focus on long-term possibilities continue to hire and fire at will and manage on personal bases. Two different labor markets emerge as a result, comprised of jobs with different characteristics.[5]

There is one final way of looking at the question of the development of formal personnel practices. That is a political answer, an attention to the role of the state in affecting private enterprise-level decision making either through legislation, regulation, example, or the demand for information. The state's role in noncapitalist settings is obvious, but cannot be ignored in situations seemingly free of political impact.[6] It is worth noting that none of the previously mentioned economic or sociological frameworks contains a political element.

A number of explanations are thus available to account for the formalization of employment practices. Although treated separately, they are by no means mutually exclusive. Standard economic arguments on the need to limit costs—caused by labor turnover, unionization, or lost productivity in general—and the Marxist emphasis on the imperatives to control labor are hardly contradictory (although certain evidence would make one view more salient than the other). Equally similar are speculations by organizational theorists and certain Marxists that emphasize the seeming omniscience and omnipotence of managers. Economic, technological, cultural, organizational, Marxist, and even political answers thus exist and will be treated as resources; the point now is to examine the actual employment practices of Philadelphia firms.

Thumbnail sketches follow of the employment histories of twenty Philadelphia firms, all of which operated at various times from the early nineteenth century through World War II. These companies were not randomly chosen; they are enterprises for which records survive.[7] They do nonetheless form a representative sample of the diverse kinds of businesses that constituted the industrial base of Philadelphia in the past.[8] Among small-scale firms with less than fifty workers, the companies include a tannery, an iron foundry, a stone carving concern, a cutlery factory, a publishing house, an insurance office, and one paint and one varnishing-producing manufactory. The five middle-level firms, with fifty to three hundred workers, include a metal works, a leatherware factory, an industrial pottery, and one carpet and one textile mill. Finally, the seven Philadelphia businesses with employment forces of more than fifteen thousand include a department store, an insurance office, a brewery, a utility company, a locomotive plant, and one precision instrument and one hatmaking concern. The objective in considering these firms is not to formulate a statistical profile; these cases will not be used to argue that certain percentages of firms in the city acted in one way or another. Rather, these companies, representing well the scale, trade, sector, and diversity of the production of goods and services in the city of Philadelphia in the period under study, provide a means of discovering the various paths actually taken in the development of personnel practices—perhaps paths not even conceived by theorists.

The twenty firms reveal a spectrum of results—from firms operating on an absolutely informal basis to businesses with highly regularized labor practices. In general, twelve of these Philadelphia enterprises conducted business with limited or moderate deliberation on personnel matters while the other eight can be characterized by industrial relations of a definite developed nature (see Table 5.1). Important distinctions are in order, however, within these broad groupings, and the case studies are best fathomed in scale or spectrum-like fashion.

Informality

An almost complete absence of formal practices is noteworthy in five firm histories. The Wetherill Paint Company provides a first example.[9] The company, which failed to survive the depression of

Table 5.1 Characteristics of twenty Philadelphia firms (by personnel arrangements)[a]

Company	Dates of operation[b]	Product/ service	Number of employees (range at peak)[c]
Wetherill Paint Co.	1784–1933	Paint	60–80
John Gay & Sons Carpet Co.	1876–1915	Carpets	50–100
William Horstmann Co.	1815–1880s	Silk products	400–500
H. Swoboda & Sons	1852–	Leather hides	30–50
Kelley & Hueber	1849–	Leather cases	100–300
Herder Cutlery Co.	1840s–	Cutlery	25–50
Lea & Febiger	1785–	Publishing	10–30
Philadelphia Contri- butionship	1752–	Insurance	15–25
Richard C. Remmey Co.	1810–	Industrial ceramics	50–100
McCloskey Varnish Co.	1854–	Varnish	50–125
Ellisco Incorporated	1843–	Sheet-metal containers	150–250
Insurance Corporation of North America	1792–	Insurance	1000–2000
Perseverance Iron	1850s–1981	Cast-iron parts	20–30
H. C. Wood Incorpo- rated	1849–	Gravestones	25–50
Christian Schmidt Brewery	1860–	Beer	1000–2000

Table 5.1   (*continued*)

Predominant skill level	Form of ownership	Organization of production	Personnel arrangements
Unskilled	Proprietorship	Single product line/ few processes	Informal
Semiskilled	Proprietorship	Single product line/ multiple processes	Informal
Semi/Skilled	Proprietorship	Multiple product line/ multiple processes	Informal
Semiskilled	Proprietorship	Single product line/ few processes	Informal
Semiskilled	Proprietorship	Single product line/ few processes	Informal
Skilled	Proprietorship	Single product line/ few processes	Informal: unsystematic paternalism
Semiskilled	Proprietorship	Single product line/ few processes	Informal: unsystematic paternalism
Semiskilled	Private corpo- ration	Single product line/ few processes	Informal: unsystematic paternalism
Semi/Skilled	Proprietorship	Single product line/ few processes	Partial formal- ization
Semiskilled	Proprietorship	Single product line/ few processes	Partial formal- ization
Semiskilled	Proprietorship/ private corpo- ration	Single product line/ few processes	Partial formal- ization
Semiskilled	Corporation	Single product line/ multiple processes	Informal/late formalization
Skilled	Proprietorship	Single product line/ multiple processes	Formal/ unionization
Skilled	Private corpo- ration	Single product line/ few processes	Formal/ unionization
Semi/skilled	Proprietorship	Single product line/ few processes	Formal/ unionization

Table 5.1   (continued)

Company	Dates of operation[b]	Product/ service	Number of employees (range at peak)[c]
John B. Stetson Hat Co.	1865–1960s	Hats	3000–5000
Brown Instrument Co.	1859–	Measuring instruments	1500–3000
Baldwin Locomotive Works	1832–1940s	Locomotives	15,000–20,000
John Wanamaker	1861–	Department store	5000–7000
Philadelphia Gas Works	1834–	Natural gas service	2500–3000

a. The firms listed here have long and evolving histories as indicated in the text. Predominant characteristics are noted.

b. Actual dates of establishment are difficult to ascertain in some instances and a general date is listed. Firms were also liquidated over periods of time; termination dates are also given in a general way in certain cases.

c. Peak employment figures are for before the 1960s.

the 1930s, dated its origin to the opening of a dry goods store in Philadelphia by Samuel Wetherill in 1784. Among other items, Wetherill sold dye colors and ground paint lead. Increased demand for paint stuffs proved an incentive to manufacture white lead directly; Wetherill subsequently established a small plant and eventually his sons abandoned retailing and built a large paint factory in the 1840s to concentrate solely on production.

The technique of manufacturing white lead at Wetherill was unchanged from the mid-nineteenth century through the company's demise in 1933. Single plant superintendents hired, fired, and supervised teams of common day laborers and a few skilled workmen in

Table 5.1 (continued)

Predominant skill level	Form of ownership	Organization of production	Personnel arrangements
Skilled	Proprietorship/corporation after 1892	Single product line/multiple processes	Formal: systematic paternalism/unionization
Semi/skilled	Proprietorship/corporation	Multiple product line/multiple processes	Formal: systematic paternalism/unionization
Skilled	Partnership/corporation after 1907	Single product line/multiple processes	Formal: systematic paternalism/unionization
Semiskilled	Proprietorship/corporation	Multiple product line/multiple processes	Formal: systematic paternalism/anti-unionization
Mixed	Semi–public agency	Single product line/multiple processes	Formal

pouring molten lead into sheets, stacking the sheets into pots of chemicals to force corrosion, and grinding the pulverized lead. Turnover was extremely high because of the perils of the work and the low compensation. Forty percent of the 3,600 men employed there between 1848 and 1896 in fact worked less than one week, and with labor costs never amounting to more than 10 to 20 percent of operating expenses the Wetherills were never moved to alleviate conditions.[10] Outside agencies did contribute to change; inspectors from both the company's insurance carrier and the Pennsylvania Department of Labor and Industry demanded improvements in working, especially in safety conditions, during the 1910s.[11] Still, Samuel Wetherill's venerable paint company is a noteworthy case for the general absence of attention to personnel matters on the part of its owners and the power accrued to and held by critical plant managers.

Two other Philadelphia firms with shorter histories than Wetherill's fit the same pattern. John Gay & Sons Carpet Company was established in 1876 and stayed in business until 1915. The firm produced worsted, velvet, and "Tapestry Brussels" carpets. The company employed a diverse work force, from highly skilled loom fixers and handloom weavers to power loom machine operatives and bobbin boys.[12] Operating in a highly competitive market, Gay & Sons sought to increase productivity through increased purchases of power looms and frequent staff and wage cuts when slack periods occurred.[13]

Turnover at John Gay & Sons was extremely high, largely because of seasonal factors and fluctuating business conditions.[14] A strong plant superintendent retained complete control over production and labor arrrangements and the owners of the concern did not develop special personnel policies to foster diligence or loyalty. (A small sales and supervisory force did receive special favors and benefits, however.)[15] Most notable in the firm's history is the extent of organized unrest. Work stoppages of one kind or another occurred in every year, with serious strikes in 1878, 1879, 1882, 1894, 1900, 1902, 1903, 1906, and 1912.[16] Wage cuts or reductions in piece rates were the most frequent causes of job actions and all grades of workers participated. The owners of the firm did join with other carpet manufacturers in the 1880s to build a united front against striking Knights of Labor–led carpet employees and agreed to the creation of citywide arbitration procedures for the industry, but the protocols were in effect for only a short period of time. John Gay & Sons offers an example of a firm in a highly competitive industry in which labor cost cutting was a daily imperative and reality; the work experience was affected accordingly.

William H. Horstmann, a German immigrant and skilled silk weaver, established a small silk weaving workshop in Philadelphia in 1815; the workshop would grow to become the highly successful William Horstmann Company. Horstmann built a fully integrated facility where raw silk was washed, twisted, dyed, and then woven into specialty items, such as tassels, fringe, and lace. Horstmann initially employed fellow German workers and operated under craft traditions with formal apprenticeship and journeyman training.[17]

In 1824, Horstmann introduced Jacquard looms to his shop, an event that immediately transformed the nature of his business. Some handloom weaving continued, but soon more than 85 percent of a growing work force would be comprised of women hired to oversee the power machinery. Craft practices were dispensed with, and in 1854 the firm, under the control of Horstmann's sons, opened a five-story factory where three to five hundred workers manufactured silk ware. A departmentalized structure of management emerged, with overseers appointed to supervise particular activities or product lines.[18]

With expansion, high turnover became a feature of employment at the firm. Between 1850 and 1875, 50 percent of those hired remained with the firm for less than one month.[19] With the exception of a few recreational outings and the creation of a company baseball team in the 1880s, there is no evidence of special initiatives taken on personnel matters by the owners of the company.[20] Adequate labor supply and a reputation as a place where German immigrants could find employment allowed the firm to operate with an inelaborate labor system throughout the period for which documentation survives.[21]

Two firms still in existence today retain features of the three formerly existing companies described above. H. Swoboda & Sons, absorbed as a division of Trans-Continental Leathers, Incorporated, in the 1960s, was established in 1852 and has survived as a producer of specialty horsehides.[22] A general absence of concern for personnel matters has marked its history. Laborers have been hired, trained informally, and supervised first by the company's founder and then by a succession of strong plant superintendents. Operations were gradually mechanized but without significant incident. In the early 1940s a personnel office was created after a successful unionization campaign by CIO organizers, but almost entirely to handle contract matters and not to usurp the powers or activities of the plant manager. (Benefit packages, for example, are only of very recent origin, and to this day the company does not require high school diplomas or any form of training on the part of its blue-collar work force.) High labor turnover has also been a constant and notable feature of the firm's history—the work, despite mechanization, is arduous, and noxious gases and the danger of chemical burns make the job fairly undesirable—but the firm has never moved or been forced to develop programs or policies to encourage greater stability.

A much less grim but in many ways similar portrait can be drawn for Kelley & Hueber, a manufacturer of specialty leather products, including eyeglass cases, its major sales item.[23] The present owners purchased the company in 1922 from a family that had established a leather case and strap concern in 1849. Production at Kelley & Hueber has remained unchanged: fully bleached and dyed hides are cut to pattern with mechanical cutting tools and subsequently sewn on industrial machines and finished. The firm is known as a producer of high-quality, small-batch, made-to-order goods.

From the 1920s through the early 1960s, one plant superintendent directed all aspects of production. He hired and trained people from the surrounding neighborhood: men generally in cutting and women in sewing and finishing. A family and personal spirit was maintained. The owners knew workers on a first-name basis and offered occasional discretionary gratuities. The plant superintendent's personal relations with and knowledge of the neighborhood and the people who came to work for the firm kept loyalty high and turnover low. Ready access to labor, in fact, represents a common aspect of production in the five least formalized cases of personnel relations considered to this point. Wetherill, Gay & Sons, Horstmann, Swoboda, and Kelley & Hueber differed somewhat in size, complexity, and spirit of operations, but the ability of their strong plant superintendents to hire help through personal, family, neighborhood, and ethnic connections appears a basic factor in their undeveloped employment practices.

Unsystematic Paternalism

Concern for labor matters but lack of formal initiatives characterizes the next three case histories; as at Kelley & Hueber, and to a greater extent, warm personal relations are noteworthy and crucial. Leopold Herder, a German immigrant, established a cutlery factory in Philadelphia in the late 1840s to manufacture custom knives and scissors.[24] Herder and later his descendants managed all aspects of production and sales. Members of the family were sent back to Germany in their early adult years to learn the cutlery trade in formal apprenticeship programs, and there they recruited skilled workers trained in metal work. Turnover was low in the firm and a protective family atmosphere prevailed. In the 1920s the Herder family, faced with competition from producers of stamped, stainless steel cutlery, closed their manufactory to concentrate solely on retailing and repairs. The firm represents a fairly typical family proprietorship, where a non-programmatic paternalism ordered relations and affairs.

A similar history is revealed in the case of Lea & Febiger, which was founded in 1785 by Matthew Carey and is the oldest existing publishing house in the United States.[25] The firm, which came to specialize in the publication of medical texts, has remained in the same family's hands for two centuries. Family members have served as editors and managers of a small office of salespeople and clerks. The office of the nineteenth century was run quite traditionally, with frock-coated male clerks who were expected to maintain prescribed high levels of decorum. College-educated women began to be hired in the first decade of the twentieth century as the office was mechanized with typewriters and billing machines.[26] The owners of the firm have been quite solicitous of their employee's needs; gifts on holidays and paid vacations were fixed practices by 1900.[27] Decorum is still an important matter at Lea & Febiger, a quaint spirit persists, and the company boasts of a loyal staff with long tenure; in short, a small office where tradition and custom have been prime motivators.

The Philadelphia Contributionship, the nation's oldest fire insurance company, founded in 1752 by Benjamin Franklin and a group of his associates, fits the same portrait, but with some differences.[28] Until 1960, the firm offered perpetual, one-payment fire insurance to customers, and the business involved minimal clerical and book-keeping tasks. Throughout the nineteenth century, an appointed chief clerk directed the work of a small staff of male clerks, mostly younger relatives of board members. Expansion in services after 1900 brought mechanization of the office and the hiring of women secretarial and clerical personnel (with a few exceptions, the women hired were high school graduates with commercial course degrees).[29] Few stayed with the company for long periods and until very recently the firm did little to encourage longer tenure. A career ladder developed, however, more through custom than deliberation, for male employees, whose clerkships have been treated as training grounds for managerial positions. (The social backgrounds of these recruits, it should be noted, have changed, but not the purposes of their apprenticeship.)[30] The Contributionship remains a small office offering two kinds of gender-specific work experiences, but to this day custom rather than deliberate initiative determines employment practices. A visit to The Philadelphia Contributionship, or to Herder Cutlery or Lea & Febriger, is an object lesson in the meaning and efficacy of tradition.

Partial Formalization

Four other of our Philadelphia firms can be characterized as having unformalized labor relations, but their histories are more complicated, with deliberate initiatives either affecting only portions of the work force or occurring only sporadically. The Richard C. Remmey Company, the first firm to be considered in this group, dates its founding to 1735 when John Remmey, a native of Germany, settled in New York City and established a pottery. Seventy-five years later a grandson of Remmey moved to Philadelphia and created a ceramics works that would prosper in the production of stoneware pitchers, plates, bowls, pipes, and fire brick for use in kilns and ovens.[31]

In the 1860s the firm, under the direction of Richard C. Remmey, moved to specialize in the manufacture of refractory materials: clay and silica fire bricks and tiles for ovens, kilns, and furnaces; large-scale crucibles for mixing and melting processes; specialized ceramic pipes; and eventually insulators for electrical use. Old craft production techniques were abandoned; mechanical shovels, conveyors, mixers, and kiln stackers were adopted; a detailed division of labor was effected; and a large twenty-five–acre facility was constructed at the turn of the twentieth century. Skills, however, were not eliminated. The Remmeys built a laboratory where college-trained engineers were hired to develop new ceramics. Model, pattern, and mold makers were still required, and here firm managers maintained formal apprenticeship programs (in fact, between 1910 and 1950, the company recruited master potters from England to train apprentices and serve as model makers).[32] The majority of other production workers, however, remained under the supervision of plant superintendents who handled personnel matters on a day-to-day basis. Until the 1960s, when the firm was absorbed into the U.S. Gypsum Company, employment practices at Remmey, which remained in spirit a family firm, were generally without procedures or rules.

The McCloskey Varnish Company, founded in 1854, provides another example.[33] Until the 1960s practically all labor at McCloskey's was hand labor. Resin, gums, and coloring were cooked in large open vats and the resulting varnish cooled, thinned, poured, canned, and labeled without the use of machinery. In an effort to increase output and market coverage, automatic reactors and filling and labeling devices were then adopted. These devices have eliminated almost all labor in basic production (but sales and clerical forces have increased proportionally). That the firm survived with primitive technology until very recently is testimony to the openness of the market and the reputation McCloskey garnered as a producer of high-quality varnishes, especially for industrial use.

Before World War II small groups of men worked in teams with little division of labor. Expansion in production during and after the war effected an initial specialization, which was formalized in 1953 when new owners hired an efficiency-minded managerial staff. To boost productivity, the company also began to offer benefits for the first time, including paid vacations, medical insurance, and pensions. The firms still operates, however, without a personnel department and without great deliberation on personnel matters. McCloskey has offered its employees steady work—the result of a stable market for its product—and its smallness has allowed a boasted-of family spirit to prevail (despite the fact that the original family has not been involved with the company for generations). Turnover remains low and the business has successfully resisted periodic efforts at unionization.

The case of Ellisco Incorporated takes the McCloskey Varnish story one step further on the path toward formalization. Ellisco dates its founding to 1843, when George Ellis established a metal works to manufacture tanners' and curriers' tools.[34] Little is known about the firm's history until World War I, when the company entered into the production of metal cans under government contract and ownership was transferred to the family that retains control to this day. Since the First World War Ellisco has become a major producer of sheet-metal milk cans, industrial waste disposals, and specialized containers for chemical and pharmaceutical processing and the handling of radioactive materials. Until World War II skilled metal workers cut and pressed objects with hand-controlled machinery; in the late 1940s the firm adopted automatic technologies. With the exception of extremely specialized items which require hand control, the machines are now tended by a work force of semi-skilled operatives.

Until 1938 recruitment and training of labor at Ellisco was completely in the hands of a strong plant superintendent. In that year an office was established to facilitate employee enrollment in the Social Security System and the gathering of data for local, state, and federal labor-related government agencies. That office evolved into a personnel department which by the late 1940s kept records, set labor policy (including new fringe benefits schedules), and controlled hiring and firing. The single plant manager, however, retained substantial control and authority. In recent years the office and sales components of the work force have increased dramatically and the firm has established formal requirements for employment, training programs, and promotion ladders for these employees. Attention to labor matters has affected white-collar workers to a far greater extent than plant employees. Control of the production work force then has been exacted through both personal and technical means; bureaucratic and organizational solutions have been forged for the office. The Ellisco example is interesting also for the way in which government orders and regulations have affected personnel arrangements. In a common but unsystematic fashion, managers at Remmey, McCloskey Varnish, and Ellisco have had to consider and implement programs for labor, but only for portions of their work forces.

The final example of a firm without a highly developed system of industrial relations is perhaps the most curious, because it involves a notably large-scale enterprise, the Insurance Company of North America.[35] Formalization emerged at INA, but at a rather late date. The company was founded in 1792 by a group of Philadelphia merchants with an eye to providing maritime insurance to the city's mercantile community. It was established as a joint stock venture and became the first capital stock insurance company in the United States.[36]

Until the 1920s, when INA's daily operations were moved into a large downtown office building, the concern was managed directly by an elected board of stockholders. One board member was selected as an operating officer of the company and assigned to direct the work of a growing office of clerks, many of whom were younger relatives of company officials. (As at the Philadelphia Contributionship, clerking was intended as an apprenticeship for eventual participation on the board.)[37]

Growth in the first decades of the twentieth century forced the board to relinquish control over operations to a staff of hired, professional managers. When the firm occupied its new large headquarters in 1924, a committee of executive officers was established to oversee personnel matters. A set of rules and regulations was issued and formal application procedures for employment initiated. Control of operations, however, remained extremely loose and in the hands of lower-level supervisors.[38]

INA did not adopt comprehensive formalized personnel practices until after World War II. The first initiative was the creation of a training school for agents; out of this effort came the creation of a full-fledged personnel department in 1956.[39] The office was given responsibility for hiring and testing employees; training; and establishing work assignments, benefit schedules, promotions, and extracurricular activities. The department, the idea of one innovative executive, represented a vast departure from the more laissez-faire practices of earlier eras.

For a firm of its size, influence, and importance, INA was late in formalizing and elaborating its personnel procedures. To this day the company acknowledges that it does not compensate its large clerical force as well as other Philadelphia white-collar employers. It tends to rely on recruiting young women from Catholic high schools with commercial course degrees and skills and expects them to remain with INA for short periods of time.[40] The less dynamic role assumed in personnel matters by the firm is a reflection of this strategy and the conservatism of its management.

Among the twelve Philadelphia businesses that have been considered unformalized with regard to personnel matters, there appear to be two patterns. Unskilled work and/or an available labor pool allowed firms as disparate as the Wetherill Paint Company and the Insurance Company of North America to conduct operations over many generations with minimal attention to labor relations. Continued family ownership and management in the absence of overt pressure by employees seems to have been responsible for the persistence of customary and personalistic methods of administration in other instances. The importance of values—the desire to maintain a certain spirit of enterprise—cannot be discounted in these cases.[41]

The question of formalization becomes clearer when we move from basically null cases to positive examples. Definitive crises, points of transformation, and initiative make for less blurred and seamless histories. Eight firms provide evidence of deliberate efforts on personnel management, but within this group, four different patterns are discernible.

Formalization from Below

In the case of three firms, order came almost unilaterally from below. Here, well-organized craft workers imposed official union work rules and procedures that led to highly regularized practices. Perseverance Iron, for example, was founded as a foundry for the manufacture of iron stoves and heaters in the early 1850s; the company remained in operation and in family hands until its closing in July of 1981.[42] The firm operated under strict craft traditions and conditions with little mechanization throughout its history. Highly skilled pattern makers, molders, kiln men, and lathe and drill press operators participated in the making and finishing of custom cast-iron parts for final assembly or replacement. Until 1916, recruitment and training were conducted by shop foremen, but the pace of production was greatly controlled by the foundry's skilled workers. In that year the firm was organized by an AFL craft union and conditions of employment—from hiring on the basis of union lists to apprenticeship arrangements, compensation, benefits, layoffs, and ultimately retirement—came under strict contract regulation. The owners of the firm never initiated personnel programs of their own accord, and the shop remained very much the province of several generations of highly permanent, kin-connected, autonomous craftsmen, and of staunch trade unionists.

H. C. Wood Incorporated, founded by Aaron Wood, a stonecutter of British descent, in the late 1840s, offers a similar history.[43] The firm produced marble front steps for Philadelphia town and row houses until after the Civil War, when a decision was made to enter the growing lucrative market for ornamental gravestones. A tradition of hiring skilled carvers of northern Italian ancestry began then and continues to this day. These workers were also organized by an AFL craft group in the 1890s and all aspects of labor relations have been handled through contracts and union rules ever since. The production of gravestones after the turn of the century became highly mechanized as sandblasting with stencils replaced handcarving. Skills have been diluted accordingly, but mechanical innovation transpired with union approval and regulation and the continuation of craft standards and procedures. The firm has been marked by low turnover, family connection in employment, and few deliberate personnel initiatives on the part of Aaron Wood and his heirs.

The case of the Christian Schmidt Brewery Company is different because the firm is decidedly on a large scale, with thousands of employees, but the basic pattern of labor relations is identical to those in the small shops of Perseverance Iron and H. C. Wood Incorporated. Christian Schmidt, a German immigrant, founded Schmidt's Brewery in 1860, and the company remained in family hands until 1976.[44] The production of beer did not change greatly at Schmidt's over the years. Ingredients were cooked and allowed to ferment in large vats; cleaning the equipment and packaging represented the only areas that underwent thorough mechanization and automation.

From the turn of the twentieth century Schmidt's also operated as a closed union shop, and unionization had a singular influence on personnel matters at the company. All hiring of non-office and supervisory staff took place through a union hiring hall and on the basis of union lists. (A personnel office was established after World War II to handle recruitment and benefits of white-collar employees.) Although standardized, customary agreements and arrangements with the union—including stipulations that sons of brewmasters have first access to job openings—resulted in the employment of successive generations of families of workers, mostly of German and Irish background. The union also strictly controlled apprenticeship procedures, wages, hours, work assignments, vacations, promotions, seniority rights, pensions, safety measures, and medical and life insurance. Schmidt's, although a family-run firm, was notably free of personnel initiatives or paternalistic programs on the part of management (at least with regard to production workers). Recreational programs were union- and not management-created and administered. The firm boasted the allegiance of its employees and pointed to low rates of turnover. The company was considered a good firm to work for, which was greatly due to the Schmidt family's willingness to deal with the strong, cohesive unions that had been a fixture in the plant and a fixture in the community of brewery workers.

Systematic Paternalism and Unionization

Unionization as a prime agent in the development of regularized personnel practices also figures in three other Philadelphia firm case studies, but only at one stage, and usually a final stage, in more complicated histories. Notable here are the efforts made by strong, morally inspired owners and managers to experiment with a gamut of programs aimed both at providing better welfare and at instilling greater loyalty and discipline among employees. Ultimately, these initiatives became less the work of charismatic figures and more bureaucratic and organizational in nature as successful union campaigns made them an integral part of union contracts.

The famous John B. Stetson Hat Company provides an almost perfect case in point. Stetson founded his company in 1865 and within fifty years his firm would grow to employ more than five thousand workers and produce one quarter of the felt hats manufactured and sold in the United States. Stetson's success was based on his deliberate strategy of using fine fur materials and marketing a varied custom product line. To render his hats distinct, Stetson also decided to sell them in specially made boxes adorned with what became the famous Stetson logo and design.[45]

In the 1870s Stetson began building a large, fully integrated factory complex. All aspects of production were conducted on the premises (including the manufacture of Stetson hat labels and boxes); fur felt was prepared, cleaned, dyed, cut, sized, shaped, sewn, trimmed, and finished within the walls of the plant. Because Stetson aimed at a custom market, much of the work involved skilled hand labor (only in the 1930s were important processes mechanized). Generally, less skilled female labor was employed in preparation and adornment, while skilled male workers attended to the cutting, sewing, shaping, and finishing of the hats.

Extremely high labor costs and a tradition of independence among hat makers forced Stetson to pay great attention to employee relations in the firm. His approach was basically paternalistic. By the 1920s, Stetson had become world famous not only for his hats but also for his various employee programs, including a cooperative store where foodstuffs could be bought at wholesale prices, language and civic courses (especially for foreign-born employees), group life insurance plans, a quarter-century club for veteran workers, a building loan association, an employees' savings bank, a Stetson chorus (which performed on local radio), Stetson baseball and track teams, a weekend lodge for workers, a profit sharing plan, a Sunday school, a hospital, a host of bonus and premium systems, and turkey giveaways on holidays.[46]

The collapse of the economy in the 1930s, however, brought great changes to the firm. Hard-pressed to return a profit to investors, firm managers furloughed workers, curbed special dispensations, hired time-and-motion consultants to define new tasks and piece rates, and began steps to mechanize various aspects of production. Workers responded by forming an independent union and then joining the United Hatters, Cap, and Millinery Workers International. A successful strike in 1936 led to union recognition and a contract providing for wage increases, a forty-hour work week, overtime compensation, abolition of time-and-motion studies, and the establishment of grievance procedures and seniority rights (union-controlled insurance plans would come later).[47]

The company in turn abandoned all paternalistic programs, upgraded supervision and the training of supervisors, continued mechanizing production, and created an Industrial Relations Department to set labor policy and bargain with the union. Stetson Hat maintained its presence in Philadelphia through the 1960s. The firm provides a good example of the limits of corporate paternalism and the roles played by economic pressure, labor strife and union contracts in spurring the growth of technical and bureaucratic personnel controls.

Although not a household word like Stetson, the Brown Instrument Company became an institution in the Philadelphia business world as a renowned manufacturer of precision gauge instruments. An evolving history of paternalistic and union-induced bureaucratic answers to personnel issues also marks this firm, though with slight variations on the Stetson theme.

The company dates its founding to 1857 when Edward Brown, inventor of the first pyrometer of American design, opened a small shop in Philadelphia to manufacture heat and liquid flow measuring devices. Within sixty years he and his son built a large-scale firm which would garner a worldwide reputation as a producer of quality custom measuring instruments. The firm was acquired by and made a division of Honeywell Incorporated in 1934.[48]

The Browns divided their growing concern into departments for engineering, purchasing, production, sales and service, and finance. The largest unit was production, which was divided into specification writing, parts manufacture, sub-assembly, and final assembly. The firm prospered by perfecting a system of specialized small-batch production, which required the employment of large numbers of skilled workers.

The Browns recruited labor primarily from the neighborhood surrounding their factory, relying on family networks and in-house training and promotion. Young men were taken on as apprentices in parts manufacture, later becoming full-time drill press and lathe operators. Young men and women were also hired for sub-assembly work; the males generally were then promoted to final assembly and specification writing, or to supervisory posts. In the 1920s, Richard Brown, son of the founder, also instituted a wide array of corporate welfare programs, including paid vacations and medical and life insurance. The firm became identified as one sensitive to the needs of its work force.[49]

The merger with Honeywell in 1934 led to significant changes at Brown Instrument. Fearing both suspension of various benevolent personnel practices and the possible closing of the plant after the new management takeover, workers at Brown began to organize. In 1936, officials from the newly formed CIO United Electrical, Radio, and Machine Workers Union were invited to assist in establishing a local at the company. Within weeks the firm's new managers agreed to recognize the union and offered the first of many contracts. It created fixed wage and incentive payment schedules, hours standards, apprenticeship arrangements, job classification and promotion schemes, grievance procedures, seniority rights, and fringe benefits.[50] In effect, union contracts formalized many of the procedures practiced by the paternally minded Browns. Office and supervisory staff, it should be noted, remained non-unionized, and Honeywell's management has repeatedly had to institute new perquisites to attract and keep these workers.[51]

Two other factors are important in understanding the work experience at Brown. The company operated in a stable, nonseasonal, well-established market; as a result, the firm never experienced financial difficulties or fluctuations and even in bad times was able to offer steady work. Second, the custom nature of the product has put a premium on skill; the firm has never operated on an assembly-line basis and workers retain substantial control over the pace of work. The company has offered its workers regular, protected employment with intrinsic and extrinisic rewards, and loyalty to the firm and tenure remain high.

The quality of the work experience—the dignity of labor offered and performed—also figures in the industrial relations history of the

Baldwin Locomotive Works, which, like Stetson, was one of Philadelphia's most famous firms. Here, too, the move from deliberate managerial initiatives to union-induced controls is evident.

Matthias Baldwin established the Baldwin Locomotive Works in the early 1830s. His plant grew into a multiblock complex comprising nineteen acres of city space, and Baldwin soon became one of the largest employers in Philadelphia. In the 1920s, the company moved its operations twelve miles outside the city to a 616-acre facility; the company could then boast a worldwide work force of close to 22,000 people.[52]

Growth, however, did not change the basic way locomotives were constructed at Baldwin. From its inception, the firm always produced engines to order, following the specifications and needs of the large number of railroads that became its customers. Specifications were turned into blueprints; drawings were then sent to the pattern shop for models to be made, which in turn went to the foundry where they were used to make molds for iron castings. Drawings also went to forge areas, where large components were shaped; to the boiler shop, where copper was cut and formed into boilers; or to the machine, tinsmith, and tender shops, where metals were cut, lathed, drilled, folded, and finished into needed components. The various parts would then be gathered in the erecting shops for assembly by skilled assemblers; carpenters and painters would put on the finishing touches.[53]

The production of custom engines required skilled workers, and firm managers from Matthias Baldwin onward devoted great time and effort to developing and maintaining the skills of their work force. Apprenticeship systems, as noted in the previous chapter, became a notable feature of the company's operations. Furthermore, the firm never adopted automated or through-process technologies (the customized nature of the product precluded such innovations). Most important, company officials never introduced experiments with scientific management, time-and-motion studies, piece-rate payments, or any kind of paternalistic programs.[54] During the late nineteenth and early twentieth centuries, certain production areas were operated on the basis of inside contracting, a form of drive system. Certain skilled workers entered into agreements with management to supervise crews in filling stipulated orders. The program, however, proved unwieldly and difficult to monitor and was ultimately jettisoned.[55] Workers laboring under subcontractors at Baldwin, it should be noted, were always compensated directly by the company according to daily wage schedules.

The Baldwin Locomotive Works represented a mammoth industrial enterprise producing a basic capital good, but one in which skill and craft were maintained (partly because of the nature of the product, but also because of deliberate company policy). Loyalty could be engendered through the work itself (and also through the high wages that were part of the firm's reputation). Baldwin never went in for paternalistic programs, despite its very visible presence in the city and the public role many of its leading executives assumed. The company was forced to recognize various craft and industrial unions and reach contracts in the 1930s and 1940s, but unionization occured without the great incident associated with New Deal–era labor campaigns. Written into agreements were procedures already practiced through custom.

Systematic Paternalism and Anti-unionism

In the cases of Stetson, Brown, and Baldwin, deliberate interventions by managers were followed by further elaboration and articulation through unionization. Another kind of history transpired in an equally famous Philadelphia enterprise, John Wanamaker's department store. Here unionization never occurred, and significant formalization of labor relations came directly through the extraordinary initiatives of one formidable figure, John Wanamaker himself.

Wanamaker opened his first retail store in 1861 at the age of twenty-three. Believing success would lie in product diversification and horizontal expansion, he continually enlargened his store; in 1875 he moved his multi-departmental retail outlet to a large railroad depot and in 1910 to the multi-story building in central Philadelphia which remains the flagship store of the large Wanamaker chain to this day.[56]

John Wanamaker was a pioneer in departmentalized approaches to management and in advertising techniques. He also developed new strategies for organizing the work of what became an army of sales and office clerks, supervisors, and buyers. Wanamaker personally attended to the structuring, training, and rewarding of his managerial staff (management training and incentive programs were a feature in the firm by the 1890s). As early as the 1880s a centralized personnel office was also established to facilitate the recruitment of sales and office help. (The firm was one of the first to use personality and aptitude tests in job placement.) For sales positions, the store preferred women from respectable homes who showed grace and decorum in interviews, dressed well, and, most important, spoke English. More significantly, Wanamaker developed a succession of programs to engender diligence and loyalty: as noted earlier, he established a store school for young employees and various in-store vocational training programs; he instituted paid vacations, the ten hour day, and the five-and-a-half-day work week in the 1880s; and he fostered a medical clinic, a savings and loan association, life and pension insurance plans, and numerous employee clubs and teams by the first decade of the twentieth century.[57] Wanamaker's reputation as a leader in corporate welfare initiatives was well deserved (he referred to his employees as "my store family"); so, too, was his reputation as a vehement opponent of trade unions.[58] Wanamaker's successors continued his basic approach to personnel matters after his death, including vigilant responses to threats of unionization; his store provides a singular example of a strong personality establishing labor control through deliberate paternalistic and bureaucratic means.

The example of John Wanamaker may please advocates of "Great Man" explanations of historical change, but other interpretations are possible and applicable. Organizational theorists would point to the obvious complexity and size of Wanamaker's operation and note that extraordinary measures were in order; similarly, a human capital theory or technology-based approach might stress that Wanamaker was faced with the problem of mobilizing and molding a new kind of task force engaged in a new skill—namely, retail selling—and that special programs and initiatives were necessary. The impact and sway of Wanamaker were so substantial, however, that attributing developments purely to his personal agency is still very compelling.

A seemingly simple answer can be found to explain the nature of labor relations at a firm such as Wanamaker's. At the upper ends of the scale of formalization, we can consider another and last case study, the Philadelphia Gas Works. The City Council of Philadelphia established the Philadelphia Gas Works in 1834 to manufacture coal gas for use in street lighting and private homes. The works first existed as a private company, then became a city-run agency; it was leased to a private concern in 1897, and finally became a municipal commission again in the early 1970s. Through all these changes, PGW has always been a major employer of Philadelphia's laboring population.[59]

Since its inception the work force at PGW has been divided into three components: production, distribution, and sales. Before 1900 the largest number of employees—common day laborers, for the most part—were occupied in the manufacture of coal gas; mechanization and automation at the turn of the century and eventual large-scale purchasing of natural gas from western suppliers in the late 1940s successively slashed and eliminated employment in production. A stable and fairly large percentage of workers have been engaged in distribution—the installation and repair of gas lines and meters—while vastly growing proportions of employees have been involved with sales (the latter including meter readers, clerks, billers, sales representatives, and accountants).[60]

Until 1897, when the Works was leased to the privately owned United Gas Improvement Company, the management of PGW's personnel was haphazard and without deliberate initiative. Appointments at all levels were tied to political patronage, and complaints by customers of uncertain service led to calls for reform in the late nineteenth century and to UGI's eventual takeover.[61]

UGI officials, trying to turn a profit, moved quickly to cut employment, fire political appointees, fully automate gas production, and mechanize the office. To gain employee loyalty, the company reduced hours from sixty to fifty a week, began a system of paid vacations, built a medical dispensary and dental clinic for workers, and established various company-sponsored recreational activities.[62] Most important, the company created a personnel department during World War I, at a moment of severe manpower shortages, and placed the department in charge of recruitment, testing applicants, training, work assignments, job classification, and promotion. This move was followed by the initiation of a wide range of paternalistic programs and the creation of an Employee Representative Committee in 1933.[63]

PGW's employment history offers a good example of efforts to establish labor control through technical means in production and bureaucratic means in service areas. Before 1897 personal connections and political favor functioned as prime motivators; UGI then sought to motivate through organizational rewards. UGI's need to return a profit (general tax revenues could be counted on to cover losses when municipal authorities ran the works); the complexity and diversity of activities at the agency; the growing white-collar, relatively autonomous component of the work force; and the public nature of operations all contributed to the deliberate personnel initiatives taken by UGI officials during the first third of the century, initiatives that affect work relations and arrangements to this very day. Of all the case histories, this is probably the most complex and stands on its own.

The particularities of each of the above twenty firm-level case studies of industrial relations in Philadelphia, and not just the Philadelphia Gas Works, militate against generalizations. Certainly no one framework adequately explains the varied histories of personnel practice and policy development seen in the enterprises. Size and complexity, for example, certainly mattered, as did the corporate form—with one exception, the Insurance Company of North America, firms characterized by informal relations were small-to-medium in size, engaged in the production of single services or products, and family owned and operated; still, in two small proprietorships, Perseverance Iron and H. C. Wood, personnel practices were extremely formalized. Similarly, consideration of costs and technological innovation spurred changes in some instances, but were not critical factors in most. Articulated conceptions of personal relations do not seem to have played a great role, but ethical standards and values affected the work experience in firms touched by the likes of John B. Stetson and the owners of Lea & Febiger.

A few common denominators can be isolated. Unskilled work, availability of labor, and/or family ownership and management were components of unformalized situations; skilled or new kinds of work and/or labor conflict and unionization marked cases noteworthy for the emergence of formal personnel policies. There is evidence in these findings to satisfy varying and vying theories, but the total portrait offered by labor market segmentation theorists, with some major provisos, seems best to fit the layered and spectrum-like quality of the results. Growing scale of operations, the corporate form, and labor pressure required or forced managers to act differently and deliberately toward labor; the persistence of firms outside this realm in turn meant the continuation of traditional, nonbureaucratic practices. Personalistic relations, however, did not preclude stable, desirable employment, as is seen in the kind of work experience offered in such family operated firms as Herder Cutlery. The question of skill and the ability of organized skilled workers to at times even unilaterally force regularization of labor policies in both large and small settings necessitate further qualification, but not dismissal, of the segmentation argument.

The twenty Philadelphia case studies also raise an interrelated issue concerning timing. Students of industrial relations history point to various critical moments in the development of modern personnel practices. Taylorism and the advent of scientific management at the turn of the twentieth century represent for some the most critical developments.[64] Other scholars discount the impact of Taylor and his disciples and look to the 1910s and World War I and to the work of the first generation of more liberal personnel management reformers.[65] The decade of the twenties similarly is frequently cited for the proliferation of experiments with corporate welfare programs,[66] and the thirties for the impact of mass production unionism.[67] Finally, others cite the forties for the role of government regulations in affecting employment policies, the growth of bureaucratic methods of labor control, or retrenchment on the part of the managerial community. (If taken to our own times, affirmative action rulings, innovations with so-called quality work teams, and recent anti-union efforts could be deemed a new stage.)[68] The existence in the literature of so many offered turning points, however, should raise suspicions about treating industrial relations history in such a developmental way.

On a note of lesser importance, the cases analyzed indicate the need to start the story of modern personnel initiatives in the 1880s. The growth of large-scale enterprises and their challenge to republican and small-producer values and visions encouraged a pioneer generation of religiously and ethically inspired enterprise-builders—the John B. Stetsons and John Wanamakers of Philadelphia and the George Pullmans of Chicago, for example—to experiment with various benevolent plans and schemes to engender greater fealty and productivity among employees. (The depression of the 1870s and such tumultuous events as the great railroad strikes of July 1877 served as definite backdrops to such steps.) Later initiatives were to follow with different means, as in the case of scientific management or recognition of unions, but with the same ends in mind. But, of greater significance, a canvass of diverse firms (not just companies famous for managerial experiments) reveals no generalized or single progression; the Philadelphia story, in fact, is notable for the persistence of old forms and old methods. Moreover, rather than a linear or stage-like progression, there is a continuity of efforts, a history of repeated crisis and response.

On the question of timing and successive if not developmental initiatives on industrial relations, a few side words on Frederick Winslow Taylor are probably in order. Certainly no history of business management in Philadelphia is complete without mention of Taylor. Taylor was the child of a wealthy and prominent Germantown family—his mother, a Quaker, was an active abolitionist—and to his parents' dismay he abandoned academic studies and became a machinist's apprentice at the age of eighteen and later a foreman and engineer at the Midvale Steel Company in the city.[69] At Midvale, Taylor began a series of experiments aimed at increasing the efficiency of the flow of goods through the productive process and the productivity of workers employed there. Although he introduced a range of managerial reforms, Taylor is most famous for his time-and-motion studies, his effort to break work into detailed, easily supervised tasks, catalogue them, establish expected rates for finishing jobs, and structure incentive schemes to boost output. Philadelphia became an important testing ground for Taylor and his principles at such firms as Midvale Steel, Tabor Manufacturing and the Link-Belt Company.[70]

Taylor and his disciples and competitors ultimately comprised a movement, dubbed scientific management, and they have been seen as critical agents in the history of the American workplace. According to the popular view, they transformed work, eliminating skills and the sway of skilled craftsmen and rendering work repetitious, without intrinsic meaning, and alienating. This vision of Taylor and his co-conspirators, however, bears little relation to the historical record, and here Philadelphia case studies confirm the need to qualify the impact of scientific management. Proponents of scientific management techniques rarely succeeded in setting their innovations in place. Resistance from foremen who were threatened by these new consultants, more notable resistance from workers, and the administrative nightmare involved in cataloguing tasks and establishing rates—particularly in firms whose product lines were always changing, as was the norm in Philadelphia—doomed most Tayloristic experiments from the start.[71] Case studies of the actual implementation of scientific management reforms confirm this conclusion. Had Taylor succeeded, in fact, industrial relations history would not be marked by further stages of development and initiative. But more important, an emphasis purely on the technical side of work overlooks the importance of social relations at the point of production. Time-and-motion studies do not by themselves define the nature of the work experience. For example, the managers at Link-Belt, who personally invited Taylor into the firm to reorganize production, at the same time introduced an impressive and effective array of paternalistic programs (the kinds of programs that Taylor detested).[72] Similarly, in firms such as Brown Instrument, time-and-motion studies became and remained a basic part of the production process, but benevolent benefits first and unionization later had a much greater impact on the nature of labor relations at the company. Taylor is a part, and a small part at that, of a larger, multi-faceted, multi-layered, and ever-contested and changing story.

The uneven history of personnel practices in Philadelphia can be seen in ongoing labor tensions in firms and management searches for solutions as well the persistence of old forms of practices and relationships. The staggered nature of change is evident in two other ways that deserve mention and emphasis. First concerns the chief agents of change. Extraordinary personalities, organization-minded bureaucrats, craft unionists, industrial unionists, and government officials played a role in the development of personnel practices in Philadelphia for the period under study. No single set of actors seems more important or dominant than another; all contributed to this history.

Second, the different kinds of personnel policies manifested within particular firms in Philadelphia add an additional element of complexity. Here, important distinctions loom between production workers and office and store staff. The former have been subject either to the personal authority and discretion of strong plant superintendents, the technical controls embedded in mechanization, or the bureaucratic controls achieved in union contracts; the latter have been encouraged over the years through organizational rewards conceived and distributed from on top. Yet, further qualifications have to be drawn between clerical and sales staffs in the office and store. The histories of such diverse firms as John Gay & Sons Carpet Company, the Insurance Company of North America, and John Wanamaker's indicate that people in sales—whether salesmen and agents on the road or saleswomen behind the counter—because of their relative autonomy, direct relations with clients and customers, and handling of monies required special interventions and inducements. In the modern, large-scale office, until very recent times, managers have been less impelled to initiate programs for their work forces behind the desk.[73] In firms employing production, sales, and clerical help—as in the case of the Brown Instrument Company—the approach to each type of worker has differed, with office people again garnering the least attention.

Firm records can reveal the oscillating, recurring, and divergent nature of personnel policies and practices in a city such as Philadelphia. The uneven history of labor relations can finally be highlighted by brief reference to an additional case study, one that will draw attention to the specific question of hiring patterns and the process of getting work. Up to this point the focus has been on employment practices in general and the issue of when and why firms in Philadelphia began to forge regularized employment procedures and in what kinds of companies and trades such practices came to prevail. The example is the Pennsylvania Railroad, a venerable employer of Philadelphia working people. The Pennsylvania Railroad (at least until its unholy demise) provides textbook writers with a textbook case of bureaucratic development.[74] By the turn of the twentieth century, the Pennsylvania had the most highly articulated hierarchies, flow charts, and systems of reports, rules, and regulations ever developed by an American enterprise. Recognition of railroad labor brotherhoods combined with increased governmental regulation of railroad labor affairs made industrial relations on the Pennsylvania quintessentially formalized. Yet, as late as the 1950s, top managers in the company were still bedeviled by what was deemed to be the chaotic nature of labor recruitment and placement on the road. Three years of committee investigation and suggestion led to the centralization of recruitment offices, the publishing of the carrier's first hiring manual, and the creation of new employment tests, forms and procedures. The story for the Pennsylvania Railroad, then, did not terminate, as others have suggested, in 1860, 1900, or 1945.[75]

The example of the Pennsylvania Railroad also reveals that hiring practices can remain highly personalized and decentralized in an enterprise where other aspects of employment have become formalized. Not only can different policies apply to the different groups of workers within firms, but mixes of policies can cut across different parts of the work experience. Hiring in general in Philadelphia appears to have remained unsystematic. This is confirmed by surveys that indicated that for the vast majority of companies the hiring function was constantly lodged in the hands of plant managers and supervisors; that 50 percent of the Philadelphians canvassed by WPA investigators in 1936 reported securing their jobs through familial and personal connections is further confirmation. In only a few case histories is there evidence of firms establishing employment offices with precise, depersonalized application procedures—the norm was for line supervisors to do the hiring, drawing on local connections. John Wanamaker and the Philadelphia Gas Works did create formal departments for employment. In such companies as Perseverance Iron and Schmidt's Brewery, where craft workers succeeded in achieving the closed union shop and control on hiring, hiring became formalized as well. This however, did not make the employment process meritocratic or impersonal, for custom and, in certain instances, written contracts, placed relatives of employees in privileged positions for hire. From the standpoint of the firm, then, securing workers (getting work from the demand side, in other words) remained unformalized through World War II with very few exceptions. Since a growing proportion of enterprises became unionized in the late 1930s and 1940s, and a growing proportion of workers came to work under union contract, the speculation that employment practices, including hiring, became more formalized in the postwar era is easy to draw; that is, among the six kinds of employment circumstances delineated in this chapter, there was a tendency toward formalization through unionization. Yet, any such prediction immediately falters; in many cases, old forms of relations persisted, and practices even in formalized situations diverged within individual firms for different employees and different aspects of the work experience. Unionization in Philadelphia did not necessarily bring greater systematization to the process of getting work, at least within private companies.

There is one form of employment, however, where every effort was made to make the hiring process extremely depersonalized and regularized, a form of employment not mentioned to this point and involving increasing numbers of Philadelphians by mid-twentieth century. Getting work in the public sector has a separate history. In a society marked by an expansive and celebrated free-enterprise system, government employment garners little attention, despite the reality that government has become a leading source of jobs for American working people. I will now turn to the state—the state both as shaper of the labor market and as direct employer.[76]

6 · The State

As early as 1920, the city of Philadelphia emerged as the single largest employer of its citizenry. Twenty thousand Philadelphians then labored in the myriad agencies that comprised city government. A study on getting work in Philadelphia cannot ignore the public sector, and the state as employer will be a major subject of this chapter. The topic of public service employment also provides an opportunity to consider and examine the question of the labor market as a political entity.

Politics and government have no necessary place in economic thinking on the labor market. For mainstream and critical economic theorists alike, the labor market operates through decisions—private decisions, that is—of suppliers and purchasers of labor acting singly or collectively in their specific best interests. That government initiatives affect transactions in the labor market is admitted—after all, government policies on, for example, immigration, schooling, old-age pensioning, trade unionism, and assistance to the disadvantaged shape total labor supply and demand and the respective leverage of workers and employers. Yet government interventions are envisioned by economists as ancillary (and, some would also argue, as meddlesome) to the system or the natural workings of the labor marketplace.

This chapter treats the labor market as a political entity, not just because state actions inevitably affect transactions in the labor market—after all, government interventions involving schooling, employment services, and even company personnel policies have already been covered. The labor market is rather discussed as inherently political because it is a community institution and one that mirrors community values and arrangements of power. Since greater social harmony rests on the proper functioning of the job market, the market also is necessarily a matter of public concern, more than just a point of intersection and negotiation for individual job seekers and employers. In Philadelphia, difficulty in securing jobs and unfair hiring practices in the private sector made for grievances and potential social unrest and demanded attention on the part of the larger community. Nowhere was the subject of obtaining work more fractious and politically heated then in the "getting" of local government positions.[1] Whether in the private or public realm, the process of getting work loomed large as a civic issue. The labor market was and is political.

From William Penn's call for trade education of the young to Progressive-era reform efforts at vocationalism and Americanization programs for immigrant children and workers, the question of the character, competence, and motivation of Philadelphia's work force made the labor market an inescapable community issue. Private attempts by managers to screen, train, and discipline recruits were naturally accompanied by demands for larger public action and collective initiatives by employers. Even when company officials introduced new practices aimed at enhancing the capacities of their personnel, they did so in a public fashion, heralding their experiments as solutions to larger societal as well as specific firm problems. Three examples from the previous chapter will serve as illustrations.

In the 1880s, John Wanamaker introduced a remarkable array of personnel reforms—from testing applicants to weekend retreats for his "store family"—that were decades ahead of their time. Ostensibly, Wanamaker had narrow intentions. The complexity of operations in his grand emporium and the need to build special incentives for salespeople required new kinds of interventions (later, the anti-union objectives of these efforts would be made more explicit). A deeply religious man—Wanamaker was a major contributor to the Presbyterian Church—his programs also reflected his beliefs in Christian charity and stewardship.[2] Yet Wanamaker did not keep his initiatives a secret. He wrote and spoke frequently about his reforms in public forums, authorized the publication of several, needless to say celebratory, store histories, and volunteered testimony to various congressional investigations on the then current state of relations between capital and labor in the United States. Wanamaker was a decidedly public figure, serving as Postmaster General of the country and as a senatorial and gubernatorial candidate.[3] He intended the administration of his department store to be testimony to the merits of a benevolent capitalism; it was a public statement.

John B. Stetson had more obvious headaches and concerns than Wanamaker. Hatmakers were a notoriously stubborn lot and staunch unionists; in fact, Stetson's hat company remained for decades one of the few non-unionized firms in this country in the trade.[4] Stetson then had clear motives for experimenting with a gamut of paternalistic programs that rivaled Wanamaker's. He, too, was a deeply religious man and an active Baptist. But he also acted for more than private reasons. Stetson intended his firm to be an example of a better way of conducting business, one that engendered greater social harmonies. Stetson's experiments with personnel reforms were well publicized and discussed in the popular press, business journals, and academic publications. In Philadelphia, the company became a community institution. Stetson built his factory complex with great attention to its physical appearance; the main building featured a magnificent clock tower that was among the city's great attractions. The firm seemed to be forever in the public eye (and ear, with the Stetson chorus on radio). During both world wars, Stetson's managers and employees assumed a leading and well-noted role in voluntary war bond and scrap material drives.[5] The firm was a model.

The personnel reforms of Wanamaker and Stetson can be approached with great cynicism: public ceremony for private gain. Such a bald interpretation misses a number of important points. The cynical argument sees Wanamaker and Stetson as straightforward profit-maximizers. But why did these two men choose to seek greater returns for their businesses through complicated and, in some instances, costly, benevolent programs? More stringent measures might have been employed in their place. Simple materialistic or so-called rational-choice explanations fail to account for variations in the behavior of employers or appreciate the social dynamics and tensions involved in organizing the productive process, motivating workers, and extracting labor. Cultural factors, such as both entrepreneurs' deeply held religious convictions, similarly are not calculated. Most important, the cynical view treats economic activity entirely as a private matter, not recognizing the public dimensions of all personal acts. Wanamaker and Stetson could not and did not operate in a void. As members of a community, they were necessarily affected by (and in turn, affected) the social norms and tensions of the society about them. They chose to respond positively as reformers, exemplifying the merits of a new benevolent capitalist order; had they fashioned their businesses on simple cash nexus relationships, that would have constituted a public commentary and statement as well.

Frederick Winslow Taylor, a third example, was also a propagandist. But that is all he shared with John Wanamaker and John B. Stetson. Taylor grew up in a Quaker household. If he had a religious sensibility at all, it was accordingly private. (Among the community of Quaker businessmen with whom Taylor associated, however, there would soon be an important movement toward outward benevolent labor practices, as will be noted shortly.) Taylor, from an early age, seemed to be grounded in the material here and now. In contrast to Wanamaker and Stetson, he introduced production and personnel reforms not in his own enterprise; he served rather as a consultant to others. And, also unlike them, he had open disdain for paternalistic efforts at engendering loyalty and discipline. His views became entirely technocratic and mechanistic. The productive process could be studied and organized in a completely efficient fashion, and with each person responsible for a highly specific task and rewarded appropriately per operation performed, a cornucopia of goods and services would flow from the system.

Taylor, however, never remained content simply to study his clients' enterprises and suggest changes to boost productivity. The main role he played in the scientific management movement of his time was as chief proselytizer. He advertised his alleged accomplishments widely, spoke to anyone who cared to listen, including congressmen and other public officials, and gathered about him a score of disciples to help spread the word and the work—characteristically, subsequent schisms among the converted would tear apart the crusade.[6] Taylor presented his techniques as more than panaceas for worker intransigence and unrest; he forecast an efficiently organized world where all material needs would be satisfied.

In their deeds and words, Wanamaker, Stetson, and Taylor, if not consciously, made the mobilization of labor and the commonweal intertwined matters. The shape of the labor market was a critical issue for them. Although their actual reforms applied to single (or in Taylor's case, sets of) enterprises, they played constant public roles. At times, concern for the character of the labor force could also impel cooperative and clearly overt action on the part of businessmen. A prime case in point is provided by the previously mentioned Metal Manufacturers' Association (MMA) of Philadelphia. The activities of this organization show hòw the labor market is fashioned by larger collective efforts as well as by seemingly private decisions.

The Metal Manufacturers' Association of Philadelphia was formed in 1904 as part of a nationwide effort of employers in the metal and machine trades to counter the growing power of unionized workers. In Philadelphia, the Iron Molders' Union had successfully organized, by the turn of the new century, more than 90 percent of the pattern makers and molders employed in the city's casting foundries; in metal tool and machine building concerns, machinists, drill press operators and others had also organized, though not as conclusively, under the banner of the International Association of Machinists. Prosperous times and an expanding economy had placed these highly skilled workers in an advantageous bargaining position. Major efforts at conciliation, including a historic nationwide agreement aimed at bringing peace to the industry, had proved unsatisfactory to all parties concerned, and by 1904 metal trades employers in Philadelphia had become collectively hardened in their thinking.[7]

Leading metal fabricating firms in the city such as the Baldwin Locomotive Works and Midvale Steel did not participate in this collective effort. The majors in the field had the resources to forestall unionization; they paid the highest wages in town and invested most heavily in training workers and maintaining their skills. The concerns enrolled in the MMA were largely small-to-medium-sized, with an average employment of seventy-two operatives.[8] Initially, too, the group had only vague intentions in mind; their founding constitution called mainly for discussion of common problems.[9] Yet within a year members of the organization had chosen and focused on a definitive strategy. Shop-floor stability could be established, they concluded, only through deliberate control of the labor market. The hiring process had to be collectively regulated and workers in the industry carefully screened. Employers in the metals industry needed no academic discourses to know that the labor market was a political and not just a private matter.

The first order of business then became the creation of the Labor Bureau of the Metal Manufacturers' Association of Philadelphia, an agency intended to monitor the labor force in the metal trade. Firms joining the association agreed to provide the secretary of the MMA with a list of all employees and information about their skills and dates of hire and severance as well as evaluations of their "industriousness and good habits."[10] As firms employed and discharged employees, they were required to update the files compiled by the bureau. In addition to serving as a data bank on employment, the Bureau also acted as an official placement service for the local industry. Workers seeking positions in the trade were informed that they should register with the Bureau and provide their personal and occupational histories, details of their prior union experience and involvement, and references. When job openings occurred in member firms, the firms alerted the Bureau and were then able to interview applicants referred to them by the office. Within a year, the labor market in the metal trades in Philadelphia (with the exception of firms such as Baldwin, Midvale, and Cramp's) became completely controlled by the local industry's association of employers.

The Labor Bureau soon played a direct role too in quelling labor unrest. A first test for the MMA occurred in 1904, when the Iron Molders' Union requested wage increases and the elimination of certain types of piecework. Surviving records of the MMA reveal how the new organization, through its Labor Bureau, assisted its president, George Cresson, in his firm's entanglement with the IMU. When iron molders in his company walked off their jobs after having their demands unmet, Cresson sought the services of the Bureau. The office supplied him with referrals, and with a new, Bureau-screened work force, he was able to maintain production during the strike. More than 250 recruits were in fact provided to Cresson and other manufacturers during the dispute, and this initiative greatly contributed to the demise of the IMU-called job action, and indeed the IMU. The Bureau monitored newly hired men so effectively that the agency was able to weed out union infiltrators. The defeat of the IMU actually allowed Cresson to declare his plant once again an open shop, and he was quite grateful. "My experience is only one of many such cases," he informed MMA members, "and what the Association has accomplished for us can be done for you likewise, and greater things also for better understanding between the employer and employees in this great manufacturing city."[11]

A precedent and pattern in the industry had thus been established. Workers went on strike and the Labor Bureau supplied nonunion workers to sustain output. Few unions in the metal trades in Philadelphia could withstand the onslaught. Here is how the secretary of the Metal Manufacturers' Association described the organization's successful campaign against the Brass Workers' Union: "As the result of the continued defeat of the Union [in strikes broken by recruits from the Labor Bureau], a large number of the better mechanics refused to continue paying dues, and its membership decreased to such an extent that about one year ago the office of [union] Business Agent was abolished, and the incumbent impelled to go to work. Since then we have had no trouble."[12]

Even companies not members of the MMA drew on its services. In July 1905, for example, machinists at Warren Webster and Company began a work stoppage for higher wages and a reduction of the work week from sixty to fifty-four hours. The Labor Bureau helped the company to hire new workers and reestablish an open shop. The firm had not been a member of the MMA. When the strike was broken, company officials decided to pay their dues, literally, and join the organization.[13]

Not every confrontation with organized metal workers in Philadelphia proved easy for the new cooperative counteroffensive of employers. In October 1905, five hundred molders and coremakers in foundries across the city went on strike on behalf of a twenty-five cent hourly increase in pay. According to surviving documents of the Metal Manufacturers' Association, the Labor Bureau provided three hundred recruits to besieged firms, but the great majority were either coaxed by union men not to cross the picket lines or else were deemed too inexperienced by employers to hold positions. Business conditions had also improved during the year and the demand for labor was high. The Labor Bureau actually made efforts to find workers in surrounding Pennsylvania cities (in Harrisburg, Steelton, Bethlehem, Easton, and Allentown) where the Iron Molders' Union had a lesser hold. The strike dragged on for more than twelve months, and in December 1906 it finally petered out as the firms involved slowly succeeded in replacing approximately three hundred workers through the continued efforts of the Labor Bureau.[14]

By 1907 the once-powerful IMU had for all practical purposes ceased to function in Philadelphia. Only four small foundries continued to bargain with the union and union membership dwindled.[15] Over the course of the next nine years, the presence of the International Association of Machinists also evaporated, and with a defeat for the organization in a strike in 1916 over the eight-hour day, the Metal Manufacturers' Association of Philadelphia reigned without contest in the entire trade (and would do so until the late 1930s, when the society would have to bow to a new inevitability and accept the reality of unionization and collective bargaining brought on by both government action and the efforts of a revitalized trade union movement).[16] In the second decade of the century, metal-worker unions began to refer to Philadelphia as "Scab City" and union officials, embarrassed by the extent of their defeats, refused even to divulge or publicize membership figures for the area.[17]

With the success of the Labor Bureau, the MMA began to refocus its attentions. Control of the labor market in the trade had been achieved. In the 1920s, the Bureau figures only cursorily in the organization's papers. Energies now centered on a range of educational efforts. The MMA established a training school for foremen and supervisors, an industry-wide cooperative apprenticeship program, and, with the support of officials of the Philadelphia Board of Education, a series of presentations for high school students on opportunities for employment in the metal trades. (The organization also advised the Board on new manual-arts training initiatives in the school system.) The MMA similarly welcomed researchers from the Wharton School at the University of Pennsylvania and opened the files of the Labor Bureau for their studies of employment patterns and trends in the city. This turn toward educational activities reflected the basic success of the organization in controlling the market for labor in the metals trade. It also mirrored the influence of Morris Leeds, a Quaker businessman who headed the prestigious firm of Leeds and Northop and who would serve in various leadership positions in the MMA in the 1910s and 1920s. Leeds represented a new breed of Quaker business figure who sought to etch a more harmonious form of labor relations, and his example and presence would alter the direction of the Metal Manufacturers' Association. Leeds also galvanized his fellow Quaker men of industry and commerce into a new group after World War I that would hold further discussions on the state of the labor market. Leeds brought the "carrot" approach to the MMA; meanwhile, the "stick" of the Labor Bureau had already accomplished the collective task of molding a compliant labor force.[18]

Concern for the composition of the city's work force then led businessmen in Philadelphia to act both as individuals and in concert, but in both instances with a constant eye to the larger community. Their personnel reforms and measures aimed at control of the labor market as well as the labor process internal to firms. For the managerial community, that represented stability. For Philadelphia's laboring people, the proper functioning of the labor market also mattered, but in an entirely different way. Stability meant employment. Were sufficient number of jobs available? Would workers have access to them?

Getting work for workers, like getting workers for employers, was more than a private matter involving just isolated job seekers. Men and women in search of employment in Philadelphia operated within networks of family and friends. Labor unions similarly attempted to control the labor market in as collusionary a way as associated businessmen, achieving stability on their own terms. But securing jobs was a public question for a more profound reason. Obstacles to employment that made for personal suffering could also spawn greater collective grievance and unrest. The proper functioning of the labor market was accordingly a community issue, requiring not just the intervention of businessmen, labor officials, and philanthropically minded citizens (who created agencies, for example, to help wayward girls and other supposedly defenseless women in their forays through the jungle of the marketplace), but also that of state officials responsible for maintaining greater social order. While government officers might face and bow to pressure from business and reform groups and even organized labor, the imperative to keep the peace demanded nonparochial views and solutions on their part—to save the interested parties from themselves if need be. Government agents had an independent role to play. The labor market as a community problem necessitating a community response is best illustrated by a series of events involving local government officials in the second decade of this century.

Several developments provide a backdrop to this Philadelphia story. During the late nineteenth and early twentieth centuries, the American economy had been in perpetual crisis—there had been major depressions between 1873 and 1879 and between 1893 and 1897, and severe recessions between 1884 and 1886 and in 1907. These downturns had been marked by extreme social dislocation and tension, producing well-warranted anxiety among property holders and government officials. In 1914, business conditions turned sour again and, in cities such as Philadelphia, unemployment grew to between 10 and 15 percent of the working population.[19] With the growth of large-scale industry, alienation on the shop floor also seemed on the rise, evident in the extraordinary rates of labor turnover, and this development spurred additional worry and discussion. Labor radicalism and socialist activity, at their peak in many parts of the country, added to a sense of turmoil. Philadelphia had remained relatively quiet—the city witnessed a short-lived tumultuous general strike in 1910 and the Industrial Workers of the World (the Wobblies) had gained support among local longshoremen—but the anti-union initiatives of the Metal Manufacturers' Association and others had had their intended sobering effects.[20] Still, mushrooming unemployment in 1914 and 1915 spelled trouble, and demands for action on the part of city officials increased. Then occupying the office of Mayor was a liberal reformer who would quickly accept the challenge.

For three decades, Rudolph Blankenburg had been the galvanizing force for reform groups in Philadelphia, groups that had tirelessly attacked corruption in city government—which had become legion—and demanded the centralization and professionalization of the provision of municipal services. In 1912, a split in the ranks of Philadelphia's party bosses led to a victory for Blankenburg in the mayoral race.[21] To bring more efficient and benign management to city government, Blankenburg made a notable appointment. He chose Morris Cooke to be Director of Public Works; it would be Cooke, with Blankenburg's encouragement, who, in response to rising unemployment in 1914, would treat the city's labor market as a definite community entity and problem.

Morris Llewellyn Cooke grew up in a Quaker household and was trained as a mechanical engineer at Lehigh University. After entering into practice as a managerial consultant, Cooke became a close associate of his neighbor, Frederick Winslow Taylor. Taylor arranged for Cooke to become director of the American Society of Mechanical Engineers, and in that position Cooke began to encourage members of the society to apply their expertise to political and social problems, to extend scientific management to the civic realm. Cooke's reputation soon grew as an advisor to the Interstate Commerce Commission and other government agencies, and on that basis Taylor personally recommended Cooke to Mayor Blankenburg for appointment as Director of Public Works. Street lighting, water supply, road construction, and garbage and snow removal would come under his purview, areas of city government notorious for boondoggles, spoilsmanship, and rampant inefficiencies. Once in office, Cooke launched a dramatic crusade, ousting political cronies from jobs, adopting new budgeting and accounting techniques, establishing monitoring systems for contracts, reclassifying and standardizing positions, and upgrading the technical resources of the department. The legend of Cooke as a progressive government manager grew and he would eventually move from Philadelphia to serve first as director of various federal emergency projects during World War I and later in Roosevelt's New Deal administration.[22]

In December of 1914, as unemployment in the city worsened, Mayor Blankenburg naturally turned to Cooke for solutions. Cooke immediately established a task force of leading Philadelphia businessmen.[23] They agreed that a full-scale study of employment trends in the city was necessary and that Cooke should appoint an expert to study the workings of the local labor market and make recommendations for public and private action. They also decided to constitute themselves as a permanent group devoted to analyzing and countering employment problems. On the basis of this mandate, Cooke conducted a search for an investigator and chose a young man, Joseph Willits, who was then an instructor in industry at the Wharton School of Finance and Commerce of the University of Pennsylvania.

The Wharton School today is commonly thought of as a training ground for future wheelers-and-dealers in finance, real estate, and industry. At the time, the school still followed the mandate of its founder, Joseph Wharton, successful Philadelphia iron and steel magnate, who hoped the institution would breed a generation of young men dedicated to virtuous and efficient administrative service, particularly in government.[24] The faculty included Simon Patten, a leading social critic, who recruited Edmund James, Leo Rowe, Clyde King, and Scott Nearing, distinguished scholars who believed society's ills could be ameliorated through investigation and government intervention. The Wharton professors also deliberately extended their activities outside the academy. They formed the American Academy of Social and Political Science, and the journal of the organization, *The Annals,* featured articles on the personnel reforms of John B. Stetson and other benevolent capitalists as well as reports on early government welfare programs in Europe and the United States. Some of the Wharton professors further lent their names and expertise to genteel reform associations, such as the Philadelphia Municipal Reform League, while others, like Scott Nearing, played active roles in more radical groups, such as the Consumers' League and the Socialist Party.[25]

Joseph Willits, however, represented a different generation of Wharton faculty members. The liberal ideas and activities of Simon Patten and his followers began to draw the fire of conservatives both inside and outside the university, and by the second decade of the twentieth century the trustees of Wharton moved to alter the direction of the institution. As Emory Johnson, their newly appointed dean of the school and a former consultant to the railroad industry, pointedly stated the case, promoters of social welfare had only been concerned with the "*distribution* of wealth"; attention now should focus on "facilitating the *production* of wealth."[26] The older generation of Wharton activists soon found their positions at the university threatened. In a series of famous incidents, Scott Nearing was fired from the school for his too-strong advocacy of child labor laws and Simon Patten for his opposition to American involvement in World War I.[27]

Joseph Willits had actually come to Wharton to study under Patten and others and he was completing his graduate work and serving as an instructor when Morris Cooke selected him to conduct research for the city on Philadelphia's labor market. Willits's reaction to the banishment of his mentors is not known, but his work was already taking a different turn. Patten and Nearing had been in the university, but not of it. They were part of a pioneer generation of Progressive-era social science investigators and critics who were bent on changing the world first and serving as academics second. By the time Joseph Willits entered graduate school, reform zeal was on the wane, radicalism was under attack, and the academic life loomed as an end in itself.

Joseph Willits throughout his life was a champion of social science research, but his career was primarily dedicated to furthering the enterprise of scholarship itself (and social change only very indirectly).[28] On the basis of his studies on employment in 1915, he received an appointment as superintendent of personnel in the Navy Yards in Philadelphia during World War I. Returning to Wharton after the war, he convinced the Carnegie Corporation to subsidize the establishment of an Industrial Research Department at the school. Willits became chief fund raiser and director of the operation, hiring a remarkable group of young women researchers, among them Gladys Palmer (to whom this book is dedicated), who conducted and produced a series of classic reports on labor market trends and changing industrial relations.[29] Willits saw his researchers as neutral observers and investigators, but he loaned the services of the IRD to the Metal Manufacturers' Association of Philadelphia in return for access to vital employment information. By the end of the 1920s, he had emerged as a expert in labor markets and labor relations and was asked to serve on a number of federal investigative committees. Willits soon moved on to more significant and greener pastures as an academic entrepreneur, accepting a position as director of social sciences for the Rockefeller Foundation, where for decades he played a powerful national role as promoter and dispenser of funds for social science research projects.[30]

Joseph Willits may not have shared the generational experiences of his mentors or their activist instincts, but he produced a report for Morris Cooke in 1915 that his teachers could applaud. *Philadelphia Unemployment with Special Reference to the Textiles Industries* is a classic study of the labor market. In a few short months, Willits completed impressive research, visiting firms and analyzing their employment and personnel records, interviewing managers and workers, and reading through government documents, trade association and union journals, and local newspapers. He framed his final report to Cooke around a singular finding. Willits had discovered a fact of economic and social existence little appreciated at the time or even now by students of American history, namely that employment in an industrial city such as Philadelphia was highly irregular. Few firms in the city operated normally fifty-two weeks a year; few Philadelphians worked even close to a full complement of possible working days. Irregular commerce in general led to fluctuations in production and employment, but as Willits noted, the problem in Philadelphia was extreme. The manufacture of custom and seasonal goods made for chronic unsteady conditions. Willits, however, did not remain content to blame the situation on unalterable market realities. Short-sighted decision making on the part of firm owners, government officials, and consumers alike exacerbated circumstances. The problem was not entirely structural; it was one also of will. As Willits wrote, "Unemployment is primarily a question of industry and industrial organization."[31] He accordingly ended his report with a lengthy set of recommendations.

Willits aimed the great majority of his suggestions at employers. He argued first that a change of attitude was imperative; then he listed his specific reforms. "At the outset," Willits began, "it must be accepted as a fundamental principle that each employing concern should regard itself as one industrial family for the welfare of whose members the concern is responsible in the way in which the head of a private family is responsible for its members."[32] In order to combat the direct and indirect costs of labor turnover, he recommended the following: that firms should analyze and monitor their production records more carefully, change their accounting systems to factor in costs of slack time, coordinate the manufacture and selling of goods more deliberately and avoid heavy reliance on sales agents, improve the accessing and flow of materials to eliminate lost time, standardize products, centralize and rationalize hiring, limit hirings and take workers on payroll only if willing to keep them on a permanent basis, train recruits in varied tasks, spread work and engage in plant repairs and new pursuits in down times, keep records on severances, and offer employees advanced notice of layoffs and financial help during furloughs.[33] More deliberation on employment matters in general was in order, and Willits advised firm owners to consider appointing a personnel manager to oversee the smooth allocation of human resources and foster ties with the community.

Government too had a role to play. Willits suggested that the city rationalize its own employment procedures to insure a steady work flow. In periods of economic contraction the city also had a responsibility to provide relief (ideally unemployment insurance) and public works jobs, but Willits argued that city officials would be better advised to enact preventive measures. He thus strongly recommended that the municipality establish a public employment bureau to facilitate contacts between job seekers and employers.[34] For Willits, access to information or the lack of it represented a key element in the problem of irregular employment. A city job placement office would be an essential clearinghouse for notices of openings; Willits's report, along with Mayor Blankenburg's and Morris Cooke's rising concern, would in fact contribute to the passage of legislation in 1915 establishing a statewide system of labor exchanges in Pennsylvania. Willits also counseled that the success of any public job placement initiative would rest on coordinating efforts with the vocational education and guidance programs of the public schools. Saturating the young with information on the labor market would smooth their transition into the work-a-day world and help them in future job searches.

Willits suggested that consumers had responsibilities as well. He pleaded with the public to refuse to "follow extreme styles." Purchasing standardized products would make for regularized production and work schedules. "Hire a man," too, in bad times.[35] Everyone, in other words, could contribute to maintaining steady and high levels of employment.

Willits submitted his extensive findings and recommendations to Morris Cooke. Cooke did not act formally on Willits's suggestions; the report's influence would be more indirect. The study, as noted, became an important ingredient in the enactment of legislation leading to the creation of public employment bureaus in Pennsylvania. The report also became a component of a larger discourse and crusade on behalf of personnel reform and the ordering of the labor market. Willits submitted his manuscript to the Wharton School to fulfill the thesis requirements of his Ph.D. degree program. The editors of *The Annals of the American Academy of Political and Social Science* then chose to publish Willits's work almost in its entirety.[36] The study thus reached a larger audience. His article in fact served as the centerpiece for a rush of essays printed in the *Annals* and other social science journals calling for the institution of rationalized employment practices by government and firm officials alike.[37] "Personnel management" became a new catch phrase, to rival "scientific management," of an emerging, well-articulated, and organized movement that included advocates of vocational education and guidance, government reformers, liberal academics, and progressive-minded business managers.[38] Public order as well as private profits, spokesmen such as Willits argued, demanded deliberate initiatives on the mobilization and allocation of labor, on the processes of getting and maintaining work.

As part of his effort unambiguously to link state action—the political—to the labor market, Morris Cooke had also established a permanent group of civic and business leaders to consider and act on employment issues. Initially dubbed "The Philadelphia Association for the Discussion of Employment Problems," its members first met in June of 1915 to consider such subjects as: "methods of securing new employees . . . selection, hiring and assignment . . . labor turnover and discharge . . . classification of work . . . training within the organization . . . conditions of work . . . vacations . . . fluctuations in employment . . . and wages and bonuses."[39] The group received and used Joseph Willits's report. Unfortunately, records for the association have not survived; its membership, activities, and even tenure are impossible to determine, although its actual creation is significant. Whatever the group's ultimate accomplishments, its work would continue and be superseded by another committee formed by leading Philadelphia citizens in 1917 to deliberate and move on employment problems. This final example involves the evolving history of Quakerism in the Quaker City and the career of another remarkable business and civic figure, Morris Leeds.

In the late nineteenth century, personnel reform had been the work (and calling) of religiously inspired businessmen such as John B. Stetson and John Wanamaker, who were Baptists and Presbyterians by and large, not Quakers. For all their reform zeal, in abolitionism particularly, Philadelphia Quakers remained surprisingly silent on the great questions of the new modern age about the respective rights and powers of Capital and Labor.[40] Philadelphia Quakers manifested notable concern for the plight of the needy and persecuted, but only those in far-off places—freedmen in the South, Native Americans in the West, and the mentally ill in asylums. Perhaps as an influential and disproportionately large component of the employer class in the city, Quakers could not reconcile their direct economic interests with their religious beliefs. The Quaker ideal of social harmony in fact led them to be sharply critical of unions and of what they perceived as the inherently antagonist stance of labor organizations.[41] Quakers characteristically did not join with the Social Gospel movement then mobilizing concerned Protestants.

In the first decades of the twentieth century, Philadelphia's Quakers began to confront social issues closer to home. They followed in this way the lead of their counterparts in Great Britain. British Quakers had not shied from the tensions of the new urban industrial age. They had translated their religious convictions into active involvement in settlement house work, social survey research and reportage, government welfare reform, and even Socialist politics. Quaker businessmen in Britain had also moved to bring their ethical beliefs and business practices into accord; a number of them instituted benefit programs and experiments in industrial democracy in their firms that attracted wide attention.[42] Morris Leeds for one came under the influence of the British Quakers and began to use the forum of Friends' meetings in Philadelphia to persuade the city's Quaker community of their immediate social responsibilities.

Morris Leeds was born in Philadelphia in 1869 and schooled in local Quaker institutions. Upon graduation from Haverford College he pursued graduate studies in biology in Germany. He returned to the United States uncertain about a career in research and teaching and went to work instead for a Philadelphia supply company of scientific instruments. In 1903 he teamed up with Edwin Northrup, a physicist and engineer, to found the firm of Leeds and Northrup, which became and remains a highly respected major producer of sophisticated electrical measuring and control devices. Leeds would eventually buy out his partner and administer the enterprise as sole proprietor.[43]

Leeds assumed a definite public persona within a short time of his entering into business. He joined the fledgling Metal Manufacturers' Association of Philadelphia, served on its executive council, and with great determination succeeded in refocusing the association's activities toward education and vocational training. Leeds used meetings of the MMA to persuade businessmen to act in more charitable ways toward labor. He used his own firm to show the way. In addition to establishing a personnel department to rationalize employment, Leeds created for his employees a stock purchasing plan, a representation committee to air grievances and suggestions, various bonus systems, and tuition subsidy and life and unemployment insurance programs. These initiatives brought him to the forefront of the emerging movement on behalf of liberal business practices. In the late 1920s and early 1930s, moreover, Leeds joined an influential group of company executives, many from the new electrical goods industry, who called for greater macro-level economic planning and cooperation between government and business officials.[44]

Leeds accepted as his public duty not only the task of persuading businessmen to effect harmonious industrial relations, but also the role of moving his fellow Philadelphia Quakers toward active concern and involvement in the social problems of their city and times. Leeds became a frequent speaker at Friends' meetings and conferences, urging his coreligionists to join the social reform movement, "to fit ourselves to play our part in helping society so to mold its conscious will that it will proceed with orderly activity to progressive steps of social betterment."[45] Leeds spoke especially of the responsibilities of the relatively large number of Quaker businessmen in the city, coaxing them to follow the example of their peers in Great Britain. During one talk before a Quaker audience he drew attention to the question of the employer's duty to maintain high levels of employment through proper administration:

> The directors of commercial enterprises may do considerable to further the cause of economic justice in spite of the limitations placed on them by general conditions. They may, for instance, see that their own establishments maintain as good standards in wages and working conditions as is possible in their trade. One of the great causes of distress among the poor is the irregularity of work. It seems to me that this might be considerably reduced if all employers recognized a responsibility to their employees and were careful to plan their enterprises with a safe margin of resources so that it would not be necessary to suddenly discontinue them on suspicion of unfavorable times.[46]

Leeds, as a single advocate and combatant, failed to generate a great change of heart among his fellow Quakers in Philadelphia. Events in Europe would serve as a better catalyst. When the United States entered the war in the spring of 1917, Philadelphia Quakers refused to take up arms. As part of their claim to conscientious objector status, they pledged service in European relief efforts. Out of this commitment emerged an organization, the American Friends' Service Committee, and it was while fulfilling their nonmilitary obligations that Quakers in Philadelphia moved toward greater social activism. Their work for the AFSC also brought them into direct contact with British Quakers, whose politics by that time had become even more radical. Morris Leeds, for one, attended a series of Quaker meetings in London devoted to discussions of social issues, including several on the inequities of the capitalist system. On the basis of his participation, Leeds returned to Philadelphia and established the Business Problems Group. Quaker businessmen, he argued in gathering support for his initiative, must "be concerned with the problems of the relations between employees and employers in industries."[47]

Fortunately, records and transcripts of meetings of the Business Problems Group survive and they reveal the labor market as a public and political matter. The BPG initially included executives from seven firms; by 1920 fifty companies were represented, and by 1924, more than one hundred.[48] Quakers comprised the vast majority of participants. Morris Leeds personally sought new members, and his letters of invitation indicate that the group operated in many respects as an extension of the Friends' meeting. To Charles Huston, Vice President and Works Manager of the Lukens Steel Company, he thus wrote: "Would thee be inclined to join the Business Problems Group . . . This group is intended to include all of the men who care to join it who are members of the Yearly Meeting and who are actively engaged in business as owners or managers . . . The whole object of our association is to try to discover what are the Christian obligations of employers to their employees and to the public."[49]

Huston accepted Leeds's offer, and although he was unable to attend many meetings, he did receive from Leeds voluminous materials, including notes of conferences. Among the documents circulated by Leeds to participants were reports on the good works of British Quaker businessmen, particularly their reform measures on wages, working conditions, security of employment, and the distribution of so-called surplus profits. The actual meetings of the Business Problems Group included formal presentations. For example, on June 8, 1920, members met at the Miller Lock Company to hear a talk delivered by company managers on recent personnel initiatives. Executives of the firm spoke at length about the costs and impact of new provisions for medical and dental care for employees, the installation of a cafeteria and recreation room, their new Participation Board (where employees aired complaints), and a recently established profit-sharing plan.[50]

On February 7, 1921, the group convened in the more comfortable quarters of the City Club to hear the redoutable Morris Cooke speak on the problem of unemployment. Cooke characteristically stressed the role employers should play in stabilizing employment through better record keeping, rationalized hiring practices, and closer attention to production scheduling.[51] The question of irregular employment appears to have been a prominent issue. Several months later,

Joseph Willits addressed the group on the same topic. His talk echoed the findings and suggestions of his 1915 report to the city, though he spoke now with even greater urgency.[52] 1921 was a particularly busy year for members of the Business Problems Group. A month before Willits's presentation, the association had heard from the great British Quaker social investigator and reformer, Seebohm Rowntree. Rowntree generated a long and agitated discussion of his talk, "The Human Factor in Business," which concerned the uncertainty and irregularity of employment.[53] In fact, this theme loomed as a common thread and concern in the seven years of BPG meetings for which records survive. The labor market did not involve just individuals, disparate suppliers and employers of labor; it was a community entity and problem.

Existing papers of the Business Problems Group offer few clues about its ultimate fate and impact. Exactly when the association disbanded is impossible to determine. Similarly, it is unclear just how many participants, Quakers or otherwise, were moved to initiate personnel reforms. It is tempting either to dismiss this venture or to overemphasize its importance. A similar temptation exists in considering the private but most public acts of a John Wanamaker, the collective interventions of the businessmen who congregated in the Metal Manufacturers' Association of Philadelphia, and the efforts of the political, business, and academic figures that culminated in Willits's report. Magnifying the significance of the above activities would be to take the pronouncements and prescriptions of elite groups and equate them with reality. Studies of the workplace, such as those briefly rendered in the previous chapter, reveal that events on the shop floor rarely transpired according to plan. Daily exigencies, constant contingencies, and personal relations—the sway of local supervisors, the informal and organized resistances of workers—made the best hopes of elites often wishful thinking.

Should we then make light of the public initiatives of business, political, and civic reformers and innovators? That tack, too, would miss a more basic point. What is significant is the dialogue itself. In Philadelphia in the late nineteenth and early twentieth centuries, a remarkable discussion unfolded, involving a circle of men whose paths crossed in church, at clubs, over lunch and dinner, at meetings and conferences, and in the pages of the newspapers and journals they read. These men of influence, particularly businessmen, began to advocate positive incentives toward labor over the simple cash nexus. They even favored government interventions to smooth the wrinkles of the labor market and the economy in general. With such actions, they were paving the way and contributing with other, often opposing, groups to the building of the (albeit hybrid and minimal) liberal, corporate, capitalist system that marks this country today—to the network of unemployment and old age assistance programs, workmen's compensation benefits, public job placement services, labor arbitration boards, and arrays of firm-level protections and benefits for workers. When elite opinion changed, institutional change was in the offing. The Stetsons, Leedses, Cookes, and Willitses played a part in ushering in the new order and also in making a matter that was latently but at base political become openly and obviously so.

The mobilization of labor entailed problems and issues beyond the ken and control of the individual employer; the competence, motivation, and even size of the work force involved decisions and developments of a societal nature. Employers had to act with an eye to the larger community in which they operated, and they often resorted to collective efforts to control the labor marketplace (as did various suppliers of labor). Social harmony, moreover, rested on the smooth workings of the labor market and government action was often necessary. Getting work, in other words, was political. For employment in the private sector, the above conclusions are not self-evident. In the realm of public service work, however, little was hidden; there, the recruitment and organization of labor was blatantly political. Public employment is an intriguing subject not just because it is a topic virtually ignored by economists and historians, but also because getting labor in public works was a repeatedly examined issue with constant initiatives and attempts to rationalize the process. There are many ironies here. In private enterprises, where competitive pressures demanded strict adherence to cost-conscious practices, personnel procedures remained remarkably informal and personalized. In the public sphere, where the profit motive did not exist, great energies have been devoted to rendering the process of labor mobilization and allocation finely meritocratic and standardized. Philadelphia provides a most colorful history of the public employment process.

In a nation that boasts openly of the wonders of the free-enterprise system, it is not surprising that public-sector work attracts so little attention. Yet it cannot be ignored, for approximately one American in five today is on a public payroll, federal, state, or local. In modern-day Philadelphia, municipal employment has always represented a major segment of available jobs. By the first decade of the twentieth century, when officials began publishing comprehensive reports on city workers, thirteen thousand Philadelphians worked directly for the municipality (this does not include seven thousand public school teachers, who came under the jurisdiction of the state education system).[54] Municipal employment (minus teachers) grew to nineteen thousand by 1925 and twenty-five thousand by 1930; already the city had become the single largest employer of its citizenry.[55] Layoffs during the years of the Great Depression brought the city's payrolls back down to twenty thousand by 1940.[56] World War II and a postwar expansion of city services allowed the numbers of local government workers to rise again to twenty-five thousand by 1950.[57] Surprisingly, there has been only a gradual increase in municipal employment since then. By the 1970s, the city of Philadelphia employed thirty thousand men and women to staff its multiplicity of agencies.[58] Expansion of public employment—the growth of the state—is often thought of as a modern or post–New Deal phenomenon, but for a city such as Philadelphia, the heart of the municipal employment force was already in place by the 1920s. Philadelphia's municipal work force also continues to represent a heavy cost to its residents. Close to 60 percent of annual tax revenues raised locally has consistently over the past century been spent on the salaries and benefits of the city's employees.[59]

The municipality hires not only a large contingent of people, but also a highly diverse occupational group. In 1920, the city published for the first time a complete list and description of positions comprising the municipal service. No less than 663 different kinds of jobs were advertised. Included were positions from ambulance chauffeur to clock attendant, herdsman, traffic statistician, and writ server.[60] The city's public work force continued to diversify. A new manual of jobs issued in 1950 contained more than nine hundred different occupational titles.[61]

City officials in Philadelphia have organized this complex work force into an ever-shifting score of agencies. In general, however, throughout the twentieth century, 25 percent of all city employees have been occupied in the maintenance of law and order, namely in the police department. Fifteen percent have been engaged in the repair and cleaning of city streets and trash removal. More than 10 percent have served in public health centers and hospitals, another 10 percent in fighting fires, 5 percent in staffing the city's court system, and 4 percent in the upkeep of Philadelphia's extensive parks. The remaining city employees have worked to maintain municipal buildings and facilities, operate the city's libraries, collect taxes, inspect buildings, provide public recreational services, guard the city's criminal inmates, handle welfare registration and check disbursement, and push paper in the countless small offices that comprise the complex of City Hall.[62]

The management of this large number of employees is a major undertaking in itself. In 1912, for example, when the city first compiled and published figures on the recruitment and allocation of municipal workers, the city received 14,000 applications, administered 193 different civil service examinations to the 4,000 applicants who reported for testing, and placed the 3,000 individuals who passed muster.[63] By the 1950s, this process had ballooned. In 1953, the city received 100,000 inquiries, processed 48,775 applications, arranged for 34,215 civil service tests, notified the 10,479 who passed of their eligibility, and appointed 4,543 to actual jobs.[64] A large staff of clerks now employed in the city's personnel department attended to recruitment, but they also had responsibility for the 5,300 transfers that had been filed in 1953 and the 5,800 separations from service (due to voluntary leaves, illness, deaths, and disciplinary discharges). City government grew just to facilitate the growth of city government.

Why did the municipal work force in a city such as Philadelphia steadily expand to the point where local government became the single largest employer of the city's working population? The increase in public workers is not a new development, associated with the rise of the modern welfare state; a large corps of workers already existed by the 1910s and 1920s. The story starts in the nineteenth century and the reasons for growth can be neatly summarized: disease, population and geographic expansion, violence, safety, commerce, economic depressions, and war.

The physical well-being of the inhabitants of the city first demanded an expansion of public services and, in turn, the creation of a public work force. From the 1790s through the 1860s, Philadelphia was plagued by repeated epidemics of cholera and other diseases. The pollution of private wells by private privy systems proved the primary cause and Philadelphia in fact became the first city in the world to develop a public water and sewer system. The building of reservoirs and filtration facilities and the laying of water and sewer lines required a large work force. Initially, private contractors conducted construction, but eventually the city assumed direct administration of the maintenance and expansion of the system. Accounting and billing alone demanded a small army of clerks—in the 1850s, for example, 700 Philadelphians each day squeezed into the main office of the city's water department to pay their bills. That department became Philadelphia's first large-scale public agency with a sizable clerical staff and crews of construction and maintenance workers. By 1920, 2,000 men and women were employed to guarantee the flow of more than 300,000,000 gallons of fresh water into and the sewage out of the homes of the city's two million people.[65]

Population expansion required expansion of the water works system and its labor force, but also placed great demands on transportation services. Private companies chartered by the city handled both street construction and the building and upkeep of the street railway system. Evidence of extraordinary corruption and poor services eventually forced public takeovers of these services. Street paving and cleaning and waste disposal became the next area for expansion of the municipal work force. By 1920, no less than 3,000 Philadelphians on the city's payroll were responsible for the 1,800 miles of streets in the city and their maintenance and sanitation.[66]

Violence in the city represented a third impetus behind the expansion of the public domain. Religious, racial, and class-based rioting in Philadelphia in the 1840s and a notable increase in personal crimes in the 1850s convinced government leaders that law and order could not be maintained by the small, locally controlled night watch and constabulary. Pressure grew for the creation of a municipal and professional police force, finally established in 1850.[67] Philadelphia's police department did not initially represent the largest contingent of public service workers in the city; by 1920, there were a few more policemen than street cleaners.[68] Relative and absolute expansion of employment in the police department is a post-1950s development; in fact, since 1950, the numbers of policemen on the beat and of staff in the municipal courts have doubled and tripled respectively, while the numbers of employees in all other agencies, with the exception of the welfare department, have remained steady or declined.[69]

Safety in the streets and safety in general led to further expansion in the civil service. The need to light public walkways at night brought into existence a large public bureaucracy, the Philadelphia Gas Works. The production of gas, the laying of gas lines, and the installation of meters required a large corps of workers; the handling of customers and accounts required another. In the 1870s, the Gas Works needed a growing clerical staff just to process the thirty thousand requests received each year for repairs and new service.[70]

Lighting the streets enabled the public to see dangers in front of them, but there were other impediments to safety and health, beyond the view of most citizens, that required local government inspection and regulation. New technologies forced the opening of municipal offices for the inspection of buildings, elevators, and boilers; the health of the population—including its moral well-being as seen by certain reformers—similarly demanded the licensing and scrutiny of restaurants and saloons.[71]

When safety measures failed or were neglected, the disasters that struck spurred public responses that contributed to the swelling of the ranks of the municipal work force. Fire proved an even greater scourge than cholera in the nineteenth-century city. Volunteer fire brigades could provide adequate service up to a point; the raucous behavior of the volunteers and their activity in local ward politics, however, brought calls in Philadelphia and elsewhere for their demise and for the creation of centralized, publicly administered fire departments. Government officials in the Quaker City established a unified and professional force in 1870, and by the first decades of the twentieth century the force numbered more than two thousand men.[72] The size of that contingent has remained fairly stable since then.

Expanded commerce also led to increases in governmental activity. Improving transportation in the city to facilitate the growing traffic of goods and people made the streets department a major agency in city government. Wharf areas also demanded attention as Philadelphia grew as a transshipment center and exporter of manufactured goods. A bequest to the city of $500,000 by the financier Stephen Girard, specifically designated for the rebuilding and expansion of the docks and warehouses along the Delaware, resulted in the 1830s in the creation of a new city agency in charge of riverside development and the employment of hundreds of new municipal workers.[73]

Prosperity could foster expanded state services, and so could economic bad times. In every major depression in Philadelphia from 1819 onward, pressure built for increased public works—in Philadelphia's federal arsenals and shipyards as well as on the city's streets.[74] The city-owned Gas Works proved a favorite place for politicians to initiate make-work projects for the unemployed.[75] Finally, war, as noted earlier, represented a basic ingredient in Philadelphia's economic history and fortunes. Military production, particularly during wartime, brought thousands of Philadelphians onto public payrolls (in this case the federal government's).[76]

The expansion of public work in Philadelphia and the number of local governmental employees thus can be understood by reference to impersonal forces such as disease, population expansion, crime, natural disasters, economic development, and war. Various urban problems emerged, particularly during the nineteenth century, that demanded public activity and an increase in the ranks of public servants. People were also deeply involved in this process and various groups in the city had every reason to support the buildup of municipal services. The great scandals that arose over the contracting out of public work to private enterprises and the persistent sentiment against the dispensing of favors by the state to private parties silenced any voices or movements on behalf of the privatization of public works. Even businessmen, who sang the praises of laissez-fairism, banded together in reform organizations to decry corruption and inefficiency in government (and high taxes), and to argue not for the withering away of the state but for better government, which invariably meant more government and more government workers.[77]

The organization of the large contingent of workers that would comprise the city's public task force by the late nineteenth century, and not its actual existence, did become a matter of political debate and tension. The recuitment of these employees—their "getting"—in particular emerged as an issue of great public concern.

Until the late nineteenth century, control over the provision of most urban services in Philadelphia resided in the city's Common Council.[78] This body of ward politicians created committees to oversee service departments; the committees appointed department heads and approved contracts with private parties. The hold that the Com-

mon Council maintained over municipal works made for some of
the great political scandals of the day. The awarding of contracts was
one major source of corruption. Councilmen, for example, avidly
sought appointment to the committee on the almshouse, but not for
altruistic reasons; that committee selected the Guardians of the Poor,
who controlled lucrative contracts to supply the almshouse. Councilmen could reward their friends and themselves.[79] The Gas Works
were the locus of even larger boondoggles. Again, councilmen appointed trustees to administer the city's gas system; that board in
turn controlled the awarding of $2 million in annual contracts.[80]

Jobs represented the other great prize; patronage served as the
means to build political machines and careers. The trustees of the
Philadelphia Gas Works, for example, appointed by the Gas Committee of Common Council, controlled more than 2,000 positions in
the 1870s and 1880s. The trustees assembled a loyal body of municipal employees who formed the ranks of the Republican Party.
Through family and friends, PGW workers directly marshaled an
estimated 20,000 votes of the total 150,000 cast in local elections in
the period.[81] Committees of Council could easily bail out a zealous
party worker when in trouble. In 1875, for example, the superintendent of the streets department hired 75 men, all political faithfuls,
after the employment of five new workers had been authorized. The
Committee on Streets quickly found funds to keep the recruits on
the city's rolls.[82] The committees of council certainly made honorable
and respected appointments—notable inventors and civil engineers
served as heads of the water and streets departments at various
times—but corruption remained pervasive.[83] Perhaps the best description of the rewarding of contracts and jobs through the committee of council system can be found in an investigative report of the
waterworks in the late 1850s:

> The office of the Chief Engineer on the Water Works is one of
> great power and patronage. That office may appoint the son of one
> member of Council a clerk in the Registrar's office; the nephew of
> another a Water Purveyor; the brother of a third, to attend an
> engine, and a brother-in-law of a fourth to report the height of
> water in a reservoir; or he may appoint one or two prominent and
> influential politicians to superintend repairs, or give them contracts
> to supply stone or oak. So with patronage and disbursements of
> the office. The brother of one member of Council may supply

tallow in large quantities, and the employer of another may supply coal. Thus every member of the Committee on Water Works may have an immediate or indirect pecuniary or personal interest in sustaining an officer that has so many sub-offices, and so much patronage to dispense, no matter what may be his misdoings or malpractices.[84]

"Corruption," of course, is a relative term. People in power—in private enterprise or the public domain—dispense favor and how that is to be interpreted remains a subjective matter. Mayor Robert Conrad appointed only native-born Protestant men to the city's newly established police force in the 1850s, and older stock Philadelphians registered no apprehension or disapproval.[85] When Mayor Richard Vaux, who owed his office to the votes of Irish immigrants, reformed and expanded the police force with Irishmen in the late 1850s, political patronage became a heated issue.[86] In Philadelphia, as in other nineteenth century American cities, politics became an avenue of opportunity for ambitious immigrants and in office they made local government responsive to the employment and welfare needs of their immigrant, working-class constituencies. This was allowed both by the increased numbers and political leverage of newer Americans and the withdrawal of traditional elites from the political life of the city and, in many instances, from the city itself.

The crisis over corruption in political life in the late nineteenth-century American city cannot be separated from the cultural and class tensions and divides of the age. The Irish succeeded especially well in staking claims in the political system. James McManes, an immigrant from Ireland who worked himself up from a textile-mill operative in Philadelphia to a mill owner and real estate developer, also rose from ward healer to a trustee of the Philadelphia Gas Works; from that post, he personally controlled between two and three thousand jobs earmarked for his fellow Irishmen. His very influence led to an exodus of Irish newcomers, especially Irish Protestants, out of the Democratic Party of Jefferson and Jackson to the new Republican Party of Lincoln that came to dominate Philadelphia politics after the Civil War.[87] But ethnic patronage knew no bounds of party. William McMullen became a kingpin maker in the Democratic Party and also an employment agent for Irish arrivals. McMullen was a second generation Irishman who grew up in the Moyamensing section of the city, an area inhabited by Irish common day laborers who worked about the docks of the Delaware River. McMullen's fighting skills brought him into politics; local Democratic officials chose the well-known brawler to serve at polling stations as a judge of voting qualifications. Through his leadership of the raucous Moyamensing Hose Company, he was able to build his own political machine, and in 1856 he was elected alderman, a post he occupied until his death in 1901. McMullen controlled a set of jobs at the Gas Works; through favors, he also had influence over more than forty positions at the Baldwin Locomotive Works. Most of the recipients of his patronage, however, received posts with the federal government. An able ally of Senator Simon Cameron, McMullen was able to place thousands of his constituents and the party faithful from his district in jobs at the Philadelphia Navy Yard and in federal Civil War pension offices in the city.[88]

With the likes of McManes and McMullen wielding power and influence, voices for reform could not be far behind. The 1870s and 1880s saw the formation of a steady stream of organizations dedicated to enobling city government and specifically to championing the end of councilman rule, establishing a strong mayor's office to administer city departments, and adopting meritocratic hiring principles. The Philadelphia Civil Service Reform League and the Committee of One Hundred led the way. These groups were characteristically comprised of leading local business figures, academicians, men of letters, church leaders, and other Philadelphians of status and standing.

In 1885, reform groups succeeded in securing passage in the state legislature of a new charter of government for Philadelphia. Henry Lea, the famous historian and publisher (of the venerable firm of Lea & Febiger) and erstwhile reformer, actually helped draft the new constitution for the city that gained acceptance in Harrisburg. The desire of state political leaders to clip the wings of McManes and others in the city helped reform forces achieve their objectives.[89] The Charter of 1885 greatly curtailed the powers of the committees of Common Council and passed the administration of municipal departments squarely to the mayor's office. Following the lead of the United States government in establishing a competitive examination system for appointment to federal jobs, the legislation of 1885 also created a Civil Service Board for Philadelphia. The board composed of the mayor and heads of municipal departments was charged with instituting tests for applicants to public employment in the city and their placement in jobs on the basis of test results.[90]

The new charter nonetheless failed to still either corruption or further calls for the cleansing of city government. Under the new legislation, committees of Common Council remained in control of more than twenty municipal agencies; the Charter of 1885 in fact succeeded in driving the council's exercise of power out of public notice. More important, the new Civil Service Board hardly curbed spoilsmanship. The mayor and his department chiefs were able to bend the system to their needs, and by 1900 an estimated ten thousand jobs in city government were still distributed to loyal party workers. In return for employment, municipal workers pledged portions of their salaries to the political machine, a longstanding practice that had not been ended with reform legislation. In 1903, investigations revealed that 94 percent of all employees in the city actually paid between 3 and 12 percent of their annual incomes to the coffers of the Republican Party organization for a total take of $349,000.[91] As Theodore Roosevelt said in 1893 as a member of the United States Civil Service Commission of the Charter of 1885, "I should rather have no law than the law you have in Philadelphia."[92]

New tales of corruption brought new calls for the reform of municipal employment. Reform forces succeeded once again in securing legislation at the state level. A bill passed in Harrisburg in 1905 accordingly established a new Civil Service Commission for Philadelphia, a seemingly more independent agency. Under the new charter, the mayor was empowered to appoint a three-member panel with no more than two members of the same party allowed to serve. The bill also provided funding for the hiring of a staff to administer competitive exams and arrange placements and to publish annually the results of their work. Staff members devoted a good deal of their time and energies in the first years to developing a battery of written tests, which were reprinted in the commission's annual report. In addition to the written exams, which tested basic knowledge and verbal, logical, and mathematical abilities, the new commission also began in 1912 to administer practical tests to measure applicants' actual skills, for example in carpentry, stenography, and even cooking. The city contracted with the department of vocational education in the public school system to conduct the testing.[93]

Statistics provided in the early reports of the new Civil Service Commission of Philadelphia offer a limited portrait of the applicants.[94] Who applied for and secured municipal employment in the early decades of the twentieth century? In 1912, the Civil Service

Commission received 14,888 applications for jobs; exams were administered to 11,889 candidates, and 7,185 passed. The group of
applicants as a whole was somewhat older than expected, with an
average age of thirty-four. They were also overwhelmingly native-
born. Ninety percent of the total number of applicants examined
were born in the United States; of applicants for clerical positions,
94 percent were native-born, and for positions as firemen, 97 percent.
Only among those seeking skilled labor positions were there substantial numbers of immigrants, with 15 percent of this pool born in
foreign countries. Place of birth figured only slightly, though, in
the appointment process. Sixty percent of American-born applicants
passed their civil service examinations, while 59 percent of the recent
arrivals to this country did as well. Native-born applicants for clerical
positions and posts in the fire department passed their tests in slightly
greater numbers than the foreign-born. Of all the examinations, the
tests for inspectors proved the most demanding, with only a third of
the examined achieving a grade that made them eligible for placement; here, too, native-born applicants succeeded in greater numbers
than their immigrant counterparts.

Educational requirements for employment in municipal service remained uneven and loose in the first decades of the twentieth century
and that is reflected in statistics provided on levels of schooling.
Fifty-five percent of all the applicants had not gone beyond grade
school; 19 percent had earned high school degrees, and 24 percent
were college graduates. Compared to an equivalent pool of recruits
in private enterprises in Philadelphia at the same time, those seeking
public jobs as a group were undoubtedly better educated; still, a
majority had completed only eight years or less of formal schooling
and educational credentialing still did not play the role that it does in
today's world. Educational achievement, however, was moderately
related to the position sought in civil service. While less than 5 percent of all applicants for police, fire, and skilled labor jobs had more
than an eighth-grade education, roughly half of those seeking clerical
and inspector positions had further schooling, another testimony to
the importance of commercial course degree training. Schooling also
helped in passing the civil service test. Only 35 percent of those
applying for clerkships with eight years or less of schooling passed
the test, while 55 percent of the high school graduates and 68 percent
with college degrees scored highly on the exam; similar patterns

existed for other positions. A college education still did not guarantee successful completion of the civil service test. Thirty-three percent of all applicants with college degrees failed Philadelphia's exams for eligibility for municipal work.

The new civil service system created by state legislation in 1905 actually proved to be the first of three major overhauls in the way the city handled the employment of its task force. A mayor-appointed commission hardly put an end to political patronage, corruption, or calls for reform. Reports that Philadelphia municipal workers contributed no less than $2 million annually to the local Republican Party machine generated a new campaign for better goverance in the Quaker City during the second decade of the twentieth century.[95] A new city charter would be written in 1919.

The 1919 charter first attended to the unworkable and unwieldy nature of the city council system. Representation in the city's two-chamber council had been based on population ratios fixed a century earlier; the councils in 1919 comprised 146 members, the largest by far in the country. The city's new consitution provided for a one-house council of twenty-one paid legislators who would serve four-year terms. The next item under scrutiny was corruption in the contracting of city services to private concerns. Articles in the charter expressly prohibited outside contracting and made administrative officials entirely and directly responsible for street cleaning, paving, and repair, and for garbage collection.[96]

The 1919 charter finally effected substantial changes in the city's civil service system. The charter created a three-member commission, this time elected by the City Council. How that would take politics out of the employment process remained to be seen. The new constitution also contained a set of sweeping prohibitions applying to city workers that was the most extensive and elaborate in the nation. Philadelphia municipal employees could no longer serve as officials in party organizations, attend political conventions, solicit funds for parties, influence voters, or even be found near polling stations except to cast their own votes.[97]

The 1919 charter also drew clear distinctions between four classes of jobs within municipal service: positions not covered under civil service procedures; posts filled only through competitive examinations; others exempt from the procedures at the discretion of the civil service commissioners; and the so-called labor class of jobs, largely unskilled manual positions, requiring only written endorsements by two citizens, the passing of physical exams, and placement according to simple waiting lists. For the great majority of positions that were to be filled through examination, the charter also specified that department heads had to chose from among the top two candidates on eligibility lists; by custom, supervisors previously had selected from among the top four, but in practice great leeway was possible.[98]

The ink was barely dry on the new charter when reform organizations began providing evidence of continued blatant corruption in the civil service and demanding another re-organization of the system; the new battle would be raged, however, over the course of thirty years. The 1919 charter clearly had shortcomings. The large number of manual jobs listed under the "labor class" remained part of the political reward system. Recommendations from political sponsors eased recruits through the physical examinations and the waiting lists.[99] A substantial number of positions remained within the prerogative of the civil service commissioners to exempt from competitive tests, and during the 1920s and 1930s the proportion of such jobs rose from 18 to 25 percent of the total positions in city government. At one point in 1932, the commission declared all jobs within the Department of Wharves, Docks, and Ferries exempt from civil service procedures, allowing department heads to employ anyone they chose.[100] The seasonal and irregular nature of the work, the commissioners explained, led to substantial turnover in the department, and supervisors could not rely on hiring through structured lists. The need to employ municipal workers on a temporary basis actually created the greatest loophole in the system, and provisional appointments became a leading point of contention for critics of Philadelphia's civil service regime in the 1930s and 1940s.

Under civil service procedures, department heads could choose to fill any position with a provisional worker for a ninety-day period. The commission justified hiring in this way because of various contingencies and the changing employment needs of city agencies. Typically, ward politicians received notice of impending vacancies and sought the placement of party loyalists in temporary posts. These workers then were at a great advantage in eventually taking examinations for full-time appointments. They became familiar with the demands of the job, the skills required, and the subjects covered on the exams. For some positions, the examination included an oral component, and provisionals again had the advantage of responding to questions delivered by department heads with whom they had had prior contact. (The oral exam itself raised basic concerns about the objectivity of the whole process.)[101]

Statistics provided by critics of the system highlighted the seriousness of the provisional worker problem. In the 1930s, 63 percent of the total number of municipal employees in Philadelphia appointed through competitive examinations had the advantage of provisional positions; moreover, 90 percent of all provisional workers succeeded in passing tests for permanent placements.[102] One study prepared in the 1940s by the Bureau of Municipal Research showed another side to the issue. Provisionals could be rehired on successive temporary appointments. The bureau found workers who had remained in service for more than ten years in acting capacities, never having to take the competitive examinations.[103]

The furor over the use of provisional apppointments that would lead to new calls for reform of Philadelphia's civil service system in the late 1940s concealed a deep-seated problem in the recruitment of municipal workers. When openings occurred, department heads or supervisors with authority to hire normally consulted the office of the civil service commissioner and the commission's eligibility lists. Lists remained in effect for two years after administered exams. High turnover or expansion of the work force in a department either on an emergency or long-term basis often exhausted the names on the list; department chiefs were then allowed to make ninety-day provisional appointments. This occurred in a sufficiently regular way to make the provisionals a sizable portion of all hires.[104]

Fluctuating demand for workers and turnover did tax the system. During and immediately after World War I, for example, the civil service commission faced a particularly difficult time in recruiting workers. No applicants actually appeared in 15 percent of all the exams administered during the period and eligibility lists were quickly exhausted; resort to provisional appointments was an imperative.[105] Ironically, the situation reversed itself immediately in the early 1920s. A period of postwar conversion led to large-scale layoffs of workers in Philadelphia manufactories, and the numbers of applicants for municipal work increased dramatically.[106]

Turnover remained high as well, forcing temporary appointments. The first comprehensive study of turnover in the city's work force, conducted in the 1930s, revealed an 11 percent total annual rate of separation from service.[107] An investigation twenty years later in 1957 recorded an identical 11 percent yearly figure for turnover.[108] Turnover, however, varied dramatically within city offices. Recreational workers and museum attendants recorded the highest rates of separation, with more than 50 percent leaving the city's employment rolls each year; clerical and then custodial jobs were the next highest in turnover. Policemen and firemen, on the other hand, recorded among the lowest figures, with 5 and 2 percent of their respective numbers taking leave of their jobs during the year.[109]

Reasons for separation from civil service posts in Philadelphia also varied. Between 40 and 45 percent of those leaving their posts resigned on their own accord for personal reasons. Fifteen to 20 percent died, 10 percent retired, another 10 percent were discharged for disciplinary reasons, and the rest left either because their positions were eliminated or because of layoffs and physical disabilities. Finally, promotions and interdepartmental shifts also brought pressure on the system. Approximately 6 percent of Philadelphia's municipal work force changed positions each year; if eligibility lists were exhausted, the city resorted to provisional appointments to fill openings.[110]

The vast use of provisionals could be explained; the tie of these appointments to politics made the practice a target for reformers. The 1919 charter had not eliminated patronage, and corruption seemed more pervasive. Matters first came to a head in 1940, when an entire new group of civil service commissioners had to be installed after a grand jury indicted the standing body for fraudulent practices in the administration of exams for police officers.[111] A threatened strike of city employees in 1947 then led to an investigation of city financing and management with various exposés of embezzlement. A new generation of reformers emerged, calling for an end to corruption, and pressure was brought in the state capital in Harrisburg for the passage of legislation allowing the city to craft its own charter for the first time. A fifteen-member nonpartisan commission appointed by Philadelphia's City Council then drew up a so-called Home Rule Charter, which was adopted in a citywide referendum in 1951. This effort coincided with the ouster of the Republican Party machine from eighty years of rule in the city and the election of a Democratic Party reform regime.

Philadelphia's fifth constitution, the 1951 Home Rule Charter, further empowered the mayor's office. It set a four-year term for the mayor, who was given veto power over city council legislation and complete administrative authority over city agencies; the size of the council was reduced to seventeen members while the number of representatives elected at large in citywide voting was increased. (City-wide elections were the latest effort to curb ward and machine politics.)[112]

Philadelphia's civil service system came under extensive overhaul again. The 1951 charter allowed for the creation of a new administrative office under the mayor, the Personnel Department, with a director of personnel. The charter made the director responsible for classifying all jobs in civil service, developing pay schemes, negotiating with municipal unions, recruiting and examining applicants, maintaining personnel files, and overseeing tests for promotion and internal shifts of workers. To deal with the critical problem of provisional appointments, the charter also provided for a system of continuous testing. The director had to abide by guidelines established by a new Civil Service Commission, a three-member body appointed by the mayor through consultation with a new Civil Service Panel of distinguished citizens; according to the stipulations of the 1951 charter, the panel included the presidents of the University of Pennsylvania and Temple University, the presidents of the Philadelphia Chamber of Commerce and Bureau of Municipal Research, and the head of the city's central trade union council. The charter withdrew day-to-day administration from the Civil Service Commission and made the body basically an advisory, oversight, policy-making, and judicial board (appeals of actions taken by the director of personnel could be taken to the commission). Pay schemes established either unilaterally by the director of personnel or through negotiation with unions and the entire budget for personnel also needed approval by a new administrative board composed of the mayor, the managing director, and the director of finance. In this way, the management of the city's work force became an administrative and no longer a legislative function. (The council's role in the staffing of the city agencies was greatly curtailed if not severed.)[113]

Formalization of the employment process—the adoption of impersonal, meritocratic practices in hiring and promotion and a deliberate attention to procedure—occurred then in the public and not the private realm of enterprise. Only a small number of firms in Philadelphia before the 1950s treated the securing and allocation of labor in a systematic fashion. With few exceptions, local supervisors retained power over recruitment and job placement, and decision making was highly personal. Adherence to procedures at times was forced from below—as in the case of unions seizing the hiring function and ordering employment according to principles of seniority. Formalized application and testing procedures emerged largely in firms seeking workers who would have direct relations with clients and relative autonomy—as in the case of salespeople—or where skills were standardized and measurable—as in clerical work.

The persistence of informal employment practices in private businesses in Philadelphia can be explained in a number of ways. Owners and high-echelon managers had little time to devote to labor matters and left decisions to lower-level supervisors; the capacities of workers were, in most instances, difficult to measure anyway; firms needed to train employees on the job as well; and, finally, businesses were not simple economic machines—they were social institutions comprised of human beings with personal needs and problems. Hiring someone from the neighborhood just because he or she was from the neighborhood made no economic sense—there were no guarantees with regard to that individual's marginal productivity. It did make social sense because social solidarities within the firm could be tightened—with possible returns in efficiency—but it frequently occurred in the course of daily events.

Formalization of the employment process occurred in the public sphere, where competitive forces did not exist to force hiring according to pure economic considerations. Cynics might argue that even in the engagement of public employees personal connections remained critical; overhaul after overhaul of the civil service system failed to eliminate politics and favoritism from the process. This argument misses an important point. The constant attempts to depersonalize recruitment are significant in and of themselves. The reasons for formalization in public employment are complex. It was not just that the public's tax dollars were involved and the public thought corruption repellent. Elite group fears of disorder in the city, their loss of power to various newcomers who manifested decidedly different lifestyles and orientations, and the actual possibilities for measuring what in most cases were standardized skills—all played a role in the institution, maintenance, and revamping of civil service systems in Philadelphia and other American cities.

Creating order represented a major motive and goal of civil service reformers. Philadelphia's municipal government by the turn of the twentieth century already comprised a dozen agencies with hundreds of different occupational positions within departments. Rationalizing employment required careful cataloguing of jobs and the creation of appropriate tests and pay schemes. The city's charter of 1919 in fact expressly ordered the commissioner of the civil service to establish a classification plan, and during the 1920s and 1930s the city contracted with consulting firms to develop one. "Standardization" became the watchword of reformers during the twenties. The labeling of positions, they insisted, should correspond precisely to the tasks performed and should hold across agencies; workers doing equivalent work should be similarly titled and compensated. Investigators in fact found ample evidence of employees listed as "patrolmen" serving as clerks, typists, janitors, motor mechanics, hostlers, printers, telephone operators, chauffeurs, deck hands, and tug boat masters. Simplification was in need as well. In 1930 in the city's guide to positions, twenty-five different titles were used for watchmen, twelve for chauffeurs and eighty-five for clerks.[114]

Two reform organizations in the city—the Bureau of Municipal Research and the Citizens' Municipal Association of Philadelphia—took up the cause of standardization and publicized numerous studies with lengthy recommendations. Albert S. Faught, head of the Citizens' Association, assumed an interesting role in this campaign. Not only did he lobby for change in the public realm, but in various speeches to business groups in the city and in publications such as *The Annals of the American Association of Political and Social Science,* he counseled managers of private firms to introduce testing procedures and classification systems developed for municipal service work.[115] Faught drew his inspiration not only from civil service reforms in Philadelphia but also from the leading role the federal government played in World War I. The government instituted aptitude tests for soldiers and civilian workers in defense plants, and its War Industries Board created job and wage classification schemes that were required in private firms receiving government contracts.[116] The public sphere thus provided an example—the state influenced the employment practices of private enterprises.

The movement for standardization reflected changing thinking on personnel management. Frederick Taylor argued that any person could fit any job; place any individual in a well-specified task with supervision and pay incentives per piece and the work would be performed efficiently. Support for testing of applicants took another stance; tests checked for the merits of recruits, but also aimed at achieving a proper fit between the abilities and disposition of the individual and the demands of the job. The search for standardized job classification systems also represented an attempt to insure that workers performing equivalent work be titled and paid equivalently—thus lessening the role of favoritism and other personal factors in job placement and compensation. Current controversial efforts at creating plans of so-called comparative worth, largely in public employment, hearken back to earlier searches and are not new in principle.

The quest for standardization also greatly influenced one last important development in municipal service work, namely unionization. Labor unions force procedures and standards on employers in the name of fairness and to blunt the capricious rule of supervisors. Such procedures existed prior to efforts to organize municipal service workers in Philadelphia, and the major union that eventually succeeded in enrolling the city's employees accordingly not only supported civil service reform, but also allowed the city's work rules to be the union's. In the private sector, by contrast, unions fight to make union work rules a part of managerial practice.

In 1937, sanitation men and street and water repair crews in Philadelphia's Department of Public Works, bitten by the wave of successful CIO–led organizing of mass production workers throughout the country, invited officials from the newly formed American Federation of State, County, and Municipal Employees (AFSCME) to help them form a union. Over the next twenty years, AFSCME would engage in a series of strikes, threatened strikes, jurisdictional battles with other unions, and legal and political imbroglios that would lead to recognition of the union by the city as the exclusive bargaining agent for all municipal employees with the exception of supervisors and uniformed personnel. (Policemen and firemen have traditionally dealt with municipal authorities through their fraternal orders, but the city still does not recognize or enter into official agreements with them.)[117]

The nature of public employment in Philadelphia made for a peculiar kind of relationship between management and labor. State laws, for example, prohibited municipal workers from striking, yet Philadelphia's civil servants frequently walked off their jobs. Local officials never moved to enjoin such actions. Challenging city workers entailed potential embarrassments; as a strategic set of voters and vote healers, city workers possessed great leverage in their dealings with city managers. Management also did not have direct power over the purse. The mayor's office reached agreements with AFSCME, but the implementation of contracts rested on funding approval by City Council and, in the case of job classification arrangements, further confirmation by the Civil Service Commissions. Once again, political pressure exerted by municipal workers and their union could matter. In certain instances, AFSCME reached beyond the Council to force new funding. In 1951, in a critical test of strength, city councilmen in Philadelphia refused to allocate money to pay for an agreement reached between AFSCME and the mayor to reduce the hours of work from forty-eight to forty. The union threatened a strike and then sought judicial help. A local court ruled that the city had to honor the bargain. The Council subsequently arranged for additional funding. Labor relations in the public sector thus had a quality of their own.[118]

AFSCME also played a minimal and non-adversarial role in the structuring of work in city government, a departure from union activity in the private sector.[119] AFSCME stood firmly, as its constitution stated, "to extend and uphold the principles of merit and fitness in public service."[120] The union campaigned for civil service reform and lobbied effectively for the Home Rule Charter of 1951. The union further accepted the initiatives of management. In 1952, the new civil service commission commenced a study of the more than twenty thousand positions in city government in order to devise a new job classification and wage schedule. More than four hundred private firms in Philadelphia and the nation were surveyed for comparative purposes. During the process, AFSCME played a silent role, rendering no general opinions or specific inputs and readily accepting the system implemented by the commissioners in 1953.[121] In private companies, unions systematically fought for clear job categories, rules to guide assignments, and fixed wage scales, all in the name of fairness and justice and in order to control management and curb arbitrary decisions, particularly of lower-level supervisors.

AFSCME similarly did not have to demand the establishment of grievance procedures, a common and critical objective of unions.

Built into the civil service system was a mechanism for discipline, complaint, and redress that the union accepted without discussion. Only at the lowest level did the union get involved. Contracts with the city called for the intervention of shop stewards when charges of poor performance were initiated by supervisors against city workers; failure to bring disputes to resolution at an early stage brought the matter up for immediate review by the civil service commission, which proceeded with clear guidelines for investigation and judgment that protected all parties. Studies conducted in the 1960s indicated that the grievance mechanisms of the Philadelphia Civil Service Commission were rarely invoked.[122] Public employees in Philadelphia automatically operated in a system of rules that coincided with union aims, and the union's input was limited accordingly.

If AFSCME took a back seat on work rules and in some ways was restricted in forcing favorable wage settlements—the city council and ultimately the public had to be convinced of the need to direct more tax payers' dollars into the paychecks of city workers—one area in which the union could and did play a forceful role was benefits. The greater part of AFSCME's energies from the early 1950s onward aimed at achieving handsome benefit packages.

The 1954 contract reached between AFSCME and the city set the precedent. The city refused to grant salary increases—in fact, in the next fifteen years of annual bargaining, the city would agree only seven times to increases in direct compensation—but began to offer substantial benefits.[123] In 1954, Philadelphia city officials agreed to pay for the costs of a health center to be used by municipal employees and their families. The work week was also lowered to thirty-seven hours and city workers were offered thirteen paid holidays, twenty days of sick leave, and two weeks of vacation during the first ten years of service (three weeks thereafter). In subsequent years, the city offered more extensive and flexible health and life insurance, school tuition plans, increased leave time, and eventually a thirty-five hour work week. By the 1970s, benefits accounted for 45 percent of the city's total payroll costs, and on all scores the benefits of Philadelphia's municipal work force far outdistanced benefits received by their counterparts in Philadelphia's private firms. (There, benefits on average represented 12 percent of the total wage bill.)[124]

Retirement packages finally also clearly marked municipal workers from employees in private companies in Philadelphia, and here developments predated union efforts by a half century. As early as 1885, state legislation in Pennsylvania provided for the creation of municipal pension funds for policemen and firemen; action was not taken in Philadelphia until 1891. In 1915, another bill passed in Harrisburg, mandating pension coverage for all municipal employees in the state. When public servants were excluded from coverage under the federal Social Security Act of 1935, Pennsylvania further moved to revamp and improve its retirement system for state and local public employees.[125] Municipal workers in Philadelphia thus did not require the assistance of AFSCME in establishing pension rights. By 1955, firemen in the city could retire at forty-five after twenty years service with practically full pay; police at fifty after twenty years on the beat at more than half compensation; and other city employees at sixty with twenty years service, also at more than half salary. Few Philadelphia workers in private enterprise could boast such benefits.[126]

Municipal employees in Philadelphia thus labored under very special circumstances. Politics in the city played a great and obvious role in their work experiences. In the nineteenth century, workers owed their employment to service to the political machine and favor from political leaders. Repeated revision of the civil service system in the twentieth century did not eliminate patronage—politicians enlisted every means such as provisional appointments to keep jobs open as rewards for loyalty and getting out the vote—but the connection between the work and politics subtly changed. Municipal workers emerged as a large and powerful voting bloc. City managers curried their support and persuaded them against job actions that could cripple the provision of urban public services. Their leverage did not necessarily translate into wages and salaries that outpaced their counterparts in the private sector, but into enviable working conditions and benefits. Finally, civil service rules, regulations, and procedures guided their initial employment and subsequent careers in municipal government. City workers were less subject to capricious decision making, and even their unions did not have to assume the role that unions representing workers in the private sector have to in securing basic protections.

The city of Philadelphia offered work of a special nature. The city also simply offered jobs—in great numbers—and for various newcomers to the city, the municipal government was a critical source of employment. For the Irish, especially, municipal service in

Philadelphia and other American cities represented a crucial means for gaining a foothold in the society. Public jobs were important for other immigrant groups as well. Here, the story of black Philadelphians diverges again, although in the case of government employment the story is only slightly different.

As far as can be ascertained, the first black person to be hired by the city of Philadelphia, with the exception of African-American school teachers who taught in segregated schools, was a black policeman employed by Mayor Samuel King in 1884 over great opposition. King had successfully courted the black vote and this move represented a reward for their support.[127] The city recruited additional black police officers in later decades for surveillance of black neighborhoods. The city did not publish statistics on the racial composition of its work force, so the black presence in municipal service is difficult to determine, but little evidence exists to indicate sizable hirings of blacks in any city agency before the end of World War II. As long as the black community was unable to exert political leverage, civil service jobs remained out of its domain. As the black population swelled and became mobilized politically during the 1920s, and more significantly during and after World War II, municipal employment emerged as a major avenue of occupational attainment. Again, the city did not publish figures on race, but the African-American presence in city jobs increased after the 1950s to the point where, in 1970, the union of city workers, AFSCME, reported that close to 80 percent of its members were black, certainly a mark of the importance of public employment for the black community.[128] In some sense, blacks in Philadelphia repeated a pattern—another in-migrant group for whom inroads were made through the civil service after a modicum of political power had been achieved—but for blacks, openings in the public system of employment came late.

The question of the state and the black community in Philadelphia is important not just for the jobs offered by government, but, more critically, for the role the state played in forcing the employment of blacks in general. The market did not work for African-Americans in the city of Philadelphia, even for skilled and educated blacks. As has been shown, institutionalized racism meant the denial of jobs for blacks in Philadelphia industries—even in menial positions—and in situations, such as hospital employment, where blacks eventually would come to dominate. Before World War II, black Philadelphians remained relegated to a separate sphere of largely low-level service sector positions. The market in theory should have opened opportunities for blacks as low-wage laborers. Racist hiring practices in effect led employers to pay an extra premium to their white workers.

If the market did not work, then extra-market forces were necessary to change the fortunes of the black community. The lobbying efforts of the Armstrong Association and the NAACP from within the ghetto pried open some doors. The crucial axe would be wielded from the outside by the state, but not by local government. Federal orders would be required before blacks gained access to municipal employment opportunities. Black economic and political progress historically has rested on the intervention of the national government. Until very recent times, when the black community has been able to achieve some leverage at the local level, local provincialism and racism have thwarted efforts at improvement. States' rights and local control have always meant for blacks retrenchment and disempowerment.

In Philadelphia, the federal government first moved on behalf of the black community in a dramatic confrontation on the city's local transit lines in August of 1944. Change was in the winds from then on. The streetcars of Philadelphia had provided the sites for a number of the most tumultuous labor-management conflicts in the city's history. A strike of streetcar workers in 1895 paralyzed the city and drew national attention; an even more momentous battle in 1910 led to a remarkable general strike that spread to workers throughout the city in all trades.[129] In 1944, the Philadelphia Transit Company, a private corporation that provided public transportation in the city, received an order from the Fair Employment Practices Commission of the United States government to hire blacks to work on buses and streetcars as motormen, conductors, and drivers. Bowing to pressure from national black organizations and from within his administration, President Roosevelt had established FEPC through executive order in 1941 to insure equal employment opportunities in wartime industries. The PTC refused to obey the ruling, arguing that a contract signed with a so-called independent company union of PTC employees prevented hiring that threatened the jobs of men on the line. In March 1944, a majority of PTC workers then voted to have a CIO union of transit workers become their official bargaining agent, and this union announced in favor of the recruitment of blacks.

On August 1, as the training of black streetcar operators began, a strike led by officers of the independent union was called, effectively shutting public transportation in the city.[130]

President Roosevelt responded to this threat to Philadelphia's wartime industries by ordering troops to the city to operate city streetcars and buses. The job action folded after ten days and management of the PTC was returned to company officials, who now directed an integrated work force. The sight of U.S. soldiers running public transportation facilities on behalf of a handful of black recruits had great symbolic value, and the 1944 federal occupation of Philadelphia became the first of several executive, judicial, and legislative initiatives by the federal government that would begin to dent racist employment practices. The move added fuel and incentive to the already mobilizing black community in Philadelphia, which would contribute equally to change through its conviction, courage, and organization.

The role of the federal government in opening job opportunities for blacks in Philadelphia brings the issue of power and the labor market to the fore. Power and politics are terms rarely invoked in discussions of the labor market. Individuals negotiate for employment in the labor marketplace and all that matters is the state of demand for their labor and their ability and desire to work and get the job done. When government intervenes on behalf of an individual or a group of people, it does so artificially and unwisely, and the normal workings of the market are disturbed. This standard view misses a crucial point: that power and politics are never divorced from the labor market and are inherent to the process of getting and maintaining work.

An individual can derive power from his or her own personal abilities and use that power to affect outcomes (for example, to get a job). A person also derives power, regardless of his or her own capacities, from membership in a group. An Irish immigrant in Philadelphia in the 1880s could find himself on the city's payroll not through his merits but through service to a ward boss and through the effective organizing of the Irish community to control the political system for the group's advantage. A German immigrant secured employment in a business owned and managed by a German-American proprietor not by ability alone, but by his ethnic heritage and the successful control of trades by his fellow countrymen; a young Quaker gentleman received a clerkship in a local bank or insurance company in similar ways. A union member received a wage or benefit increase not necessarily for his or her performance, but because of the collective sway of his or her fellow unionists. An employer today similarly stops to think about denying employment or a promotion to a black person or a women—all hell could break loose; that hesitation occurs because of the leverage gained, though still in a limited way, by African-Americans and women in recent times. The common denominator in all these situations is organized power; at issue is which groups can operate in the public arena and coalesce to set apart their labor, an opportunity historically open only to professionals and skilled and eventually production-line workers, who were white and male. The labor marketplace involves transactions of individuals who affect outcomes partly through their abilities but also by their membership in groups that have achieved power generally—that goes for both employers and the employed.

People who are used to getting their way never quite understand the role of collectivities in the labor market, or that the labor market is a social institution that reflects values and power arrangements of the society at large. "We are all individuals, after all." "If I made it, why can't everyone?" These are common refrains. In a competitive and unequal world, people with lesser means and impact rely on all available resources—personal ones, their group membership, and the state, if need be. The intervention of the state is not unnatural; government after all is inherently involved in the labor market in the task of maintaining social order and peace; how the state acts, negatively or positively, necessarily affects the powers of the parties bargaining in the labor marketplace, and securing the favor of government—which requires organization—is always crucial. People who have an impact in a city such as Philadelphia have the luxury of not considering how their social identities—their whiteness, or maleness, or particular ethnic heritage, for example—and their own organizations and access to the levers of government have benefited them.

The labor market then is no empty stage. An ideological backdrop is in place, notions of the value of different kinds of work and who should work. The state serves as stage manager. And the players are in position. Particular characters enter the limelight by their pluck and ability and also by the forces they marshal. Getting work is political.

7 · Losing Work and Coping

The smooth workings of the labor market: for employers in Philadelphia, that meant the recruitment of suitable workers; for trade unionists, the controlling of jobs; for politicians, reformers and academics, the achievement of greater social harmony or justice. In each instance, the labor market emerged as more than a simple arena for the private negotiations of suppliers and purchasers of labor. It was a public problem requiring collective and institutional responses—the creation of an employment agency by a trade association, for example, a union hiring hall or vocational guidance programs for the schools. For William Rees, Timothy Ragan, Jean Bally, William Deacon, and their fellow laboring Philadelphians, the workings of the labor marketplace also had definite personal meaning; their survival and that of their families depended on eased access to employment. The issue took on even greater personal significance, for few workers in the Quaker City enjoyed long tenures of employment. For reasons of choice and circumstance, separations from jobs were frequent and getting work a constant process. When economic downturns cut people from the employment rolls, moreover, Philadelphians had to develop various coping strategies. Institutional support was available in a vast array of public and private relief services, but, as in the case of their forays into the job market—where schools, employment bureaus, help-wanted advertising, and other agencies existed to facilitate the securing of work—Philadelphians also had to fend for themselves and rely on their own resources. They acted personally but also always within a social realm.

The unsteady nature of employment in Philadelphia in the nineteenth century and the first decades of the twentieth is revealed in a series of documents. A payroll register for the silk textile firm of William Horstmann, for example, details the work experiences of 1,680 workers employed in the company from the 1850s through the mid-1870s.[1] Contemporary newspaper accounts depicted Horstmann's as a desirable place for employment. One reporter stated: "Young females who are anxious for situations will wait for months for a vacancy [at the firm], if they are so fortunate as to obtain a recommendation that will secure them admission."[2] Potential employees may have been knocking zealously at the door, but the register reveals that once inside they did not stay long. Nor did they come back. Turnover was extremely high.

Employees at Horstmann's remained on payroll an average of eighteen months, but close to 50 percent of the those hired stayed for less than five months, 20 percent for less than one month. Moreover, workers generally did not come back to serve the successive stints that are commonly found or assumed in textile work. Only 10 percent of those listed in the company's register chose to return to Horstmann's at least once after an initial severance, only 1 percent for two or more shifts. The firm could boast of a small veteran force, however. Better than four hundred of Horstmann's employees worked for the firm for more than a year and a half; twenty-four true veterans labored for more than ten years, two loyal workers remained for twenty-two.

Turnover was even more extreme at the Wetherill Paint Company. Surviving ledger books for the concern show that between 1848 and 1896, 3,673 different individuals passed through the firm's gates. Forty percent of this total stayed less than one week with the company, many of them for no more than one day! Severance rates reached levels of 400 and 500 percent in the 1880s and 1890s. In the year 1890, for example, Wetherill had on the rolls on any given day an average of fifty-five workers; during that year, 303 men entered into hire in the firm. Turnover apparently increased over the course of the century. In 1848, 33 percent of the labor force worked at least forty-eight weeks during the year; such "full-timers" represented 10 percent of the total by the early 1890s.[3] These statistics are all the more remarkable because Wetherill offered steady employment. Seasonality was not a factor in operations at the firm. As noted in an earlier chapter, the perils and difficulty of the work at Wetherill probably account for the extreme turnover.

Irregular employment did not abate in the first decades of the twentieth century. When Joseph Willits prepared his study on employment patterns in Philadelphia for Morris Cooke and the city government, he gained access to the personnel and membership records of several companies and unions. In the Axminster Carpet Mill for the period from 1907 to 1915, he found that between 40 and 50 percent of the men and women hired by the firm had worked there for ten weeks or less, approximately 70 percent for less than one year.[4] A study of the hiring hall lists of the Lacemakers' Union for the period from 1909 to 1914 similarly revealed that 40 percent of the membership worked half the number of what was considered a year's full complement of days.[5]

Willits's research and general concern for high rates of turnover spurred an additional spate of studies on employment patterns during World War I and the 1920s; these studies recapitulated the results of earlier investigations. In 1917, the Philadelphia Electric Company released figures showing 200 to 300 percent annual turnover rates for the company.[6] A large-scale study of the metal-works industry likewise noted that only 40 percent of the men in the trade in Philadelphia experienced steady employment (defined as employment for one full year with one employer).[7]

The Industrial Research Department of the Wharton School of the University of Pennsylvania, established and directed by Joseph Willits, conducted the most prodigious research on the subject. In a study of twenty-four Philadelphia firms during the years 1921 to 1924, investigators for IRD discovered 100 percent rates of turnover on average; turnover was explicitly defined as a ratio of the number of terminations from employment recorded for a given period of time divided by the average daily number of workers on payroll.[8] Concerned to place their findings in some historical perspective, researchers for Willits's organization also examined the surviving personnel records of Philadelphia shipbuilding firms for the late 1850s and early 1860s. Slightly higher employee turnover figures were calculated, but by and large there appeared to be no great difference in employment patterns in the city between the mid-nineteenth century and the third decade of the twentieth.[9]

The Great Depression generated a new series of labor force studies, and into the IRD's net in 1936 came William Rees, Timothy Ragan, Jean Bally, William Deacon, and 2,500 other Philadelphia workers. The employment histories of these respondents to the WPA/IRD survey can only be characterized as unsteady and irregular.[10] During the ten-year period from 1926 to 1935, for example, the men and women questioned had been hired on average by three different employers, worked for these employers for an average of three and a half years, changed both their occupational titles and trades at least once, and been unemployed an average of fifteen months (with the average span of unemployment lasting nine months). Since the survey included the years of the depression, unsteady work profiles would be expected. Yet the survey extended over the entire course of these individuals' careers. Two-thirds of the sample had begun their working lives before the turn of the twentieth century, and they had experienced on average eleven changes of one form or another in job status.

Of course, scattered evidence exists of Philadelphia workers who enjoyed long and presumably satisfying tenures at work. In 1915, for example, firm executives of the famed Disston Saw Company could boast in a company history that two-thirds of the 2,200 employees then on payroll had served with the concern for more than ten years, and that twenty men had actually been in service for more than half a century.[11] A surviving employee roster of the Farmers' and Mechanics' Bank in Philadelphia for the period from 1871 to 1905 indicates that the bank's clerical and bookkeeping staff stayed an average of six years.[12] In the small varnish concern of Christian Schrack, account books similarly reveal that the work force remained practically unchanged for ten years at a time.[13] Unfortunately, there is no single document, such as the United States Population Census, that can provide a comprehensive portrait of employment patterns in Philadelphia—to determine, for example, overall figures for job changes and tenure. A composite view, however, gleaned from a range of records and surveys, establishes fairly conclusively that for the vast majority of workers in the city frequent employment shifts and irregular work histories were the norm.

High levels of geographic mobility are a feature of American life that has been duly noted by American social historians. Only recently have the clearly interrelated issues of job mobility and uneven patterns of employment been recognized and appreciated as well. The conclusion (confirmed here) that unsteady work marked working people's experiences in the United States at least before World War II, however, should not serve as an end point for investigation.[14]

Why was job tenure so short? Did workers leave in great numbers simply of their own accord or did uneven employment histories reflect the fluctuating business conditions of the times? Moreover, did all segments of the laboring population in a city such as Philadelphia experience irregular work patterns? Fortunately, records from Philadelphia firms and social science surveys survive to provide valuable insights into these additional questions.

The Horstmann Company employee roster is an intriguing document, for it lists reasons for the termination of employment. The record indicates that tenure in the firm between the 1850s and 1870s varied by gender, occupational position, and family connections (that is, whether workers had relatives working for the company).[15] While men worked an average of three years for Horstmann, women generally remained with the firm for fourteen months. Similarly, skilled repair mechanics stayed about a year longer on average than those employed as weavers and two years longer than workers in unskilled positions. Employees with kin in the firm had longer tenures by ten months than those not working with family members. In multivariate analysis, however, gender emerged as the critical factor in length of employment. Marked differences between men and women on job tenure existed across occupational levels and regardless of kin connection. Men and women thus had different employment histories at the Horstmann Company; though female employees could be found in every aspect of production save highly skilled repair work, they did disproportionately occupy the most tedious and low-paying jobs and apparently had much looser ties to the firm. Gender distinctions are also evident in the reasons for job severance.

Notations for why workers left Horstmann appear for 82 percent of the close to 1,700 employees listed in the company's register. Eight of these employees died (at least one gruesomely; as noted for Louis Lamind, he "died in our blade at 2:20"). A large number, 36 percent of the total, were laid off (or, as the Horstmann record aptly noted, "out of work"). While business downturns in certain particularly bad years, 1868 and 1873, for example, forced a great number of layoffs, even in other years the number of furloughs was sizable, particularly during November and December. Horstmann operated in seasonal and fluctuating markets even in normal times and employment was affected accordingly.

For 48 percent of the workers, however, leave-taking was a voluntary act—employees just quit or, as appeared in the register most often, "gave notice." When more was specified, the reasons varied greatly. Leaving to take another job, start a business, learn a trade, or go to school were cited most often, with health reasons a close second. Complaints about poor pay were voiced next in frequency and getting married (or "Got Married"), fourth. Moving from the area proved an almost equally important refrain. John and Emma Mettauser are thus listed as returning to Switzerland in May of 1874 after putting in twenty-five years between them on the firm's power looms. Not everyone moved as far, of course. Many Horstmann employees are simply listed as moving "to the country," "out west," or to adjoining states. Finally, family problems and concerns ("was compelled to stay home," "her mother needed her to do house-work") and general dissatisfactions with the job were also reasons, though the least frequently cited, for leave-taking. (James Lindsey quit his job in the machine shop "because he did not want to clean oil cups, said it was colored work.")

Forty-eight percent of those listed with reasons for severance thus quit the Horstmann Company and 36 percent were laid off. The remaining 16 percent were fired. Discharges occurred with various justifications, but dissatisfaction with job performance ("Poor Work") was cited most frequently by far. Conduct such as quarrel-ing, going to the dressing room too often, or being impudent, indo-lent, or disobedient warranted dismissal as well. Finally, failure to conform to certain moral standards could invite discharge. Annie Parker, employed one month in the office during the spring of 1872, was "too lively." Sarah Cain, employed for sixteen years in the sew-ing room, was let go when it was "heard she was living with another woman's husband." Paul Volker lasted six months in the sword shop (making silk scabbards); he "paid no attention to his work and too much to the girls." Alexander Smith, in a supervisor's training posi-tion, was similarly dismissed because he was "not a suitable person to take charge of girls."

Of course, overt resistance to managerial authority received quick action as well. Maggie Hiltner was fired when she threw "peelings" on the floor at the feet of her supervisor. Mary and Alice Brennan received notice in 1871 over a "disturbance with Mr. Sichnel." (Their ousting prompted a walkout by several of their co-workers on the spooling frames in a show of solidarity.) Two other women were discharged in August 1873 when it was learned that they planned to "strike for $7.00 per week." More cryptic is the case of Margaret Crocke, who was fired for "raising disturbances with the hands."

The examples of female employees listed as fired and involved in disturbances raise questions about gender differences and severance. Actually, men and women behaved fairly similarly in terms of reasons for leaving the Horstmann Company. Practically equal proportions of men and women quit or were fired or laid off; in this respect, female employees were as likely to raise disturbances or present problems to management as the males. Differences emerged, though, in reasons for leaving voluntarily. Women were much more likely to quit for personal and family reasons, men to pursue better occupational opportunities. Of the 167 employees who cited personal reasons, 90 percent were women; of the 22 moving out and hopefully up occupationally, 82 percent were men. The unique jottings in the Horstmann employee register provide evidence on this score that Frederick Schurmann left to keep a beer saloon, Louis Schultz to start a shooting gallery, Louis Wacker, a grocery business, and other men to learn new trades and to go on to school. The register also reveals that of the four women leaving to take higher-level positions, three actually returned to their old jobs with the firm within a year. The Horstmann Company employee register thus offers details on the extent of turnover, the respective place of layoffs, quittings, and firings, and the differential experience of men and women in the job market in mid-nineteenth century Philadelphia. Other records for later eras, though none with the anecdotal richness of the Horstmann register, replicate many of the patterns of job serverance found in the firm.

In the early 1920s, investigators at Joseph Willits's Industrial Research Department had at their disposal the payroll records of twenty-four companies. They too found higher rates of separation and shorter tenures at work for women than for men; with access to more extensive socioeconomic and demographic information, they were also able to establish irregular employment patterns as more common to younger workers than old, unskilled than skilled, and immigrants, particularly new arrivals from southern and Eastern Europe, than the native-born. Workers with the greatest number of years of schooling surprisingly, or perhaps not surprisingly when reasons for leave-taking are analyzed, had higher turnover rates than

Philadelphians with little or no formal education.[16] Unfortunately, researchers for IRD did not engage in the kinds of statistical analyses that would have determined the relative importance of these different social factors in accounting for varying employment histories.

Turnover rates, however, remained high for all groups of workers—highly skilled men had to be replaced at firms in relatively smaller numbers than their unskilled counterparts, but the differences were not dramatic. Here, the differing reasons for job separation shed light on a multifaceted process. Researchers for IRD found that the proportions of workers leaving companies because of voluntary resignations, layoffs, and disciplinary discharges changed constantly. In 1921, for example, at a time of economic recession in Philadelphia, 50 percent of all the job terminations recorded in the twenty-four firms under investigation were attributable to layoffs, 42 percent to resignations, and 8 percent to discharges. Three years later, with the return of better business conditions, furloughs accounted for 30 percent of all listed severances, voluntary quitting for 55 percent, and dismissals for 15 percent. (A follow-up study conducted five years later under the aegis of the IRD saw layoffs rise once again to 55 percent of all employment separations.)[17] The numbers clearly differ from year to year, though from the Horstmann records for the 1850s through the mid-1870s and the IRD surveys of the 1920s, it appears generally that in nearly half of the cases workers took leave of their jobs on their own accord and in more than half severances from work were due either to plant shutdowns or to disciplinary actions.

The 1920 turnover studies of the Industrial Research Department also drew connections between reasons for leave-taking and age, nativity, schooling, and occupational position. Younger workers and immigrants in Philadelphia tended to quit or be laid off or dismissed in similar proportions to their respective counterparts. Differences emerged between skilled and unskilled, with the latter losing work in great numbers through layoffs, the former generally taking leave of their employers to seek better situations. Interesting dissimilarities were also recorded for workers of different educational backgrounds; those with the greatest number of years of schooling had among the highest rates of turnover and invariably left work on their own volition in search of greener pastures; a separation from work for Philadelphians with little or no formal education usually meant a layoff.

Finally, IRD investigators drew no distinctions between men and women and whether they resigned or were discharged or laid off in different proportions, but among workers taking leave of their own accord, women were much more likely to give marriage and family duties as their reasons, results that match the Horstmann Company records.[18]

The 1936 WPA survey adds extra dimensions and complexities to an examination of job stability and severance, particularly concerning the factor of career time. Tenure at work and reasons for leave-taking were affected by general economic conditions as well as by the social backgrounds and occupations of the workers involved. As the stage in the working life cycle was important in the means by which laboring people secured employment, so it was in the way people lost work.

Unsteady employment generally marked the work experiences of the Philadelphians interviewed by Gladys Palmer and her IRD associates, but within the cohort there was considerable variation. Age in 1936 proved to be the most salient factor in employment history.[19] Older workers tended to be both employed and unemployed for longer periods of time and to have experienced the greatest number of job shifts. Because they had spent more years in the work force, that was to be expected. Apparent distinctions in steadiness of employment between men and women respondents, married and single workers, and among Philadelphians of different nationality and educational backgrounds, moreover, tended to disappear when age was considered. There is one exception to this pattern, and that involves employment experience during the years of the Great Depression. When the 1930s alone are considered, it was the youngest workers in the WPA survey, not the oldest, who reported the highest number of job changes. They were not mobile by choice, either; when reasons for shifts are examined, the most recent entrants to the labor market comprised the group most susceptible to layoffs.

Two other factors besides age were related to steadiness of employment, but in lesser ways. Workers who had obtained their jobs through family connections generally had more stable careers than those relying on personal initiative or institutional means (a link between employment stability and family employment networks was also discovered in the personnel records of the Horstmann Company).[20] WPA survey respondents utilizing kin networks had fewer

Table 7.1   Reasons for job change, Philadelphia workers, 1870–1936

Reason	First Job		Second Job		Third Job		Fourth Job		Fifth Job	
	N	%	N	%	N	%	N	%	N	%
Emigrate to America	124	6	73	4	46	3	28	2	16	1
Military service	29	2	78	4	84	5	60	4	41	3
Better position	799	42	576	30	447	24	346	21	253	18
Promoted	178	9	171	9	128	7	119	7	85	6
Quit	205	11	191	10	154	9	148	9	110	8
Laid off	269	14	523	27	679	38	740	45	761	53
Fired	13	1	18	1	14	1	11	1	9	1
Finished apprenticeship	173	9	135	7	74	4	40	3	28	2
Personal reasons	84	4	67	4	70	5	52	3	42	3
Illness	16	1	23	1	25	1	27	2	24	2
Strike	12	1	42	2	49	3	41	3	42	3
Other	22	1	19	1	24	1	17	1	15	1

Source: See Table 2.5.

job shifts on average and were employed for longer periods of time; this suggests that they were tied to their work in a different manner than other workers (although the actual mechanisms of this tie remain unclear).

A third important ingredient in job history was apprenticeship. Philadelphia workers having the advantage of apprenticeship training generally had much steadier work histories than those not similarly trained.[21] They also had strikingly greater success in rising to skilled positions.

On reasons for job change, the WPA study is also insightful, because information was recorded across careers. On first job shift, the numbers are quite at odds with those discovered elsewhere. Eighty-five percent of the WPA respondents reported leaving their first positions voluntarily, rather than 40 or 50 percent, while only 14 percent were laid off and 1 percent fired (see Table 7.1). The great majority of those voluntarily leaving their first jobs did so to accept better positions in other firms. The next largest group chose to shift because of internal company promotions; residential change, personal concerns, health problems, military service, and poor working conditions represented other chosen reasons for severing employment.

Over career time, however, the results change dramatically, with a notable increase in involuntary losses of jobs; here the WPA canvass begins to look entirely similar to the Horstmann Company records and the IRD studies of the 1920s. Between first and fifth job change, the percentage of those answering "to take a better position" successively declined from 42 percent to 18 percent. Conversely, the percentage of survey members laid off from their jobs rose progressively from 15 percent to a 53 percent majority. All other categories remained constant. Late in careers, in other words, a job change meant forced unemployment for the Philadelphians sampled, and shifts into better positions were only possible for most early in their working lifetimes. This pattern, that layoffs increased as the reason for job severance over career time, held for all generations of workers surveyed, but the situation was particularly dire for those young Philadelphians who entered the job market just prior to and during the Great Depression. Whether it was their first job change or their fifth, they experienced job layoffs in the greatest numbers (see Table 7.2). Layoffs then have a personal and generational dimension; involuntary leave-taking increased for Philadelphia workers in general as they aged, and those entering the world of work in poor economic times were especially liable to being let go.

Age also affected reasons for job separation. For example, when all age categories were considered together, the strongest distinctions were found between men and women. In their first employment, young women were much more likely to be laid off than men and were more likely to quit for personal rather than professional reasons, a result found in other studies. Differences on layoffs and voluntary leaves between men and women, however, generally evaporated when the factor of age was considered.[22] Distinctions between first- and second-generation immigrants dissolved in a similar fashion. One notable distinction did remain constant with regard to first job experience involving industry of employment. Thirty-nine percent of the Philadelphians engaged in building and construction lost their initial jobs to layoffs, a far greater figure than the average of 15 percent. The seasonal and fluctuating nature of employment in this trade made furloughs a basic component of the job.

When varying reasons for job separation are examined in later work experiences, no significant differences emerged between different groups of Philadelphia workers except on the factor of generation;

Philadelphians entering the job market in the era of the Great Depression continued to have a difficult time holding their jobs. Women once again were laid off in greater numbers than men on fifth job experience, but their younger ages played a role here; distinctions surfaced between different immigrant groups and between workers in different trades, yet these differences were slight and not warranting of generalization. It appears that late in their careers Philadelphians of different backgrounds were equally at risk in losing work involuntarily.

A final issue on reasons for job separation concerns disciplinary discharges. When early payroll records are examined, between 8 and 16 percent of all severances can be attributed to disciplinary actions. Less than 2 percent of the 2,500 workers canvassed in the WPA study of 1936, however, reported losing their jobs because they were fired. The disparity in these results obviously calls into question the reliability of personal surveys. In the material available, moreover, no group of workers stands out as experiencing discharges in disproportionate numbers. Men and women, immigrant and native-born, unschooled and educated proved equally capable of being thorns in the sides of management.

Philadelphians then, at least before World War II, went in and out of work with great frequency. Women workers, young entrants to the labor market, the unskilled, new immigrants, and people laboring not alongside kin tended to have the most unstable employment histories, with short tenures at work and numerous shifts. Becoming part of the labor force in poor economic times did not bode well, either. Reasons for changes in job status also varied. In general, slightly more than 50 percent of all employment shifts experienced by Philadelphia workers for the time period under study can be attributed to forced layoffs and disciplinary dismissals, the rest to a range of voluntary decisions made by individual workers. Career time proved critical here. Philadelphians were most likely to leave their jobs for positive reasons early in their working lives and to be severed from employment for circumstances beyond their control late in careers. Some groups of workers, women and new immigrants, for example, were more likely to be laid off than others during all stages of their occupational lifetimes, but the cohort of workers continually at the greatest risk of layoffs was the generation

Table 7.2 Reasons for leaving work, first job and fifth, by various factors, Philadelphia workers, 1870–1936

Variable/Category	Reasons for leaving first job (%)			
	Voluntary leave	Laid off	Fired	V (sig)
Year of Birth				
After 1907	68	32	1	
1892–1907	91	8	1	
Before 1892	94	5	1	.24 (.00)
Sex				
Male	87	12	1	
Female	75	24	1	.14 (.00)
Place of Birth				
Philadelphia	80	19	1	
Rest of USA	86	13	1	
Germany	96	4	0	
Germ.-Am.	88	12	0	
Italy	100	0	0	
Ital.-Am.	78	22	0	
E. Europe	97	3	0	
E. Eur.-Am.	91	9	0	
Britain	98	2	0	
Brit.-Am.	92	8	0	
Ireland	100	0	0	
Irish-Am.	75	25	0	
Other	100	0	0	
Other-Am.	85	15	0	.13 (.00)
Years of Schooling				
0–5	91	8	1	
6	90	10	0	
7	85	14	1	
8	82	17	1	
9–16	79	20	1	.08 (.06)
Industry				
Textiles	89	10	1	
Hosiery	81	18	1	
Metal	69	30	1	
Other Manuf.	84	14	2	
Bld. Const.	61	39	0	
Commerce	93	0	7	
Government	96	0	4	
Service	83	17	0	
Agriculture	97	3	0	
Other	83	17	0	.17 (.00)
Skill Level				
Skilled	80	19	1	
Semiskilled	83	16	1	
Unskilled	91	8	1	.07 (.04)

Source: See Table 2.5. Coefficient V is given as measure of association with level of significance noted in parentheses.

Table 7.2 *(continued)*

Variable/Category	Reasons for leaving fifth job (%)			
	Voluntary leave	Laid off	Fired	V (sig)
Year of Birth				
After 1907	29	71	6	
1892–1907	45	54	1	
Before 1892	55	44	1	.15 (.00)
Sex				
Male	48	51	1	
Female	25	75	0	.20 (.00)
Place of Birth				
Philadephia	40	59	1	
Rest of USA	49	50	1	
Germany	55	45	0	
Germ.-Am.	71	29	0	
Italy	28	72	0	
Ital.-Am.	53	47	0	
E. Europe	52	48	0	
E. Eur.-Am.	25	75	0	
Britain	50	50	0	
Brit.-Am.	62	38	0	
Ireland	71	29	0	
Irish-Am.	50	50	0	
Other	71	29	0	
Other-Am.	25	75	0	.14 (.00)
Years of Schooling				
0–5	47	53	0	
6	44	55	1	
7	38	61	1	
8	47	53	0	
9–16	38	61	1	.07 (.47)
Industry				
Textiles	49	50	1	
Hosiery	26	73	1	
Metal	43	56	1	
Other Manuf.	44	56	0	
Bld. Const.	35	65	0	
Commerce	57	43	6	
Government	57	43	0	
Service	60	40	0	
Agriculture	44	56	0	
Other	55	45	0	.14 (.07)
Skill Level				
Skilled	50	49	1	
Semiskilled	37	63	0	
Unskilled	52	48	0	.10 (.01)

that came of working age in the 1920s and 1930s as the nation entered its most severe and longest economic depression.

The leaving and losing of work was as complicated a matter as the getting of work. When Philadelphians left their jobs on their own accord, for example, they moved for a host of reasons. Even when they gave notice to "take a better position elsewhere," as it was listed in personnel records and recorded in survey research, this did not necessarily mean that they acted for simple material gain. For some workers, particularly skilled craftsmen, job hopping was part of an occupational ethos and practice. Investigators from the Industrial Research Department at the Wharton School during the 1920s thus found to their surprise that tool and diemakers and other skilled metal workers in Philadelphia frequently transferred from shop to shop. Interviews revealed that for men in the metal and machine trades, changing jobs represented a stage in their trade education. "After a man completes his apprenticeship, he stands a better chance of becoming a first-class tool and diemaker by working in as many shops as he can for a period of about ten years," IRD researchers concluded. "The things that [he] will learn in shifting around are many and varied. He will learn different shop practices, and many new ways of doing his work by coming in contact with the methods of different workmen."[23] The motivations behind even obvious positive job changes could thus vary. Of course, not every voluntary employment shift effected by a Philadelphia worker involved happy or satisfying circumstances. Young women had to leave the job market to assume family care and maintenance responsibilities; men and women both had to terminate employment by their own choosing for sickness and infirmity (and with increasing probability as they became older).

Qualifications are thus in order when considering the various reasons workers privately chose to leave their employers. The matter of the forced severing of employment is even more complicated. In a small percentage of cases, firms discharged workers for what was perceived as poor, negligent, or unruly behavior. In the vast majority of instances, companies in Philadelphia unilaterally dismissed their employees because of various problems they faced in maintaining operations. Layoffs could occur, however, for quite idiosyncratic reasons. In 1926, for example, the famed Dobson Mills, once employing more than five thousand textile operatives, closed its doors when its proprietor, James Dobson, died with no heir to assume ownership and command of the firm. The reluctance of living children or grandchildren to take managerial roles in enterprises established by their forebears led to the boarding up of other Philadelphia factories as well.[24] Fires similarly could take their toll on businesses and employment. Employees could also lose their jobs when their employers from either personal or business concerns, opted to cease production in the area and move their companies elsewhere.

Highly particular answers can be found for the forced unemployment of Philadelphia workers. Losing work proved a pervasive problem and experience, however, for more general economic reasons. Structural changes in the economy, or, simply, the wholesale disappearance of trades, placed people on the unemployment line. Changes in fashion and consumer demand decimated the fancy carpet industry in Philadelphia during the 1920s, jeopardizing the jobs of 30,000 city wage earners; nylon similarly wiped out Philadelphia's prosperous silk hosiery trade in the 1940s, forcing whole neighborhoods of workers to find new occupations.[25] Large-scale shifts in demand thus could lead to the folding of particular industries. Periodic general losses in purchasing and investment power, of course, could result in the many "great" general depressions that inundated Philadelphia seemingly every twenty years in the nineteenth and first half of the twentieth centuries: from the depression of 1819 that placed 20,000 people out of work to the economic crises of 1836–1845, 1857–1859, 1873–1880, 1893–1897 (with 60,000 Philadelphians unemployed), and 1929–1940, when, at its peak, 360,000 people, more than 40 percent of the city's labor force, were idle.[26]

Occupational shifts and general economic downturns represent the great jolts, when unemployment became massive, widespread, well reported, and a social problem and threat that demanded the attention of civic and political leaders. But employers were forced to lay off workers for a third kind of economic circumstance that had even more pervasive effects and implications. Temporal shifts in demand and production faced by firms operating in seasonal and specialized markets—characteristics of the Philadelphia industrial order—made irregular work loads and uncertain employment a constant. When Philadelphia businesses closed down periodically—to retool or wait for new orders and warehoused goods to be sold off—Philadelphia workers received layoff notices; a promise to be rehired represented no guarantee of future employment and searches for new jobs were imperative.

Unemployment was thus a chronic reality and problem, not an experience just faced during notable bad times. Building and construction in the city generally came to a halt during the winter months and hence the employment of workers in the trade.[27] The head of a stevedore firm in the city similarly told Joseph Willits that he did "not believe that dock-hands ever average over two days [of work] a week."[28] In the textile industry in the early twentieth century, managers estimated that their looms were down at least 35 percent of possible operating time.[29] A typical weaver in the upholstery trade during the 1920s could thus report the following schedule of lost work and pay:

January
  2nd week. No Work
  3rd week. No Work
  4th week. No Work
  5th week. Warp Out

March
  2nd week. Warp Out
  3rd week. Warp Out
  4th week. Change Loom

April
  5th week. Warp Out

May
  3rd week. Leave of Absence
  4th week. Leave of Absence
  5th week. Leave of Absence

June
  2nd week. Worked 1 Day
  3rd week. Worked 5 Days
  4th week. No Work

July
  1st week. Worked 4 Days
  2nd week. No Orders
  3rd week. No Orders
  4th week. Worked 4 Days
  5th week. Warp Out 2 Days

August
  1st week. Warp Out
  4th week. Change Loom

September
  2nd week. Change Loom
  3rd week. Change Loom

December
  1st week. Change Loom
  4th week. Trouble with Loom
  5th week. Loom Broke Down[30]

The singular importance of temporary layoffs in the lives of the working people of Philadelphia was probably best voiced and explained by Robert Bradford, the director of a settlement house in the

textile manufacturing district of Kensington. As he testified to Joseph
Willits:

> We make the mistake of assuming that unemployment is a ques-
> tion solely of severe bad times. It is true that conditions are worse
> at such times—they even approach the destructiveness of a flood
> or an earthquake. But it is true that unemployment and part time
> employment is a situation that is with us to a very considerable
> degree practically without cessation. If it is not one industry, it is
> another. If one mill escapes, another is hit. The fear of unemploy-
> ment hangs a permanent pall over [the community].[31]

When the term "laid off" appears in company personnel records
or in tables compiled by social science researchers, the actual circumstances under which an individual or group of workers has been let
go by their employers are rarely clear. Philadelphia workers received
notices for the termination of employment in odd situations as well
as when particular industries or the economy in general were falter-
ing. Even in seemingly good times, layoffs were common because
of seasonal factors. Clarifying the varying dynamics of job loss, however, should not lose sight of one essential matter. Philadelphia workers may have been laid off by their employers because of either economic downpours or showers, but unemployment always meant the
same thing: crisis for themselves and their families, surviving some-
how, and getting new work.

Irregular work took its toll on all concerned. For businessmen in
Philadelphia, high employee turnover and the frequent furloughing
of workers meant inevitable and critical losses in productivity and
profits. The manager of the largest tool-making concern in the city
thus told Joseph Willits in 1915, "After a period of unemployment,
it takes the employer three weeks to get his force and plant up to the
point where it can turn out orders with normal efficiency." A foreman at the Axminster Textile Mill echoed his words, "Even if the
same weaver comes back to the same loom, after a long period of
lost time, it takes three weeks before the loom will run again as well
as it did before we shut down."[32] For government leaders, of course,
unemployment and uncertain employment posed dangerous threats
to social peace and harmony within the city. The issue could not be
and was not taken lightly—witness the intense dialogue on worker
turnover that occurred in Philadelphia during the second and third

decades of the twentieth century and the calls for rationalized personnel management and public employment services. Business and political leaders had to cope.

For laboring people in the city, new managerial practices and conferences and research on unemployment may have been beside the point. The loss of a job for whatever reason had immediate consequences. Coping with layoffs was also made all the worse for the individuals and families involved because there was no telling when rehirings would occur. Reports generated by concern for the social upheavals of irregular employment in fact indicate that Philadelphians once out of work remained so for long periods of time.

To supplement the research of Joseph Willits, Mayor Rudolph Blankenburg and Director of Public Works Morris Cooke in March of 1915 asked the Metropolitan Life Insurance Company to conduct a survey of the firm's policy holders in Philadelphia to determine levels of employment. Agents for Metropolitan Life canvassed 79,000 families and secured information from more than 137,000 adult wage earners. Seventy percent of the company's clients reported being employed on a full-time basis; 20 percent were working only part-time; and 10 percent were unemployed and looking to be hired. Fifty-five percent of those out of work had actually been idle for over ninety days; 40 percent had been in search of a job for 120 days, while 22 percent had been unemployed for more than half a year. Male workers reported being out of work for longer periods of time than women, with 75 percent of the former not having worked for sixty days and 67 percent of the women out a similar two months. Twenty-four percent of the men had been out for half a year, a situation faced by 16 percent of the women. Workers formerly holding positions as "laborers" tended to be out of work longer than others, though in 1915 Philadelphians in building and construction and the locomotive industry experienced particularly long bouts of unemployment. In general, the families of about half of those out of work in 1915 had to figure on the loss of one-fourth of the annual earnings of their main breadwinners.[33]

In April of 1929, the U.S. Department of Labor conducted an even more extensive survey of employment conditions in Philadelphia, a good half year before the nation would begin its plunge into a ten-year period of severe economic depression. Bad times had already come to the Quaker City. Department of Labor investigators found

10 percent of the work force out of work, a figure identical to that calculated by the Metropolitan Life Insurance Company fourteen years earlier.[34]

Once again, unemployed Philadelphians reported being out of work for long periods of time. Fifty percent had been idle for a least ninety days, 29 percent had been unemployed for more than half a year, 12 percent for at least a full year (the latter figures indicate that slightly higher percentages of Philadelphians experienced truly long periods of unemployment in April of 1929 than in March of 1915).[35] As in 1915, women in Philadelphia were unemployed for shorter periods than men, with 23 percent of the men remaining unemployed for six months and only 17 percent of the women.

The Department of Labor study was also one of the first to report in a comprehensive way on the employment situations of black Philadelphians; racial discrimination not only kept African-Americans in the city out of the industrial fold, but it also kept them absent from most social survey research of the time. Levels of unemployment in Philadelphia were twice as high for blacks as for whites, yet blacks tended to be out of work for shorter periods of time. While 25 percent of the whites surveyed had been unemployed for at least six months, 16 percent of the blacks similarly reported being without work for at least a half a year. Department of Labor investigators surmised that the average shorter periods of unemployment experienced by women and blacks—and their higher rates of unemployment in general—reflected their disproportional numbers in domestic service and light industrial jobs, occupations where both layoffs and rehirings occurred frequently. In typical white male occupations (for example, building and construction and the machine trades), figures for 1929 duplicate those for 1915, showing longer bouts of unemployment for workers in those trades.[36]

In 1915 and 1929, when the first extensive figures on duration of unemployment are available for Philadelphia, a majority of those out of work could count on remaining unemployed for at least three months; 25 percent faced the prospect of not being hired again for half a year. 1915 and 1929 can be taken as normal or normal "bad" times. Circumstances could certainly prove worse in the midst of a total economic collapse. As the Great Depression of the 1930s unfolded, the numbers of unemployed grew—to between 40 and 50 percent of the working population in Philadelphia—and the percent-

age of workers facing excruciatingly long periods of job loss esca-
lated. In 1931, investigators at state employment bureaus in the city
discovered that 21 percent of the unemployed had been out of work
for more than one year, a figure not far different from that compiled
by the Department of Labor in 1929. That proportion then climbed
to 39 percent in 1933, 60 percent in 1934, and 69 percent in 1935,
then "leveled off" at 63 percent in 1936, 62 percent in 1937, and 48
percent in 1938! In 1935, 33 percent of the unemployed in Philadelphia actually reported not holding a job for three or more startlingly
long years.[37]

An economic crisis on the order of the total disintegration of the
American economy in the 1930s demanded extraordinary measures,
in the public realm, of course, but also privately, by families of the
unemployed. Yet even in normal times the unemployment of a major
breadwinner for periods of three or six months wreaked havoc and
required special strategies and actions on the part of the family and
all family members.

In the nineteenth century and the first decades of the twentieth,
working people in Philadelphia had a difficult time making ends
meet. Figures on income and expenditures for the 1880s, for example,
indicate that even if a skilled worker labored a full complement of
days during the year, his or her wages would cover less than 90 percent
of the expenses needed by a typical family of five simply to survive;
for the unskilled, full-time employment would have yielded less than
60 percent of the money needed to match the costs of basic needs.[38]
Since few workers in the city worked on a regular basis and received
regular income, few families could rely on the earnings of one breadwinner. Matters did not improve in the twentieth century. An extensive survey of the budgets of families of textile workers in Philadelphia conducted in 1919 revealed that on average the incomes of heads
of households comprised less than 80 percent of normal expenditures
and that only 14 percent of the families canvassed could amass any
savings.[39] The uncertain income-producing abilities of the male heads
of these households was a critical factor in the problem. In the early
1920s, the plight of newly arriving black families from the South was
even more extreme. Survey research conducted during the decade
with these latest arrivals to the city indicated that only 40 percent of
the families studied could survive at minimal subsistence levels on
the income of the leading breadwinner.[40]

The traditional answer for making ends meet when the head of household's irregular and low earnings could not match family expenditures was to place more family members into the labor force. At least before World War II in Philadelphia, older children went first. As shown earlier, the percentage of young people twelve to seventeen years of age at work increased at each age level over the course of the nineteenth century and only gradually declined in the twentieth, even with compulsory school attendance laws and expansion in school facilities. The availability of light industrial jobs in this city of diversified manufacture presented opportunities for teenage employment, but as important, if not more, was the critical contribution that young people could make to family income and survival. Families on the lowest rungs of the economic ladder and across all ethnic groups, with one important exception, were the most likely to have their older sons and daughters in the labor market. Black teenagers, as noted earlier, faced severe obstacles in securing jobs; they stayed in school and their place in producing income was assumed by their mothers.

The income brought into the household by young men and women represented a substantial part of the family's total monetary resources. In the late nineteenth century, German and Irish immigrant teenagers whose fathers were unskilled workers contributed more than 40 percent of the family income.[41] The relative share of children's earnings declined in the twentieth century as child labor declined. Still, researchers in 1919 found that, among families of textile workers in Philadelphia, earnings of children still amounted to 10 percent of family income on average. This figure varied according to the occupational status of the head of household, but did not reach the proportions evident for the period fifty years earlier. Notable in 1919 was a rise in the place of the earnings of working mothers.[42]

Children's income could also be as uncertain and irregular as their parents. High turnover and frequent layoffs marked their work as well. Legislation passed in 1889 by Pennsylvania required that businesses employing workers under the age of sixteen maintain a separate register recording their positions and attendance. A surviving record book for the textile firm of William Whitaker & Sons during the period from 1890 to 1922 shows that teenagers were engaged on an uneven basis for the company. Twenty-five percent of those employed stayed less than one month, 60 percent worked at Whitaker's for just three to six months. A small number, 10 percent, did remain on the rolls for more than two years.[43] Children's labor proved vital for family survival in Philadelphia during the nineteenth and early twentieth centuries, though their work proved to be no less unstable than that of the adults whose incomes they had to supplement.

Families placed older children in the work force to balance income with expenditures as a matter of course in the nineteenth century and first decades of the twentieth. Great reluctance was shown, on the other hand, in having married women work outside the home, except in the case of black married women. The labor-force participation rates of white married women remained distinctively low through the 1930s. In the late nineteenth century, census enumerators reported that only between 3 and 5 percent of all white married women in Philadelphia held jobs outside the home.[44] Married women's so-called gainful employment increased during the early twentieth century, with 9 percent of them working for wages by 1910, 10 percent by 1920, and 14 percent by 1930. In contrast, throughout this period between 50 and 60 percent of all single white women in the city earned income as employees of Philadelphia enterprises. Native- and foreign-born married women entered the labor force in the exact same proportions.[45] Black women in Philadelphia, though, had notably different employment histories. In 1880, 22 percent of all married black women worked outside the home; by 1930, 40 percent were in the labor force. Three to four times as many black married women labored for wages as white; single black women similarly could be found gainfully employed in greater numbers than their single white counterparts.[46]

A paucity of evidence prevents a definitive explanation for the markedly low rates of labor-force participation of married white women in Philadelphia, a city whose light and diversified manufacturing base encouraged women's work outside the home. The ability of older white sons and daughters to secure employment certainly allowed their mothers to stay at home and attend to child care and household production activities. Discrimination against black youths in hiring undoubtedly contributed to the greater numbers of married black women at work away from the family. Whether white married women remained outside the labor force in attempts to maintain some ideal of the proper household is difficult to affirm without substantial qualitative evidence. In Philadelphia and elsewhere, unionized male workers raised the demand for the so-called family wage, that is, compensation adequate to keep their children and wives at home and protected from the alleged physical and social evils of the workplace.[47] Whether this represented a purely strategical and rhetorical device on the part of labor leaders or a true reflection of values shared among working people is also a matter without a clear answer.

Focusing on the cultural or economic reasons that led families, that is, white families, to limit the labor force participation of mothers and wives places the onus solely on the supply side. The employers who barred married women from employment in a number of instances must also be taken into account. The firing of women school teachers after they married is a classic example, but in other pursuits as well employers either officially or informally adopted the practice of letting go and not hiring married female employees and job applicants. In 1930, investigators from the Women's Bureau of the Department of Labor interviewed executives of forty-four firms in Philadelphia that employed great numbers of female clerical workers. The investigators found that twelve, or 22 percent, had strict policies barring married women from employment; seventeen (39 percent) noted that they never retained a single female employee if she did get married.[48] A larger follow-up study in 1940, this time involving 279 companies with sizable white-collar work forces, revealed that 39 percent of the firms never hired married women and that 15 percent made a definite practice of letting their newly married female employees go.[49]

Companies justified the official policy of barring married women from employment on the grounds that child rearing made for unpredictable tenures at work; firms could not risk the costs of training and turnover. In white-collar work, bald sexist attitudes may have also played a role. Testimony of personnel managers in Philadelphia in the 1950s indicated that male executives preferred hiring young single female secretaries; they felt less able to exert and maintain authority over older married women.[50] Oddly, such cultural stereotyping could work to the advantage of some married women in their searches for employment. Researchers from the Women's Bureau of the Department of Labor in the late 1920s found employers in Philadelphia favoring certain immigrant married women for custodial jobs. One foreman of an office cleaning crew testified that he only hired married Slavic women because "they work hard, don't object to scrubbing floors on their knees. They still like brooms and are afraid of vacuum cleaners." Another manager of a manufacturing firm noted that he favored Polish married women: "They are hard workers, solid—equal to heavy jobs. We have no Italians or Jews here. We do not like the excitable Italian type for work and the Jews cannot satisfy their ambition in this plant as there is no chance for progress in skill or wages."[51] On such attitudes, employment decisions were made.

Choices, by families and employers, limited the gainful employment of the great majority of married white women. When they did work outside the home, it usually involved desperate circumstances. Black women labored long hours in wage labor to compensate for continuing job discrimination against adult black males and older black children; preferences by white employers for black women as domestics and in such arduous and poorly paid work as laundries allowed them a place, if lowly, in the job market. Before World War II, the entrance of white married women into the labor market normally signified a severe crisis in the earning powers of their husbands. When a group of 728 working mothers in Philadelphia were asked by investigators in the early 1920s why they worked, only 10 percent answered out of personal preference. The largest number, 30 percent, cited the irregular and insufficient incomes of the male heads of households, a mark of the role that underemployment played in the family economy; another 22 percent attributed their working to the death of a husband, 14 percent to his illness. The desertion of families by husbands led to the employment of married women in another 13 percent of the cases, and the reneging on support by men who had already abandoned their families accounted for the remaining instances.[52]

Under normal circumstances, when white married women worked they contributed a small percentage of the family income—an estimated 3 percent as revealed in budget studies of Philadelphia families conducted after World War I.[53] In crisis situations, the money earned outside the home by working mothers rose to a least 50 percent of the total monetary resources of the family.[54] White families placed women in the work force reluctantly, at least before World War II, but when circumstances warranted—invariably when the male head of household's contribution to family income precipitously declined—mothers entered into gainful employment as a matter of course.

A general trend toward the greater labor-force participation of white married women is evident as early as the first decades of the twentieth century. Rapid and substantial increases in the number of these women at work outside the home would not occur until after World War II, and particularly in very recent decades. Labor shortages may have played as important a role here as changes in attitude and the family economy. When department stores in Philadelphia, for example, built their first suburban outlets in the 1950s, they faced severe problems in filling sales clerk positions. They were forced to revise their employment policies and tap into a new labor pool, suburban housewives who were willing to work part-time. Part-time employment of white married women during the labor-scarce decade of the 1950s represented the first step to their fuller engagement in work outside the home.[55]

An interesting inverse relationship exists historically, though, between the labor-force participation of children and that of married women: as the former declined, the latter increased. Families in a city such as Philadelphia apparently have always had a difficult time making ends meet or matching income with rising levels of consumption. In the nineteenth century, families typically placed older children into the work force to compensate for the inadequate or irregular earnings of fathers. In the twentieth, with legal proscriptions on child labor, compulsory school-attendance laws, and eventually the increased role played by educational credentialing in occupational achievement—which did not become a widespread issue in Philadelphia until after World War II—there occurred a simple substitution of mother's gainful employment for children's.

The decision of mothers to work outside the home, of course, raised the critical matter of child care. Working families in Philadelphia in the nineteenth century and first half of the twentieth did not have access to the institutionalized day-care facilities that are just developing in our own times. A study conducted in 1930, for example, revealed that only twenty-one nurseries then operated in the city, serving less than 900 families; six of these day-care centers catered to black working women.[56] Without community-based support, reliance had to be placed almost entirely on relatives and friends. A survey of approximately 1,200 married women who were forced to work outside the home in the 1920s accordingly indicated that in 28 percent of the cases children were sent during the day to relatives' or neighbors' homes; in 18 percent, relatives assisted with child care directly in the home; unemployed fathers assumed care of children in 14 percent of the instances and older siblings in 10 percent. Twenty-five percent of the working women reported relying on schools, and, in a small percentage of cases, children were simply left at home by themselves.[57] Obviously, leaving the home for work was not an easy matter for working mothers, certainly one reason the percentages of married women in the work force remained relatively low. This places the plight of black working women in even graver perspective.

Married women, however, could contribute to family income without leaving the home, thus avoiding the crisis of child care. Their unpaid labor in home maintenance, production of goods for direct household use (most notably clothes and food), and child-rearing alone constituted a vital savings and subsidy for the family economy. Married women in Philadelphia also worked in the home for wages through the putting-out system. Domestic outwork is often portrayed as a stage in industrial development leading to the emergence of full-fledged factories. The coming of the factory system in Philadelphia, however, did not spell the end of the placing of work in homes, but rather led to a vast expansion in outwork. Merchants traditionally organized putting-out; in the 1780s, for example, Samuel Wetherill circulated broadsides throughout the small commercial city of Philadelphia announcing that he would deliver wool and flax "to good Women . . . who want Employment in the Business of Spinning"; the cloth they manufactured in their homes would be sold in his store.[58] In the modern industrial era, factory owners replaced merchants as the operators and sustainers of the domestic outwork system. The home emerged as an ancillary to the factory, in effect, as manufacturers attempted to reduce costs by limiting the number of permanent plant employees on the rolls and farming out certain aspects of production to homeworkers on a piece-work basis as needed.

Domestic outwork persisted as a subterranean part of the economy and went largely unmeasured. Census enumerators compiling information about households for the population census did not raise questions about work conducted within the home; their counterparts gathering data from businesses for the manufacturing census did not bother to ask about workers not directly employed. Determining a precise number or percentage of married women involved in out-work for any period in Philadelphia's history is impossible. Firm executives themselves often had no idea of how many people were engaged. A study conducted on domestic industry in the 1910s revealed that manufacturers left the recruitment of home workers entirely in the hands of contractors and they themselves, as one testified, "[had] no means of knowing how many people our contractors employ[ed]."[59] Even the contractors did not keep close tabs. One agent described his operations as follows: "I go out on Christian Street and pick up a couple of Italian women that know how to finish trousers." The agent reported that he never learned their names, nor how they went about finding and organizing relatives, friends, and neighbors in helping to finish his orders. This was a labyrinthine system.[60]

If numbers on domestic outworkers are unavailable, it is clear that putting-out persisted and expanded in Philadelphia largely on the strength and place of the garment trades in the city's economy. A survey of close to three hundred women regularly engaged at home in putting-out work in 1916 found that upwards of 67 percent worked on men's clothing and another 20 percent on women's and children's garments. A small number performed finishing tasks on rugs, and the rest were engaged with a range of miscellaneous non-textile wares.[61] Since the vast majority of outworkers were involved with the apparel trade, it is possible to place a low and rough estimate on the number of Philadelphians earning money at home through domestic outwork in the first decades of the twentieth century. Studies of the city's garment industry during the period established that 60 percent of the labor involved in the production of apparel generally occurred within the confines of factories and the balance in homes.[62] With the census reporting near forty thousand Philadelphians directly employed by garment companies in the city in 1920, simple calculations place the number of outworkers at approximately twenty-six thousand—or twenty-six thousand families who relied on the income earned by wives laboring on piece-work in the home.[63]

The earnings derived from domestic outwork played a critical role in family survival. When researchers asked Italian immigrant married women why they brought needle trades work into their homes, the most common response by far was to compensate for the income lost by their husbands' seasonal or irregular employment.[64] Domestic outwork persisted and expanded in Philadelphia because the city's garment industry supplied opportunities and also because there existed a pool of laboring women who wanted to work at home to ease the problem of child care while earning extra monies to deal with the uncertain job prospects chronically faced by first breadwinners in the Philadelphia economy.

The prevalence of outwork in the city also provided the fuel for social protest. In the Progressive era, muckraking journalists and social science researchers brought to the public devastating stories and statistics on the conditions under which women toiled on piece-work in the home and the exploitative practices of the outwork contractors. Exposes during the period failed to bring reform or regulation of the institution. In the 1930s, the putting-out system came under new attack, receiving fatal blows first from organized labor and next from the federal government. In 1933, the Amalgamated Clothing Workers Union, which had secured a strong foothold in the garments trade in Philadelphia during the 1920s, launched a concerted effort to abolish outwork; as long as manufacturers could shift production to non-unionized workers and work sites, the organization's leverage remained precarious. After massive picketing and demonstrations, the union succeeded in reaching an agreement with an association of outwork contractors that established fixed and improved wage scales for home workers. The agreement effectively spelled an end to the system. With increased outside labor costs, manufacturers now determined to keep all aspects of production under factory roofs with centralized and more easily supervised work forces.[65] In 1938, Congress passed the Fair Labor Standards Act, which outlawed most work contracted out in homes, particulary in apparel manufacture.[66] Domestic outwork probably would have disappeared in Philadelphia with the almost complete collapse of the garment industry after World War II, but union and government initiatives officially dealt its demise in the 1930s. Families in the city accordingly lost an important source of income, earnings that helped tide them over when husbands and fathers were unemployed. The issue of whether married women should be allowed to work in the home under contract has reemerged as a sensitive question in our own day.

Work, then, was brought into the home to supplement family

income. But the home itself could also serve as an important resource in family survival. No history of Philadelphia is complete in this respect without treatment of the widespread ownership of homes and its implications for working people. As early as the 1870s, writers had dubbed Philadelphia "The City of Homes," with such renowned social investigators as Carroll Wright claiming that at least one in four of the city's "industrial classes" owned the homes in which they lived; another respected researcher, Lorin Blodget, placed the figure at 50 percent.[67] Home ownership was even touted at the time as a prime reason for the supposed conservativism of Philadelphia's laboring population. "Trade unions could not possibly succeed in Philadelphia," one editorialist blithely wrote in the *Public Ledger* in 1893, because "the separate home feature of the city detracts very much from the attractiveness of union headquarters, and once there, with his working clothes off and his slippers on, the average workingman is just as likely to stay in as he is to go out." Directors of the Philadelphia Society for Organizing Charity similarly applauded the role played by the numerous building and loan associations in the city. In enabling families to own their own homes, they helped "make men independent . . . self-helpful . . . steady, thrifty, forehanded and domestic in habits."[68] Philadelphia businessmen such as John B. Stetson established company savings and home loan plans for their employees in the belief and hope that home ownership would curtail both labor turnover and radicalism.[69]

Accurate statistics compiled by census takers in the early twentieth century lend substance to the appellation "City of Homes." In 1920, census enumerators reported that 40 percent of all families in the city then resided in homes they owned, the highest percentage among the nation's largest cities. That figure grew to 52 percent by 1930 and dipped to 39 percent in 1940, a mark of the mortgage foreclosures suffered by Philadelphians during the Great Depression. By mid-twentieth century, home ownership in the city stood at 50 percent of all families, once again highest among the country's leading municipalities.[70]

A number of factors have contributed to the continued prevalence of home ownership in Philadelphia. Available land is one simple consideration. While Philadelphians had eighty-three thousand acres on which to build their venerable row houses, New Yorkers had twenty-five thousand dearer acres; population pressure and limited space there would lead to multistoried tenement and apartment build-ing development.[71] A custom of ground rents established by William Penn and extended into the nineteenth century further facilitated the construction of private homes. Prospective home owners did not have to purchase land; they could rent the land on long-term leases and needed only to finance the costs of building.[72] The availability of materials, notably bricks and lumber, and of skilled labor also kept construction costs relatively low.[73] Critically important was the remarkable spread of building and loan associations in Philadelphia. The first such institution in the nation formed in the city in 1831. By the 1920s, the city housed 2,600 saving societies for home construc-tion and purchase, one-fourth the number in the entire United States.[74] Typically, Philadelphians bought shares in these associations and they were allowed to borrow up to their matured value at moder-ate interest rates. Between 1850 and 1875, Philadelphia's building and loan societies pumped $50 million into home construction and the practice became so popular that by the 1920s more than one million Philadelphians had invested their savings in local associations.[75] The building and loan societies were particularly effective in offering their members low-interest second mortgages to supplement the limited mortgages that established banks offered to working families.[76] This two-tiered system of financing, labeled the "Philadelphia Plan" in the real-estate industry, was frequently cited as a prime contributor to expanded home ownership in the city.[77]

Not every family, of course, could afford to own its own resi-dence. While Carroll Wright and Lorin Blodget spoke of between 25 and 50 percent of the citizens of Philadelphia owning homes, surveys by state officials in the late nineteenth century placed the number at a more realistic 10 percent.[78] Moreover, studies in the twentieth cen-tury revealed a clear relationship between occupation, income, and race and ability to own a home. While 63 percent of all professionals in the city owned their own residences in 1940, less than 30 percent of those listed as "laborers" in the census were similarly endowed; similarly, twice the number of high-income as of low-income Phila-delphians owned their own homes; and on average, while 40 percent of all white families lived in homes they owned, more than 90 percent of the black community were renters. Income may have been a more important fact than race, however. Black families of means in Phila-delphia owned homes in similar proportions to their white counter-parts.[79]

Foreign-born Philadelphians became home owners in even greater numbers than older-stock city dwellers and this trait held across income categories. In 1940, 55 percent of all naturalized immigrants and 44 percent of the yet-to-be naturalized lived in residences they owned, both higher figures than the 40 percent calculation for Philadelphians born in the United States.[80] Did greater property ownership among foreign immigrants to the city represent some cultural propensity, a mark of their alleged traditional values and peasant backgrounds? Researchers thought not. The purchase of homes by the foreign-born seemed more of an instrumental act, a means to guarantee family survival.[81] The home existed as an income-producing resource; work and, more important, boarders, could be brought into the home to augment earnings, particularly in slack times. As home ownership constitutes a hedge against inflation for present-day Philadelphians, in the late nineteenth and early twentieth centuries owning a home served as insurance against irregular employment.

Before World War II, taking in boarders was a common practice in urban areas in the United States and an important means of supplementing family income.[82] In Philadelphia during the late nineteenth century, lodgers could be found in more than one in six of all the households in the city.[83] While the boarding of strangers did not vary significantly by the incomes of heads of households, the taking in of lodgers by low-income families, who on average lived in the most cramped quarters, must have entailed great disruption and sacrifice. Foreign-born Philadelphians housed boarders also in equal proportions to native-born whites. The greatest distinction occurred between black and white families; lodgers were present in one-third of all African-American households in the city.[84] Female-headed households also listed boarders in disproportionate numbers, as did older families who rented rooms emptied by grown children.[85]

In the late nineteenth and early twentieth centuries, families could earn between $20 and $100 a month through boarding, as high as 15 percent of the total family income.[86] Boarding could prove so essential to survival that even firms resorted to housing workers in slack times as a means of raising needed revenues.[87] For families in Philadelphia, the taking in of lodgers probably made the difference in many instances in whether wives and mothers would have to work outside the home and served as an essential source of income in the absence or decline of earnings contributed by the main breadwinner.

Boarding could also affect the labor-force participation of older daughters, who were needed to help with the extra work now involved in household maintenance.[88]

The family and home thus represented a first line of defense against irregular income. Older children could be placed in the work force; in extremely desperate times white married women, and in normally desperate times black married women, could find work outside the home; work and boarders also could be brought into the home. Philadelphians faced with uncertain employment could also fend for themselves and their families by hustling odd jobs, working as migrant laborers on truck farms in New Jersey, tending bar, shining shoes, selling door-to-door, and performing day labor work in construction and on the railroads.[89] Unemployed or underemployed skilled workers could also take a chance on opening their own businesses. During the depression of the 1930s, laid-off machinists in Philadelphia set up small shops of their own in basements and garages to fill small-batch orders from metal-works companies in their neighborhoods.[90]

Families trying to make ends meet in normal or extremely bad times relied first on their own resources. Assistance could also be sought in the larger community. Local unions, for example, provided relief to their members. Labor organizations in Philadelphia fought for higher wages and shorter hours, but an equal effort was devoted to instituting measures that cushioned the blow of fluctuating employment conditions. Unions aimed to regulate the labor market and distribute work equitably by establishing seniority rights, grievance procedures, hiring hall practices, work sharing, and controls on apprenticeship. Unions also specifically sought to take power over hiring and laying off workers in slack times from those foremen and plant superintendents who acted in capricious and nepotistic ways. Unions in Philadelphia in the nineteenth and early decades of the twentieth centuries had limited funds to offer direct aid to their unemployed members, but they could work to regularize and impart fairness to the employment process.

Trade unions in Philadelphia through the 1920s only lent services to an elite of the city's working population, largely skilled white male workers of old-American and old-immigrant stock backgrounds. Beyond fending for themselves, for the larger mass of laboring people, there existed a growing network of private and public relief agencies.

In the nineteenth century, charitable organizations emerged in Philadelphia for the express purpose of aiding the unemployed. The Philadelphia Society for the Employment and Instruction of the Poor, for example, was established in 1847. For Philadelphians out of work, the society offered free medical care, bathing and laundry facilities, groceries at cost, vocational training courses, short-term lodging between jobs, and, of course, prayer meetings. Between 1861 and 1880, surviving ledgers for the association indicate that more than fifty-five thousand Philadelphians sought the organization's assistance. The records of the society also show that its clientele varied with changing economic circumstances. In the winter months, dock workers and other outdoor laborers flooded the agency, seeking relief during periods of seasonal unemployment. During major business downturns, in the late 1850s and from 1873 to 1879 specifically, the rolls of the society swelled with skilled mechanics and even white-collar workers.[91]

The Philadelphia Society for the Employment and Instruction of the Poor developed into a major operation. Smaller relief organizations also proliferated. The Spring Garden Soup Society, for example, established in 1853, emerged as the first of twelve soup kitchens that offered food to families of the unemployed in late nineteenth-century Philadelphia.[92] Other associations formed to provide clothing and medical care. The spread of relief services occurred unsystematically, and to bring order to the general effort, a group of reformers founded the Philadelphia Society for Organizing Charitable Relief in 1878. The organization assumed as its principal task the coordination and sponsorship of private assistance to families in need. A catalogue produced in 1879 reported no less than 270 societies, serving, with public relief agencies, an estimated one in seven Philadelphia families.[93]

From the early colonial period, state and local authorities also offered various kinds of assistance to families and individuals in distress without adequate means of support. Government officials supervised public alms and work houses and offered so-called outdoor relief grants. Throughout the nineteenth century, great pressure existed for an expansion of a public role in assisting the needy of Philadelphia. Private charities could not handle the demand, nor did they readily open their doors to new immigrants or to families whose appearance and behavior in the eyes of private charity givers marked them as "undeserving." During economic depressions in particular, the city witnessed demonstrations calling on public authorities to establish soup kitchens, shelters, and works projects. Government assistance to families of the unemployed grew in the nineteenth and early twentieth centuries, but in as haphazard a manner as private relief. More systematic assistance would only be afforded with the passage of the Social Security Act in 1935, when the federal government assumed the role of organizing and directing state governments in the dispensation of unemployment insurance and aid to dependent families.

Local provision of relief still mattered before the implementation of federal welfare measures. In the early 1930s, surveys in Philadelphia indicated that no less than 50 percent of all households in the city with an adult unemployed member had applied for assistance to the Philadelphia County Relief Board.[94] Help from the community—public or private—however, remained an uncertain matter throughout the nineteenth century and first decades of the twentieth; families in Philadelphia faced with irregular employment and incomes wisely and necessarily kept relying on their own resources.

Federal fiscal and monetary policies to regulate and pattern economic activity; the maintenance of high levels of aggregate demand through government deficit-financed spending for public works and military goods manufacture; the bolstering and sustaining of consumer purchasing power through government assistance and insurance programs for farmers, the unemployed, the disabled, the retired, and dependent mothers and children; union protections for mass production workers; diversified corporations operating in international markets and able to balance and regulate production schedules; increased communications and accounting capacities through computerization; personnel practices that encourage long-term tenure; the spread of stable white-collar jobs; the forty-hour week, fifty-week a year work regimen—all these are facets of present-day life in Philadelphia. Such benefits, to be sure, are still not shared by all members of the community, but they are features that had absolutely no part in the lives of William Rees, Timothy Ragan, Jean Bally, and William Deacon. In their world, uncertain employment was the norm.

The measures that have been taken for more regularized work are now under attack. For conservatives, government spending policies and welfare programs promote laxity, stifle initiative, lower productivity, and boost inflation. For critics from the left, these efforts at greater social security are haphazard at best; they tend to placate rather than empower people and cover only a portion of the working population; they do not attend to the dilemmas faced by women, African-Americans, and other minorities. The consequences of the practices and institutions that mark Philadelphia in the late twentieth century are not at issue here, but rather their genesis. Efforts to regularize employment came as part of concerted attempts by various, often contending, groups in the society—businessmen, politicians, trade unionists, academics, and reformers—to bring administration to an unstable capitalist order. Major and minor economic crisis upon crisis demanded change. More concretely, the impetus for reform of the system can be found in the lives of William Rees and our other erstwhile Philadelphians, and particularly in their constant losing and constant having to get work.

Conclusion

A young man or woman needs a job; an employer needs new workers. The parties to this transaction meet and assess their respective interests and requirements. Bargaining ensues, an accord is eventually reached and an employment contract signed. Another hiring in the job marketplace. A simple matter indeed.

The history rendered in this book proves otherwise. The existing state of labor supply and demand; the given occupational structure or the kinds of jobs that are available; the attitudes and expectations of the job seeker; the recruitment practices and general personnel policies of the prospective employer; the question of skill and whether training can occur prior to employment or must be on the shop, sales, or office floor; the potential role of unions; whether agencies operate to facilitate contacts between suppliers and purchasers of labor; the possible impact of government regulations; who has the power to force decisions on employment and even to define which labor in the society is to be valued—this is just a partial list of considerations, of factors shaping the hiring process. Transactions in the labor market are never simple.

This book has peeled away various layers embedded in the question of the getting of work. The individual chapters in the volume form complete stories—the role of schooling in occupational attainment, the place of mediating agencies in the labor market, the impact of government interventions. The task now remains to weigh the parts—to counterpoise the structural with the personal and institutional, to reiterate findings and draw conclusions.

The institutional, those organizations and programs created by various groups and individuals in Philadelphia that directly or indirectly affected outcomes in the labor market, can serve as a starting point. The role of institutions at first glance seems of little note. At least before 1950, for example, private and public employment bureaus

256

and newspaper help-wanted advertising figured in less than 10 percent of all job searches; these agencies in fact provide more interest
for what they reveal about elite fears of social disorder in the city
than they do about the actual workings of the labor marketplace.
Yet, the specific role that employment bureaus and help-wanted ads
played in the lives of black Philadelphians and older, immigrant
workers with limited years of schooling should not be ignored; nor
should the impact that a Labor Bureau of the Metal Manufacturers'
Association of Philadelphia could have on employment in a trade. A
balanced view of the place of unions is similarly in order. Before the
great upsurge of labor organization in the late 1930s, the trade union
movement reached and enrolled only a small percentage of workers
in the Quaker City, but the controls on labor recruitment and allocation achieved by various unions of skilled workmen in the city deserve emphasis as well.

An even more ambiguous (and complex) assessment is due on the
question of schools and work. Every effort was made in Philadelphia
to have the schools linked to the world of work; the ideal of a classical
education commanded few adherents and never gained full sway in
the city. Yet fiscal stringency, class tensions, the democratic ethos,
and intellectual confusion guaranteed a loose commitment to education in general and to vocationalism specifically. As important, if not
more so, the plight of working families in Philadelphia in making
ends meet—a problem exacerbated by chronic irregular employment—meant that vast numbers of young boys and girls developed
only fragile ties to the school order. Family survival demanded their
foregoing formal education for work.

The general conclusion that a golden age of American schooling
never existed, that the role of the schools in occupational achievement
in the past should not be overestimated—the schools may have
helped many who entered, but the point is that not all stayed and
attended—has to be counterbalanced by other intriguing findings of
this study. Commercial course degree programs clearly mattered.
The implementation of commercial courses transpired without the
ideological and political dilemmas entailed in industrial education;
white-collar, presumed upwardly mobile jobs were involved. The
schools could also train students in the standardized skills that employers needed and had no interest in providing themselves. The
commercial course degree was a good ticket to employment. The

role of Catholic schools in Philadelphia in this respect is of definite interest. Significantly, system-building in both the public and parochial schools in the city involved centralization and the deliberate curtailing of local community controls, related professionalization, and also vocationalism. For the latter, parochial and public school administrators rested the survival and success of their institutions on attracting students with the promise of a practical education. The Catholic schools not only chose the practical appeal, but also placed great resources into commercial education, and there were payoffs in the employment of their graduates, particularly of young Catholic women. Private trade schools in fact represented the only domain where mechanical arts schooling prevailed in a meaningful way. Any evaluation of the role of schools in getting work must draw distinctions, then, between forms of vocationalism and the respective and different educations afforded in public, parochial, and private trade schools.

One additional and crucial distinction is in order with regard to schooling and work, and that involves formal schooling and apprenticeship. Apprenticeship as an institution survived in Philadelphia—in changed form to be sure—and served as a decided advantage in employment experience (more so than schooling, apparently). This finding raises fundamental questions about the learning process in modern societies. Schools are a remarkably new institution, dating in most instances from the mid-nineteenth century. With the exception of the private tutorials and academies attended by the children of the rich, most young people in the past learned through direct observation and in apprenticeship, not through schooling. Schools remained tangential in the experiences of most adolescents during the late nineteenth and early twentieth centuries and by every indication the relationship between schools and urban teenagers today is no stronger. (If there is a crucial difference of course, it is that jobs were available for those young men and women who left or were forced to leave schools a century ago.)

A new look at apprenticeship is suggested by this study. If one public policy recommendation is in order from this work, it would involve a call for reviving the institution of apprenticeship on a massive scale. Tax incentives, for example, could be offered to firms operating in and near cities such as Philadelphia to take sizable numbers of young people from disadvantaged neighborhoods into employment. They could be assigned mentors who would be responsible for their attendance, training, and progress. The apprentices would be released from their jobs during the day for schooling in basic academic subjects, either on company premises or in central locations. Mentors would oversee school work and compensation would be based on successful class and work performance. Critics may interpret this suggestion as just another example of an effort to mold a disciplined work force for business, but that would miss an important point. The workplace has served and can serve as a major site of learning, not just technical but general and social as well. The kinds of relationships that are structured at work—be they participatory or hierarchical—are another matter. The history of apprenticeship reminds us that education need not be an artificial or divorced experience for young people.

The role of institutions in getting work is then mixed. In Philadelphia, at least for the period under study, neither schools, unions, employment bureaus, or help-wanted advertising had a singular or definitive impact on labor market transactions. The exceptions to this statement—with apprenticeship serving as a notable case in point—do deserve highlighting. Similar results emerge from an excursion into the realm of the personal—telling insights are afforded but still no general conclusions. There is, though, at least one unique story here.

To give weight to the personal is to render agency to the subjects of analysis. Philadelphians were not merely acted upon by economic forces and institutions; working people in the city acted on their own behalfs and on the basis of closely held values and ideals. Evidence of personal initiative abounds. Families in Philadelphia employed every means available to insure survival, for example; family was both a resource and motivating principle. Philadelphians also used personal connections as a key method in getting work and in sharing work formally and informally on the job. Individual employers, in a similar vein, deliberately structured their businesses with benevolent standards in mind.

Personal considerations, however, do not bear full explanatory power, because few distinct patterns of behavior are discernible. Philadelphians acted in more similar ways than dissimilar. Native-born Philadelphians and their immigrant counterparts, for example, basically secured and lost work in like manners. They sent their children to schools and into the labor market in common fashion (class proved more important here than any particular cultural disposition). True, women's laboring experience varied distinctly from that of men— women attended schools and participated in the labor force at different rates, found employment by slightly different means, occupied a separate set of jobs, and their severances from work followed different paths. Distinctions on this order could be drawn between young and old workers as well. These differences deserve absolute recognition, yet they appear less remarkable when two definitely odd situations are considered: the first, the less than obvious case of German-Americans, and second, the too obvious example of Philadelphians of African-American descent.

As for the German-Americans, they do appear different and possibly represent the clearest instance where distinct cultural values led to distinct behaviors. The extremely low rates of school attendance among German-American boys and girls, their relatively large presence in the work force, their engagement in apprenticeship, and the dominance of older members of the community in the skilled trades marks this group. Here personal agency is important. The distance between German-Americans and other ethnic groups on labor market experience may not have been as great as that measured between men and women and young and old—the point is arguable—but what makes the German-American case different is the deliberate nature of activity; this is a group that made its own history.

The African-American experience in Philadelphia stands out even farther as a separate story—other differences between groups do not seem as remarkable when the black/white divide is studied—but here history remained more dictated than made. Black Philadelphians remained frozen out of industrial employment (and white-collar jobs, for that matter) into the fourth decade of the twentieth century; no other group experienced that fate. Even the skilled and schooled among them could not find work outside the African-American community. The ways in which they secured and lost work and their general employment histories—and black women stand out here— followed vastly different paths (as, ironically, did the school attendance of black youngsters). Black Philadelphians had physically the greatest access to jobs and socially, the least. African-Americans were not simply the last in-migrants to the city with the marketplace ultimately pushing them up the social ladder; they had in fact inhabited the city in sizable numbers generations before most white immigrant groups had arrived. Nor was it just that the same manufacturing jobs which had benefited various other newcomers began to disappear when the black migration reached its peak during and after the 1920s—these jobs had never been available to them. Racism made the black experience in Philadelphia extraordinary and extraordinary measures—lobbying from within the community, federal government interventions from afar—were necessary for a different history even to begin. Government in this respect had an impact on the job market in Philadelphia in various ways—the state created jobs, brought the issue of the rationalization of employment to the fore, and affected both directly and indirectly the personnel policies of private firms—but nowhere was the state more important than in rulings and actions that began to break the cycle of racial discrimination.

To look to the personal is to look for difference, to see the labor market as involving more than a faceless, homogeneous mass. Various differences in experience are noteworthy, but when the German-American case in the late nineteenth and early twentieth centuries (an example of a group clearly charting a distinct course) and, much more significantly, the African-American Philadelphia story through the 1940s (a group denied an indistinct history) are considered, other differences merit display under a smaller spotlight.

Institutions mattered, the personal mattered, but neither in a conclusive fashion; the historical record is complicated on both scores. The structure of economic activity, on the other hand, weighed heavily on the lives of William Rees, Timothy Ragan, Jean Bally, and William Deacon. Philadelphians like these labored in a city with a particular character. Philadelphia in the nineteenth and first half of the twentieth centuries was a diversified, light-industrial manufacturing center dominated by specialized small-to-medium-sized family owned and operated firms. Continued demand for nonstandardized goods and a many-layered marketplace allowed for the survival and expansion of the Philadelphia production system—the enterprise and innovative spirit of its immigrant and native-born proprietors and the skills and hard labor of its work force also contributed to the overall record. The city prospered and jobs were created, jobs for succeeding waves of newcomers from Western and Eastern Europe and for most young people. Young white men and women went to work and not to school in great numbers because their incomes were indispensable to their families, but also because vast employment opportunities existed for them.

Philadelphia's specialized manufactories were also located in residential areas; the city was comprised of distinct manufacturing neighborhoods. The physical and social distances between work and home remained small into the first decades of the twentieth century. This allowed for family, ethnic, and neighborhood networks of hiring—a reason why personal connections loomed so large in the securing of employment and why Philadelphia firms generally maintained highly informal recruitment practices. Plant superintendents knew how and who to hire.

The particular economic structure of the city impinged on all its citizens in another crucial way. Custom production fostered prosperity but also insecurity. Philadelphia's specialized proprietary firms went in and out of business with great frequency (and for a variety of reasons), making uncertain employment a norm of working-class life in the city. As has been shown, this reality had enormous implications for family dynamics and economy.

The hold of the structure on people's lives can be fully appreciated by comparing Philadelphia's past with its present. Since World War II, Philadelphians have lived in a city where the national government plays a key role in flattening the ups and downs of the business cycle, forestalling utter economic collapse, regularizing and improving employment conditions, and placing a floor, as low as it is, on social suffering. A more standardized national and increasingly international marketplace—the death knell of Philadelphia's specialized industrial production system—and the extended corporate order have contributed to stabilization as well. Irregular employment is no longer the norm in the city; for discriminated-against segments of the laboring population, however, there is a new norm of long-term unemployment.

The location of work has also changed, with serious ramifications. The increase in white-collar jobs in center city offices has created a new dynamic in getting work. The role of schools has always been different with regard to office employment. White-collar employers historically have relied on outside agencies for the training of prospective employees in standardized office skills—thus the relative importance of the commercial course degree. The situation may actually be changing in subtle ways. With new technologies and more specialized work in the office, white-collar employers may find them-selves in a similar situation to that of Philadelphia manufacturers—there may be no substitute for on-the-job training, and the merits of the educational credential may lessen. The role of training prior to employment, however, in white-collar work will probably always remain important, and as office work has replaced factory labor, differences between the pre–and post–World War II era are clear.

The true distinction, though, may lie not in the occupational shift, but rather in the locational. Downtown hiring on a massive scale represents a fundamental change, necessarily lessening the role of neighborhood hiring and of personal connections. Physical distance and the drawing of labor from disparate parts of the city (and region, with suburbanization) make for formalized procedures, reliance on educational requirements, reference checking, extended interviews, and personnel testing. No doubt, friends (and probably not relatives) still help in securing employment; this may be particularly true for women, who now occupy clerical positions in great numbers. ("My girlfriend is looking for a new job" may be as common a refrain as it was in industrial neighborhoods fifty and a hundred years ago.) Still, Philadelphians inhabit a very different world today, with the prevalence of downtown white-collar employment, and the hiring process and experience have been affected accordingly.

Context, time, and place, then, count—another way of saying that the structural weighs more heavily than the personal and institu-tional. That is a major conclusion of this study. An investigation of another city or era would probably qualify various findings revealed here. A reader who has picked up this book in hope of receiving some practical suggestions for securing employment and who has read this far might be rather disappointed now. Knowledge that the total situation is important is difficult to translate into a definitive course of action. The unfortunate truth is that transactions in the labor marketplace, in the past, present, and no doubt future, are always complicated—consider just the issue of power in society and who has the power to define the nature of social relationships. The labor market is thus reduced to supply and demand curves on a blackboard or political nostrums on individual enterprise at the risk of great intellectual (and practical) vacuity. Getting work is no mundane matter.

Primary Sources

Archives of the Board of Education of the City of Philadelphia

Hagley Library, Wilmington, Delaware

Broadside and Pamphlet Collection
Christian Schrack Company Papers
Disston Saw Company Papers
E. C. Beetem & Sons Company Papers
E. I. DuPont & Company Papers
Luken Steel Company Papers
Mr. and Mrs. Thomas Savery Papers
Penrose R. Hoopes Papers
Pennsylvania Railroad Company Papers
Philadelphia National Bank Papers
William Whitaker & Sons Company Papers

Historical Society of Pennsylvania, Philadelphia, Pennsylvania

Baldwin Locomotive Company Papers
John Gay & Sons Company Papers
Philadelphia Board of Trade Papers
Philadelphia Chamber of Commerce Papers
Samuel Vauclain Papers
William Horstmann Company Papers

National Archives, Washington, D.C.

Records of the Women's Bureau of the Department of
Labor

Pennsylvania Economy League Library, Philadelphia, Pennsylvania

Albert S. Faught Papers

University of Pennsylvania, Philadelphia, Pennsylvania

Gladys Palmer Papers, in custody of Professor Ann Miller
Wetherill Paint Company Papers, Lippincott Library

Urban Archives, Temple University Library, Philadelphia, Pennsylvania

Armstrong Association of Philadelphia (Urban League) Papers
International Union of Electrical Workers Local 105 Papers
Metal Manufacturers' Association of Philadelphia Papers
1936 Gladys Palmer Survey for the Works Progress Administration
Operative Plasterers' and Cement Masons' International Union, Local #8
    Papers
William Beyer Papers

Firms in Philadelphia with Accessible Archival Records

Brown Instrument Company of Honeywell, Incorporated, Fort Washington, Pennsylvania
Insurance Company of North America, now Connecticut Insurance Group of North America (CIGNA)
Lea & Febiger
Philadelphia Contributionship
Philadelphia Gas Works
Richard Remmey Son Company
Swoboda and Sons of Transcontinental Leather, Incorporated
H. C. Wood Incorporated

Notes

Preface

1. In one of the more extreme variants of standard economic thinking, which bears directly on the subject matter of this study, even unemployment is seen as a kind of occupation: a period of job search when decidedly savvy souls measure whether delaying re-entrance to work might be more pleasurable or more profitable than returning immediately, with more leisure or better offers to come. See Steven Lippman and John McCall, "The Economics of Job Search: A Survey," *Economic Survey*, 14 (June 1976), pp. 155–189; 14 (September 1976), pp. 347–368.

2. Walter Licht, *Working For The Railroad: The Organization of Work in the Nineteenth Century* (Princeton, 1983).

1. Particularities

1. In 1936, the Works Progress Administration contracted with researchers at the Wharton School of the University of Pennsylvania to conduct surveys on employment patterns in Philadelphia. Original questionnaires and transcripts can be found in Interview Schedules, 1936 Gladys Palmer Survey for the Works Progress Administration, Urban Archives, Temple University.

2. For Philadelphia's rise as a commercial center during the colonial period see Thomas M. Doerflinger, *A Vigorous Spirit of Enterprise: Merchants and Economic Development in Revolutionary Philadelphia* (Chapel Hill, 1986); Gary Nash, *The Urban Crucible: Social Change, Political Consciousness, and the Origins of the American Revolution* (Cambridge, Mass., 1979); and Russell E. Weigley, ed., *Philadelphia: A 300-Year History* (New York, 1982), pp. 1–154.

3. Gladys Palmer, *Philadelphia Workers in a Changing Economy* (Philadelphia, 1956), pp. 6–7; Diane Lindstrom, *Economic Development in the Philadelphia Region, 1810–1850* (New York, 1978), chapter 2; Sam Bass Warner, Jr., *The Private City: Philadelphia in Three Periods of Its Growth* (Philadelphia, 1968), chapters 1–2; Weigley, *Philadelphia*, pp. 209, 212, 266.

4. Bruce Laurie and Mark Schmitz, "Manufacture and Productivity: The

Making of an Industrial Base, Philadelphia, 1850–1880," in Theodore Hershberg, ed., *Philadelphia: Work, Space, Family and Group Experience in the Nineteenth Century—Essays Toward an Interdisciplinary History of the City* (New York, 1981), pp. 44–47.

5. Philip Scranton, *Proprietary Capitalism: The Textile Manufacture at Philadelphia, 1800–1885* (New York, 1983), pp. 47, 100, 179, 417.
6. Laurie and Schmitz, "Manufacture and Productivity," pp. 53–66; Philip Scranton and Walter Licht, *Work Sights: Industrial Philadelphia, 1890–1950* (Philadelphia, 1986) contains photographs that illustrate the diversity of work settings in Philadelphia.
7. Laurie and Schmitz, "Manufacture and Productivity," p. 59; Scranton and Licht, *Work Sights,* pp. 71–75; Palmer, *Philadelphia Workers,* pp. 8–9; Rosara L. Passero, "Ethnicity in the Men's Ready-Made Clothing Industry, 1800–1950: The Italian Experience in Philadelphia" (unpublished Ph.D. dissertation, University of Pennsylvania, 1987), pp. 163–166.
8. Palmer, *Philadelphia Workers,* pp. 8–9; Scranton, *Proprietary Capitalism,* p. 95.
9. Scranton and Licht, *Work Sights,* pp. 181–213.
10. Laurie and Schmitz, "Manufacture and Productivity," p. 52.
11. Scranton, *Proprietary Capitalism,* p. 189.
12. Ibid., p. 311.
13. Palmer, *Philadelphia Workers,* p. 25; Scranton, *Proprietary Capitalism,* pp. 247–251.
14. Lindstrom, *Economic Development,* chapters 2–4.
15. Scranton, *Proprietary Capitalism,* p. 48; Weigley, *Philadelphia,* p. 269.
16. Palmer, *Philadelphia Workers,* p. 24.
17. Weigley, *Philadelphia,* p. 75; Christian Schrack Company Papers, Hagley Library, Accession 712, Box 2.
18. Scranton, *Proprietary Capitalism,* pp. 132–134.
19. E. Digby Baltzell, *Puritan Boston and Quaker Philadelphia* (New York, 1979).
20. Scranton, *Proprietary Capitalism,* p. 134.
21. Ibid., p. 46; Palmer, *Philadelphia Workers,* p. 13.
22. Scranton, *Proprietary Capitalism,* pp. 63–64, 127–129, 283–284; Palmer, *Philadelphia Workers,* pp. 13–15.
23. Weigley, *Philadelphia,* p. 558; Scranton and Licht, *Work Sights,* pp. 44–47, 227–246.
24. Weigley, *Philadelphia,* pp. 482–483.
25. Gladys Palmer and Ada Stoflet, *The Labor Force of the Philadelphia Radio Industry in 1936* (Philadelphia, 1938), pp. 2–3.
26. Weigley, *Philadelphia,* p. 597.

27. Sophia T. Cambria, "Youth in the Philadelphia Labor Market" (unpublished Ph.D. dissertation, Bryn Mawr College, 1945), p. 27; Joseph Willits, *Philadelphia Unemployment with Special References to the Textile Industries* (Philadelphia, 1915), p. 23.
28. Palmer, *Philadelphia Workers,* pp. 56–57.
29. Scranton and Licht, *Work Sights,* pp. 266–270.
30. Deindustrialization is seemingly a late twentieth-century phenonomen; yet in Philadelphia the process can be traced to the 1920s. The ingredients of Philadelphia's early industrial decline are also slightly different from such declines in our own times. It is common to blame either foreign competition or high wages (or both) for current losses in American industry. These factors hardly figured in Philadelphia. The growth of a standardized marketplace proved to be the critical blow to Philadelphia's production system. Recently Philip Scranton has added a new twist to this argument by citing the impact on Philadelphia's specialty firms of the new merchandizing practices of the large retail outlet firms that emerged in the 1920s. See Philip Scranton, *Figured Tapestry: Production, Markets, and Power in Philadelphia Textiles, 1885–1941* (New York, 1989), chapter 6.
31. Scranton, *Proprietary Capitalism,* p. 42.
32. Palmer, *Philadelphia Workers,* pp. 22, 45.
33. Ibid., p. 10.
34. Sam Bass Warner, Jr., "If All the World Were Philadelphia: A Scaffolding for Urban History, 1774–1930," *American Historical Review,* 74 (October 1968), pp. 40–41; William Martin Hench, "Trends in the Size of Industrial Companies in Philadelphia From 1915 through 1930" (unpublished Ph.D. dissertation, University of Pennsylvania, 1938), pp. 9–18; Palmer, *Philadelphia Workers,* p. 25.
35. Weigley, *Philadelphia,* p. 533; Palmer, *Philadelphia Workers,* p. 25.
36. Scranton and Licht, *Work Sights,* pp. 219–220; Palmer and Stoflet, *The Labor Force,* pp. 2–3.
37. Warner, *Private City,* p. 51.
38. Theodore Hershberg et al., "A Tale of Three Cities: Blacks, Immigrants, and Opportunity in Philadelphia, 1850–1880, 1930, 1970," in Hershberg, ed., *Philadelphia,* p. 465.
39. Laurie and Schmitz, "Manufacturing and Productivity," pp. 46–47.
40. Ibid.
41. Irwin Sears, "Growth of Population in Philadelphia: 1860 to 1960" (unpublished Ph.D. dissertation, New York University, 1960), p. 95.
42. Richard Juliani, "The Social Organization of Immigration: The Italians in Philadelphia" (unpublished Ph.D. dissertation, University of Pennsylvania, 1971), pp. 112–115.

43. Palmer, *Philadelphia Workers,* p. 8.
44. Caroline Golab, *Immigrant Destinations* (Philadelphia, 1977), pp. 30–31, 42, 106–110.
45. Laurie and Schmitz, "Manufacturing and Productivity," p. 47.
46. Dale Light, "Ethnicity and the Urban Ecology in a Nineteenth-Century City: Philadelphia's Irish, 1840–1890" (unpublished Ph.D. dissertation, University of Pennsylvania, 1979), p. 8.
47. Ibid., p. 17.
48. Scranton, *Proprietary Capitalism,* pp. 338–339, 347.
49. Palmer, *Philadelphia Workers,* p. 26.
50. Scranton, *Proprietary Capitalism,* p. 214.
51. Palmer, *Philadelphia Workers,* p. 11; Hench, "Trends in the Size of Industrial Companies," pp. 21, 41.
52. Statistics on irregular employment and unemployment will be presented and discussed in Chapter 7.
53. Palmer, p. 29.
54. The question of homeownership will be dealt with in Chapter 7.
55. The response of business leaders and politicians to employment problems in Philadelphia will be discussed in Chapter 6.

2. Entering the World of Work

1. Joseph Speakman, "Unwilling to School: Child Labor and its Reform in the Progressive Era" (unpublished Ph.D. dissertation, Temple University, 1976), pp. 163–167.
2. Ibid., p. 212.
3. Ibid., p. 297.
4. Ibid., pp. 179–180.
5. Ibid., pp. 159–169.
6. This discussion of the labor force participation of children will treat only youngsters twelve years of age and above. Less than 3 percent of all nine to eleven year olds were in the labor force during the nineteenth century; their rates, though low, also rose over the course of the century. The focus on older children is warranted not just because of their greater numbers at work. Parents of children in these age categories had choices to make between schooling and work for their offspring. The variance in behaviors is a subject worthy of further study.
7. Sophia T. Cambria, "Youth in the Philadelphia Labor Market" (unpublished Ph.D. dissertation, Bryn Mawr College, 1945), p. 258.
8. Michael Katz, "School Attendance in Philadelphia, 1850–1900" (unpublished paper, University of Pennsylvania, 1982; copy in my possession), pp. 18–19.

9. Ibid., pp. 15–17, 38; Claudia Goldin, "Family Strategies and the Family Economy in the Late Nineteenth Century: The Role of Secondary Workers," in Theodore Hershberg, ed., *Philadelphia: Work, Space, Family, and Group Experience in the Nineteenth Century—Essays Toward an Interdisciplinary History of the City* (New York, 1981), pp. 289–296, 304. The high rates of school attendance of children from families of upper-class standing will be further dealt with in Chapter 3.

10. Lesley Ann Kawaguchi, "The Making of Philadelphia's German-American Ethnic Group and Community Development, 1830–1883" (unpublished Ph.D. dissertation, University of California, Los Angeles, 1983), pp. 124–125.

11. The finding that rates of school attendance for immigrant Russian Jews were closely correlated with class position has been confirmed in the most rigorous historical analysis of this subject to date. See Ari Joel Perlmann, "Education and the Social Structure of an American City: Social Origins and Educational Attainments in Providence, R.I., 1800–1925" (unpublished Ph.D. dissertation, Harvard University, 1980), pp. 202–230.

12. Katz, "School Attendance," pp. 13–14.

13. Cambria, "Youth in the Philadelphia Labor Market," p. 28.

14. Michael Haines, "Poverty, Economic Stress, and the Family in a Late Nineteenth-Century American City: Whites in Philadelphia, 1880," in Hershberg, *Philadelphia*, pp. 253–258.

15. Goldin, "Family Strategies," p. 204.

16. Michael Katz, "Work, Household, and the Transition to Adulthood" (unpublished paper, University of Pennsylvania, 1982; copy in my possession), p. 35.

17. A technological argument for reductions in child labor has been argued most notably by Paul Osterman in *Getting Started: The Youth Labor Market* (Cambridge, Mass., 1980), pp. 58–61. There is no evidence that this kind of argument can apply to Philadelphia and its particular industrial system.

18. Cambria, "Youth in the Philadelphia Labor Market," p. 67.

19. Ibid., pp. 36–37.

20. Interview Schedules, 1936 Gladys Palmer Survey for Works Progress Administration, Urban Archives, Temple University. The information in this survey has been computerized and a computer tape is in my possession.

21. The WPA survey provides more precise information on age of entrance to the work force than is afforded by the aggregated census statistics reported in Tables 2.1–2.4; the latter offer only percentages of specific age groups in school or work. The WPA figures mirror census results,

showing a gradual decline in teenage labor force participation in the twentieth century; they show too how schooling delayed entrance to work across all generations. Ethnic differences apparent in the census data are also manifest in the WPA survey; for example, youngsters of German heritage (and British) began working at distinctly younger ages, a reflection of their fathers' dominance in skilled trades. The WPA survey also provided the means to compare age of labor force entry between first and second generation immigrants. A statistically significant difference emerged in the interval between leaving school and securing first jobs; the time elapsed was three times greater for immigrants whose initiation to work occurred in their native lands—a reason perhaps for their migration.

22. A number of recent social history studies have emphasized the instrumental role of families in job procurement. These works include: Michael Anderson, *Family Structure in Nineteenth-Century Lancashire* (London, 1971); Tamara Haraven, *Family Time and Industrial Time: The Relationship Between the Family and Work in a New England Industrial Community* (New York, 1982); and John Bodnar, Roger Simon, and Michael Weber, *Lives of Their Own: Blacks, Italians, and Poles in Pittsburgh, 1900–1960* (Urbana, 1982). None of these works had access to materials that would place precise figures on the relative importance of family connection in hiring; none has considered the issue of change in methods of finding work over working lifetimes.

23. The padrone system will be discussed in Chapter 4. All indications are that padrones did not operate in Philadelphia as in other cities; see Russell Weigley, ed., *Philadelphia: A 300-Year History* (New York, 1982), p. 491.

24. This finding is confirmed in another study conducted by the Industrial Research Department of the University of Pennsylvania, the group responsible for the 1936 WPA survey. See Dorothea De Schweinitz, *How Workers Find Jobs: A Study of Four Thousand Hosiery Workers in Philadelphia* (Philadelphia, 1932), p. 93. The problems older immigrants experienced finding work in Philadelphia are poignantly described in a 1905 letter of a sixty-three year old Irish day laborer. He had lived in the city for forty-two years and wrote to his sister in Belfast that he had been unemployed for six months: "There is a great deal of work going on here at present but the employers prefer younger men to do this work. Old people are thought very little of in this country, especially poor ones that have made no provision for old age. Not even their families have any regard for them when they become played out from age and my own experience is no exception." The quote appears in Dale Beryl Light, "Ethnicity and the Urban Ecology

in a Nineteenth-Century City: Philadelphia's Irish, 1840–1890" (unpublished Ph.D. dissertation, University of Pennsylvania, 1979), p. 60.

25. "Pennsylvania Employers Survey—State Employment Survey," typescript, Gladys Palmer Papers, University of Pennsylvania, in custody of Professor Ann Miller, Box 170, pp. 1–2.

26. Gladys Palmer, "War Labor Supply Problems of Philadelphia and its Environs" (unpublished paper, University of Pennsylvania, no date; copy in my possession), pp. 24–28.

27. Charlotte Thomas, "A Study of the One-Clerk Office in Large Office Buildings in the City of Philadelphia, Pennsylvania" (unpublished M.A. thesis, Temple University, 1939), p. 33.

28. Barbara Mary Klaczynska, "Working Women in Philadelphia, 1900–1930" (unpublished Ph.D. dissertation, Temple University, 1975), p. 5.

29. A review of these surveys can be found in David Stevens, "A Reexamination of What is Known About Jobseeking Behavior in the United States," in National Commission for Manpower Policy, *Labor Market Intermediaries* (Washington, D.C., 1978), pp. 55–104. The Department of Labor conducted a large-scale study of methods of getting work in 1975. The results are published in U.S. Department of Labor, Bureau of Labor Statistics, *Bulletin 1886: Jobseeking Methods Used by American Workers* (Washington, D.C., 1975).

30. W. E. B. DuBois, *The Philadelphia Negro: A Social Study* (New York, 1967), pp. xviii–xix.

31. Ibid., p. 111.

32. On the faith of the Philadelphia African-American community in education, see Vincent P. Franklin, *The Education of Black Philadelphia: The Social and Educational History of a Minority Community, 1900–1950* (Philadelphia, 1979), chapter 4.

33. The most precise figures on ethnic discrimination in hiring in Philadelphia and the special case of black workers can be found in Theodore Hershberg et al., "A Tale of Three Cities: Blacks, Immigrants, and Opportunity in Philadelphia, 1850–1880, 1930, 1970," in Hershberg, *Philadelphia,* pp. 461–491. See also Roger Lane, *Roots of Violence in Black Philadelphia, 1860–1900* (Cambridge, Mass., 1986), pp. 6–44.

34. "Report Dealing with Activities in the City of Philadelphia, April 11–19, 1941," Urban League Papers, Urban Archives, Temple University.

35. Charles Johnson, *To Stem This Tide: A Survey of Racial Tension Areas in the United States* (Boston, 1943), p. 18.

36. Klaczynska, "Working Women In Philadelphia," p. 60.

37. Ibid., p. 57.

38. Philip Scranton and Walter Licht, *Work Sights: Industrial Philadelphia, 1890–1950* (Philadelphia, 1986), pp. 244–245.

39. Sadie Tanner Mossell, "The Standards of Living Among One Hundred Negro Migrant Families in Philadelphia," *Annals of the Academy of Social and Political Science,* 98 (November 1921), p. 174; Walter Licht, *Working For The Railroad: The Organization of Work in the Nineteenth Century* (Princeton, 1983), pp. 223–224.

40. Mossell, "The Standards of Living," p. 175.

41. DuBois, *The Philadelphia Negro,* pp. xxxvii–xxxviii.

42. Ruth Frances Paul, "Negro Women in Industry: A Study of the Negro Industrial Woman in the Clothing, Cigar, and Laundry Industries" (unpublished M.Ed. thesis, Temple University, 1940), pp. 20–21.

43. Consumers' League of Eastern Pennsylvania, *Colored Women as Industrial Workers in Philadelphia* (Philadelphia, 1919), p. 15; Mossell, "The Standards of Living," p. 174.

44. *Industrial Opportunities for Negroes in Philadelphia: Report of the Educational Committee of the Armstrong Association of Philadelphia* (Hampton, Va., 1911), pp. 18–19, 24.

45. Theodore Hershberg, "Free Blacks in Antebellum Philadelphia: A Study of Ex-Slaves, Freeborn, and Socioeconomic Decline," in Hershberg, *Philadelphia,* p. 376.

46. *Industrial Opportunities,* p. 22.

47. Committee of Teachers of the Philadelphia Public Schools, *Negro Employment: A Study of the Negro Employment Situation and its Relation to the School Program* (Philadelphia, 1941).

48. DuBois, *The Philadelphia Negro,* pp. 428, 431; Franklin, *The Education of Black Philadelphia,* pp. 60–62.

49. David McBride, "Black Health Care Labor and the Philadelphia Medical Establishment, 1910–1965" (unpublished Ph.D. dissertation, Columbia University, 1980), p. 27.

50. DuBois, *The Philadelphia Negro,* p. 480.

51. Katz, "Work, Household, and the Transition to Adulthood," p. 13.

52. McBride, "Black Health Care Labor," pp. 245, 250.

53. Quoted in Eudice Glassberg, "Philadelphians in Need: Client Experiences with Two Philadelphia Benevolent Societies, 1830–1880" (unpublished D.S.W. dissertation, University of Pennsylvania, 1979), p. 106.

54. Ibid., p. 100.

55. Hershberg, "Free Blacks in Antebellum Philadelphia," p. 376.

56. Ibid., p. 376.

57. Irving Lewis Horowitz, *The Metal Machinery Trades in Philadelphia: An Occupational Survey* (Philadelphia, 1939), pp. 59–60.

58. Richard R. Wright, Jr., *The Negro in Pennsylvania: A Study in Economic History* (New York, 1969), pp. 95–97.
59. DuBois, *The Philadelphia Negro,* pp. 227–228.
60. Paul, "Negro Women in Industry," p. 15.
61. Charles Leese, *Collective Bargaining among Photo-Engravers in Philadelphia: Ordinary Methods Applied to an Occupation Which is Both Art and a Manual Trade* (Philadelphia, 1929), p. 101.
62. Consumers' League of Eastern Pennsylvania, *Colored Women,* p. 34.
63. For a historical overview of the role played by black organizations in petitioning for the hiring of black women in one firm, see "Interview with Mr. P. N. Bohn, Wage and Salary Administrator, SKF Industries, March 18, 1957," Gladys Palmer Papers, Box 167, p. 6.
64. Joseph Willits, *Philadelphia Unemployment with Special Reference to the Textile Industries* (Philadelphia, 1915), p. 6.
65. Hershberg et al., "A Tale of Three Cities," p. 470.
66. Ibid., p. 470.
67. Theodore Hershberg et al., "The 'Journey-to-Work': An Empirical Investigation of Work, Residence and Transportation, Philadelphia, 1850 and 1880," in Hershberg, *Philadelphia,* pp. 135–147.
68. De Schweinitz, *How Workers Find Jobs,* p. 58.
69. Gwendolyn S. Hughes, *Mothers in Industry: Wage-Earning by Mothers in Philadelphia* (New York, 1925), p. 36.
70. Eugene Ericksen and William Yancey, "Work and Residence in an Industrial City" (unpublished paper, Temple University, 1976; copy in my possession), pp. 33–34.
71. Stephanie W. Greenberg, "Industrial Location and Ethnic Residential Patterns in an Industrializing City: Philadelphia, 1880," in Hershberg, *Philadelphia,* pp. 210–214; Kawaguchi, "The Making," pp. 440, 461, 464.
72. For a discussion of the changing geography of Philadelphia industry, see Scranton and Licht, *Work Sights,* pp. 62–71, 154–155.
73. Ericksen and Yancey, "Work and Residence in an Industrial City," p. 4.

3. Schools and Work

1. For a succinct review of issues in the history of American education, see Daniel Rodgers and David Tyack, "Work, Youth, and Schooling: Mapping Critical Research Areas," in Harvey Kantor and David Tyack, eds., *Work, Youth, and Schooling: Historical Perspectives on Vocationalism in American Education* (Stanford, Calif., 1982), pp. 270–294.

2. John Curran, "Workers' Education in the Philadelphia Industrial Area" (unpublished M.A. thesis, University of Pennsylvania, 1951), p. 1.

3. Joseph Leigh Altadoona, "The School, Curriculum, and Community: A Case Study of the Institutionalizing of Industrial Education in the Public Schools of Philadelphia, 1876–1918" (unpublished Ed.D. dissertation, Columbia University, 1983), p. 26.

4. Ibid., pp. 65–69; Edward Meredith Fee, "The Origin and Growth of Vocational Industrial Education in Philadelphia to 1917" (unpublished Ph.D. dissertation, University of Pennsylvania, 1938), pp. 88–89.

5. David Hogan, "The Examination System, the Meritocratic Project and Common Schooling: Philadelphia, 1838–1868" (unpublished paper, University of Pennsylvania, 1987; copy in my possession), pp.4–5.

6. Ibid., pp. 5–6.

7. David Labaree, "The People's College: A Sociological Analysis of the Central High School of Philadelphia, 1838–1939" (unpublished Ph.D. disseration, University of Pennsylvania, 1983), pp. 30–40.

8. Ibid., pp. 45–46, 396.

9. Ibid., pp. 49–52.

10. Ibid., pp. 57–64, 90, 408–409, 432–439.

11. Fee, "The Origin and Growth of Vocational Industrial Education," pp. 176–177.

12. William Donald Ashbrook, "The Development of Industrial Education in the Schools of Pennsylvania" (unpublished Ph.D. dissertation, University of Pittsburgh, 1953), p. 33; Leo Dushoff, "Evening Public Schools of Philadelphia, 1850–1930" (unpublished M.Ed. thesis, University of Pennsylvania, 1932), pp. 9–12, 18–19, 31, 39–43, 46, 63, 95.

13. Altadoona, "The School, Curriculum, and Community," pp. 31–33.

14. Fee, "The Origin and Growth of Vocational Industrial Education," pp. 180–181.

15. Ashbrook, "The Development of Industrial Education," pp. 76, 180–181.

16. "School of Industrial Arts" (unpublished article, Archives of the Board of Education of the City of Philadelphia, no date; copy in my possession), p. 201.

17. Ashbrook, "The Development of Industrial Education," pp. 78–79.

18. Fee, "The Origin and Growth of Vocational Industrial Education," p. 186.

19. *Annual Report of the President of the [Philadelphia] Board of Education,* 67 (1885), pp. 15–25.

20. *Annual Report of the President of the [Philadelphia] Board of Education,* 62 (1880), pp. 14–15.

21. Ashbrook, "Development of Industrial Education," p. 112; *Annual Report of the President of the [Philadelphia] Board of Education,* 74 (1892), pp. 12–21.

22. Ashbrook, "The Development of Industrial Education," pp. 90–91; William Issel, "Modernization in Philadelphia School Reform, 1882–1905," *The Pennsylvania Magazine of History and Biography,* 94 (July 1970), pp. 360–366; Philip C. Garrett, *Progress of Industrial Education* (printed paper delivered at the meeting of the Philadelphia Social Science Association, 1883; copy in my possession).

23. Labaree, "The People's College," pp. 62, 75–88.

24. Altadoona, "The School, Curriculum, and Community," pp. 176–178, 183; Dushoff, "Evening Public Schools of Philadelphia," p. 121; Issel, "Modernization in Philadelphia School Reform," p. 358.

25. Altadoona, "The School, Curriculum, and Community," p. 96.

26. Ibid., p. 159.

27. Issel, "The Modernization in Philadelphia School Reform," pp. 73–76, 79–81; Thomas J. Donaghy, *Philadelphia's Finest: A History of Education in the Archdiocese of Philadelphia* (Philadelphia, 1972), p. 139.

28. Altadoona, "The School, Curriculum, and Community," pp. 176–178.

29. Ibid., p. 114.

30. Ibid., pp. 111–113; Fee, "The Origin and Growth of Vocational Industrial Education," pp. 183–185.

31. Altadoona, "The School, Curriculum, and Community," pp. 116–119.

32. Ibid., pp. 123–124, 136–137.

33. Business leaders also argued that vocational classes would fill a vacuum created by the dissolution of apprenticeship programs and practices. See Ashbrook, "The Development of Industrial Education," pp. 80–81; George Sikes, "Apprentice System in the Building Trades," *Journal of Political Economy,* 2 (June 1894), p. 411; Minutes of the Philadelphia Board of Trade, Volume 123, pp. 136–139, Philadelphia Board of Trade Papers, Historical Society of Pennsylvania; Minutes of the Board of Directors of the Philadelphia Chamber of Commerce, December 14, 1922, p. 225, and January 11, 1923, p. 23, Philadelphia Chamber of Commerce Papers, Historical Society of Pennsylvania.

34. Edward Bemis, "Relation of Labor Organizations to the American Boy and to Trade Instruction," *Annals of the American Academy of Political and Social Science,* 5 (September 1894), pp. 81–82; "Testimony of Mr. John H. Phillips, *Report of the United States Commission on Industrial Relations, Volume 3* (Washington, D.C., 1916), p. 2979.

35. Judith Goldberg, "Strikes, Organizing and Change: The Knights of

Labor in Philadelphia, 1869–1890" (unpublished Ph.D. dissertation, New York University, 1985), pp. 11–12.

36. Ashbrook, "The Development of Industrial Education," pp. 101–108, 110–111.

37. Fee, "The Origin and Growth of Vocational Industrial Education," pp. iii, 161, 198; Ashbrook, "The Development of Industrial Education," pp. 114–116.

38. Fee, "The Origin and Growth of Vocational Industrial Education," pp. 190–191; Ashbrook, "The Development of Industrial Education," p. 111.

39. Altadoona, "The School, Curriculum, and Community," p. 188.

40. Ibid., pp. 196–197.

41. *Annual Report of the President of the [Philadelphia] Board of Education,* 97 (1915), p. 20.

42. Labaree, "The People's College," p. 122; Fee, "The Origin and Growth of Vocational Industrial Education," pp. 208–209; Sophia T. Cambria, "Youth in the Philadelphia Labor Market" (unpublished Ph.D. dissertation, Bryn Mawr College, 1945), pp. 86–87.

43. *Philadelphia School Survey* (Philadelphia, 1922), pp. 190–196; Ashbrook, "The Development of Industrial Education," p. 188; Cambria, "Youth in the Philadelphia Labor Market," p. 81; Altadoona, "The School, Curriculum, and Community," pp. 242–243.

44. Donaghy, *Philadelphia's Finest,* pp. 95–96.

45. Karen Mittelman, "Training Philadelphia's Girls for Home, Factory, and School: The Evolution of Girls' High, 1887–1893" (unpublished paper, University of Pennsylvania, 1983; copy in my possession), pp. 2–4.

46. *Report of the Select Committee of the Board of Controllers in Relation to Changing the Model School into a Normal School for Qualifying Female Teachers* (Philadelphia, 1847).

47. Mittelman, "Training Philadelphia's Girls," pp. 10–11.

48. Ibid., pp. 13–17; *Report of the Commission on Industrial Education, made to the Legislature of Pennsylvania* (Harrisburg, 1889), pp. 417–419.

49. *Annual Report of the Philadelphia Public Education Association, 1889* (Philadelphia, 1889), p. 20.

50. Mittelman, "Training Philadelphia's Girls," p. 18.

51. Ibid., pp. 21–23.

52. Elizabeth Ortleib, "The Origins and Development of Commercial Education in the Philadelphia High Schools" (unpublished M.Ed. thesis, Temple University, 1930), pp. 11–14.

53. Cheesman Herrick, *William Penn High School for Girls: Some Early Beginnings* (Philadelphia, 1935), pp. 12–13.

54. Ortleib, "The Origins and Development of Commercial Education," p. 19; Cambria, "Youth in the Philadelphia Labor Market," pp. 96–99.

55. For the impact of compulsory school attendance laws on Philadelphia public school vocational guidance services, see *Annual Report of the [Philadelphia] Board of Education, 1929* (Philadelphia, 1929), pp. 484–488; "Testimony of Mr. Henry J. Gideon," *Report of the United States Commission on Industrial Relations* (Washington, D.C., 1916), vol. 3, p. 2931; Bruce Watson, "Street Trades in Pennsylvania," *American Child,* 4 (August 1922), pp. 3–6.

56. Nan Martin, "The Opportunity for Employment of Juniors in Retail Establishments in Philadelphia" (unpublished M.A. thesis, Temple University, 1938), pp. 1–2; *Annual Report of the [Philadelphia] Board of Education, 1919* (Philadelphia, 1919), p. 143; Cambria, "Youth in the Philadelphia Labor Market," pp. 117–122.

57. *119th Annual Report of the White-Williams Foundation, 1919* (Philadelphia, 1919), pp. 5–11; "Vocational Guidance and Junior Placement," *Children's Bureau [of the United States Department of Labor] Publication No. 149* (Washington, D.C., 1925), p. 225.

58. *120th Annual Report of the White-Williams Foundation, 1920* (Philadelphia, 1920), pp. 19–31.

59. Rebecca Leaming, "Tests and Norms for Vocational Guidance at the Fifteen-Year-Old Performance Level," *The Psychological Clinic,* 14 (December 1922), pp. 192–193.

60. Cambria, "Youth in the Philadelphia Labor Market," p. 134; "Vocational Guidance," pp. 223, 253–259; Fee, p. 194; Ashbrook, "The Development of Industrial Education," p. 113.

61. "Vocational Guidance," p. 253; Ruth Woodruff, "The Hosiery Industry," *Bulletin Series No. 5, Junior Employment Service, Board of Education of Philadelphia* (Philadelphia, 1925), foreword.

62. Dorothea De Schweinitz, *How Workers Find Jobs: A Study of Four Thousand Hosiery Workers in Philadelphia* (Philadelphia, 1932), pp. 131–141.

63. Quoted in Cambria, "Youth in the Philadelphia Labor Market," p. 134.

64. "Vocational Guidance," pp. 261–262.

65. Donaghy, *Philadelphia's Finest,* pp. 24, 47.

66. Ibid., pp. 44–47.

67. John E. O'Breza, "The Philadelphia Parochial School System from 1830 to 1920: Growth and Bureaucratization" (unpublished Ed.D. dissertation, Temple University, 1979), pp. 31–33.

68. Ibid., pp. 38, 154, 162, 177; Donaghy, *Philadelphia's Finest,* p. 63.

69. O'Breza, "The Philadelphia Parochial School System," pp. 163–164; Donaghy, *Philadelphia's Finest,* pp. 154–155.

70. Sister Terence Marie Harte, "The Development of the Business Department in Five Catholic High Schools for Girls in the Philadelphia Diocesan System of Education" (unpublished M.A. thesis, Catholic University, 1958), pp. 8–18; O'Breza, "The Philadelphia Parochial School System," pp. 65, 78, 83, 163–165.

71. Ibid., p. 163–164; Donaghy, *Philadelphia's Finest*, pp. 154–155.

72. Ibid., p. 162.

73. Ibid., pp. 96, 151, 177.

74. Harte, "The Development of the Business Department," pp. 20–21.

75. Ibid., p. 27.

76. Ibid., pp. 42–53.

77. Ibid., p. 67.

78. Fee, "The Origin and Growth of Vocational Industrial Education," pp. 118–120; Ashbrook, "The Development of Industrial Education," pp. 17–20.

79. Fee, "The Origin and Growth of Vocational Industrial Education," pp. 134–146.

80. Ibid., pp. 127–129.

81. Ibid., pp. 129–133; A. J. Rowland, "Vocational Education in Philadelphia and Vicinity," in *Transactions of the American Institute of Electrical Engineers* (New York, 1913), pp. 1416–1418.

82. Ashbrook, "The Development of Industrial Education," p. 23; Fee, "The Origin and Growth of Vocational Industrial Education," pp. 108–117.

83. Fee, "The Origin and Growth of Vocational Industrial Education," p. 99; Ashbrook, "The Development of Industrial Education," p. 22.

84. Fee, "The Origin and Growth of Vocational Industrial Education," pp. 103–108; Ashbrook, "The Development of Industrial Education," p. 26; Edwin Craig, "A Survey of the Graduates of Girard College from February 1933 to June 1934, Inclusive" (unpublished M.Ed. thesis, Temple University, 1941), p. 13.

85. Ashbrook, "The Development of Industrial Education," p. 26.

86. *Annual Report of the Spring Garden Institute, 1892* (Philadelphia, 1892), p. 1; *Catalogue of the Spring Garden Institute, 1922–23* (Philadelphia, 1922), pp. 6–7; Fee, "The Origin and Growth of Vocational Industrial Education," pp. 121–127.

87. Fee, "The Origin and Growth of Vocational Industrial Education," pp. 162–167.

88. Ibid., pp. 86–87, 146–154, 168–169.

89. Vincent Franklin, *The Education of Black Philadelphia: The Social and Educational History of a Minority Community, 1900–1950* (Philadelphia, 1979), pp. 30–31.

90. Ibid., pp. 32–33.

91. Ibid., pp. 35–51.

92. Harry Silcox, "The Search by Blacks for Employment and Opportunity: Industrial Education in Philadelphia," *Pennsylvania Heritage,* 4 (December 1977), pp. 41–43.

93. Franklin, *The Education of Black Philadelphia,* p. 55.

94. Silcox, "The Search by Blacks for Employment," pp. 38–39; *Industrial Opportunities for Negroes in Philadelphia: Report of the Educational Committee of the Armstrong Association of Philadelphia* (Hampton, Va., 1911), pp. 6–7.

95. Silcox, "The Search by Blacks for Employment," p. 39.

96. Ibid., pp. 40–41; *Industrial Opportunities,* pp. 7–8.

97. Dorothy DuPont, "A Study of Private Vocational Schools in Philadelphia, Pennsylvania" (unpublished M.Ed. thesis, Temple University, 1937), pp. 16–48.

98. United States Commission of Education, *Education Report, 1887–88* (Washington, D.C., 1888), pp. 938–939.

99. DuPont, "A Study of Private Vocational Schools," pp. 25–30.

100. Labaree, "The People's College," p. 302.

101. David Hogan, "Enrollment, Achievement, and Curricula Choice in Philadelphia High Schools, 1885–1940" (unpublished paper, University of Pennsylvania, no date; copy in my possession), pp. 53–55.

102. Ibid., pp. 31–32.

103. *When Philadelphia Youth Leave School at 16 and 17* (Philadelphia, 1941), p. 9.

104. Nellie A. Laird, "A Study of Pupils Dropped from the Roll of the Kensington High School" (unpublished M.Ed. thesis, Temple University, 1938), p. 12.

105. Duncan E. Grizelli, "Certain Phases of Pupil Elimination Related to a Class in Germantown High School in Philadelphia" (unpublished manuscript, Temple University, 1932; copy in my possession), p. 58.

106. Hogan, "Enrollment, Achievement, and Curricula Choice," pp. 28–29.

107. *119th Annual Report of the White-Williams Foundation* (Philadelphia, 1919), p. 16.

108. Laird, "A Study of Pupils Dropped from the Roll," p. 12.

109. Charles Young, "A Survey of the Industrial Curricula at Northeast High School, Philadelphia" (unpublished M.A. thesis, Temple University, 1928), p. 28.

110. Rowland, "Vocational Education in Philadelphia," p. 8.

111. Ernest Kohl, Jr., "Influences Contributing to the Adjustment and Retention of Pupils in the Edward Bok Vocational-Technical School"

(unpublished Ed.D. thesis, University of Pennsylvania, 1949), pp. 15–16.

112. Henry Menken, "A Comparative Study of the Social and Educational Status of the 8B Grade Academic and Industrial Boys at the Furness Junior High School, Philadelphia" (unpublished M.Ed. thesis, Temple University, 1935), pp. 101–106; Cambria, "Youth in the Philadelphia Labor Market," p. 85.

113. *120th Annual Report of the White-Williams Foundation* (Philadelphia, 1920), p. 65.

114. *Report of the Philadelphia School Survey, Volume 3* (Philadelphia, 1922), p. 268.

115. Laird, "A Study of Pupils Dropped from the Rolls," pp. 32–33.

116. Leaming, "Tests and Norms for Vocational Guidance," p. 214; Labaree, "The People's College," p. 308; David Hogan, "Philadelphia High School for Girls, 1901–1922: Attendance and Achievement" (unpublished manuscript, University of Pennsylvania, no date; copy in my possession), pp. 56–57.

117. Lorinda Perry, *The Millinery Trade in Boston and Philadelphia: A Study of Women in Industry* (Binghamton, N.Y., 1916), pp. 96–99, 105–109.

118. Irving Lewis Horowitz, *The Metal Machine Trades in Philadelphia: An Occupational Survey* (Philadelphia, 1939), pp. 42–44, 56, 63–66.

119. Albert Johann, "Job Training of Production Workers By Philadelphia Area Industries" (unpublished M.B.A. thesis, University of Pennsylvania, 1946), p. 23.

120. William Ash, "Continuation Class for Printers in the Philadelphia Trades School," *National Association of Corporation Schools Second Annual Convention* (Philadelphia, 1914), p. 369.

121. Anna Owers, "What are the Trade Schools Contributing to the Equipping of this Area with a Supply of Trained Foremen?" (unpublished paper, University of Pennsylvania, 1929; copy in my possession), p. 1.

122. Ken Fones-Wolf, "Employer Unity and the Crisis of the Craftsman," *The Pennsylvania Magazine of History and Biography,* 107 (July 1983), pp. 449–455; Earl Sparks, "The Metal Manufacturers' Association of Philadelphia: A Review of Activities, 1903–1953," typescript, Metal Manufacturers' Association of Philadelphia Papers, Urban Archives, Temple University, Box 1, p. 4; Cooperative Apprentice Plan of the Metal Manufacturers' Association of Philadelphia, ibid., Box 4; Secretary's Report for the Commmittee of Vocational Education [of the Metal Manufacturers' Association of Philadelphia], December 9, 1925, ibid., Box 4.

123. Personal interview with Percy Lanning, President of Perseverance Iron, April 1982. The firm of Perseverance Iron participated in several failed cooperative training programs between the Philadelphia school system and businesses in the area. The firm's personnel history is described in Chapter 5.

124. Fee, "The Origin and Growth of Vocational Industrial Education," pp. 172–174.

125. *When Philadelphia Youth,* pp. 54–55.

126. Paul Ryan, "Job Training, Employment Practices, and the Large Enterprise: The Case of Costly Transferable Skills," in Paul Osterman, ed., *Internal Labor Markets* (Cambridge, Mass., 1984), pp. 191–230; Beatrice G. Reubens, "Vocational Education for All in High School," in James O'Toole, ed., *Work and the Quality of Life* (Cambridge, Mass., 1974), p. 308.

127. Survey Materials for Bulletins Nos. 120 and 188 of the Women's Bureau of the U.S. Department of Labor, National Archives, Records of the Women's Bureau of the Department of Labor, Group 86.

128. Benjamin Shapiro, "A Study of the Duties Performed by Bookkeepers in Business Establishments in the City of Philadelphia" (unpublished M.A. thesis, Temple University, 1933), pp. 60–61.

129. Harriet Bryne, "Women Office Workers in Philadelphia," *Bulletin of the Women's Bureau [of the United States Department of Labor],* 96 (Washington, D.C., 1932), pp. 5–6.

130. Interview with H. W. Flecktner, Personnel Department, Bayuk Cigars, Inc., April 17, 1957, Gladys Palmer Papers, University of Pennsylvania, in custody of Professor Ann Miller, Box 167, p. 5.

131. Interview with Mabel McMurray, Personnel Assistant, Smith, Kline, and French Laboratories, May 1, 1957, ibid., p. 4; interview with S. H. Kirkpatrick, Personnel Manager, American Stores, March 22, 1957, ibid., p. 4; personal interview with Claudette John, archivist of the Insurance Company of North American, and Lee Corak, Assistant Director of Training, INA, May 1982. INA is now Connecticut Insurance Group of North America (CIGNA).

132. Cambria, "Youth in the Philadelphia Labor Market," p. 122.

133. Horowitz, *The Metal Machinery Trades in Philadelphia,* pp. 65–66.

134. *When Philadelphia Youth,* p. 33.

135. Charles Johnson, "The Armstrong Association of Philadelphia (A Social Study and Program Evaluation), March 31, 1942," typescript, Armstrong Association of Philadelphia Papers, Urban Archives, Temple University, pp. 79–82.

136. *How Fare Philadelphia Public School Graduates* (unpublished paper, no

author listed, 1939; copy in my possession), pp. 1–22; *When Philadelphia Youth,* pp. 3, 52–62, 66–67.

4. Agencies

1. Paul Douglas, *American Apprenticeship and Industrial Education* (New York, 1921), pp. 12–16.
2. Ian Quimby, *Apprenticeship in Colonial Philadelphia* (New York, 1985), pp. 5–9.
3. Ibid., pp. 9–11; Douglas, *American Apprenticeship,* pp. 25–26.
4. Quimby, *Apprenticeship in Colonial Phildelphia,* pp. 16–17, 30–31, 41, 106–107; Richard McLeod, "The Philadelphia Artisans, 1828–1850" (unpublished Ph.D. dissertation, University of Missouri, 1975), pp. 58, 70–71.
5. Quimby, *Apprenticeship in Colonial Philadelphia,* pp. 3, 140–156; William J. Rohrbaugh, *The Craft Apprentice: From Franklin to the Machine Age in America* (New York, 1986), pp. 16–75.
6. Edward Meredith Fee, "The Origin and Growth of Vocational Industrial Education in Philadelphia to 1917" (unpublished Ph.D. dissertation, 1938), pp. 52–55.
7. Ibid., pp. 49–51.
8. Douglas, *American Apprenticeship,* p. 17.
9. Dennis Clark, "Babes in Bondage: Indentured Irish Children in Philadelphia in the Nineteenth Century," *The Pennsylvania Magazine of History and Biography,* 101 (October 1977), pp. 475–486.
10. Rick Halpern, "Industrial Apprenticeship in Nineteenth-Century Philadelphia" (unpublished paper, University of Pennsylvania, 1984; copy in my possession), pp. 12–13; Apprentice Rosters, Baldwin Locomotive Company Papers, Historical Society of Pennsylvania.
11. Halpern, "Industrial Apprenticeship In Nineteenth-Century Philadelphia," pp. 13–14.
12. Matthias Baldwin to J. A. Escheverres, October 9, 1851, Outgoing Letters, Baldwin Locomotive Company Papers, Historical Society of Pennsylvania.
13. Halpern, "Industrial Apprenticeship In Nineteenth-Century Philadelphia," p. 14.
14. Ibid., pp. 18–20.
15. N. W. Sample, "Apprenticeship System at the Baldwin Locomotive Works, Philadelphia," *The Annals of the American Academy of Political and Social Science,* 33 (1909), pp. 175–177.
16. Ibid., p. 177.

17. "Testimony of Mr. Alba Johnson," *Report of Commission on Industrial Relations, Volume 3* (Washington, D.C., 1916), p. 2823.
18. Raghvendra Tripatri, "A Study of Labor Skills Required for Specific Production Jobs at the Baldwin Locomotive Works" (unpublished M.B.A. thesis, University of Pennsylvania, 1949), pp. 19–20.
19. Albert Freeman, "The Labor System of the John B. Stetson Company," *The Annals of the American Academy of Political and Social Science,* 22 (November 1903), pp. 34–35; "The Disston History, Volume 2," typescript, Disston Company Papers, Hagley Libary, Accession 1567, p. 20.
20. Public Education and Child Labor Association of Pennsylvania, *Survey of Opportunities for Vocational Education in Pennsylvania* (Harrisburg, 1929), pp. 153–166; A. J. Rowland, "Vocational Education in Philadelphia and Vicinity," *Transactions of the American Institute of Electrical Engineers* (1913), pp. 1424–1426; Carroll D. Wright, *The Apprenticeship System in Its Relations to Industrial Education* (Washington, D.C., 1908), pp. 49–50.
21. The following two extensive biographies provide a wealth of information on Wanamaker and his store: Herbert Adams Gibbon, *John Wanamaker* (New York, 1926, 2 volumes) and Joseph Appel, *The Business Biography of John Wanamaker* (New York, 1930).
22. Herman Stern, "The Present Union-Management Relationship in Philadelphia Central City Department Stores" (unpublished M.B.A. thesis, University of Pennsylvania, 1942), pp. 33–35.
23. Gibbons, *John Wanamaker,* vol. 2, pp. 284–285; Appel, *The Business Biography of John Wanamaker,* pp. 428–430; John Wanamaker, "The John Wanamaker Commercial Institute—A Store School," *The Annals of the American Academy of Political and Social Science,* 23 (1909), pp. 151–154.
24. Quoted in Appel, *The Business Biography of John Wanamaker,* p. 434.
25. Donald Freud, "A Critical Analysis of Methods Employed by the 'Big Five' Philadelphia Department Stores in Recruiting, Selecting, Training, and Evaluating the Performance of Their Sales Trainees" (unpublished M.B.A. thesis, University of Pennsylvania, 1955), pp. 71–100.
26. Harriet Fox, "The Strawbridge & Clothier School," *The National Association of Corporation Schools Bulletin,* 4 (December 1917), p. 30–33.
27. Benjamin Cadbury, "A Plan for Educational Work in a Small Corporation," *The National Association of Corporation Schools Bulletin,* 1 (June 1914), pp. 33–37; Rowland, "Vocational Education in Philadelphia," pp. 1424–1426.
28. Douglas, *American Apprenticeship,* pp. 214–215.

29. Public Education and Child Labor Association of Pennsylvania, *Survey*, pp. 153–166; "Apprentice Program, 1926," typescript, Metal Manufacturers' Association of Philadelphia Papers, Urban Archives, Temple University, Box 3; "Cooperative Apprentice Plan," ibid., Box 4; Secretary's Report for the Committee on Vocational Education, December 9, 1925, ibid., Box 4.

30. Fee, "The Origin and Growth of Vocational Industrial Education," pp. 172–175; *Philadelphia Naval Shipyard Beacon*, November 30, 1974, p. 4; Irving Lewis Horowitz, *The Metal Machinery Trades in Philadelphia: An Occupational Survey* (Philadelphia, 1939), p. 64.

31. James M. Motley, *Appprenticeship in American Trade Unions* (Baltimore, 1907), p. 31.

32. McLeod, "The Philadelphia Artisans," p. 62.

33. Motley, *Apprenticeship in American Trade Unions*, pp. 60–61.

34. Ibid., p. 62.

35. Charles Leese, *Collective Bargaining among Photo-Engravers in Philadelphia: Ordinary Methods Applied to an Occupation Which is Both Art and a Manual Trade* (Philadelphia, 1929), pp. 75, 89–92, 96.

36. Public Education and Child Labor Association of Pennsylvania, *Survey*, pp. 153–166.

37. Dorothea De Schweinitz, *How Workers Find Jobs: A Study of Four Thousand Hosiery Workers in Philadelphia* (Philadelphia, 1932), p. 65; "Standards of Apprenticeship of International Resistance Company of Philadelphia, In Formulation by a Joint Apprenticeship Committee Representing the International Resistance Company and the United Electrical, Radio & Machine Workers of America Local 105," International Union of Electrical Workers Local 105 Papers, Urban Archives, Temple University, Box 4.

38. F. E. Wolfe, *Admission to American Trade Unions* (Baltimore, 1912), p. 47.

39. Motley, *Apprenticeship in American Trade Unions*, p. 77.

40. Wolfe, *Admission to American Trade Unions*, p. 42.

41. Ibid., p. 42.

42. "Agreement between Local 8 and Contracting Plasterers and Lathers, 1958," Operative Plasterers' and Cement Masons' International Union, Local #8 Papers, Urban Archives, Temple University, Box 7.

43. Interview Schedules, 1936 Gladys Palmer Survey for the Works Progress Administration, Urban Archives, Temple University.

44. *Industrial Opportunities for Negroes in Philadelphia: Report of the Educational Committee of the Armstrong Association of Philadelphia* (Hampton, Va., 1911), p. 24.

45. In crosstabulating a number of independent variables with the depen-

dent variable of occupational mobility, gender proved to have the highest relationship (Contingency C was .40 at the .01 level of significance); apprenticeship training was next in importance (C was .25 at the .01 significance level) and years of school proved to be absolutely random (C = .07 at the .71 level of significance).

46. The greater importance of apprenticeship than schooling in occupational achievement revealed in the 1936 WPA Survey points to another bind faced by young black Philadelphians. They stayed in school in great numbers, largely because of limited access to apprenticeship programs and jobs, but schooling did not insure success in the labor market. Such were the odds encountered by black youth. These results bring into question the basic premises of so-called human capital theory, which argues for returns on personal investments in education.

47. Gladys Palmer, *Philadelphia Workers in a Changing Economy* (Philadelphia, 1956), pp. 16–17; Russell Weigley et al., *Philadelphia: A 300-Year History* (New York, 1982), pp. 279–280, 433–436.

48. Palmer, *Philadelphia Workers,* p. 17; Weigley, *Philadelphia,* pp. 338, 548.

49. *Daily Record,* January 14, 1946, p. 14; Richard Lester, *Hiring Practices and Labor Competition* (Princeton, 1954), p. 21.

50. Anne Bezanson, *Earnings and Working Opportunity in the Upholstery Weavers' Trade in 25 Plants in Philadelphia: An Experiment in Co-operative Research* (Philadelphia, 1928), p. xv; Leese, *Collective Bargaining among Photo-Engravers in Philadelphia,* pp. 33, 68, 131.

51. Ken Fones-Wolf, "Employer Unity and the Crisis of the Craftsman," *The Pennsylvania Magazine of History and Biography,* 107 (July 1983), pp. 449–455.

52. Gladys Palmer, *Union Tactics and Economic Change: A Case Study of Three Philadelphia Textile Unions* (Philadelphia, 1932), pp. 22–29.

53. Motley, *Apprenticeship in American Trade Unions,* p. 51.

54. Fred Lauterwasser, "Employment Work by Trade Unions and the Public Employment Office System," *American Federationist,* 40 (December 1933), pp. 1305–1306.

55. John Seybold, *The Philadelphia Printing Industry: A Case Study* (Philadelphia, 1949), p. 24.

56. Lauterwasser, "Employment Work by Trade Unions," pp. 1306–1307; Leese, *Collective Bargaining among Photo-Engravers in Philadelphia,* pp. 101–103.

57. Lauterwasser, "Employment Work by Trade Unions," pp. 1307–1308.

58. Elden LaMar, *The Clothing Workers in Philadelphia: History of their Struggles for Union and Security* (Philadelphia, 1940), pp. 103, 113, 192–

193, 199–203; Richard Biegel, "Union Management Relations in the Men's Tailor-made Clothing Industry in Philadelphia: A Case Study" (unpublished M.B.A. thesis, University of Pennsylvania, 1962), p. 49.

59. LaMar, *The Clothing Workers in Philadelphia,* pp. 130–131.

60. Judith Goldberg, "Strikes, Organizing and Change: The Knights of Labor in Philadelphia, 1869–1890" (unpublished Ph.D. dissertation, New York University, 1985), chapter 9, pp. 20–21.

61. Palmer, *Union Tactics,* pp. 29–44.

62. Lauterwasser, "Employment Work by Trade Unions," p. 1306.

63. Goldberg, "Strikes, Organizing and Change," chapter 9, p. 16.

64. Leese, *Collective Bargaining among Photo-Engravers in Philadelphia,* pp. 141–143.

65. Joseph Willits, *Philadelphia Unemployment with Specific Reference to the Textile Industries* (Philadelphia, 1915), p. 34.

66. Sumner Slichter, *Union Politics and Industrial Management* (Washington, D.C., 1941), p. 126.

67. Gladys Palmer and Ada M. Stoflet, *The Labor Force of the Philadelphia Radio Industry in 1936* (Philadelphia, 1938), pp. 32–33.

68. Interview Schedules, 1936 Gladys Palmer Survey for the Works Progress Administration.

69. W. E. B. DuBois, *The Philadelphia Negro: A Social Study* (New York, 1967), pp. 227–228; Richard R. Wright, Jr., *The Negro In Pennsylvania: A Study in Economic History* (New York, 1969), pp. 95–97; Ruth Francis Paul, "Negro Women in Industry: A Study of the Negro Industrial Woman in the Clothing, Cigar and Laundry Industries" (unpublished M.Ed. thesis, Temple University, 1940), p. 15; *Industrial Opportunities,* p. 18; Leese, *Collective Bargaining among Photo-Engravers in Philadelphia,* p. 101.

70. Male-dominated unions did in certain instances initiate policies that restricted female employment. The Upholsters' Union in Philadelphia, for example, reached an agreement with manufacturers in the trade that placed limitations on hiring women as weavers. See Palmer, *Union Tactics,* p. 59. This was the exception more than the rule.

71. Fones-Wolf, "Employer Unity and the Crisis of the Craftsman," p. 454; "Testimony of Mr. Edward Keenan," *Report of the Commission on Industrial Relations, Volume 3* (Washington, D.C., 1916), p. 2882; "Testimony of Mr. Henry Morgan," ibid., pp. 2909, 2913. The papers of the Metal Manufacturers' Association of Philadelphia, housed in the Urban Archives of Temple University, provide extensive documentation on the Association's Labor Bureau. The annual reports of the president and secretary of the organization in Box 1 are particularly illuminating.

72. Weigley, *Philadelphia,* p. 76.
73. James Stewart, "The DuPont Company and Irish Immigration, 1800–1857: A Study of the Company's Efforts to Arrange for the Families of its Workmen" (unpublished paper, University of Delaware, 1976; copy in my possession), pp. 1–4, 7, 15, 17, 20–24, 33–34; Robert Taylor to E. I. Dupont de Nemours, October 28, 1847, E. I. DuPont & Company Papers, Hagley Library, Accession 500, Series I, Part 1, Series B, Box 386; George McHenry to E. I. DuPont de Nemours, August 26, 1851, ibid., Box 253; Andrew Craig to John Peoples, January 6, 1847, ibid., Box 70; A. J. Catherwood to E. I. DuPont de Nemours, January 1, 1849, ibid., Box 56.
74. John Koren, "The Padrone System and Padrone Banks," *Bulletin of the Department of Labor,* 4 (March 1897), pp. 113–115.
75. Ibid., pp. 118, 123, 125; Richard Juliani, "The Social Organization of Immigration: The Italians in Philadelphia" (unpublished Ph.D. dissertation, University of Pennsylvania, 1971), p. 208–218.
76. Frances Kellor, *Out of Work: A Study of Employment Agencies: Their Treatment of the Unemployed, and the Influence Upon Homes and Businesses* (New York, 1904), p. 104; Dorothea De Schweinitz, *How Workers Find Jobs: A Study of Four Thousand Hosiery Workers in Philadelphia* (Philadelphia, 1932), p. 118.
77. "C. G. Odell & Co.'s Employment Bureau," broadside, Broadside and Pamphlet Collection, Hagley Library.
78. Advertisements from these firms can be found in the E. C. Beetem & Sons Business Papers, Hagley Library, Accession 1178, Series V, Files 336–337.
79. Barbara Klaczynska, "Working Women in Philadelphia, 1900–1930" (unpublished Ph.D. dissertation, Temple University, 1975), p. 52; Wright, *The Negro in Pennsylvania,* p. 73.
80. Klaczynska, "Working Women in Philadelphia," p. 52; Kellor, *Out of Work,* pp. 19, 28.
81. Charles Johnson and Associates, "The Armstrong Association of Philadelphia," typescript, Armstrong Association Papers, Urban Archives, Temple University, pp. 62–69, 79–82; Klaczynska, "Working Women in Philadelphia," p. 53; John Emlen, "The Movement for the Betterment of the Negro in Philadelphia," *The Annals of the American Academy of Political and Social Science,* 49 (September 1913), p. 91.
82. Interview with P. N. Bohn, March 18, 1957, Gladys Palmer Papers, University of Pennsylvania, in custody of Professor Ann Miller, Box 167, p. 6.
83. Amey E. Watson, "Household Employment in Philadelphia," *Bulletin of the Women's Bureau. No. 93* (Washington, D.C., 1932), p. 56; "Stan-

dards of Placement Agencies for Household Employees," *Bulletin of the Women's Bureau. No. 112* (Washington, 1934), pp. 10–12.

84. De Schweinitz, *How Workers Find Jobs,* pp. 116–118.
85. Ibid., pp. 118–124; Edwin Craig, "A Survey of the Graduates of Girard College from February 1933 to June 1934, Inclusive" (unpublished M.Ed. thesis, Temple Univerity, 1941), p. 93; "Affidavit—Occupational Classification (Industrial), Selective Service System," Penrose R. Hoopes Collection, Hagley Library, Accession 1344, Box 26.
86. Kellor, *Out of Work,* pp. 86, 158, 227.
87. Leonard Adams, *The Public Employment Service in Transition, 1933–1968: Evolution of a Placement Service into a Manpower Agency* (Ithaca, N.Y., 1969), p. 26.
88. *Monthly Bulletin of the Pennsylvania Department of Labor and Industry,* 7 (December 1920), p. 154; Willits, *Philadelphia Unemployment with Special Reference to the Textile Industries.*
89. *Monthly Bulletin of the Pennsylvania Department of Labor and Industry,* 2 (December 1915), p. 21.
90. *Monthly Bulletin of the Pennsylvania Department of Labor and Industry,* 4 (April 1917), p. 56.
91. Adams, *The Public Employment Service in Transition,* pp. 23–26.
92. Figures on registrations at Philadelphia offices of the Pennsylvania State Employment Service are available in the *Monthly Bulletin of the Pennsylvania Department of Labor and Industry* from 1915 through 1932. Additional figures can be found in Gladys Palmer, *The Search for Work in Philadelphia, 1932–36: An Analysis of Records of the Philadelphia State Employment Office* (Philadelphia, 1939), p. 11; Gladys Palmer, "Labor Market Functioning: Philadelphia Labor Market Studies" (unpublished paper, University of Pennsylvania; copy in my possession); Gladys Palmer, "War Labor Supply Problems of Philadelphia and Its Environs" (unpublished paper, University of Pennsylvania, 1942; copy in my possession), pp. 23–28.
93. Gladys Palmer, "Depression Jobs: A Study of Job Openings in the Philadelphia Employment Office, 1932–1933" (unpublished paper, University of Pennsylvania, 1934; copy in my possession), pp. 4, 12. Figures listed in the *Monthly Bulletin of the Pennsylvania Department of Labor and Industry* from 1915 through 1932 on the operations of the state employment bureaus include number of registrants, job openings, referrals, and positions filled. Although the numbers fluctuated, generally a two-to-one ratio existed between listed openings and actual jobs secured.
94. Palmer, *The Search For Work,* pp. 16–17.
95. Ibid., pp. 17–18.

96. Gladys Palmer, *Recent Trends in Employment and Unemployment in Phila-delphia* (Philadelphia, 1937), pp. 19–21.

97. Palmer, "Depression Jobs," p. 6.

98. Palmer, *The Search For Work,* pp. 9, 23; Palmer, *Recent Trends,* p. 18.

99. Palmer, *Recent Trends,* pp. 19–21.

100. Interview Schedules, 1936 Gladys Palmer Survey for the Works Progress Administration, Urban Archives, Temple University.

101. For the purposes of this analysis, the author counted and categorized want ads found in the *Public Ledger, Bulletin,* and *Inquirer* in the May 1 editions for 1850, 1860, 1870, 1880, 1890, 1900, 1910, 1920. May 1 was chosen after investigations revealed that advertisements tended to be the greatest in number during that month.

102. *Public Ledger,* November 18, 1905, p. 9.

103. Anne Bezanson, *Help-Wanted Advertising as an Indicator of the Demand for Labor* (Philadelphia, 1929), pp. 1–16; Palmer, "War Labor Supply Problems of Philadelphia and its Environs," p. 24.

104. Palmer, *Philadelphia Workers,* p. 179.

105. Bezanson, *Help-Wanted Advertising,* pp. 70–72.

106. Ibid., pp. 4, 16, 25.

107. D. F. Garretson to E. C. Beetem & Son Company, March 17, 1913, E. C. Beetem & Son Company Papers, Hagley Library, Accession 1178, Series V, File 363.

108. A. E. Griggs to E. C. Beetem & Son Company, March 16, 1913, ibid.

109. Herbert Zachery to E. C. Beetem & Son Company, March 16, 1913, ibid.

110. A. M. Merchant to E. C. Beetem & Son Company, March 16, 1913, ibid.

111. William Sargent to E. C. Beetem & Son Company, March 17, 1913, ibid.

112. C. A. Laird to E. C. Beetem & Son Company, March 16, 1913, ibid.

113. *Bulletin,* May 1, 1910, p. 14.

114. *Inquirer,* May 1, 1920, p. 26.

115. Interview Schedules, 1936 Gladys Palmer Survey for the Works Progress Administration, Urban Archives, Temple University.

116. Consumers' League of Eastern Pennsylvania, *Colored Women as Industrial Workers in Philadelphia* (Philadelphia, 1919), p. 34.

117. Isabel Eaton, "Special Report on Negro Domestic Service in the Seventh Ward, Philadelphia," in W. E. B. DuBois, *The Philadelphia Negro: A Social Study* (New York, 1967), p. 436.

118. "Pennsylvania Employers Survey," typescript, Gladys Palmer Papers, University of Pennsylvania (copy in my possession).

119. Ibid., De Schweinitz, *How Workers Find Jobs*, pp. 131, 140–141; Horowitz, *The Metal Machinery Trades in Philadelphia*, pp. 65–66.

5. Firms

1. The question of barring married women from employment will be treated in detail in Chapter 7.
2. Had Alfred Chandler in his various seminal writings on managerial history chosen to deal with labor affairs, this kind of organizational perspective would probably have been in the offing. See especially Alfred Chandler, *The Visible Hand: The Managerial Revolution in American Business* (Cambridge, Mass., 1977).
3. This top-down form of Marxist argument has been best articulated by Harry Braverman. See Harry Braverman, *Labor and Monopoly Capital: The Degradation of Work in the Twentieth Century* (New York, 1974).
4. For this more dialectical viewpoint see, Michael Burawoy, *Manufacturing Consent: Changes in the Labor Process under Monopoly Capitalism* (Chicago, 1980); Walter Licht, *Working for the Railroad: The Organization of Work in the Nineteenth Century* (Princeton, 1983); and Sanford Jacoby, *Employing Bureaucracy: Managers, Unions, and the Transformation of Work in American Industry, 1900–1945* (New York, 1985).
5. Richard Edwards, *Contested Terrain: The Transformation of the Workplace in the Twentieth Century* (New York, 1979); David Gordon, Richard Edwards, and Michael Reich, *Segmented Work, Divided Workers: The Historical Transformation of Labor in the United States* (New York, 1982).
6. The impact of the state on personnel practices has recently been emphasized in James Baron, Frank Dobbin, and P. Devereaux Jennings, "War and Peace: The Evolution of Modern Personnel Administration in U.S. Industry," *American Journal of Sociology*, 92 (September 1986): 350–383; and in Jacoby, *Employing Bureaucracy*, chapters 5 and 8.
7. I selected the firms discussed in this chapter in the following way. First, I conducted a search in local archives for company records; quantity and quality of materials pertaining to personnel matters determined choices, and I located six case studies in this manner. Second, I sent letters to more than three hundred firms that had been in business in the city of Philadelphia for at least one hundred years; a listing provided by the Philadelphia Chamber of Commerce facilitated this mailing. Responses from forty-two firms and subsequent visits to twenty-six established possibilities for research in fourteen businesses. Surviving documents and opportunities to interview veteran and retired workers, supervisors, and owners determined this selection.

8. For confirmation, see Gladys Palmer, *Philadelphia Workers in a Changing Economy* (Philadelphia, 1956), pp. 5–60.

9. A history of the Wetherill Paint Company can be found in Miriam Hussey, *From Merchants to "Colour Men:" Five Generations of Samuel Wetherill's White Lead Business* (Philadelphia, 1956).

10. Ibid., pp. 16, 97–102.

11. Medical Records, M-52-ABC, Wetherill Paint Company Papers, Lippincott Library, University of Pennsylvania; Safety Committee Records, ibid.

12. "Journal of Daily Occurrences," John Gay & Sons Carpet Mill, 1876–1916, Historical Society of Pennsylvania, December 1, 1882; January 17, 1883; February 21, 1884.

13. Ibid., June 12, 1892; March 10, 1896; Lorin Blodget, *The Textile Industries of Philadelphia* (Philadelphia, 1880), pp. 45–50.

14. "Journal of Daily Occurrences," John Gay & Sons Carpet Mill, November 5, 1878; August 19, 1881; March 31, 1884; March 29, 1889; June 12, 1892; March 10, 1896; May 14, 1906; September 3, 1908; November 9, 1909; March 29, 1915.

15. Ibid., December 3, 1878; December 10, 1878; December 18, 1880; May 3, 1893; December 27, 1914.

16. Entries in the "Journal of Daily Occurrences" of the John Gay Company reveal frequent job actions in the years listed.

17. Scrapbook, Newspaper Clippings, 1867–1888, William H. Horstmann Company Papers, Historical Society of Pennsylvania, article dated August 21, 1873; undated article from the *American Cabinet Maker;* article dated December 9, 1869, "The Silk Manufacturers of Paterson, N.J."; "American Silk Manufacturer," *Commercial Advisor,* May 17, 1875.

18. Ibid., *The Daily Register,* October 22, 1853; *American Gazette,* June 27, 1860; *Daily Chronicle,* May 20, 1870.

19. Computerized analysis of Horstmann and Company Employee Register, 1850–1875, William H. Horstmann Company Papers, Historical Society of Pennsylvania.

20. Scrapbook, Newspaper Clippings, 1867–1888, assorted invitations, ibid.

21. Ibid., article from *American Gazette,* June 27, 1860. From numerous other clippings in the Horstmann Scrapbook, it is clear that William H. Horstmann played a leading role in the German-American community in Philadelphia.

22. This case study is based on interviews with George Kallish, manager of Swoboda & Sons for Trans-Continental Leather, Inc., and on a small file of historical papers and items kept in the vault in Mr. Kallish's office (including a typewritten history of the firm prepared in the 1960s; no author listed).

23. This case study is based on extensive interviews with Edward K. Hueber, former owner and operating manager of Kelley & Hueber; Mr. Hueber referred to a few surviving papers and files of the firm.

24. This case study was compiled through interviews with Mrs. Lynne Walker, general manager of Herder Cutlery and descendant of Leopold Herder, and with Otto Schwartz, a grinder who started working with the firm in 1924.

25. This case study is based on interviews with Christian Spahr, one of the four owners of Lea & Febiger and a descendent of Matthew Carey, the founder of the company. I also consulted assorted records and materials deposited in the vault of the firm.

26. Roll of Employees, 1890–1910, Lea & Febiger, vault.

27. Ibid.

28. A basic history of the Philadelphia Contributionship can be found in Nicholas Wainwright, *The Philadelphia Contributionship for the Insurance of Houses from Loss by Fire* (Philadelphia, 1952).

29. Carol Wojtowicz, "Office of the Philadelphia Contributionship," *227th Annual Report of the Philadelphia Contributionship* (Philadelphia, 1979).

30. Interviews with Carol Wojtowicz, Curator and Archivist, Philadelphia Contributionship, and Walter Smith, Secretary Treasurer, Philadelphia Contributionship.

31. The basic business and production history of Richard Remmey and Company can be found in the following articles supplied to the author by John Remmey, former president of the firm: W. Oakley Raymond, "Remmey Family: American Potters," *Antiques* (June 1937), pp. 296–297; W. Oakley Raymond, "Remmey Family: American Potters, Part II," *Antiques* (September 1937), pp. 132–134; "Laboratory Control and Flexible Operation Allow Wide Variety of Refractions," *Brick & Clay Record* (August 1940), pp. 44–46; "Remmey Refractories," *The Noreaster* (February 1948), pp. 7–8; "The Remmeys and the Refractory Industry," *Reading Railroad Magazine* (no date), pp. 10–11, 24.

32. Interview with John Remmey.

33. This case study is based on interviews with S. E. Firestone, President of McCloskey Varnish, and Alice Carducci, whose father began working for the firm in the 1920s and who began working there herself in the early 1950s and has held various production and clerical jobs.

34. This case study is based on interviews with A. K. Taylor, Chairman of the Board of Directors of Ellisco Incorporated, and Robert Taylor, his son, who serves as vice president of the firm. Both informants studied their files after I submitted a long agenda of questions; I was not allowed direct access to written material.

35. The Insurance Company of North America is now Connecticut Insurance Group of North America (CIGNA).
36. For an overview of INA's history see Thomas Montgomery, *A History of the Insurance Company of North America* (Philadelphia, 1885); Marquis James, *Biography of a Business, 1792–1942* (New York, 1942); and William Carr, *Perils Named and Unnamed* (New York, 1967).
37. Directors' minutes, Archives of the Insurance Company of North America, Philadelphia, Pennsylvania, Volume 7, September 4, 1877, p. 9; February 5, 1878, p. 16; March 5, 1870, p. 18; April 5, 1881, p. 67; Volume 9, October 1, 1895, p. 24; January 13, 1897, pp. 68–69. See also James, *Biography of a Business,* pp. 104–107, 160; Montgomery, *A History of the Insurance Company of North America,* p. 47; Carr, *Perils Named and Unnamed,* p. 7.
38. "New Building Instructions, October 29, 1925," Record Group 9/14; untitled memorandum from Home Office Service Committee, Record Group 9/12.4; "Employment Application," Record Group 9/14, Archives of the Insurance Company of North America.
39. Record Group 9/6, ibid.
40. "Philadelphia Salary Market Analysis," Record Group 9/13, ibid.; interviews with Claudette Johns, archivist of INA, and Lee Corak, Assistant Director of Training at INA; "Interview with Harris Ebenbach, Personnel Department, Insurance Company of North America, September 12, 1956," Gladys Palmer Papers, Box 167, University of Pennsylvania, Philadelphia, Pennsylvania (in custody of Professor Ann Miller).
41. For a recent study that emphasizes the role of culture in affecting industrial relations, see Charles Dellheim, "The Creation of a Company Culture: Cadbury's, 1861–1931," *American Historical Review,* 92 (February 1987): 13–44.
42. This case study is based on interviews with Percy Lanning, president of Perseverance Iron, and perusal of assorted papers in his possession, as well as on informal interviews with veteran workers.
43. This case study is based on interviews with Harvard Wood and Harvard C. Wood, Jr., president and vice-president of H. C. Wood Incorporated. Their responses were based on memory and their searches of surviving records.
44. This case study is based on extensive interviews with William Hipp, Vice President of Production at Schmidt's Brewery. Mr. Hipp's grandfather and father worked as brewmasters at Schmidt's, a position he also occupied before promotion to general plant manager. Mr. Hipp permitted the author access to various company papers, including union contracts and several unpublished company histories. Since the

research and basic writing of this book were completed, Schmidt's Brewery has closed its production plants in the city.

45. Edward Pry, "Analysis of Employer-Employee Relations in the John B. Stetson Company" (unpublished M.A. thesis, University of Pennsylvania, 1941), pp. 2–15.

46. Ibid., pp. 15–25; "Employee Relations of the John B. Stetson Company," *National Association of Corporation Schools Bulletin,* 12 (December 1917), pp. 22–25.

47. Pry, "Analysis of Employer-Employee Relations in the John B. Stetson Company," pp. 27–44.

48. "Brown, Richard Percy," entry in *The National Cyclopedia of American Biography,* Volume G (1943–46), pp. 112–113; "Edward Brown: Pacesetter," *Delaware Valley Announcer,* November 1959, pp. 28–29 (articles found in a vault at Honey Incorporated, Fort Washington, Pennsylvania).

49. Interviews with Carl Wagenhals (former production manager at Brown), Jack Wiley (veteran product line manager), Charles Cusick, John Moore, and James Cameron (retired engineers), Frank Rae (former chief of production at Brown), and Stuart Smith (director of personnel at Honeywell).

50. "Brown Instrument Co. and United Electrical, Radio, and Machine Workers of America (CIO)," printed article without references located in vault of Honeywell Incorporated, Fort Washington, Pennsylvania; copy in my possession.

51. Interviews with Stuart Smith and Carol Holcombe (veteran secretary at Brown).

52. Basic histories of the Baldwin Locomotive Works can be found in *Memorial of Matthias Baldwin* (Philadelphia, 1867); William Brown, *The History of the First Locomotives* (New York, 1871); *History of the Baldwin Locomotive Works, 1831–1923* (Philadelphia, no date or author listed); and *The Baldwin Locomotive Works of Philadelphia: The Story of Eddystone* (Philadelphia, 1928).

53. *The Baldwin Locomotive Works,* pp. 63–73.

54. Samuel Vauclain, *Optimism* (Philadelphia, 1924), pp. 45–46. This printed address was located in the files of the Samuel Vauclain Papers, Historical Society of Pennsylvania.

55. On the subcontracting system at Baldwin see the journal notes of William Austin, 1910, William Liseter Austin Collection, Box 5, Hagley Library, Wilmington, Delaware.

56. The following two extensive biographies provide a wealth of information on John Wanamaker and his store: Herbert Adams Gibbons, *John Wanamaker* (New York, 1926, 2 volumes); Joseph Appel, *The Business Biography of John Wanamaker* (New York, 1930).

57. See especially Gibbons, *John Wanamaker,* vol. 2, pp. 261–264, 272–279, 284–285; Appel, *The Business Biography of John Wanamaker,* pp. 428–430; John Wanamaker, "The John Wanamaker Commercial Institute—A Store School," *The Annals of the American Academy of Political and Social Science,* 33 (1909), pp. 151–154.

58. Appel, *The Business Biography of John Wanamaker,* p. 434; Herman Stern, "The Present Union-Management Relationship in Philadelphia Central City Department Stores" (unpublished M.B.A. thesis, University of Pennsylvania, 1943), pp. 33–35.

59. Walton Forstall, "One Hundred Years of Philadelphia Gas Supply" (unpublished manuscript in possession of the Public Relations Department of the Philadelphia Gas Works, 1935), pp. 2–10.

60. *The Philadelphia Gas Work News,* 22 (July-August 1950), pp. 4–41, 58.

61. Forstall, "One Hundred Years of Philadelphia Gas Supply," pp. 153–159.

62. Ibid., pp. 162–172; *The Philadelphia Gas Work News,* 22 (July-August 1950), pp. 42–49, 54, 60; Circular Letters 3093–3097 of Personnel Office, Archives of Philadelphia Gas Works, Philadelphia, Pennsylvania.

63. *The Philadelphia Gas Work News,* 22 (July–August 1950), p. 54; Forstall, "One Hundred Years of Philadelphia Gas Supply," pp. 255–258.

64. Harry Braverman, *Labor and Monopoly Capitalism.*

65. Sanford Jacoby, *Employing Bureaucracy.*

66. David Brody, "The Rise and Decline of Welfare Capitalism," in Brody, *Workers in Industrial America; Essays on the 20th Century Struggle* (New York, 1980), pp. 48–81.

67. David Brody, "The Emergence of Mass-Production Unionism," ibid., pp. 82–119.

68. James Baron, Frank Dobbin, and P. Devereaux Jennings, "War and Peace"; Richard Edwards, *Contested Terrain;* and Howell John Harris, *The Right to Manage: Industrial Relations Policies of American Business in the 1940s* (Madison, Wis., 1982).

69. For the most up-to-date biography of Taylor, see Daniel Nelson, *Frederick W. Taylor and the Rise of Scientific Management* (Madison, Wis., 1980).

70. Daniel Nelson, *Managers and Workers: Origins of the New Factory System in the United States, 1880–1920* (Madison, Wis., 1975), pp. 56–58, 62–63, 71–73.

71. Ibid., pp. 68–78; Edwards, *Contested Terrain,* pp. 97–104.

72. Kathy Burgess, "Self-Help and Scientific Management at the Link-Belt Company, 1890–1915" (unpublished manuscript, University of Pennsylvania, 1983; copy in my possession).

73. Employers of clerical help faced little pressure, at least before 1950, to innovate in personnel relations. They relied on outside agencies,

namely schools, for training clerks in typing, stenography, filing, etc.; since these skills were standardized, in-house training programs were unnecessary. Since there apparently was also a ready supply, particularly of young women with commercial course degrees, little concern existed to encourage long tenure. The situation for production workers and sales forces was different. Human capital theory is helpful in this instance in understanding various strategies toward labor. See Jurgen Kocka, *White Collar Workers in America* (London, 1980).

74. Chandler, *Visible Hand,* pp. 105–109; Licht, *Working for the Railroad,* pp. 16–17, 83.

75. "Data on Hiring in System Departments in Philadelphia," box marked "Personnel Records: Employee Recruitment and Hiring," Pennsylvania Railroad Company Papers, Hagley Library, Wilmington, Delaware; "A Program of Employee Selection, 1956," ibid; "A Report on the Personnel Program, The Pennsylvania Railroad," box marked "Personnel Records: Personnel Department," ibid; "Hiring Manual," Vice President for Operations Files, Box 5, ibid.

76. A question can be raised about whether the patterns in personnel practices noted in this chapter are unique to Philadelphia. In some sense, this comment misses the point; the discussion here aimed at identifying various possibilities. In other places, the proportions of firms with particular personnel histories might be different; qualifications would be in order if patterns not noted here were discernible and discovered elsewhere. Is the typology rendered here inclusive, in other words?

The particular distribution of practices described in this page, admittedly, is very much a mirror of particular aspects of Philadelphia's economic and social history. The Quaker influence in the city is obvious; that ethical values played a role in firm personnel histories in many instances is not surprising. Custom goods production dominated in the city and a high proportion of the work involved skilled labor; that skilled workers played an important role in fixing practices is also not surprising. Family owned and operated firms also were common to the city; this, too, made for cases of nonprogrammatic paternalism. Philadelphia similarly was composed of distinct and stable manufacturing districts; family and ethnic ties also affected personnel matters within companies. An appreciation of Philadelphia's particular industrial history can be found in Philip Scranton and Walter Licht, *Work Sights: Industrial Philadelphia, 1890–1950* (Philadelphia, 1986).

The ultimate point, however, is not whether the findings are representative, but whether they comprise the full gamut of personnel histories manifest in American business enterprises. That remains for other researchers to confirm or refute.

6. The State

1. Government employment will be treated as municipal employment in this chapter. The city of Philadelphia employed more people than the state and federal governments combined. To look at the politics of state and federal employment would also take this study far afield to Harrisburg and Washington, D.C. The issues raised in this chapter are illustrated well at the level of city government.
2. Kenneth Fones-Wolf, "Trade Union Gospel: Protestantism and Labor in Philadelphia, 1865–1915" (unpublished Ph.D. dissertation, Temple University, 1985), p. 143.
3. On John Wanamaker, see Herbert Adams Gibbons, *John Wanamaker* (New York, 1926, 2 volumes); Joseph Appel, *The Business Biography of John Wanamaker* (New York, 1930).
4. On hat makers and trade unionism, see David Bensman, *The Practice of Solidarity: American Hat Finishers in the Nineteenth Century* (Urbana, Ill., 1985).
5. Fones-Wolf, "Trade Union Gospel," p. 139; Philip Scranton and Walter Licht, *Work Sights: Industrial Philadelphia, 1890–1950* (Philadelphia, 1986), pp. 155–170.
6. On Frederick Winslow Taylor and his movement, see Daniel Nelson, *Frederick W. Taylor and the Rise of Scientific Management* (Madison, Wis., 1980).
7. David Montgomery, *The Fall of the House of Labor: The Workplace, the State, and American Labor Activism, 1865–1925* (New York, 1987), pp. 261–269; Kenneth Fones-Wolf, "Employer Unity and the Crisis of the Craftsman," *Pennsylvania Magazine of History and Biography,* 107 (July 1983), p. 454; Howell Harris, "Solidarity Forever: The Metal Manufacturers' Association of Philadelphia, 1900–1930" (unpublished paper, University of Durham, no date; copy in my possession), pp. 20–23; Earl Sparks, "The Metal Manufacturers' Association of Philadelphia: A Review of Activities, 1903–1953," typescript, Metal Manufacturers' Association of Philadelphia Papers, Urban Archives, Temple University, Box 1, File 2, p. 1; D. H. McPherson, "Secretary's Report, 1904," ibid., File 12.
8. G. D. Brooks, "Protection from Labor Troubles: Workers' Control and the Metal Manufacturers' Association of Philadelphia" (unpublished paper, University of Pennsylvania, no date; copy in my possession), pp. 12–13; Fones-Wolf, "Employer Unity," p. 454.
9. "Constitution of the Metal Manufacturers' Association," Metal Manufacturers' Association of Philadelphia Papers, Box 1, File 1.
10. On the workings of the Labor Bureau of the Metal Manufacturers'

Association of Philadelphia see "Testimony of Justus Schwacke," *Industrial Relations: Final Report and Testimony Submitted to the Congress by the Commission of Industrial Relations, Volume III* (Washington, D.C., 1916), p. 2890; "Testimony of Henry Morgan," ibid., pp. 1903–1905; Sparks, "The Metal Manufacturers' Association of Philadelphia," pp. 1–2.

11. "Secretary's Report, 1905," Metal Manufacturers' Association of Philadelphia Papers, Box 1, File 12, p. 4.

12. "Secretary's Report, 1904," p. 2.

13. "Secretary's Report, 1905," p. 4.

14. Brooks, "Workers' Control and the Metal Manufacturers' Association of Philadelphia," pp. 20–21.

15. Fones-Wolf, "Employer Unity," p. 454.

16. Minutes from special meetings of the Metal Manufacturers' Association for June 7, 1916, June 19, 1916, June 23, 1916, and July 10, 1916, Metal Manufacturers' Association of Philadelphia Papers, Box 2; "Secretary's Report, 1917," Box 1, File 12.

17. Brooks, "Workers' Control and the Metal Manufacturers' Association of Philadelphia," p. 22.

18. Sparks, "The Metal Manufacturers' Association of Philadelphia," pp. 3–10; "History of the Metal Manufacturers' Association, 1903–1945," typescript, Metal Manufacturers' Association of Philadelphia Papers, Box 1, File 3, pp. 10–33.

19. Joseph Willits, *Philadelphia Unemployment with Special Reference to the Textile Industries* (Philadelphia, 1915), pp. 127–150.

20. Russell F. Weigley, *Philadelphia: A 300-Year History* (New York, 1982), pp. 548–550.

21. On political reform movements in Philadelphia during the Progressive era, see Donald Dishbrow, "Reform in Philadelphia under Mayor Blankenburg, 1912–1916," *Pennsylvania History*, 27 (October 1960), pp. 379–396; Arthur Dudden, "Lincoln Steffen's Philadelphia," *Pennsylvania History*, 31 (October 1964), pp. 449–458; and David Pivar, "Theocratic Businessmen and Philadelphia Municipal Reform, 1890–1900," *Pennsylvania History*, 33 (July 1966), pp. 189–307.

22. Jean Christie, *Morris Llewellyn Cooke: Progressive Engineer* (New York, 1983), pp. 1–18, 23–30.

23. Willits, *Philadelphia Unemployment*, pp. 3–4.

24. Jeffrey Feld, "The Whartonians: An Examination of the Relationship between Philadelphia Municipal Reform and Professors of the Wharton School, 1906–1916" (unpublished paper, University of Pennsylvania, 1980; copy in my possession), pp. 18–19.

25. Ibid., pp. 17–48.

26. Ibid., p. 97.
27. Ibid., pp. 94–96.
28. Howell Harris, "War in the Social Order: The First World War and the Liberalization of American Quakerism" (unpublished paper, University of Durham, no date; copy in my possession), pp. 38–39, 43–45.
29. Gladys Palmer, *Philadelphia Workers in a Changing Economy* (Philadelphia, 1956), pp. vii–viii.
30. Harris, "War in the Social Order," p. 47.
31. Willits, *Philadelphia Unemployment*, p. 67.
32. Ibid., p. 68.
33. Ibid., pp. 6–7, 69–109.
34. Ibid., pp. 9, 110–119.
35. Ibid., p. 9.
36. Joseph Willits, "Steadying Employment, with a Section Devoted to Some Facts of Unemployment in Philadelphia," *The Annals of the American Academy of Political and Social Science*, 65 (May 1916), supplement.
37. The entire 1916 issue of the *Annals*, ibid., was devoted to studies in personnel management.
38. For a history of the personnel management movement, see Sanford Jacoby, *Employing Bureaucracy: Managers, Unions and the Transformation of Work in American Industry, 1900–1945* (New York, 1985).
39. Willits, *Philadelphia Unemployment*, pp. 169–170.
40. For a thorough study of the Quaker community in Philadelphia in the late nineteenth and early twentieth centuries, see Philip S. Benjamin, *The Philadelphia Quakers in the Industrial Age, 1865–1920* (Philadelphia, 1976).
41. Harris, "War in the Social Order," pp. 7–12.
42. Charles Dellheim, "The Creation of a Company Culture, Cadbury's, 1861–1931," *American Historical Review*, 92 (February 1987), pp. 13–44.
43. Harris, "War in the Social Order," pp. 15–16.
44. Daniel Nelson, "'A Newly Appreciated Art': The Development of Personnel Work at Leeds & Northrup, 1915–1923," *Business History Review*, 44 (Winter 1970), pp. 520–535.
45. Quoted in Harris, "War in the Social Order," p. 25.
46. Ibid., p. 23.
47. Ibid., pp. 28–30, 31–34, 36.
48. Ibid., p. 36.
49. Morris Leeds to Charles Huston, February 4, 1920, Charles Huston Correspondence, I-H (1919–1920), Lukens Steel Company Papers, Hagley Library, Accession 50.

50. "Meeting of the Business Problems Group, June 8, 1920," ibid.
51. "Minutes of the Meeting of the Business Problems Group, February 7, 1921," Charles Huston Correspondence, H–O (1919–1922).
52. "Meeting of the Business Problems Group, December 19, 1921," ibid.
53. "Report of Address by B. Seebohm Rowntree on the Human Factor in Business, at the Meeting of the Business Problems Group, October 26, 1921," ibid.
54. *Fifteenth Annual Report of the Civil Service Commission of the City of Philadelphia for the Year Ending September 31, 1920* (Philadelphia, 1920), p. 14; Lynn J. Barnard and Jessie Evans, *Citizenship in Philadelphia* (Philadelphia, 1925), p. 147; *An Outline of City and County Organization Shown in Charts and Text* (Philadelphia, 1949).
55. *Twentieth Annual Report of the Civil Service Commission of the City of Philadelphia for the Year Ending September 31, 1925* (Philadelphia, 1925), p. 14; *Philadelphia's Quota of Government Employees: 1930* (Philadelphia, 1930), p. 3.
56. United States Department of Labor, *State, County and Municipal Survey, Government Employment and Pay Rolls, 1929 through 1938: The City of Philadelphia and Philadelphia County, Pennsylvania* (Washington, D.C., 1941), pp. 1–10.
57. Edwin Rothman et al., *Philadelphia Government, 1956* (Philadelphia, 1956), p. 34.
58. *Trend of Philadelphia Municipal Employment* (Philadelphia, 1967), pp. 3, 6–15.
59. Rothman et al., *Philadelphia Government*, p. 301.
60. *Classification of Positions in the Classified Service of the City of Philadelphia, 1920* (Philadelphia, 1920).
61. Rothman et al., *Philadelphia Government*, p. 301.
62. *Trend of Philadelphia Municipal Employment*, pp. 6–15.
63. *Fifteenth Annual Report*, p. 12.
64. *Annual Report of Personnel Department of City of Philadelphia, 1953* (Philadelphia, 1953), p. 24.
65. John William Crum, "The Citizen vs. The City: Municipal Bureaucracy in Nineteenth-Century Philadelphia" (unpublished Ph.D. dissertation, University of Delaware, 1980), p. 163; Barnard and Evans, *Citizenship in Philadelphia*, p. 60.
66. Crum, "The Citizen vs. The City," pp. 100, 107; Barnard and Evans, *Citizenship in Philadelphia*, pp. 81–83.
67. Weigley, *Philadelphia*, p. 359.
68. Barnard and Evans, *Citizenship in Philadelphia*, p. 124.
69. *Changes in Philadelphia City Employment Between 1953 and 1979: A Review of Municipal Personnel Trends in the Past Quarter Century* (Philadelphia, 1980), pp. 10, 19.

70. Crum, "The Citizen vs. The City," p. 171.

71. Ibid., pp. 175–176.

72. Weigley, *Philadelphia*, p. 438; William Beyer, *Personnel Administration in Philadelphia* (Philadelphia, 1937), pp. 4–5.

73. Crum, "The Citizen vs. The City," pp. 37–38.

74. Eudice Glassberg, "Philadelphians in Need: Client Experiences with Two Philadelphia Benevolent Societies, 1830–1880" (unpublished Ph.D. dissertation, University of Pennsylvania, 1978), p. 99.

75. Walton Forstall, "One Hundred Years of Philadelphia Gas Supply" (unpublished manuscript in possession of the Public Relations Department of the Philadelphia Gas Works, 1935), pp. 153–159.

76. Weigley, *Philadelphia*, p. 558.

77. The notion that even businessmen who espoused laissez-fairism contributed to the expansion of municipal government through their calls for reform is dealt with in an intriguing way in James Allen Scott, "The Businessman, Capitalism and the City: Businessmen and Municipal Reform in Philadelphia from the Act of Consolidation (1854) to the Bullitt Bill (1885)" (unpublished Ph.D. dissertation, University of Delaware, 1977), especially pp. 174–175.

78. Weigley, *Philadelphia*, pp. 26–27, 166–167; Rothman et al., *Philadelphia Government*, pp. 15–17; Crum, "The Citizen vs. The City," pp. 11–12, 17.

79. Howard Frank Gillette, Jr., "Corrupt and Contented: Philadelphia's Political Machine, 1865–1887" (unpublished Ph.D. dissertation, Yale University, 1970), p. 37.

80. John D. Stewart II, "Philadelphia Politics in the Gilded Age" (unpublished Ph.D. dissertation, St. John's University, 1973), p. 105.

81. Ibid., pp. 161–162; Weigley, *Philadelphia*, pp. 438–439.

82. Stewart, "Philadelphia Politics in the Gilded Age," pp. 158–159.

83. Crum, "The Citizen vs. The City," pp. 68–76.

84. As quoted in Crum, "The Citizen vs. The City," pp. 79–80.

85. Harry Silcox, *Philadelphia Politics from the Bottom Up: The Life of Irishman William McMullen, 1824–1901* (Philadelphia, 1989), pp. 20–21.

86. Weigley, *Philadelphia*, p. 369.

87. Silcox, *Philadelphia Politics from the Bottom Up*, p. 28; Weigley, *Philadelphia*, pp. 439–441, 497.

88. Silcox, *Philadelphia Politics from the Bottom Up*, pp. 16–17, 34–35, 39, 85–87, 116–118.

89. Weigley, *Philadelphia*, p. 497.

90. Rothman et al., *Philadelphia Government*, pp. 19–20; Crum, "The Citizen vs. The City," p. 20; Bernard and Evans, *Citizenship in Philadelphia*, pp. 337–338.

91. Weigley, *Philadelphia*, p. 539.

92. Quoted in *Annual Report of the Civil Service Commission to His Honor, The Mayor for the Year Ending December 31, 1906* (Philadelphia, 1907), p. 11.

93. Ibid., pp. 9–11; Beyer, *Personnel Administration in Philadelphia*, p. 71; *Seventh Annual Report of the Civil Service Commission to His Honor, The Mayor for the Year Ending December 31, 1912* (Philadelphia, 1913), pp. 15–16.

94. *Seventh Annual Report of the Civil Service Commission*, foldout tables, nos. 1–5.

95. Weigley, *Philadelphia*, p. 546.

96. Ibid., pp. 563, 570; Crum, "The Citizen vs. The City," p. 20; Bernard and Evans, *Citizenship in Philadelphia*, pp. 364–366; Rothman et al., *Philadelphia Government*, pp. 20–21.

97. Beyer, *Personnel Administration in Philadelphia*, pp. 6, 37–39, 43, 58–59, 64.

98. Francis L. Reinhold, *The Provisional Appointment in City Civil Service Systems with Special Reference to the Philadelphia Civil Service* (Philadelphia, 1937), pp. 6–8, 11.

99. Rothman et al., *Philadelphia Government*, p. 22.

100. Rheinhold, *The Provisional Appointment in City Civil Service Systems*, pp. 10–11.

101. Ibid., pp. 24–26.

102. Ibid., pp. 26–30, 55, 90.

103. Peter Korn, "Recruitment of College Graduates for Careers in Local Government with Particular Emphasis on the City of Philadelphia" (unpublished M.G.A. thesis, University of Pennsylvania, 1962), pp. 57–59.

104. Rheinhold, *The Provisional Appointment in City Civil Service Systems*, pp. 20–33.

105. *Fifteenth Annual Report of the Civil Service Commission of the City of Philadelphia for the Year Ending September 31, 1920* (Philadelphia, 1920), p. 4.

106. *Sixteenth Annual Report of the Civil Service Commission of the City of Philadelphia for the Year Ending December 31, 1921* (Philadelphia, 1921), p. 3.

107. Rheinhold, *The Provisional Appointment in City Civil Service Systems*, p. 16.

108. William Beyer, *Employee Turnover in the City Service* (Philadelphia, 1958), p. v.

109. Ibid., pp. 14, 18.

110. Rheinhold, *The Provisional Appointment in City Civil Service Systems*, p. 18.

111. Weigley, *Philadelphia,* p. 623.
112. Rothman et al., *Philadelphia Government,* pp. 24–30.
113. Ibid., pp. 303–307; Weigley, *Philadelphia,* pp. 654–655; Korn, "Recruitment of College Graduates for Careers in Local Government," p. 67.
114. Rheinhold, *The Provisional Appointment in City Civil Service Systems,* pp. 67–68; *Philadelphia's Quota of Government Employees,* p. 14.
115. The papers of Albert S. Faught, Secretary of the Pennsylvania Civil Service Reform League, can be found in the library of the Pennsylvania Economy League in Philadelphia. Boxes marked 1912–1921, 1922–1927, 1928–1929, N.C.S.R.L. (National Civil Service Reform League), and Correspondence, 1911–1925, contain Faught's extensive unpublished and published writings and speeches on standardization in civil service and the need of private companies to follow the example of city government. See also Albert S. Faught, "Employment Tests in the Public Service," *The Annals of the American Academy of Political and Social Science,* 113 (May 1924), pp. 311–321. William Beyer, Director of the Bureau of Municipal Research, prepared numerous position papers on standardization for the Bureau. His papers are deposited at the Urban Archives of Temple University. Box 3 in this collection includes Beyer's writings on this subject.
116. Paul Douglas, "Plant Administration of Labor," *Journal of Political Economy,* 27 (July 1919), pp. 548–550, 553.
117. Harriet F. Berger, "The Grievance Process in the Philadelphia Public Service: A Problem in Public Personnel Policy" (unpublished M.A. thesis, University of Pennsylvania, 1958), pp. 6–7; James Edward Conlin, "An Analysis of Municipal Labor Relations: City of Philadelphia and District #33 of the American Federation of State, County and Municipal Employees, 1925–1956" (unpublished M.B.A. thesis, University of Pennsylvania, 1958), pp. 1–2, 9, 34–35, 78–82; Donald Marquis, "The Status of Municipal Employee Organizations with Emphasis on Philadelphia" (unpublished M.G.A. thesis, University of Pennsylvania, 1961), pp. 42–43, 59–60; *Background for Decision: A Union Shop for Philadelphia's City Employees?* (Philadelphia, 1960), pp. 1–2.
118. Conlin, "An Analysis of Municipal Labor Relations," pp. 3–5.
119. David T. Stanley, *Managing Local Government Under Union Pressure* (Washington, D.C., 1972), p. 107.
120. As quoted in Berger, "The Grievance Process in the Philadelphia Public Service," p. 8.
121. *Background for Decision,* p. 6; Conlin, pp. 40–41.
122. Marquis, "The Status of Municipal Employee Organizations," p. 70;

Berger, "The Grievance Process in the Philadelphia Public Service," pp. 12–18, 41, 49, 53–55, 60; Stanley, *Managing Local Government Under Union Pressure,* pp. 42, 55.

123. Conlin, "An Analysis of Municipal Labor Relations," pp. 73–74; Stanley Spero and John Capozzola, *The Urban Community and Its Unionized Bureaucracies: Pressure Politics in Local Government Labor Relations* (New York, 1973), p. 225.

124. *Benefits of City of Philadelphia Employees Compared with Benefits in Private Industry: 1980* (Philadelphia,1980), pp. v–vi.

125. Gerald Robert Davis, "Financing Municipal Retirement Systems with Emphasis on the Philadelphia Municipal Pension Fund" (unpublished M.G.A. thesis, University of Pennsylvania, 1965), pp. xiv, 2, 11–12; Rothman et al., *Philadelphia Government,* pp. 294–296.

126. Rothman et al., *Philadelphia Government,* p. 296.

127. Weigley, *Philadelphia,* p. 493.

128. Spero and Capozzola, *The Urban Community and Its Unionized Bureaucracies,* pp. 125–126.

129. Thomas Roberts, "A History of Labor-Management Relations in the Philadelphia Transit Industry" (unpublished Ph.D. dissertation, University of Pennsylvania, 1959), pp. 2–61.

130. Weigley, *Philadelphia,* pp. 642–644.

7. Losing Work and Coping

1. Horstmann and Company Employee Register, William Horstmann Company Papers, Historical Society of Pennsylvania.

2. *American Gazette,* July 27, 1860, Scrapbook, Newspaper Clippings, 1867–1880, William Horstmann Company Papers.

3. Miriam Hussey, *From Merchants to "Colour Men": Five Centuries of Samuel Wetherill's White Lead Business* (Philadelphia, 1956), pp. 97–102.

4. Joseph Willits, *Philadelphia Unemployment with Special Reference to the Textile Industries* (Philadelphia, 1915), p. 81.

5. Ibid., pp. 22–33.

6. *The National Association of Corporation Schools Bulletin,* 4 (November 1917), p. 42.

7. Irving Lewis Horowitz, *The Metal Machinery Trades in Philadelphia: An Occupational Survey* (Philadelphia, 1939), p. 76.

8. Anne Bezanson et al., "Four Years of Labor Mobility: A Study of Labor Turnover in a Group of Selected Plants in Philadelphia, 1921–1924," *The Annals of the American Academy of Political and Social Science,* 119 (May 1925), supplement, pp. 17, 134–135.

9. Anne Bezanson, "Some Historical Aspects of Labor Turnover," in

Arthur H. Cole, ed., *Facts and Factors in Economic History* (Cambridge, Mass., 1932), p. 701.

10. Interview Schedules, 1936 Gladys Palmer Survey for the Works Progress Administration, Urban Archives, Temple University.

11. "The Disston History, Volume 2," typescript, Disston Saw Company Papers, Hagley Library, Accession 1567, p. 94.

12. "Instructions to Employees, 1871–1905, Farmers' and Mechanics Bank," Philadelphia National Bank Company Papers (uncatalogued), Hagley Library.

13. Pay Book, 1911–1916, Christian Schrack Company Papers, Hagley Library, Accession 712, Box 3.

14. For a recent key historical work on employment patterns of American workers, see Alex Keyssar, *Out of Work: The First Century of Unemployment in Massachusetts* (New York, 1986).

15. A computerized data set derived from the employee register of the Horstmann Company is available from the author. Kin connections were established as follows. Workers with similar surnames who worked in similar positions and entered the firm on the same day were considered kin. Possible pairs of workers with very common names were not considered as kin. This produced a conservative estimate of 8 percent for the number of employees working alongside relatives in the firm.

16. Bezanson et al., "Four Years of Labor Mobility," pp. 70–72, 96, 110–115, 118–119, 123–125.

17. Ibid.; Burton Morley, "Occupational Experience of Applicants for Work in Philadelphia" (unpublished Ph.D. dissertation, University of Pennsylvania, 1930), pp. 104–109.

18. Bezanson et al., "Four Years of Labor Mobility," p. 47.

19. In crosstabulations of age, sex, place of birth, years of schooling, marital status, apprenticeship training, occupation, and methods of securing employment with a range of measures for employment history—such as number of jobs held, length of work stints, and months unemployed—age consistently correlated most strongly (contingency $C = .77$, for example, for age and years employed in regular occupation). Other factors, such as sex, correlated much less highly ($C = .24$ for the above example) and in multivariate analysis completely dissipated in importance when controls for age were introduced.

20. Workers in the WPA survey who secured employment through family connections had longer stints (by an average of five months) than their counterparts who found work through other means; recorded differences were statistically significant.

21. Workers in the WPA survey who had the advantages of apprenticeship

training had longer stints (by an average of six months) than their counterparts not apprenticed; recorded differences were statistically significant.

22. In Multiple Classification Analysis, differences among age cohorts with regard to percent laid off were not eliminated with controls for sex, nativity, years of schooling, or skill level. Differences between men and women disappeared completely when age was factored.

23. Bezanson et al., "Four Years of Labor Mobility," p. 71.

24. Philip Scranton and Walter Licht, *Work Sights: Industrial Philadelphia, 1890–1950* (Philadelphia, 1986), pp. 266; Philip Scranton, *Proprietary Capitalism: The Textile Manufacture at Philadelphia* (New York, 1983), pp. 175, 202, 206, 278.

25. Gladys Palmer, *Ten Years of Work Experience of Philadelphia Weavers and Loom Fixers* (Philadelphia, 1938), pp. 3–4.

26. Gladys Palmer, *Philadelphia Workers in a Changing Economy* (Philadelphia, 1956), p. 13.

27. Willits, *Philadelphia Unemployment,* p. 40.

28. Ibid., p. 28.

29. Ibid., p. 32.

30. Anne Bezanson, *Earnings and Working Opportunity in the Upholstery Weavers' Trade in 25 Plants in Philadelphia: An Experiment in Co-Operative Research* (Philadelphia, 1928), p. 69.

31. Quoted in Willits, *Philadelphia Unemployment,* p. 17.

32. Quoted in ibid., pp. 58–59.

33. Ibid., pp. 127–150.

34. J. Frederic Dewhurst and Ernest A. Tupper, "Social and Economic Character of Unemployment in Philadelphia: April, 1929," *Bulletin of the United States Bureau of Labor Statistics No. 520* (Washington, D.C., 1930), p. 17.

35. Ibid., p. 6.

36. Ibid., pp. 19–25, 32–33.

37. Gladys Palmer, *Recent Trends in Employment and Unemployment in Philadelphia* (Philadelphia, 1937), pp. 5–10.

38. Eudice Glassberg, "Philadelphians in Need: Client Experiences with Two Philadelphia Benevolent Societies, 1830–1880" (unpublished D.S.W. dissertation, University of Pennsylvania, 1978), p. 39.

39. William Beyer, *Workingmen's Standard of Living in Philadelphia: A Report by the Bureau of Municipal Research of Philadelphia* (New York, 1919), p. 30.

40. Frederic Miller, "The Black Migration to Philadelphia: A 1924 Profile," *The Pennsylvania Magazine of History and Biography,* 108 (July 1984), pp. 338–339.

41. Claudia Goldin, "Family Strategies and the Family Economy in the Late Nineteenth Century: The Role of Secondary Workers," in Theodore Hershberg, ed., *Philadelphia: Work, Space, Family and Group Experience in the Nineteenth Century—Essays toward an Interdisciplinary History of the City* (New York, 1981), p. 284.

42. Beyer, *Workingmen's Standard of Living in Philadelphia,* p. 30.

43. "Record Book, Children Under 16 Years of Age Employed in This Establishment," 1890–1922, William Whitaker & Sons Company Papers, Hagley Library, Accession 1471, File 200.

44. U.S. Bureau of the Census, *Eleventh Census of the United States: 1890. Population. Volume 1, Part 2* (Washington, D.C., 1895), p. cxxvii.

45. Joseph A. Hill, *Women in Gainful Occupations, 1870 to 1920, Census Monograph, IX* (Washington, D.C., 1929), pp. 269–275.

46. Goldin, "Family Strategies and the Family Economy," pp. 297–298; Hill, *Women in Gainful Occupations,* pp. 269–275.

47. For a review of the literature on the "family" wage, see Maurine Weiner Greenwald, "Working-Class Feminism and the Family Wage Ideal: The Seattle Debate on Married Women's Right to Work, 1914–1920," *Journal of American History,* 76 (June 1989), pp. 118–149.

48. Survey Material for Bulletin No. 120 of the Women's Bureau of the U.S. Department of Labor, National Archives, Women's Bureau Record Group 86.

49. Survey Material for Bulletin No. 188 of the Women's Bureau of the U.S. Department of Labor, National Archives, Women's Bureau Record Group 86.

50. Interview with Mabel McMurray, Personnel Assistant, Smith, Kline and French Laboratories, May 1, 1957, Gladys Palmer Papers, University of Pennsylvania, in the custody of Professor Ann Miller, Box 167, p. 3.

51. Quoted in Barbara Klaczynska, "Working Women in Philadelphia, 1900–1930" (unpublished Ph.D. dissertation, Temple University, 1975), p. 47.

52. Gwendolyn Salisbury Hughes, *Mothers in Industry: Wage Earning by Mothers in Philadelphia* (New York, 1925), p. 22.

53. Beyer, *Workingmen's Standard of Living in Philadelphia,* p. 30.

54. Hughes, *Mothers in Industry,* pp. 118–119.

55. Interview with Peter Torrey, Assistant Store Manager, Lord & Taylor, October 30, 1956, Gladys Palmer Papers, Box 167, p. 2.

56. Klaczynska, "Working Women in Philadelphia," pp. 180–181.

57. Caroline Manning, *The Immigrant Woman and Her Job* (New York, 1970), pp. 39–41.

58. "Philadelphia. To the Good WOMEN in the city and County adjacent,

who want Employment in the Business of SPINNING," broadside of Samuel Wetherill, Broadside and Pamphlet Collection, Hagley Library.

59. Agnes M. H. Byrnes, *Industrial Home Work in Pennsylvania* (Harrisburg, 1921), p. 110.
60. Ibid., p. 111.
61. Ibid., p. 23.
62. Rosara Lucy Passero, "Ethnicity in the Men's Ready-Made Clothing Industry, 1880–1950: The Italian Experience in Philadelphia" (unpublished Ph.D. dissertation, University of Pennsylvania, 1978), pp. 163, 166.
63. Palmer, *Philadelphia Workers*, p. 179.
64. Passero, "Ethnicity in the Men's Ready-Made Clothing Industry," p. 292.
65. Scranton and Licht, *Work Sights*, pp. 28–31.
66. Eileen Boris, "Regulating Industrial Homework: The Triumph of 'Sacred Motherhood,'" *Journal of American History*, 71 (March 1985), pp. 745–763.
67. Eudice Glassberg, "Work, Wages and the Cost of Living: Ethnic Differences and the Poverty Line, Philadelphia, 1880," *Pennsylvania History*, 46 (January 1979), p. 29.
68. Quoted in John Fulton Sutherland, "City of Homes: Philadelphia Slums and Reformers" (unpublished Ph.D. dissertation, Temple University, 1973), pp. 15–16.
69. William N. Loucks, *The Philadelphia Plan of Home Financing: A Study of the Second Mortgage Lending of Philadelphia Building and Loan Associations* (Chicago, 1925), p. 40.
70. Henry McCulley Muller, "Urban Home Ownership: A Socio-Economic Analysis with Emphasis on Philadelphia" (unpublished Ph.D. dissertation, University of Pennsylvania, 1947), p. 78.
71. Sutherland, "City of Homes," p. 14.
72. Muller, "Urban Home Ownership," pp. 73–74.
73. Theodore Hershberg et al., "The 'Journey-to-Work': An Empirical Investigation of Work, Residence and Transportation, Philadelphia, 1850 and 1880," in Hershberg, *Philadelphia*, p. 151.
74. William J. Carson, *Savings and Employee Savings Plans in Philadelphia: An Analysis of Savings and Types of Plans to Encourage Savings and Thrift Among Employees of Industrial Plans in Philadelphia* (Philadelphia, 1932), pp. 10–13.
75. Sutherland, "City of Homes," p. 14; Loucks, *The Philadelphia Plan of Home Financing*, p. 2.
76. Muller, "Urban Home Ownership," pp. 78–79.

77. Fredrick J. Shoyer, "Importance of Building and Loan Associations in Making Philadelphia the City of Homes," *Real Estate Magazine,* 6 (August 1925), pp. 16–17, 54.
78. Glassberg, "Work, Wages and the Cost of Living," p. 29.
79. Muller, "Urban Home Ownership," pp. 39, 89–91.
80. Ibid., pp. 29, 82.
81. Ibid., p. 27.
82. John Modell and Tamara K. Hareven, "Urbanization and the Malleable Household: An Examination of Boarding and Lodging in American Families," *Journal of Marriage and the Family,* 35 (August 1973), pp. 467–479.
83. Goldin, "Family Strategies and the Family Economy," p. 282.
84. Ibid., p. 282.
85. Ibid., pp. 286–292.
86. Michael Haines, "Poverty, Economic Stress, and the Family in a Late Nineteenth-Century American City: Whites in Philadelphia, 1880," in Hershberg, *Philadelphia,* p. 265.
87. Scranton, *Proprietary Capitalism,* pp. 112–115, 201–208.
88. Goldin, "Family Strategies and the Family Economy," p. 292.
89. Willits, *Philadelphia Unemployment,* p. 153; Richard N. Juliani, "The Social Organization of Immigration: The Italians in Philadelphia" (unpublished Ph.D. dissertation, University of Pennsylvania, 1971), pp. 194–195.
90. Helen Hermann, *Ten Years of Work Experience of Philadelphia Machinists* (Philadelphia, 1938), pp. 4–5.
91. Glassberg, "Philadelphians in Need," pp. 34, 266, 285–312.
92. Ibid., pp. 31, 55–56.
93. Ibid., pp. 125–126.
94. Palmer, *Recent Trends in Employment and Unemployment,* pp. 15–17.

Index

African-Americans, 22–27, 32–33, 36, 43–53, 239; and schooling, 83–85, 96; apprenticeship of, 112–113; and employment bureaus, 125–126, 131–132; and help-wanted advertising, 139; and public employment, 216–218; women workers, 242–246; home ownership, 250; boarding of lodgers, 251. *See also* Domestic service work; Trade unions

Age as factor in employment, 39–40, 138, 215, 227–234, 272n24

Amalgamated Clothing Workers' Union, 118–119, 248

American Academy of Social and Political Science, 184, 188

American Federation of State, County, and Municipal Employees (AFSCME), 212–216

Apprenticeship, 47–48, 154, 229; early history of, 98–99; in the nineteenth century, 99–104, 108–110; professional, 100; public, 100; management controlled programs, 101–108; in the twentieth century, 104–108, 110–114; union controlled programs, 108–111; and occupational attainment, 111–114; and women, 112–113. *See also* African-Americans; Baldwin Locomotive Works; German immigrants; Italian immigrants; Philadelphia Navy Yard; Russian immigrants; Trade unions

Armstrong Association of Philadelphia (Urban League), 126

Bache, Alexander, 61

Baldwin Locomotive Works, 6, 45, 54, 163–164, 178, 202; apprenticeship programs, 101–104

Bayuk Cigar Company, 95

Beetem (E. C.) & Son Company, 137–138

Berean Training School, 85

Blankenburg, Rudolph, 183–184, 187, 238

Blodget, Lorin, 249

Boarding of lodgers, 251–252

Bok (Edward) Vocational School, 89

Breck, Samuel, 60

Brill (J. G.) Company, 45, 92

British immigrants, 14, 32–33, 35–36

Brown Instrument Company, 161–162

Brumbaugh, Martin Grove, 67–68, 83, 87

Budd Manufacturing Company, 45, 104

Building and construction industry: hiring practices, 41, 116–117; employment patterns, 230, 236

Bureau of Municipal Research of Philadelphia, 207, 209, 211

Business Problems Group, 191–193

Business schools, 86

Cameron, Simon, 202

Centennial Exhibition, 62

Central High School for Boys, 60–61, 64, 68, 70–71, 88

Central Manual Training High School, 89

Child care, 245–246

Child labor as reform issue, 18–19. *See also* Youth employment

Commercial course programs, 71–72, 94–96

313